CHRISTIAN HERITAGE COLLEGE

2100 Greenfield Dr.
El Cajon, CA 92021

A Variorum Commentary on

the Poems of John Milton

MERRITT Y. HUGHES
General Editor

THE COMPLETE SERIES

A Variorum Commentary on

The Poems of
John Milton

Volume Two

THE MINOR ENGLISH POEMS

A. S. P. WOODHOUSE *and* DOUGLAS BUSH

Part One

New York

COLUMBIA UNIVERSITY PRESS

1972

First published 1972 by
Columbia University Press, New York
Copyright © 1972 Columbia University Press
International Standard Book Number: 0 231 08880 9
Library of Congress Catalog Card Number: 70 129962
Printed in Great Britain

Publication of this VARIORUM COMMENTARY ON THE POEMS OF JOHN MILTON was made possible by funds granted by the Carnegie Corporation of New York. That Corporation is not, however, the author, owner, publisher, or proprietor of this publication, and is not to be understood as approving by virtue of its grant any of the statements made or views expressed therein.

The Varsity Fund of the University of Toronto has generously provided, in honor of the late A. S. P. Woodhouse, additional funds which have helped to make possible publication of this volume.

Contents

v

Contents

Contents

Preface

A. S. P. Woodhouse, of the University of Toronto, who had undertaken to prepare the volume of the Variorum Commentary devoted to Milton's minor English poems, died suddenly on 31 October 1964. He had for many years been the distinguished head of the department of English, and had been very actively involved in the concerns of his University, notably in the development of graduate studies, and also in scholarly and educational affairs in Canada at large. His *Puritanism and Liberty* (1938; 2nd ed., 1950) was from the first accepted as a standard work of fresh and prime importance. A large selection from his published and unpublished writings on Milton is now being edited, as *A Preface to Milton*, by H. R. MacCallum. His last discussion appeared in his Weil lectures, a survey of religion in English poetry called *The Poet and his Faith* (1965).

Other pressing claims on Woodhouse's time and energy had delayed the progress of his work on this Commentary, and he left a large but far from completed manuscript which was given to me to revise and finish. The work he had done was, as we should expect, substantial, precise, and judicious, marked by the combination of religious, philosophical, and literary insight with historical knowledge which he had displayed through many years of study and writing. The manuscript was a first draft, ranging in various parts from approximately finished form to pencilled notes. In the most extensive area, annotation of individual poems, Woodhouse had come nearest to completeness. More or less introductory material had been assembled for a number of poems, especially *Comus* and *Lycidas* and some sonnets. Apart from particular discussions in the notes, and a few scattered items, no digests of criticism had been made for any poem except *Comus*, and that critical section was presumably regarded as only a nucleus. There has accordingly been much to add in many places, since in recent decades scholarship and criticism have been so very active. Most small additions (often in the way of references) have been made silently, but, where it seemed desirable, small as well as large additions have been indicated by square brackets or the initials 'D.B.' Woodhouse's own insertions, in excerpts he quoted, are enclosed in pointed brackets (⟨ ⟩). While I have been very reluctant to change what he wrote, it has often seemed necessary, as the manuscript grew in bulk, to omit, condense, or otherwise alter; in the nature of the case, most such changes have likewise had to be made silently. In general, the effort to revise and complete the work of another man, especially of a very old and much admired friend, has involved endless difficulties. I cannot claim to have resolved them without various kinds and degrees of awkwardness; but I hope that my editorial operations have not blurred or misrepresented Woodhouse's insights and opinions. The larger part of the material remains in essentials what he put together.

The digests of criticism are intended only to provide a conspectus of recent developments, not substitutes for the complete originals, and of course the better the criticism the more inadequate the summary. Modern criticism of Milton's poetry has achieved an altogether new level of insight and precision, as we all gratefully recognize; at the same time these summaries (and the notes likewise) may suggest that, along with much that is new and valuable, there has been some that is merely new or that repeats old error. While discrimination is incumbent upon a compiler, it has seemed better to err on the side of inclusiveness than of exclusiveness, since even notable Miltonists—not to mention lesser ones —can maintain what seem to other people inexplicable aberrations. Further, the summaries do aim at objectivity, though not even a computer could attain that; and, if one proceeded on the assumption that all ideas are born free and equal, an unsophisticated reader might well feel lost, like Milton's Lady in the dark wood. Without preempting the roles of the first and second Brother, still less that of the Attendant Spirit or Jove, Woodhouse and I have sometimes questioned critical opinions, and I have sometimes felt obliged to question his—and these editorial comments may in turn be questioned by readers.

The very important and complex subject of metrics and rhythm in all Milton's English poetry (and such related matters as pronunciation) will be treated in essays and notes in a separate volume by Edward Weismiller, but he contributes to the present work a substantial review of prosodic studies of the minor poems; and a few of his incidental notes (labeled 'E. W.') have been appropriated.

The Columbia edition of Milton's complete works (20 vols., New York, 1931–40) is the text used for all references and quotations; it is cited as *Works*. Since the Columbia abbreviations for the titles of Milton's poems and prose writings (Index, 1, xiii–xvi) necessitate continual recourse to the code, the Variorum editors devised a set that would be immediately intelligible. These are listed, along with the Columbia set, at the beginning of this volume.

For almost all references to and quotations or translations from the ancient Greek and Roman authors, the volumes in the Loeb Classical Library (L.C.L.) are used. For some authors, such as Claudian, the number of the volume and the page may, for the reader's convenience, be added to the usual reference. For titles of classical works the standard abbreviations are commonly used.

Later authors, Continental and English, are cited from early or standard modern editions. The same practice is followed with phrases or excerpts quoted by the older commentators, from Newton and Warton[1] onward, who commonly drew upon editions now obsolete (and who assembled a large proportion of the canonical illustrative parallels, ancient and modern). In quotations from English authors of the sixteenth and seventeenth centuries, and from Milton himself, the frequent italics of the originals are not ordinarily reproduced. Since Du Bartas' very popular epic of creation serves as a repository of common ideas, and since Sylvester's often flamboyant translation attracted the young Milton and has general illustrative value for diction, it is often quoted; quotations are taken from the 1621 edition of Sylvester's works, but, to save space and aid the curious reader, references are given to the

---

[1] For a judicious appreciation of Warton's editorial work see L. C. Martin, 'Thomas Warton and the Early Poems of Milton,' *Proc. of the British Academy 1934*, vol. 20, 25–43. A full and precise general account is Ants Oras, *Milton's Editors and Commentators from Patrick Hume to Henry John Todd (1695–1801)*, Dorpat and London, 1931.

Preface

Complete Works of Joshuah Sylvester, ed. A. B. Grosart (2 vols., 1880), in which lines are numbered.

When Milton's editors, from Newton and Warton onward, are cited in the notes, a reference is not ordinarily given, since the number of the line is enough. A list of all editions cited is given in the Index, under Milton.

When illustrative works (apart from the ancient classics) and Miltonic critics are cited for the first time, a full bibliographical reference is usually given but is not repeated in the Index. Subsequent references are not listed.

The initials used for the titles of periodicals and serials are normally the standard ones listed and used in the annual bibliographies of the Modern Language Association of America and the Modern Humanities Research Association. A list of those frequently cited here is included in the front matter.

The editorial board of the Variorum Commentary is deeply grateful to the University of Toronto for contributing, through the instrumentality of Professor Clifford Leech, the handsome sum of $4000 toward the expense of printing this volume.

I must acknowledge several personal debts of gratitude: to the late William R. Parker (whose untimely death on 28 October 1968 was a great loss to scholarship and to our editorial board) and the Clarendon Press for being provided, a long time in advance of publication, with proofs of his massive and invaluable *Milton: A Biography* (1968); to the American Council of Learned Societies and the Harvard Graduate Society for Study and Research for grants which covered many miscellaneous expenses; and, as often before, to the abundant helpfulness of the staff of the Widener, Houghton, and other Harvard libraries and, in the summer, of the Dartmouth College Library.

I am indebted also to Mr Henry H. Wiggins of the Columbia University Press and to the much-tried but almost imperturbable buoyancy of the general editor, my old friend Merritt Hughes (who, I grieve to say, has died since those words were written).   D.B.

ABBREVIATIONS FOR THE TITLES
OF MILTON'S WRITINGS

Variorum *Commentary*		*Columbia* *Works*
Acced	Accedence Commenc't Grammar	G
AddCM	Additional Correspondence and Marginalia	ACM
AddCorr	Additional Correspondence	AC
Animad	Animadversions upon the Remonstrants Defence	A
Apol	An Apology against a Pamphlet	AP
Arc	Arcades	ARC
Areop	Areopagitica	AR
Asclep	'Asclepiads' (called 'Choriambics,' *Works* 1, 327)	
BrNotes	Brief Notes upon a late Sermon	BN or N
Bucer	The Judgement of Martin Bucer, concerning Divorce	M
CarEl	Carmina Elegiaca	CE
Carrier 1, 2	On the University Carrier; Another on the same	UC
CharLP	Milton's Character of the Long Parliament	TC
Circum	Upon the Circumcision	CI
CivP	A Treatise of Civil power	CP
Colas	Colasterion	C
ComBk	Commonplace Book	CB
Comus	Comus	CO
DDD	The Doctrine and Discipline of Divorce	*D. and D.*

Abbreviations: Titles of Milton's Writings

Variorum Commentary		Columbia Works
DecDut	Declaration against the Dutch	DEC
Def 1	Pro Populo Anglicano Defensio (First Defence of the English People)	1D
Def 2	Pro Populo Anglicano Defensio Secunda (Second Defence)	2D
Defpro Se	Pro Se Defensio	SD
DocCh	De Doctrina Christiana	CD
EC	English Correspondence	EC
Educ	Of Education	E
EffSc	In Effigiei Eius Sculptorem	IEE
Eikon	Eikonoklastes	K
El 1, &c.	Elegia 1, &c.	EL
Eli	In obitum Praesulis Eliensis	PE
EpDam	Epitaphium Damonis	ED
Epistol	Familiar Letters of Milton	FE
EProl	Early Prolusion by Milton	EP
EpWin	Epitaph on the Marchioness of Winchester	EM
FInf	On the Death of a fair Infant	I
Hirelings	Considerations touching The likeliest means to remove Hirelings out of the church	H
HistBr	History of Britain	B
HistMosc	Brief History of Moscovia	HM
Hor	Fifth Ode of Horace	HOR
Idea	De Idea Platonica	IPA
IlPen	Il Penseroso	IP

Abbreviations: Titles of Milton's Writings

Variorum Commentary		*Columbia Works*
InvBom	In inventorem Bombardae	IB
L'All	L'Allegro	L'A
Leon 1, &c.	Ad Leonoram Romae canentem	LR
LetFr	Letter to a Friend	LF
LetMonk	Letter to General Monk	LM
LetPat	A Declaration or Letters Patents of the Election of this Present King of Poland	LP
Log	Art of Logic	LO
Lyc	Lycidas	L
Mansus	Mansus	MA
Mar	Marginalia	MAR
May	Song. On May Morning	MM
MC	Miscellaneous Correspondence	MC
Nat	On the Morning of Christ's Nativity	N
Naturam	Naturam non pati senium	NS
NewF	On the new forcers of Conscience	FC
OAP	Observations on the Articles of Peace	O
Passion	The Passion	PA
Patrem	Ad Patrem	ADP
PE	Of Prelatical Episcopacy	P
PhilReg	Philosophus ad Regem	PAR
PL	Paradise Lost	PL
PR	Paradise Regain'd	PR
Procan	In obitum Procancellarii medici	PM
ProdBom 1, &c.	In Proditionem Bombardicam 1, &c.	PB

Abbreviations: Titles of Milton's Writings

Variorum Commentary		Columbia Works
Prol 1, &c.	Prolusions 1, &c.	PO
Propos	Proposalls of Certaine Expedients for the Preventing of a Civill War Now Feard	PRO
Ps 1, &c.	Psalms 1, &c.	PS
QNov	In quintum Novembris	QN
RCG	The Reason of Church-governement Urg'd against Prelaty	CG
Ref	Of Reformation Touching Church-Discipline in England	R
REW	The Readie & Easie Way to Establish a Free Commonwealth	W
Rous	Ad Joannem Rousium	JR
RH	Apologus de Rustico et Hero	RH
SA	Samson Agonistes	SA
Salmas 1, &c.	On Salmasius 1, &c.	
Sals	Ad Salsillum poetam Romanum	AS
Shak	On Shakespear. 1630	SH
SolMus	At a solemn Musick	SM
Sonn 1, &c.	Sonnet 1, &c.	S
Tetr	Tetrachordon	T
Time	On Time	TI
TKM	The Tenure of Kings and Magistrates	TE
TR	Of True Religion, Haeresie, Schism, Toleration	TR
Vac	At a Vacation Exercise in the Colledge	V

ABBREVIATIONS FOR TITLES OF PERIODICALS, ETC.

AJP   *American Journal of Philology*
AN&Q   *American Notes and Queries*
CL   *Comparative Literature*
ELH   *Journal of English Literary History*
ELN   *English Language Notes*
ES   *English Studies*
Essays and Studies   Essays and Studies by Members of the English Association
Explic.   *The Explicator*
Facs.   Vol. 1 of H. F. Fletcher's facsimile ed. (see Index, under Milton)
HLQ   *Huntington Library Quarterly*
JEGP   *Journal of English and Germanic Philology*
JHI   *Journal of the History of Ideas*
JWCI   *Journal of the Warburg and Courtauld Institutes*
MiltonN *Milton Newsletter* (1970 f., *Milton Quarterly*)
MLN   *Modern Language Notes*
MLQ   *Modern Language Quarterly*
MLR   *Modern Language Review*
MP   *Modern Philology*
N&Q   *Notes and Queries*
PBSA   *Papers of the Bibliographical Society of America*
PMLA   *Publications of the Modern Language Association of America*
PQ   *Philological Quarterly*
RES   *Review of English Studies*
SCN   *Seventeenth-Century News*
SEL   *Studies in English Literature*
SB   *Studies in Bibliography*
SP   *Studies in Philology*
TLS   [London] *Times Literary Supplement*
TSLL   *Texas Studies in Literature and Language*
UTQ   *University of Toronto Quarterly*
V.C.   *Variorum Commentary*

I	II	III
El 3 (Andrewes d. 25 Sept. 1626; funeral 11 Nov.)	Oct.–Nov. 1626	
QNov	Before 5 Nov. 1626 (early autumn and perhaps summer)	
Eli (Felton d. 5 Oct. 1626)	Oct.–Nov. 1626	
Prol 1–5		1626–9? 1631–2?
Hor		1626–9?
El 4 (to T. Young)	March–April 1627	
FInf (on niece buried 22 Jan. 1628?)		22 Jan.–9 April 1628? 1625–6?
El 7		1 May 1628 (or 1627? 1630?)
Sonn 1–6		1628–30
Naturam		June 1628?
Prol 6; *Vac*	July(?), 1628	
M. takes B.A. degree	26 March 1629	
El 5	April–May 1629	
May		1 May 1629?–31?
Idea		*c.* 1629–31?
M. buys works of G. della Casa	December 1629	
Nat	Christmas 1629	
El 6	Dec. 1629–Jan. 1630	
Epilogue appended to *El* 7		1630–45
Passion	*c.* 26–8 March 1630	

Chronological Table

I	II	III
Shak	1630–24 March 1631	
Carrier 1, 2	Jan.–Feb. 1631	
EpWin	April–May 1631	
L'All; *IlPen*	Summer 1631 (or 1632?)	
Prol 7		1631–2?
Patrem		1631–2? (1634–7?)
Arc		1632? (1629–33?)
M. takes M.A. degree	3 July 1632	
M. at home (Hammersmith)	July 1632–35	
M. begins to record poems in Cambridge MS.		1632? 1637?
Sonn 7 (on 24th birthday)	9 Dec. 1632	
Time		Dec. 1632? (1630?)
Circum		1 Jan. 1633 (1631?)
'Letter to an Unknown Friend'		Jan.–Feb.?, 1633
SolMus		Feb.–Mar. 1633?
A Mask (*Comus*)	Performed 29 Sept. 1634	
Ps cxiv (Greek trans.)	Nov. 1634	
M. at home (Horton)	1635–April 1638	
Milton's mother d.	3 April 1637	
Comus pub. (ed. Lawes)	1637–March 1638	

3

I	II	III
Important letter to Diodati (*Works* 12, 22–9)	Dated 23 Sept. 1637 (probably should be 23 Nov.)	
Star Chamber decree on censorship	11 July 1637	
Edward King drowned	10 August 1637	
Lyc written	November 1637	
Lyc pub. (*Justa Edouardo King*)	1638	
Sir Henry Wotton's letter to M. (prefixed to *Comus*, 1645)	13 April 1638	
M. in Paris	April?–May 1638	
M. journeys through France to Nice; sails to Genoa	May–June 1638	
M. in Florence (*c.* 2 months)	July?–Aug.–Sept. 1638	
C. Diodati buried	27 Aug. 1638	
M. in Rome (*c.* 2 months)	Oct.–Nov. 1638	
Sals written	Nov.(?), 1638	
M. in Naples	December 1638	
Mansus written	Dec. 1638–Jan. 1639	
M. in Rome again (*c.* 2 months)	Jan.–Feb. 1639	
Leon 1, etc., written	1639?	
M. in Florence again (*c.* 2 months)	March–April 1639	
M. in Venice (a month)	April?–May 1639	
M. in Geneva	June 1639	

I	II	III
M. returns to England	July–Aug. 1639	
M. in lodgings in London, near Fleet Street	1639?–40 (nearly a year)	
EpDam written	Late 1639–early 1640	
EpDam privately printed		1639–45
Long Parliament meets	3 Nov. 1640	
M. living in Aldersgate Street	1640 (autumn?)–1645	
M. sets down list of subjects for tragedies		*c.* 1641
Ref pub.	May 1641	
PE pub.	June–July 1641	
Animad pub.	July (?), 1641	
RCG pub.	Jan.–Feb. 1642	
Apol pub.	April 1642	
M. marries Mary Powell	*c.* 29 May–1 June 1642 (French, *L.R.* 2, 61); 'probably early in July' (Parker, 230; cf. 862–74)	
Mrs Milton returns to parents' home	Probably 'not long before 22 Aug.' (Parker, 873, n. 21)	
Outbreak of Civil War	22 Aug. 1642	
Sonn 8	*c.* 13 Nov. 1642	
Sonn 9–10		1642–5
Parliamentary ordinance on censorship	14 June 1643	

5

I	II	III
Westminster Assembly convened	1 July 1643	
DDD pub.	*c.* 1 Aug. 1643	
DDD (2nd ed., revised and enlarged)	Jan.–Feb. 1644	
Educ pub.	*c.* 4–5 June 1644	
Bucer pub.	August 1644	
Areop pub.	November 1644	
Attacks on M.'s divorce tracts. Controversy on toleration	1644 f.	
Acced written?		1645?
Tetr and *Colas* pub.	*c.* 4 March 1645	
M. and wife reunited	1645 (before November)	
M. living in Barbican	Sept.–Oct. 1645–Sept. (?), 1647	
Sonn 11 and 12	1645–6	
Poems (dated 1645) pub.	On or before 2 Jan. 1646	
M. working on *HistBr* (bks. 1–4) and *DocCh*	1646–9	Parker, Shawcross, and Carey would include *SA*
Sonn 13 (to Lawes)	9 Feb. 1646	
Daughter Anne b.	29 July 1646	
Sonn 14 (on Mrs Thomason)	December 1646	
NewF		1646–7
Rous	23 Jan. 1647	

I	II	III
J. Milton senior d.	March 1647	
M. living in High Holborn	Aug. (?), 1647–March 1649	
Log and *HistMosc* written?		*c.* 1648? (Parker)
Ps 80–88 versified	April 1648	
Sonn 15 (Fairfax)	14 June–17 Aug. 1648	
Daughter Mary b.	25 Oct. 1648	
King Charles executed	30 Jan. 1649	
Eikon Basilike (by J. Gauden) pub.	1–9 Feb. 1649	
TKM pub.	*c.* 13 Feb. 1649	
M. appointed Secretary for Foreign Tongues to Council of State	15 March 1649 (held office till 1659; as a Latin Secretary, 1654–9)	
OAP pub.	May 1649	
Eikon (reply to *Eikon Basilike*) pub.	*c.* 6 Oct. 1649	Or *c.* 6 Nov. (Parker)
M. living in Scotland Yard	Nov. 1649–Dec. 1651	
Period of the Commonwealth	1649–53	
Def 1 pub.	24 Feb. 1651	
Son John b. (d. June 1652)	16 March 1651	
M. licenser of newspaper *Mercurius Politicus*	23 Jan. 1651–22 Jan. 1652	
M. becomes completely blind	Nov. 1651–Feb. 1652	
M. living in Petty France, Westminster	Dec. 1651–1660	

I	II	III
Sonn 19 ('When I consider')		1652–5
Daughter Deborah b.	2 May 1652	
Mary Powell Milton d.	5 (?) May 1652	
Sonn 16 (Cromwell)	May 1652	
Sonn 17 (Vane)	3 July 1652	
Ps 1–8	August 1653	*Ps* 1 earlier?
Period of Cromwell's Protectorate	1654–8	
Def 2 pub.	*c.* 30 May 1654	
Sonn 18 (Piedmont)	May–June 1655	
Sonn 20–2		1654–6
Def pro Se pub.	*c.* 8 Aug. 1655	
M. marries Katherine Woodcock (b. 1628)	12 Nov. 1656	
Daughter b. (d. 17 March 1658)	19 Oct. 1657	
Katherine M. d.	3 Feb. 1658	
Sonn 23	1658	Before 12 Nov. 1656 (Parker)
Cromwell d.	3 Sept. 1658	
Cromwell's funeral: M. presumably in procession with Marvell and other secretaries	23 Nov. 1658	
M. working on *HistBr*, *DocCh*.	1655–60	
PL begun		1658?
CivP pub.	Feb. 1659	
Hirelings pub.	August 1659	

Chronological Table

I	II	III
REW pub.	3 March, or slightly earlier, 1660	
LetMonk	March 1660	
BrNotes; *REW* (enlarged)	April 1660	
Charles II enters London	29 May 1660	
M. secluded by friends in Bartholomew Close	Summer 1660	
Parliamentary order for M.'s arrest and burning of *Eikon* and *Def* I	16 June 1660 (public proclamation, concerning books only, 13 Aug.)	
M. not named among those excepted from Act of Pardon	29 Aug. 1660	
M. in custody	Some period between 13 Sept. and release (15–17 Dec. 1660)	
M. living in Holborn		Sept. (?), 1660– early 1661 (Parker)
M. living in Jewin St.		1661–3 (French, *L.R.* 4, 388); till *c.* 1669–70 (Parker, 608, 1125)
M. marries Elizabeth Minshull (b. 1638)	24 Feb. 1663	
PL finished	1663?–5	
M. and family at Chalfont St Giles (because of plague)	July 1665–Feb. (?), 1666	
Great Fire in London	2–5 Sept. 1666	

I	II	III
PL (in 10 bks.) pub.	August (?), 1667	
Acced pub. (see under 1645 above)	June 1669	
M. living in Artillery Walk, Bunhill Fields		From *c.* 1669–70 (Parker, 608) or 1663 (French, *L.R.* 4, 388) till 1674
HistBr (6 bks.) pub.	1670	
PR and *SA* pub.	1671	
Log (written *c.* 1648?) pub.	1672	
TR pub.	1673	
Poems (2nd ed., enlarged)	1673	
Epistol and *Prol* pub.	July (?), 1674	
PL (2nd ed., in 12 bks.)	July 1674	
Milton died	8 (?) Nov. 1674	
M. buried in St Giles Cripplegate	12 Nov. 1674	
CharLP (omitted from *HistBr* of 1670) pub.	1681	
HistMosc (written *c.* 1648?) pub.	1682	
Letters of State, ed. E. Phillips (incl. *Sonn* 15, 16, 17, 22)	1694	

CHRONOLOGICAL SURVEY[1]

The non-chronological order in which the poems are treated in this volume is that of the Columbia edition, which follows the second and fuller edition of Milton's *Poems* (1673). While some of the poems can be dated with entire certainty, for many others the dates and the order of composition are beset with problems, problems which modern scholarship has done much both to clarify and to complicate, so that in many cases expert conjectures may differ considerably. [The range of conjecture could only now and then be suggested in the Chronological Table which precedes this Survey. That Table is a mere skeleton, less ambitious than Woodhouse's, though a number of entries have been added (and a number altered).]

I

We may recognize seven types of evidence (not to mention ambiguity) available, and these differ in the degree of significance they carry and of certainty or probability they yield.

(1) A number of poems are dated in the editions of 1645 and 1673 and occasionally in the Cambridge MS. (on this MS. see section II of this Survey and *Arcades* 1 below). Sometimes the year is given (e.g. *Nativity*, *Comus*, *Lycidas*). Often it is the year of the poet's age, with the phrase *Anno aetatis*; Milton evidently used *Anno aetatis 17*, for example, not to mean 'In his seventeenth year' but 'At the age of 17.' This is clearly shown by the dates of some events commemorated, e.g. in elegies on notable persons; and there is no ground for supposing that in this matter Milton's practice was not constant [though the variation in the dating of *Elegy* 7 is unique and ambiguous]. This

---

[1] [Woodhouse's draft of this Survey has been much abridged, especially through the shifting of parts of it to the introductions to individual poems, where such material may be more convenient for the reader; these and other changes it has not been possible to indicate, though some are noted. Woodhouse's line of argument is in the main that of his 'Notes on Milton's Early Development,' *UTQ* 13, 1943–4, 66–101 (cited hereafter as 'Notes').]

interpretation of *Anno aetatis*, suggested by Masson (*Poetical Works*, 3 v., London, 1890, 1, 116), was established by W. R. Parker ('Some Problems in the Chronology of Milton's Early Poems,' *RES* 11, 1935, 276–83); [it was disputed by E. Sirluck ('Milton's Idle Right Hand,' *JEGP* 60, 1961, 781–4), but is cogently restated by Parker (*Milton: A Biography*, Oxford, 1968, 784–6), who notes that Milton 'was simply conforming to common usage, even that of official records': this biography is henceforth cited as 'Parker.'] Milton's dates, where he provided them, appear to be mainly accurate, though his memory certainly misled him in one case, perhaps in two (*Procan*: Parker, 731, 785; *Fair Infant*: ibid. 738, 785).

(2) Some poems may be placed within narrow limits by the known dates of the events that called them forth, such as the deaths of Hobson the carrier and the Marchioness of Winchester.

(3) A theme or title may fix the season but not the year (e.g. *In quintum Novembris*, *Elegies* 5 and 7, *The Passion*, *Upon the Circumcision*), and other evidence may help to suggest the year.

(4) Sometimes a reference in one poem to another gives us not only a *terminus a quo* for the former but suggests its date: e.g. references to the *Nativity* date *Elegy* 6 and, less certainly, *The Passion*.

(5) The order and state of poems in the MS. provide—not without debatable complexities—valuable indications of the order of composition (e.g. *Arcades*, *Time*, *Circumcision*, *Solemn Musick*); likewise the numbering of the sonnets in the MS. and in 1673 when collated with dates attached to some of them and inferred for others [but the dates of two great sonnets, 'When I consider' and 'Methought I saw my late espoused Saint,' remain subjects of debate]. The absence of poems from the MS. may also be evidence (e.g. *L'Allegro*, *Il Penseroso*). The order of poems in the collected editions (1645, 1673) is not as a whole chronological, but it is apparently intended to be so within certain groups (Grierson, *Poems*, London, 1925, 1, x; Parker, *RES* 11, 1935, 279–80), such as the sonnets [but see the headnotes to *Sonnets* 19 and 23, cited above. J. T. Shawcross (*SEL* 3, 1963, 77: title under *Horace* below) sees

four groupings within the English (and Italian) poems, and two groupings within the Latin and Greek poems: those with religious connotation (*Nativity Ode* through *At a solemn Musick*), secular poems (*Epitaph on the Marchioness* through *Il Penseroso*), the sonnets, and pastoral works (*Arcades, Lycidas, A Mask*); poems in elegiac meter, and those in other meters (*sylvae*). Exceptions exist: at least *Epitaph on the Marchioness* is out of order, the *Nativity Ode* was placed first to achieve a notable beginning, and the three 'pastorals' were arranged apparently by increasing length. The second edition of 1673 repeats the 1645 arrangement but adds poems written both before and after 1645. The *Fair Infant Elegy*...was printed in chronological order among the religious poems, sonnets were added, three poems were included between the sonnets and *Arcades*, two sets of psalm translations were appended to the English poems in reverse order of composition....

Parker (762, n. 53) gives this view of the problem:

Masson assumed that the order in which poems appear in the Manuscript is the order of their composition, regardless of the order in which Milton arranged them for printing. Grierson corrected this misapprehension, emphasizing the fact (which one may observe by examining the Manuscript) that most of the poems there are either transcripts or fair copies of poems composed elsewhere, or else poems so nearly completed elsewhere that the poet wanted a clean copy to see how the verses read. Grierson therefore concluded, correctly I feel sure, that we can infer nothing confidently from the absence of any poem from the Manuscript, and that the Manuscript's order is not to be preferred to Milton's arrangement of the printed editions.]

(6) Statistical study of the verse, a method used with some success in nineteenth-century work on Shakespearian chronology, confronts a different set of conditions in Milton, where the poems belong to different genres and demand different metrical effects, which his virtuosity seems always able to supply. Such evidence, valuable for its objectivity, can be misleading if taken by itself.

(7) More subjective and hence more speculative is the kind of evidence seen in the character of the poem, its degree of maturity in thought and artistry, and its similarity or dissimilarity in theme and manner to Milton's other poems. However speculative, this type of evidence is based directly on the poetry; and it would be odd indeed if in dating

poems one paid attention to everything except the poems themselves. [These remarks are of course quite sound, and a wise warning against excessive or exclusive faith in bibliographical evidence, which can be highly speculative too. Yet, if we did not know, e.g., that the *Passion* followed the *Nativity*, its poetic character would certainly place it earlier; so that we cannot assume an unfaltering advance in maturity.]

Finally, it may be asked whether, in the poems that can be certainly dated, any recognizable pattern of development is indicated, and whether this pattern is consonant with Milton's own utterances (e.g. his repudiation of the elegiac in *Elegy* 6; his retrospective account of his changing interests in the *Apology for Smectymnuus*; the resolution taken in *Sonnet* 7). If such a pattern can be established, it supplies a framework in which the other poems may be fitted (with of course scrupulous regard to all the existing evidence); and the result will be the most probable chronological sequence at present obtainable.

II

With two certain and two [four?] probable or possible exceptions, all Milton's extant poems were written after he took up residence at Cambridge (about Easter, 1625). The two certain exceptions are the paraphrases of Psalms 114 and 136, which he said, in printing them in *Poems* (1645), 'were done...at fifteen years old,' that is, between 9 December 1623 and 8 December 1624. Two probable exceptions are the Latin *Carmina Elegiaca* and 'Asclepiads' (*Works* 1, 326–9: [where the latter is wrongly labelled 'Choriambics': see H. W. Garrod in *Poetical Works*, ed. H. Darbishire, Oxford, 1952–5, 2, 371]). These— which Milton never printed—were found on a loose leaf along with Milton's Commonplace Book in 1874; on the reverse side was a short Latin essay called by the Columbia editors 'An Early Prolusion' (*Works* 12, 288–91). The three pieces, all on the subject of early rising, were probably exercises done at St Paul's School; at any rate they may be roughly dated 1624–6. [Two other pieces of verse possibly—some would say probably—done at school, pieces Milton included in his *Poems*, are

14

the Latin *Apologus de Rustico et Hero* (1673) and the Greek *Philosophus ad Regem* (1645, 1673). This last W. R. Parker (144, 796, n. 67), who suggests that it refers to the younger Alexander Gill's clash with Laud and the Star Chamber, would date in December 1634 or 'perhaps much later.' See *V.C.* 1, 152, 259.]

Elegy 1, a Latin epistle to his friend Diodati, Milton did not date, but all the known evidence points to the spring of 1626, the short period of his [apparent] rustication from Cambridge at the end of his first academic year. In the autumn of 1626 Milton produced in rapid succession five Latin poems, four of them obituaries (*Procan, El* 2 and 3, *Eli*), and the small epic *In quintum Novembris*; [this last he might have written during the summer and early autumn, since the celebration of November 5 was an assured annual prospect]. The Latin epigrams on the Gunpowder Plot and the one on the inventor of gunpowder are usually bracketed with the little epic, but for no other reason than the subject; they may have been written in 1626 or at intervals over several years [see Parker, 732, n. 28]. The second epigram may possibly belong to November 1625, since it alludes to King James's death (27 March 1625).

The five longer Latin poems were exercises in craftsmanship [though not merely that], and they were all written with an academic audience in view. However, in the next year, 1627, Milton produced only *Elegy* 4, addressed to his old tutor in Hamburg, and in this he was completely silent about his own activities in Cambridge [*Elegy* 7, on his encounter with Cupid, commonly dated 1628, may belong to the spring of 1627: see below]. The ebb and flow of Milton's early academic verse, whatever other causes are taken into account, seem to coincide with his consciousness of hostility or friendliness on the part of his fellow undergraduates. The first evidence of his awareness of hostility appears in *Prolusion* 1, which may thus be tentatively assigned to the last months of 1626 or the beginning of 1627. *Prolusion* 3 (*Against the Scholastic Philosophy*) bears on the disagreement regarding the course of study which Milton assigns as the reason for the hostility to him (*Prol* 6, *Works* 12, 206); [there was also his fastidious aversion to some kinds of student licence]. And *Prolusion* 4 would seem to mark the cessation of that hostility and *Prolusion* 6 the healing of the breach.[2] [Since conjectural dates for the Prolusions differ widely, as this long footnote indicates, and since conjectural dates for a number of poems also differ widely, the relating of Milton's early

[2] Sir John Sheppard ('Milton's Cambridge Exercises,' *Music at Belmont and Other Essays and Addresses*, London, 1951, 152–62) denies that the Prolusions afford any evidence of a rift between Milton and his audience: Milton's diatribes, he maintains, are spoken in jest and in the spirit of the occasion. This explanation might possibly serve for *Prol* 1 were it not for Milton's quite definite statements in *Prol* 6, but these cannot be ignored.

Since there seems no reason to doubt that they were printed (in 1674) in the order of composition, as Milton remembered it, we have in fact a satisfactory (though not of course certain) dating for *Prolusions* 1–6 as delivered at intervals between late 1626 or early 1627 and the beginning of the long vacation of 1628. Masson took the seven Prolusions to 'extend pretty equally over Milton's University course' (*Life*, 1, rev. ed., London, 1881, 275). At first glance this seems reasonable, but it will not square with the evidence of *Prol* 6, which demands that it should be preceded by at least two others, *Prol* 1 and the Prolusion referred to as favourably received (probably 4). The subject and tone of *Prol* 3 make it almost certain that it preceded the Prolusion favourably received. Thus the assumption of a chronological order in the printed text is confirmed for four of the six Prolusions; and there is no reason (other than a desire for more equal distribution) to withdraw 2 and 5 from the series and assign them to the long gap between 6 and 7. Tillyard (*Milton: Private Correspondence and Academic Exercises*, Cambridge, 1932, xxv) argues that the subject of *Prol* 2, the music of the spheres, places it near the *Nativity* (Christmas 1629); but this kind of argument would push *L'All* and *IlPen* back to the period of *Prol* 1, i.e. at least to 1627, which he does not contemplate. The editors of the *Complete Prose Works* (New Haven, 1, 1953, 211–306: this work, in progress, is cited hereafter as *C.P.W.*) offer no discussion of dates, but in a chronological table (xv) adopt '1628?–1632,' citing as authority for this impossibly late beginning J. M. French's admittedly arbitrary distribution of the Prolusions in his *Life Records* (New Brunswick, 1, 1949, 101, etc.: this work is cited hereafter as *L.R.*).

[All attempts to date the Prolusions are necessarily speculative. Woodhouse's theory strains probability (cf. Parker below) by confining six of the seven Prolusions within one early period, from late 1626 to July 1628. If it was Milton who in 1674 collected these Prolusions and had a written record at hand, the sequence would be reliable, though dates would still be lacking; otherwise, it obviously would not be. We have only one certain date: *Prol* 6 (to which *Vac* was attached) belongs to July (?), 1628; also, most scholars take *Prol* 7, the last of the printed series, to be Milton's valedictory to Cambridge and to belong to 1631–2. Otherwise we are left to doubtful inference. M. Y. Hughes (*Complete Poems and Major Prose*, New York, 1957: henceforth cited as 'Hughes') prudently gives no dates except those just cited for *Prol* 6 and 7. H. F. Fletcher, after special study of the curriculum, disregards the printed order and assigns all the Prolusions, even the seventh, to 1628–9 (*Intellectual Development of John Milton*, 2, Urbana, 1961). J. T. Shawcross ('The Dating of Certain Poems, Letters, and Prolusions Written by Milton,' *ELN* 2, 1964–5, 261–6) takes the printed sequence as 'evidently haphazard and not made by Milton,' dates the Prolusions in 1628–32, mostly in 1628–9, and sees their chronological order as 1, 4, 6, 3, 2, 5, 7. Parker (53, 774–5, n. 80) likewise disregards the printed order but assigns all the extant Prolusions except the sixth to Milton's post-baccalaureate years, 1629–32. M.A. exercises involved 'three Responsions in the Schools, two in the College, and one College

prose and verse is a ticklish matter; moreover, like other writers, Milton can repeat favourite ideas and images, sometimes after long intervals. At any rate it is clear, from his own words, that he did have a period of unpopularity, although it is a question if that temporarily chilled his poetic vein.]

The year 1628 brought a renewal of poetic activity, of which the chief products were two poems in English, the earliest extant specimens of original verse in Milton's native tongue. [Some scholars, e.g. Hanford (*Poems*, 2nd ed., New York, 1953) would include here *Sonnets* 1–6, that is, 'O Nightingale' and the Italian pieces: see below.] One poem, the *Fair Infant*, Milton apparently misdated, assigning it to 1626; Parker (*TLS*, 17 December 1938, 802; *Milton*, 738, n. 46) showed that the subject was almost certainly the infant niece who was buried on 22 January 1628—a date which better fits the quality of the poem. [The innocently erotic *Elegy* 7, written on May Day, was given a unique form of dating, *Anno aetatis undevigesimo*. On the strength of Milton's normal use of a cardinal numeral, this phrase is commonly taken to mean 'at the age of 19,' i.e. 1628; but, if the peculiar phrase is taken literally, it means 'at the age of 18,' i.e. 1627 (Parker, 785). Parker ('Notes on the Chronology of Milton's Latin Poems,' *A Tribute to George Coffin Taylor*, ed. Arnold Williams, Chapel Hill, 1952, 113–31) argued ingeniously but, one may think, unconvincingly, for 1630; the argument and date are supported by J. T. Shawcross (*Complete English Poetry*, New York, 1963, 57, 548: this edition is cited hereafter as *C.E.P.*) and are reaffirmed in Parker's *Milton*, 77, 754, n. 35.]

Another Latin poem, *Naturam non pati senium* (*That Nature Submits Not to the Decay of Old Age*), probably belongs to the early summer of 1628. At least it seems most likely to be the set of verses Milton mentioned in a letter to the younger Gill as written for the use of a Fellow of the College at Commencement on 1 July, and, according to custom, printed for distribution among the audience (*Epistol* 3, 2 July 1628,

oration,' and, apart from the special *Prol* 6, Milton's others consisted of just those items: 'it seems reasonable to suppose that Milton chose to print, not his undergraduate efforts, but his more mature work.']

Works 12, 11). This piece fits the circumstances better than any other extant poem except possibly the burlesque *De Idea Platonica*. If *Naturam* is correctly related to the Commencement of 1628, the *Idea* may well have been produced for a similar occasion [or for that one, instead of *Naturam*] and in response to a similar request, and the most likely time for a second request would be the following year. [*Naturam* is, in mythological terms, a declaration on the 'modern' and 'progressive' side in the protracted European debate on the supposed decay of nature—a subject lately examined in George Hakewill's huge reply (1627) to the deteriorationists. Shawcross (*ELN* 2, 1964–5, 262–4) assigns *Epistol* 3 to 2 July 1631, and dates both *Naturam* and the *Idea* in June 1631. Parker (43–4, 104, 773, n. 79), who would dissociate both poems from Milton's letter, assigns them to 'the period 1630–2'. It may be added, although a caution has already been lodged against repetition in Milton as evidence for dating, that there is a rather remarkable parallelism between the numerous classical allusions in *Naturam* and those in the *Fair Infant* (see *V.C.* 1, 211), both of which seem to belong most probably to the first half of 1628.]

Apart from its intrinsic significance, we can welcome a poem of apparently certain date (July?, 1628), the English *At a Vacation Exercise* (published in 1673 as written *Anno Aetatis 19* but not included in the *Poems* of 1645). The poem was composed for delivery with *Prolusion* 6, as its title and the *Prolusion* make clear.

Milton's translation of the fifth ode of Horace is one of the poems that have occasioned the widest span of conjecture, but probability would seem to place it among the Cambridge exercises of 1626–9, perhaps in the spring of 1628. [See the headnote to the translation. Parker (57–8, 746, n. 4) would tentatively link the piece with *Elegy* 5 of the spring of 1629.]

Milton's dating of *Elegy* 5 (*Anno aetatis* 20) places it in the spring of 1629 and seems to be generally accepted. The little English poem, *Song. On May Morning*, is, because of its similarity of spirit, commonly assigned to the same year and season. [Recent opinion has inclined to 1629–30 or 1630–1. In *Poems* (1673) it follows the first poem of a secular group, the *Epitaph on the Marchioness of Winchester* (April–May 1631) and precedes *On Shakespear*, which Milton dated 1630 (i.e. 1630–24 March 1631); but the *Epitaph* appears to be out of order (Shawcross, *SEL* 3, 77, above). Parker (768–9, n. 60) argues for May 1631 (see headnote to the *Song* below).]

With the *Nativity* we are happily on solid ground. It was 'Compos'd 1629' (*Poems*, 1645), just after Milton's twenty-first birthday; in *Elegy* 6.79–88 he told Diodati that he had written the poem as a birthday gift for Christ, adding that the first light of Christmas morning brought him his theme. The *Nativity* is only Milton's third original English poem, and by far the most ambitious. It is also the first to deal with a specifically religious theme; and, read in the light of *Elegy* 6, it is seen to mark an important moment in Milton's early evolution—in fact, to reveal a new element in its pattern (see III below).

The dating of *The Passion* is not quite so certain, but, from the pointed reference to the *Nativity* with which it opens, critics have agreed in inferring that it was written for the ensuing Good Friday (which in 1630 fell on 26 March). The poem breaks off abruptly at the end of the eighth stanza, with an apologetic note from the author. It is the only unfinished work in the Miltonic canon. The failure, coupled with the fact that Milton chose to print the fragment in his *Poems*, raises a question which touches the whole pattern of his early development and which is discussed below by critics of the poem.

Sonnet 1, in English, is followed in the *Poems* by *Sonnets* 2–6 and a *Canzone*, in Italian, and the seven poems are linked together by their amatory themes as well as their position. The old assignment of the Italian pieces to Milton's Continental journey (1638–9) was tentatively questioned by Masson (*P.W.* 1, 209) and demolished by D. H. Stevens (*MP* 17, 1919–20, 25–33) and J. S. Smart (*Sonnets of Milton*, Glasgow, 1921; repr., Oxford, 1966), but their date is a matter of inference and depends partly on one's reading of Milton's early evolution. [The problem is discussed in the headnote to *Sonnet* 1. Tillyard, Woodhouse ('Notes,' 1943–4, 81–3), and Hughes date the whole group, Parker (78, 755) the Italian poems, in 1630; Hanford, in '1628?' (*Poems*, 1953).

(In 'The Youth of Milton,' *Studies in Shakespeare, Milton and Donne*, New York, 1925, 121, he had favoured 'between the spring of 1629 and the winter of 1629–30'; this canonical essay is quoted throughout from the *Studies*, but it has been reprinted in *John Milton poet and humanist: essays by James Holly Hanford*, Cleveland, 1966.) J. Carey (*RES* 14, 1963, 383–6) assigned the group to 1629, just before the *Nativity* (see headnote to *Sonnet* 1 and *El* 6.89 n.). E. A. J. Honigmann (*Milton's Sonnets*, London and New York, 1966) revives the old idea of 1638–9 (see below, *Sonnets* 1). Parker (57–8, 746, n. 6) links *Sonnet* 1 with *Elegy* 5 as of 1629.]

The next group of poems can be dated with certainty. The lines *On Shakespear* Milton dated 1630, and that, as Grierson noted (*Poems* 1, x), may mean as late as March 1631, if the date is Old Style. The two epitaphs on Hobson, the University carrier, must have followed closely upon his death (1 January 1631). The same inference holds for the *Epitaph on the Marchioness of Winchester*; the Marchioness died on 15 April 1631. [The *Epitaph*, as we noted above (Shawcross), is out of order in its group.] All four poems are exercises in composition: the first in the serious employment of poetic wit; the second and third in the comic or mock-serious; and the fourth in the Jonsonian lyric mode [but Milton's feelings are surely engaged in the first and fourth].

The affectionately adroit and biographically valuable poem *Ad Patrem* was assigned to *c.* 1632 by Masson (*Life*, 1, 334). At least since Grierson (1, xxii) it has been commonly dated 1637—or 1634 (favoured by Parker)—for what may be thought an odd reason: that Milton had not made up his mind about his vocation until the publication or the writing of *Comus* committed him—as if he had been aimlessly drifting through all the preceding years, ever since he had declared his ambitions in the *Vacation Exercise* of 1628. [In his 'Notes' (84–95) Woodhouse dated *Ad Patrem* in Milton's last year at Cambridge, 1631–2, but gave better reasons than Masson's for the early date. Debate was briefly summarized by Sirluck (*JEGP* 60, 1961, 784–5), who upheld 1637. Woodhouse's date was supported by Bush ('The Date of Milton's *Ad Patrem*,' *MP* 61, 1963–4, 204–8; cf. headnote to that poem, *V.C.* 1,

232–40). Parker (788–9) restates his arguments for 1634. These may be thought stronger against 1637 than against 1631–2; indeed some of them, like Milton's use of Latin, support the earliest date. (Parker is, by the way, surely mistaken in saying, 789, n. 26, that the allusion to Clio in line 14 'refers to the study of history which...Cambridge did not provide...but is now [in the Hammersmith period] possible': Clio is mentioned only as the traditional chief of the Muses, named first in Hesiod's list in *Theog.* 77.) What Parker calls 'post-graduation talk' would more naturally precede graduation: would father and son wait for two years—or, as others would have it, for five—to talk about the son's profession? And to say that Milton's career in the ministry 'is simply assumed' is to ignore the wholly secular substance and tone of the poem, which is the work of a Renaissance humanist—a young one —intent on literary fame; it is hard to believe that Milton could have written in such a vein after *Sonnet* 7 and the religious poems that followed, up to *Comus.*] But these questions belong to his development and are discussed further in section III below.

L'Allegro and *Il Penseroso* of course go together, although the one is light and secular and the other not only serious but religious, and both have been traditionally assigned to 1632, the year in which Milton received his M.A. (July) and left Cambridge for his father's house— that is, the beginning of the so-called Horton period (1632–8), [though 'Horton' now appears to be partly a misnomer (see Chronological Table above and, below, the first paragraph of the introduction to the twin poems)]. Some scholars may stick to 1632; the majority seem to follow Tillyard in favouring the summer of 1631, Milton's last long vacation (see the introduction just cited, and Parker, 769–70).

Arcades, the date of which is a problem in itself, brings us to the whole set of problems connected with the order and state of poems in the Cambridge or Trinity College MS. (cited in the present volume simply as 'MS.'), in which Milton kept copies of most of his minor poems from *Arcades* onward. [The MS. was reproduced in facsimile by W. A. Wright (Cambridge, 1899), but is now most conveniently available in *John Milton's Complete Poetical Works Reproduced in Facsimile,* ed. H. F. Fletcher, 1 (Urbana, 1943), cited in this Commentary as *Facs.*] The first poems in the MS. are, in this order: *Arcades*; two drafts of *At a solemn Musick*, without title, and a fair copy with the title; two drafts of the prose 'Letter to a Friend,' both referring to *Sonnet 7* and one of them containing a fair copy of it; *On Time*; *Upon the Circumcision*. [Detailed discussions appear below under these poems, especially *Arcades* and *On Time*; the introduction to the latter includes a summary of Shawcross's radical argument (*MLN* 75, 1960, 11–17) for dating the first part of the MS. (*Arcades* to *Lycidas* inclusive) in 1637. Conjectural dates for *Arcades* have ranged between 1630 (or even 1629, an alternative in Parker, 80, 755, who prefers 1630) and 1634; Woodhouse sees 1632 as alone satisfying all the known evidence.]

Sonnet 7 ('How soon hath time') has been traditionally assigned to Milton's twenty-third birthday (9 December 1631), and has by many editors been given titles to that effect, titles that have no authority. But W. R. Parker (*RES* 11, 1935) argued, very convincingly, that the sonnet was written a year later, on Milton's twenty-fourth birthday. The importance of this redating, both for the background and import of the sonnet itself and for the general pattern of Milton's early development, is shown in III below and in the headnote to the poem.

The two great English poems of the rest of the decade present almost no problems of chronology. *A Mask* (*Comus*) was written for performance at Ludlow Castle 'On Michaelmasse night' (title page, 1637), 'the 29th of September 1634' (Bridgewater MS.), and must have occupied Milton through most of the spring and early summer. Some important additions were made between its composition and its publication by Lawes in 1637–8 (see below, *Comus* V, notes on 778–805 and 999–1010, [and Sirluck under 1961 in *Comus* IV]). On the evidence of the MS. Milton wrote no more poetry until *Lycidas*, which in the MS. he dated 'Novemb: 1637.' Edward King had been drowned on August 10.

In April or May, 1638, Milton set off on his Continental tour. His sojourns in Florence, Rome, Naples, and other cities do not concern us here; the immediate poetical fruits of his travels were all in Latin: *Ad Salsillum*, three epigrams *Ad Leonoram Romae canentem*, and

Mansus, one of his best Latin poems. Milton returned to England in July or August, 1639. While abroad he had had news of the death of his closest friend, Charles Diodati (August 1638). His elaborate pastoral elegy, *Epitaphium Damonis*, was written after he was settled at home, late in 1639 or early in 1640. It counts as the last of his early poems.[3]

III

By his own account (*RCG, Works* 3, 242) Milton went up to Cambridge with the intention, his parents' and his own, that he should enter the ministry of the Established Church. He was probably destined, as William Haller has argued (*Rise of Puritanism*, New York, 1938, 288–323), for a place in the brotherhood of Puritan preachers whose operations within the church had been largely directed from the University. But that from the first he also entertained poetic ambitions is clear from the *Vacation Exercise* (1628) and from his eager quest of practice in writing (at first in Latin), which had commenced two years earlier and went on through the rest of the Cambridge period (1626–July 1632). There was ample precedent for the dual aim in such admired figures as Giles and Phineas Fletcher, not to mention such greater poets as Donne, George Herbert, and Herrick, if Milton at that time was aware of them.

Some of Milton's earliest Latin poems—memorials to conspicuous episcopal and academic personages—were in the main poetical exercises [although it may be noted that the elegies on the two bishops embody the young poet's first ecstatic visions of heaven]. The religious feeling of *In quintum Novembris* (1626) was more earthly and patriotic anti-Catholicism. *Elegy* 4 (1627) pictured Milton's former tutor, Thomas Young, as a Puritan exile and martyr. The young man's delight in reading and imitating 'the smooth Elegiack poets' (*Apology, Works* 3,

---

[3] [A separate printing of the poem was discovered by L. Bradner (*TLS*, 18 Aug. 1932, 581); the text is reproduced in Fletcher, *Facs.* 355 f. Fletcher (*JEGP* 61, 1962, 788–96) dated this printing after the *Poems* of 1645. J. T. Shawcross (*SB* 18, 1965, 262–5) argued that 'certain textual and compositional matters show that the separate printing was a source for the text of 1645,' that the separate text 'is frequently altered in 1645 to improve certain readings.']

302)—that is, the Roman love-poets, Ovid, Propertius, and Tibullus, and, evidently also, such modern Latinists as George Buchanan—found 'pagan' expression, equally intense and innocent, in *Elegy* 7 and the astonishing *Elegy* 5 (*On the Coming of Spring*). Poems of such diverse or contradictory character were not of course insincere; they represent both inbred piety and natural impulse—'most agreeable to natures part in me' (*Works* 3, 302)—and always poetic decorum. They all express facets of the youthful poet's personality and aesthetic experience.

The elegiac was, however, a passing phase. In *Elegy* 6 (December 1629–January 1630), if Milton half playfully endorses the poetry of love and wine, the note deepens as he turns to celebrate the poetry of heroic themes and describes the ascetic Pythagorean discipline that must prepare the poet therefor. Then with a sudden transition comes the announcement that he is writing the *Nativity* (Christmas 1629)— an earnest (for how else can we take it?) of the higher poetry that he hopes to compose. The epic ambitions revealed in the *Vacation Exercise* now have a religious context. For the *Nativity*—as positive and joyful an affirmation of Christianity as *Elegy* 5 was of naturalism—teaches us not only to take seriously the repudiation of the elegiac in *Elegy* 6 [which Parker (68–70) still declines to do], but to translate the heroic priestly bard who breathes forth Jove into the Christian poet-priest whose inspiration is kindled from God's 'secret Altar.' We have here recorded the beginning of a religious experience which, when completed, was to have a profound effect on Milton's poetry.

We do not know when he began to turn away from the idea of entering the ministry (perhaps not until he was about to quit Cambridge in July 1632), or when his decision became final. Ultimately he was to recognize that poetry might be 'of power beside the office of a pulpit,' might be 'doctrinal and exemplary to a Nation' and foster 'the seeds of vertu, and publick civility' (*Works* 3, 237–8), and was to substitute (in Haller's words) the poetry for the rhetoric of the spirit. Whenever these thoughts germinated, it is clear that the experience recorded—perhaps *realized* would be a better word—in the *Nativity* and *Elegy* 6 had a bearing upon them.

Some three months later Milton sought to renew that experience in *The Passion*, and the fragment, an avowed failure, shows that the subject cannot capture and control his imagination, which lies open to the crowding in of all the vagrant thoughts and feelings appropriate to his youthful sensibility. Similar feelings, secular and amatory, are in the ascendant in *Sonnets* 1–6, 'O Nightingale' and the Italian pieces [which Woodhouse, Hughes, and Parker (*Sonnets* 2–6) associate with the spring and summer of 1630, but which some others put in 1628–9, before the *Nativity*].

The common mark of the next group of poems (*On Shakespear* and the epitaphs on Hobson and the Marchioness of Winchester) is that, far more than the poems that preceded them, they are impersonal, remote from Milton's inward experience, as if he were holding his deeper feelings in abeyance and deliberately excluding them from his verse. Nor does this character altogether disappear from poems of 1631–2: *L'Allegro*, *Il Penseroso*, *Ad Patrem*, and *Arcades*. [For diverse views on the dates of these poems, see II above, and, in fuller detail, the introductions to the several poems.]

Arcades, probably the latest of these, is a piece of pure aesthetic patterning, a secular, courtly compliment, and bears no other reference of any kind. One proof is that Milton's favourite image of the music of the spheres is here used without any of the moral and religious implications it carries everywhere else, and is directed solely to the purpose of compliment [but see *Arcades* 69–77 n. and the postscript to Woodhouse in *Arcades* II]. This is not surprising in a poem written to order for a special occasion in which the poet had no share. It becomes matter for comment only when we compare *Arcades* with *Comus*, written for a similar occasion but freighted with doctrine, bent to Milton's personal interests and concerns, the record and realization of a profound inward experience. In *Arcades* Milton enters fully into the Arcadian mood— for the last time.

L'Allegro and *Il Penseroso*, whatever else criticism may discover in them, are certainly elaborate exercises in aesthetic patterning; nor is it easy to find in *L'Allegro*, taken by itself, much more than that. In *Il*

Penseroso there are indeed overtones from Milton's moral and religious preoccupations, but they are at most overtones and uttered with a reserve quite foreign to the earlier *Nativity* and the later *Comus* and *Lycidas*. Again it is not surprising that such overtones should be heard in *Il Penseroso*, since, like *Prolusion* 7 and *Ad Patrem*, it bears, if only indirectly, on Milton's cherished hope of retirement to his father's house to enjoy leisure for learning and to complete the learning necessary for poetry. But nothing in any of the three pieces would warrant us in supposing Milton already aware that the poetry is to be exclusively or predominantly religious or that the preparation will involve the degree of moral and religious as well as intellectual discipline which the years at [Hammersmith and] Horton actually afforded. The accent falls on learning as delightful (*Il Penseroso*), as useful (*Prolusion* 7), as essential to high achievement in poetry of any sort (*Ad Patrem*). There is a sense of the interdependence of intellect and morals (*Prolusion* 7) and of the way in which knowledge may mature to inspiration—'Till old experience do attain / To something like Prophetic strain' (*IlPen* 173–4). *Ad Patrem* continues to talk of poetry in general terms and predominantly classical images, as the *Vacation Exercise* did; and only the overtones of *Il Penseroso* give a hint, perhaps unconscious, of what is to come. There is no such indication as *Sonnet* 7 will provide, of Milton's final decision to dedicate his life to God's service in poetry: presumably because the decision is not yet irrevocably taken, but also because, though he is now writing on subjects bearing quite closely on his own career, he is still as it were holding experience at arm's length and not letting his deeper feelings find utterance. [J. T. Shawcross ('Milton's Decision to Become a Poet,' *MLQ* 24, 1963, 25) reaches the astonishing conclusion that 'None of the works before 1637 which have usually been adduced to indicate leanings toward a poetic career prove so under scrutiny.... It was not until 1637 that he recognized this calling and took steps to become more fit'—that is, near the end of the Horton period! Parker (125–7), imagining a crisis between father and son over the writing of a masque (1634), sees open conflict in *Ad Patrem*, 'one of the crucial moments in Milton's development'; this crisis other readers may be unable to discern in what Parker rightly calls a 'smiling, urbane' poem. Moreover, it seems very strange to disregard Milton's own clear, positive, and famous statement of his early ambition: that not long after his youthful preoccupation with the Roman love-poets he was 'confirm'd' in the opinion that, if he was to become a true poet, he 'ought him selfe to bee a true Poem' (*Apol*, Works 3, 303).]

The corrected dating of *Sonnet* 7 ('How soon hath time') has served, as we noted briefly, to resolve more than one problem in chronology; it has also clarified the pattern of Milton's development in the time between the *Nativity* (December 1629) and the *Solemn Musick* (February–March 1633?). After leaving Cambridge in July 1632, Milton, so far as we know, wrote nothing for some five months. Then, on his twenty-fourth birthday, 9 December 1632, he broke his silence with *Sonnet* 7. Nothing could be more natural in the circumstances than that he should thus pause to take stock of his resources and his future. Here we encounter for the first time a characteristic of Milton's more mature poetry: not the unembarrassed affirmation of *Elegy* 5 or the *Nativity*, nor the implications and overtones of *Il Penseroso*, but the formulation of a pressing problem which is resolved, or, better, transcended, as the poem proceeds to its close. [Woodhouse's fuller comment appears under *Sonnet* 7.] This is the mode of *Lycidas*, of *Sonnet* 19 ('When I consider'), and of yet more complex examples.

From the vantage point of *Sonnet* 7, we can see Milton's decision taken in the *Nativity* and *Elegy* 6 as ultimately significant indeed, but premature and followed first by failure (*The Passion*), then by some degree of hesitation and retreat (*Sonnets* 1–6), then by a turning to indifferent themes remote from his inward experience and deeper feelings (*On Shakespear* and the epitaphs, and we may add *L'Allegro* and *Arcades*), while even with subjects more immediately personal something of reticence remains (*Ad Patrem* and *Il Penseroso*). But now, after months of silent meditation, his poetry becomes once more the uninhibited expression of Milton's inner experience and deepest feeling; for he has reached his final decision, the act of dedication from which there will be no looking back.

That this is the significance of *Sonnet* 7 is confirmed by the three poems which almost certainly followed in close succession: *On Time*, *Upon the Circumcision*, and *At a solemn Musick*. Their religious themes link them with *Sonnet* 7, the first religious poem written since *The Passion*. *On Time* celebrates the Christian's triumph over time and is connected in subject with the sonnet. By its subject and its treatment the *Circumcision* is calculated to make good the failure of *The Passion*. The event commemorated, the first wounding of Christ, is prophetic, as Milton bids us remember (17–28), of the Crucifixion. Like *The Passion*, the poem opens with a memory of the joyous Nativity, then turns to mourn—this time more adequately. The notable differences are the unified and concentrated effect and the sense of man's sin as the cause of Christ's affliction. *At a solemn Musick* returns to the kind of *On Time* and renews its triumphal note; but the poem bears a subtler relation to the *Nativity*, touching again on some of its leading ideas and completing them with a stronger sense of sin and a more ecstatic hope of heaven. It is the decisive clarifying of Milton's own position in *Sonnet* 7 that enables him thus to repair the failure of *The Passion* and to clarify and complete at certain points the ideas of the ode. But more than this: except for a handful of occasional poems scattered over the next twenty-five years, the resolution taken in the sonnet leaves its mark on the whole of Milton's later poetry: it is all written 'As ever in my great task Masters eye.'

With these three poems setting as it were the seal upon his resolution, Milton turned to his studies. At Cambridge he had embraced every opportunity to write. At [Hammersmith and] Horton he systematically prepared himself for the great poems he hoped to produce, and meanwhile, as he wrote to Diodati in 1637, let his wings grow. Only twice in the next five years did he compose poems, *Comus* in 1634 and *Lycidas* in 1637, and the latter with signs of reluctance that were more than conventional. [Parker (126), speaking in italics of this long silence, sees Milton, after the 'conflict' stated in *Ad Patrem*, still supposedly expecting to be a clergyman and 'studying, at his father's expense—at his father's wish.'] Whatever critical disagreements there have been about *Comus*, or even *Lycidas*, no one could fail to detect the maturing of

Milton's thought, feeling, and artistry or the way in which he writes into these poems the concerns that are occupying his mind.

The Italian journey (1638–9: [see Parker, 169–82, 818–31]) is at once the completion of Milton's conscious preparation for his life work and an interlude both in his studies and (in a subtler sense) in his rigorous self-discipline. Bating no jot of his principles—*Coelum non animum muto dum trans mare curro* [cf. Horace, *Ep.* 1.11.27]—he responds to the social life, the literary culture, the Platonic idealism of the academies, courtly and popish though they were. One has only to read *Epitaphium Damonis* or the letter to Carlo Dati of 20 April 1647 (*Epistol* 10, *Works* 12, 44–53; Parker, 934, n. 57) to realize how vividly those golden days lingered in Milton's memory and affections. But the immediate experience yielded only one significant poem: in *Mansus*, addressed to his Neapolitan host, Milton expressed his proud conscious- ness of English culture and his sense of belonging to it, and also revealed his hope of writing an English epic, an *Arthuriad*. This, though it was to be abandoned, marks a phase in Milton's development. In the absence of other claimants, we may suppose that the *Arthuriad* was the work he was meditating, the work for which he was letting his wings grow, when he wrote to Diodati in the autumn of 1637 (*Epistol* 7, *Works* 12, 26–7); [more immediate meditations may have focused on *Lycidas*, which Milton dated in November 1637]. That was still his ambition when he wrote the *Epitaphium Damonis* in 1639–40.

IV

Milton had abridged his travels because of news from home of mounting troubles in church and state (*Def* 2, *Works* 8, 125), and although, by his own account, he did not hurry his return, such a decision was a first indication that service to the Puritan cause—a cause vehemently asserted in *Lycidas*—might postpone the great work in poetry for which his plans had been crystallizing. The continuance of his large poetic ambitions was recorded (*c.* 1641) in the list of subjects for tragedies pre- served in the MS. and in the personal passage in his fourth anti-episcopal tract, published early in 1642 (*RCG, Works* 3, 235–42). But after that tract we hear no more of such ambitions: the great work was evidently to be postponed *sine die*. [We may remember Edward Phillips' statement that part of Satan's address to the sun (*PL* 4.32–41) had been written quite early for the opening speech of a tragedy; and there are also the outlines of dramas on the story of Adam and Eve (*Works* 18, 228–32).]

On or before 2 January 1646, Milton's *Poems* appeared (dated 1645: see Parker, 300, 918, n. 1), at an unpropitious time, in the middle of the Civil War; the publication may be read as Milton's recognition that sustained poetic effort was no longer conceivable and that it might be well to gather the fruit of happier days. [On the reception of the *Poems* Parker (898–9, n. 121) assembles the evidence, mainly echoes in contemporary writers; to the names he there mentions may be added Marvell (ibid. 1023, n. 39), whose apparent echoes are chiefly from *Lycidas*. It may seem odd to us that a second edition did not appear until 1673. During 1650–60 the publisher, the highly literary Humphrey Moseley (d. 1661) listed the *Poems* in nine editions of the catalogue of his publications included in two dozen of his books (J. M. French, 'Moseley's Advertisements of Milton's Poems, 1650–1660,' *HLQ* 25, 1961–2, 337–45).]

Between 1642 and 1658 Milton composed, so far as we know, seventeen sonnets (8–23, and *On the new forcers of Conscience*), all occasional pieces, public or private; the Latin ode to John Rous, written to accompany a gift of the *Poems* to the Bodleian Library (23 January 1647); and the metrical paraphrases of two groups of Psalms (April 1648; August 1653). It would seem that preoccupation of mind rather than the lack of time accounts for the smallness of Milton's poetical output in this period, for there were two fairly long intervals in his pamphleteering, 1645–8 and 1655–8. Because of his blindness, which became complete about the beginning of 1652, and of the large works he wrote in defence of the Commonwealth (1649–54), he had been increasingly relieved of his duties as Latin Secretary [though he continued to perform some up through 1659]; but he was engaged on the huge *De Doctrina Christiana* (completed *c.* 1658–60) and, apparently from about 1658 onward, on

Paradise Lost. In the earlier period, 1645–8, Milton had been working on the *History of Britain* and probably several other things. A. H. Gilbert (*PQ* 28, 1949, 98–106) would push the composition of *Samson Agonistes* from the Restoration period back to *c*. 1642–3, and Parker [supported by Shawcross and Carey] back to 1647 f. [Parker's latest and fullest argument (313–21, 903–17) may be thought no more convincing than it was before, though some readers may be converted.]

It is significant that, after a ten-year interval, Milton should turn back to the sonnet form in 1642, when public causes and the war claimed his energies and attention. From that year until 1658 the sonnet was the principal, almost the only, form he employed; but when he turned seriously to the composition of *Paradise Lost* he found apparently no further need for it. All the sonnets at least from 7 onward are occasional, and hence add to their poetic interest a marked biographical value. The largest group (8, 11, 12, *On the new forcers of Conscience*, 15, 16, 17, 18, 22) tell us of Milton's public concerns and thus provide memorable supplements to the prose works and concentrated documentation for the development of his opinions on toleration and the separation of church and state. There were of course phases of public affairs and private interest on which the sonnets do not touch, notably the theological studies that issued in *De Doctrina Christiana*. But the private sonnets tell us of his friendships (9, 10, 13, 14, 20, 21, 22), of his reactions to the affliction of blindness (19, 22), and of the anguish attending his greatest domestic bereavement (23). The sonnets also prove that the poetic impulse was not wholly dormant during 1642–58; and they strikingly manifest one constant quality of Milton's poetry, the ability to re-create traditional forms with powerful originality.

v

Although there is room for difference of opinion regarding the precise order and the dates of a number of poems, the general pattern of Milton's development up to 1658 is reasonably clear and self-consistent. In retrospect it may be briefly summarized as follows:

(1) In his earlier years at Cambridge (1626–9), while destined, as he

thought, for the ministry, Milton was already ambitious to be a poet as well (*Vacation Exercise*, 1628), and to this end gave himself eagerly to practice in poetic composition, chiefly in Latin. With *Elegy* 6 (December–January, 1629–30) he concluded his initial experiments in Latin, and, having made two essays in English, launched upon a series of English poems with the *Nativity* (December 1629), which was also his first English poem on a religious theme. After the failure of his second essay, *The Passion* (1630), his remaining time at Cambridge (1630–2) was given to secular subjects, possibly commencing with the Italian sonnets (1630?) and probably including a brief return to Latin (*Ad Patrem*, 1631–2?). But his main efforts were in English: several epitaphs, in different styles (1630–1), and probably *L'Allegro* and *Il Penseroso* (1631–2?), and *Arcades* (1632?).

(2) After some months of retirement at home came the religious resolution of *Sonnet* 7 (December 1632). This was followed by three religious poems (*On Time, Circumcision, Solemn Musick*, December 1632–early 1633?). Thereafter, until the Italian tour of 1638–9, there were only two poems, written at request, though both profoundly personal in their moral and religious implications (*Comus*, 1634; *Lycidas*, 1637). The character of the period 1632–8 is thus very different from that of the Cambridge years. Milton is consciously preparing himself for his life work with a new sense of dedication, which leaves its mark on all the poems of this second period and with a deepening intensity on almost everything he was to write.

(3) During the Italian tour and for a while afterward Milton thought much about the subject and form of a projected major poem, considering first a national and Christian epic on Arthur (*Mansus, Epitaphium Damonis*), perhaps in a manner akin to Tasso's *Jerusalem Delivered*. Then he set down a variety of dramatic subjects from scriptural and British history, the theme of *Paradise Lost* receiving a prominent place among the former; but, finally, he still gave open-minded consideration to the merits and sanctions of various poetic forms (*RCG, Works* 3, 237–8). There is ample confirmation for Milton's later phrase about his epic—'long choosing, and beginning late' (*PL* 9.26).

[Of all the motives that inspired Milton throughout his life, perhaps the most constant, comprehensive, and urgent was his religious vision of perfection—a vision which included, but transcended, the beauties of earth. In the earlier poems, from the elegies on Bishops Andrewes and Felton through the *Nativity, Il Penseroso, On Time, At a solemn Musick, Comus,* and *Lycidas,* it was, quite literally, a vision of heaven. Then, in the great body of prose written during the Puritan Revolution, Milton was intent upon translating the vision into actuality, upon establishing the holy community, Christ's kingdom, on earth. As he said in *Of Education (Works* 4, 277),

The end then of Learning is to repair the ruines of our first Parents by regaining to know God aright, and out of that knowledge to love him, to imitate him, to be like him, as we may the neerest by possessing our souls of true vertue, which being united to the heavenly grace of faith makes up the highest perfection.

The public sonnets of that period are acts as well as poems, the acts of a man deeply committed to religious and civil freedom, a man who, committed as he also was to being God's poet, was yet impelled to postpone his great work and his hopes of poetic immortality in order to battle for God's cause in the dust and heat of immediate strife. But in *Paradise Lost,* turning away from the mass of men and militant action, he increasingly admitted, or proclaimed, that the grand reformation he had so long laboured to bring about would be realized only after the Day of Judgment, when 'God shall be All in All.' In the two epics and in *Samson* the disillusioned idealist limited his vision, in its earthly meaning, to the possibilities of humble strength and regeneration, aided by grace, in the individual soul.][4]

[4] [Thomas Greene (*The Descent from Heaven: A Study in Epic Continuity,* New Haven, 1963, 394) remarks: 'The youthful optimism of his Christian Humanism is reflected in the soaring visions of redemption which conclude *On Time, At a Solemn Musick, Epitaph on the Marchioness of Winchester, On the Death of the Bishop of Winchester, Manso, Damon's Epitaph, Lycidas,* and *Comus.* The same optimism informs the visionary conclusion of his first published prose work, *Of Reformation in England.'* With this attitude Greene contrasts the 'downward movement' at the end of the *Ready and Easy Way* and *Paradise Lost.*]

On the *Morning* of *Christ's Nativity*

※

I. DATE AND CIRCUMSTANCES

This, Milton's first great poem, was his first original English poem on a purely religious subject. It was written, or presumably begun, on Christmas Day, 1629, less than three weeks after Milton had become 21, and while he was at home in London for the holidays. The first light of Christmas morning brought him his theme, and he conceived the poem as a birthday gift for Christ (*Elegy* 6.87–8). Its place in his development is indicated in the Chronological Survey above; some critical comment is summarized in section III below.

The poem is not in the Cambridge MS., in which the first item is *Arcades*. It was first printed in the *Poems* of 1645 and was there significantly given first place. There is only one noteworthy alteration in the text of the 1673 edition (see 143–4 n.).

II. LITERARY BACKGROUND AND SOURCES

As a Christmas poem the ode takes its place in a very large class, although it bears no close relation to the traditional carol or Christmas hymn. It presents some interesting features for comparison and contrast with other seventeenth-century poems on the Nativity, such as Crashaw's. But the tradition to which it belongs is clearly that inaugurated by Virgil's fourth or 'Messianic' *Eclogue*, which heralds the return of the Golden Age under Augustus and associates it with the birth of a child— perhaps a son of Pollio, in whose consulship, in 40 B.C., the poem was written, [or perhaps a child of Octavian (Augustus) and Scribonia or of Antony and Octavia, or a vague reflection of Jewish speculations (see, e.g., M. Hadas, *History of Latin Literature*, New York, 1952, 144)].

34

On the Morning of Christ's Nativity

Through many centuries of the Christian era Virgil's poem was interpreted as an unconscious prophecy of the birth of Christ.

While invoking the pastoral Muses, the *Eclogue* announces a loftier strain and thus gives precedent for a combination of the pastoral with something approaching the heroic (cf. *Eclogue* 5 [and 6]). In the *Nativity* the combination is fortified by the inevitable role of the shepherds in a Christmas poem, which must yet deal with the second of the three supreme events in history [the other two being the Creation and the Day of Judgment, both of which come into Milton's poem]. The presence of the shepherd as a central figure in classical and in Christian imagery is one of the great points of contact and of union between the two; the *Nativity* itself affords striking illustration, since Milton links the shepherds with those of the pastoral tradition and Christ, the Good Shepherd, with Pan (85–92 and notes). Nor is this all. It is clear from the terms used in *Elegy* 6, as was remarked above (Chronological Survey), that Milton thinks of the *Nativity* as the first essay of one pledged to heroic poetry and an earnest of what he will attempt; and this too is in line with a tradition going back to Virgil's career and revived by Renaissance poets. But it is the elaboration of the return of the Golden Age (133–48) that binds Milton's poem (as it will also bind Pope's *Messiah*) most securely to the Messianic *Eclogue*, although Milton establishes the bond only to break it with 'But wisest Fate sayes no' (149) and press on to the new heaven and new earth that follow the Day of Judgment, the full Christian equivalent, or rather transcendence, of the restored Golden Age (165–6).

Other poems intervened between the Messianic Eclogue and the *Nativity*, to which the latter has been related. [A number are surveyed by J. B. Broadbent (III below, under 1960).] A. F. Leach ('Milton as Schoolboy and Schoolmaster,' *Proc. Brit. Acad.*, 3, 1907–8, 15–16) pointed to Prudentius, the inaugurator in the early fifth century of the Christian tradition in poetry, whose poems appeared in Colet's curriculum for St Paul's School and were probably still read there in Milton's day. It is likely that he would have read the hymns for Christmas and the Epiphany in Prudentius' *Liber Cathemerinon*, and in the *Nativity*

2-2

(173–80, 189–96) he might well have owed something to Prudentius' account of the silencing of the oracles in his *Apotheosis* (435–43, 474–8). Milton is, to be sure, letting his imagination play (as Prudentius did) on the Christian view of the data recorded by Plutarch in his *Obsolescence of Oracles* (*Moralia*, L.C.L. 5: see below, notes on 173 f.) and in other sources. [Donald L. Clark (*John Milton at St. Paul's School*, New York, 1948, 125–6) points out the lack of evidence for the reading of Prudentius, Mantuan, and Lactantius at St Paul's, though later Milton had more or less knowledge of these authors. John Carey (*Poems of John Milton*, ed. J. Carey and A. Fowler, London, 1968, 98), while taking account of Clark, recognizes 'striking' similarities between Milton and parts of Prudentius' *Apotheosis*. A. S. Cook's citations from Prudentius —and Mantuan—are recorded in the notes below.

Sir Herbert Grierson (*First Half of the Seventeenth Century*, New York, 1906, 182; *Metaphysical Lyrics & Poems of The Seventeenth Century*, Oxford, 1921, xlviii) was perhaps the first to suggest another possible model, Tasso's *Sopra la Cappella del Presepio fatta costruire da papa Sisto V in S. Maria Maggiore* (*Opere di Torquato Tasso*, ed. G. Gherardini, 5 v., Milan, 1823–5: 4, 579–82; also, with variant punctuation, in *Opere*, ed. G. Rosini, 33 v., Pisa, 1821–32: 6, 63–6). In this Christmas *canzone* of 120 lines Tasso celebrates the God who made the world and preserved the children of Israel, and the Son who was born in a time of universal peace and whose uniting of divinity and humanity evokes contrasts between his celestial glory and his humble and sacrificial life on earth. Such themes remind us of passages in Milton's ode, but they were the common property of the Christian tradition and are not proof of Tasso's influence.

Perhaps less central and familiar in poetry is the motif of Tasso's lines 73–90, the overthrow of the Greek, Roman, and Egyptian deities with the advent of the one true God:

> Già divien muto Apollo, e l'antro e l'onde,
>   E gli Dei falsi e vani,
>   La cui morte nel canto egli predisse;
>   Nè Dafne nella quercia altrui risponde

Più con accenti umani,
Ma quel fine ha lo spirto, ond' ella visse,
Ch' agli idoli superbi il Ciel prescrisse;
E giace Amón nella deserta arena,
Ove tempesta face Austro spirando,
Pur come soglia in procelloso Egéo;
Co' tempi di Mitréo
Giace il gran carro; ove legò domando
Berecintia i leoni, or non gli affrena;
Giacciono o sono in bando
I Coribanti ancor di Creta e d' Ida
Che rimbombò di strida;
E dagli altari suoi dolente fugge
Api ed Anubi, e più non latra o mugge.

Yet this theme too was a part of the tradition, and some illustrations—for example, from Ralegh's *History of the World*—are cited in the notes. It is probable enough that such a lover of Italian literature as Milton would have read Tasso's poem, and he might have got hints from it, especially for the last third of his own, but internal evidence in such a case is not at all conclusive. Carey—who does not mention Grierson—cites the same poem of Tasso under the title '*Nel giorno della Natività* (*Rime* (Venice 1621) viii 63–7),' and thinks it was 'in some part' a likely inspiration for Milton. He speaks of the resemblances noted above and others—'Nature's awe,' and Tasso's conclusion, in which he offers his humble poem as a gift like 'the "odours sweet" (*odori*) that the wise men bring.' (Cf. below, the end of *Nat* 23 n.)

B. Feinstein ('On the Hymns of John Milton and Gian Francesco Pico,' *CL* 20, 1968, 245–53) argues for the influence of Pico's *Hymnus ad Christum* (*Hymni heroici*, Milan, 1507). She groups parallels under five topics: (1) 'the noiselessness of the battle between Christ and the Roman leaders'; (2) the 'imagery of sun, thunderbolt, and trump of doom' used 'to convey the destruction of the oracles'; (3) 'the silencing of the oracles and their retreat, accompanied by howling and lamentations'; (4) the descriptions of rituals and deities; (5) the withdrawal of Pico's 'Tartarean shadows' like clouds thinned by the sun, which is

37

likened to Milton's 'shadows' trooping to the infernal jail 'as the sun is curtained by clouds.' Mrs Feinstein names many of the closer and more familiar sources and analogues cited by Cook, Patrides, and others, but hardly takes sufficient account of them. Pico's hymn is another illustration of the widespread traditions, but this argument for its influence on the *Nativity* may be thought unconvincing.

Giles Fletcher's *Christs Victorie, and Triumph* (1610) has yielded numerous phrases to commentators on the *Nativity*, as the following notes indicate, but M. M. Mahood (*Poetry and Humanism*, London, 1950, 171–5) sees Fletcher as inspiring 'far more of the Nativity Ode than an occasional conceit or personification. The whole mood and tone of Milton's poem belong to the same Baroque tradition. The Ode has a Baroque amplitude of conception, for it embraces the complete history of the world from its creation to its final dissolution. Like all the finest seventeenth-century works of art in the grand style, it is saved from turgidity by the vigour of its movement.... The matter of the poem is no less Baroque, for it offers as complete a fusion of classical mythology with Christian themes as the seventeenth century could desire'—a fusion more lusciously exemplified in Fletcher. (Miss Mahood is quoted also in III below, under Broadbent, 1960.)

References for and comment on the music of the spheres and the whole musical-metaphysical tradition are given below in the note on lines 125–32.]

III. CRITICISM [D.B.]

After a paragraph on the early ode as a genre, this section summarizes and excerpts comments on the *Nativity* from the following critics, in chronological order: G. Saintsbury; S. G. Spaeth; J. H. Hanford; E. M. W. Tillyard; G. N. Shuster; A. Barker; A. S. P. Woodhouse; M. M. Ross; Rex Warner; M. Mack; C. Brooks and J. E. Hardy; L. Stapleton; D. C. Allen; L. L. Martz; L. Nelson; F. T. Prince; K. Muir; D. Daiches; R. Tuve; J. B. Broadbent (and M. M. Mahood); M.-S. Røstvig; H. Frazier; L. L. Martz; I. G. MacCaffrey; C. A. Patrides; F. S. Kastor; J. S. Lawry; B. Rajan; J. Carey; P. Cullen.

On the *Morning* of *Christ's Nativity*

When the young Milton wrote the *Nativity*, 'almost at a single bound the English ode' sprang 'into full-blown life' (Robert Shafer, *The English Ode to 1660*, Princeton, 1918, 94). The ode (a term Milton used in line 24) was during the previous generation only beginning to crystallize as a distinct lyrical and reflective genre. In his famous letter to Milton of 1638 Sir Henry Wotton, a poet himself, could speak of 'a certain Dorique delicacy' in the 'Songs and Odes' of *Comus*. The ancient models, Pindar, the Anacreontea, and Horace (who alone offered a wide variety), might well obstruct the crystallizing process, and their modern continental imitators contributed in various ways to both laxity and neoclassical strictness. Spenser's *Fowre Hymnes* we might be inclined to call odes, and the label 'hymn' was a common equivalent or approximation in the period after him; his *Epithalamion* was of course an ode of a special and fully recognized genre. Drayton in his score of odes was a conscious innovator; his chief models were Horace, Ronsard, and Skelton. He conceived of the ode as a song, a lyrical address of some length, on either an exalted and public or private and amatory theme and written in a high or middle strain; such odes as *To the Virginian Voyage*, *The Ballad of Agincourt*, and *To his Coy Love* exemplify Drayton's fluid notion of 'a mixed kinde' (*Complete Works of Michael Drayton*, ed. J. W. Hebel, K. Tillotson, and B. H. Newdigate, 5 v., Oxford, 1931–41, cited hereafter as 'Drayton': 2, 345). About the time of Milton's *Nativity*, Ben Jonson (whose other odes were especially Horatian) produced his formal—and neoclassical—Pindaric on Sir Lucius Cary and Sir Henry Morison, and gave the English ode the dominant pattern it was to follow, strictly or more often loosely, for over a hundred years. The *Nativity* did not of course attempt the Pindaric form, although it 'brilliantly illustrated some features of Pindar's style and the manner in which Pindar disposed the materials of his poems' (Shafer, 7). Milton's ode has been called Spenserian, Italianate, Baroque, or Mannerist—as some of the following pages will indicate. Later Milton himself, surveying the genres in his defence of the religious and moral aims of poetry, spoke of both classical and biblical models and linked odes with hymns: 'Or if occasion shall lead to imitat

39

those magnifick Odes and Hymns wherein Pindarus and Callimachus are in most things worthy, some others in their frame judicious, in their matter most an end [i.e. for the most part] faulty: But those frequent songs throughout the law and prophets beyond all these, not in their divine argument alone, but in the very critical art of composition may be easily made appear over all the kinds of Lyric poesy, to be incomparable' (*RCG, Works* 3, 238).

On the character and development of the genre four books, of varying scope, are: Shafer (above); G. N. Shuster, *The English Ode from Milton to Keats* (New York, 1940); Carol Maddison, *Apollo and the Nine: A History of the Ode* (London, 1960); Kurt Schlüter, *Die englische Ode* (Bonn, 1964).

George Saintsbury ('Milton,' *Cambridge History of English Literature*, 7, 1911, 125–6) saw Milton's originality first displayed, 'in the most striking fashion,' in the *Nativity*. 'Most striking—for the opening stanzas of the proem, though much finer than anything he had done, were still not quite Milton. Not merely Spenser, but the greater Davies, either Fletcher, several other poets actually or nearly contemporary, might have written them. *The Hymn* itself, in its very first lines, not merely in metre but in diction, in arrangement, in quality of phrase and thought alike, strikes a new note—almost a new gamut of notes. The peculiar stateliness which redeems even conceit from frivolity or frigidity; the unique combination of mass and weight with easy flow; the largeness of conception, imagery, scene; above all, perhaps, the inimitable stamp of phrase and style—attained, chiefly, by cunning selection and collocation of epithet—give the true Milton.... The piece gives us all its author's poetry *in nuce*—his union of majesty and grace, his unique and all-compelling style, his command of "solemn music" such as had never before been known.'

In his pioneer and still useful book, *Milton's Knowledge of Music: Its Sources and Its Significance in his Works* (Princeton, 1913: cited hereafter as *Music*), Sigmund G. Spaeth (90–2) remarks that 'Milton's sense for sound is most marked' in the *Nativity*. 'The entire poem seems to move upon an undercurrent of music.' It 'falls naturally into three parts which are distinguished through the characterization of sounds.' The opening description of universal peace 'creates a background of complete silence' or of 'the gentle sounds of nature.' Then the birth of Christ is welcomed by universal harmony, the music of the angels joined with that of the spheres. 'Milton seems to feel himself the leader of a tremendous orchestra, which responds to every suggestion of his imagination.' The third part brings 'an abrupt transition from the celestial to the infernal, from the harmonious to the discordant.' The overthrow of the pagan gods 'is portrayed chiefly by the silencing of characteristic sounds connected with their rites,' and by shrieks, laments, sighs, moans, 'Cymbals ring' and 'Timbrel'd Anthems dark.' 'Thus, from beginning to end, the *Nativity Hymn* is built up on suggestions of sound. Its lyric effectiveness lies largely in this preference of the audible to the visible.'

J. H. Hanford ('Youth,' 1925, 122–4) saw the *Nativity* as a conspicuous milestone in Milton's development. Both it and the sixth *Elegy* (which followed immediately) are examples of his habit of stocktaking. Although in his Latin epistle to Diodati Milton could write sympathetically of the festive poetry of wine and love, he set above that the ascetic ideal of the heroic poet, the poet-priest. The very different *Nativity* was also an indirect dedication of his talents to the most exalted kind of poetry. Milton had lately come of age, and 'the coincidence of his birthday with the Christmas season explains the mood in which he took up the subject of the Nativity.

'The poem itself, as all critics have recognized, strikes a new note in the poetry of Milton.' While it is still in the Spenserian line, 'it quite transcends the earlier [English] poems in elevation and poetic fervor. We feel that here, for the first time, we have the genuine and characteristic reaction of Milton's personality upon a serious religious subject. He contemplates the event, not at all with the loving surrender of a Catholic poet to its human sweetness, but with an austere intellectualized emotion stirred in him by the idea of its moral significance. Christ is, for him, not a babe, nor indeed a person at all, but a symbol of purity and truth, that truth which "came once into the world with her divine Master, and was a perfect shape most glorious to look on." The pagan deities are multiform ugliness of error.... The poet completely identifies himself with his conception and this identification calls forth all his imaginative and expressive powers. However much Milton's precise theological ideas may have changed in later life and his ethical sense become enriched with the content of experience, his attitude retains to the end the form which it assumes in the *Nativity Ode*. The poem is the lyric prelude of *Paradise Lost* and in an exacter sense of *Paradise Regained*.'

E. M. W. Tillyard (*Milton*, London and New York, 1930, 35–42) quoted two opposed judgments, only a generation apart in time: Warton, while praising some stanzas (especially 19–26), described the rest as chiefly 'a string of affected conceits, which his early youth, and the fashion of the times, can only excuse'; and Henry Hallam pronounced the *Nativity* 'perhaps the finest [ode] in the English language' [*Literature of Europe*, ed. 1839–40, 3, 515]. Tillyard thinks 'the general tissue of conceit must either be justified or condemned.' His justification is that the conceits partly create the 'unique charm' of the ode, 'the clean exuberance of the best primitive art,' as in a fifteenth-century Italian painting of the Nativity. 'The essence of the poem is not stateliness excusing conceit [Saintsbury], but homeliness, quaintness, tenderness, extravagance, and sublimity, harmonised by a pervading youthful candour and ordered by a commanding architectonic grasp.' The poem has a 'combination of qualities' not found in the later Milton. In the *Nativity* 'he seemed to write with a pulse beating quicker, with a mind more alert, more varied, more susceptible to fancy as well as to imagination, less censorious, tenderer, less egotistical, than when he wrote any other poem before or since.' Tillyard follows Hanford in invoking both the sixth *Elegy* and the later *Apology for Smectymnuus* and in seeing the *Nativity* as Milton's 'mental dedication of himself to the high calling of epic poet,' 'a deep committal, fervently and whole-heartedly made,' that brings serenity with it. There is also the hope, the Christian hope, of human progress. There is finally, Tillyard feels, 'something of sex,' not demonstrable but implicit in 'the run of the verse, the dance of that incomparable stanza.'

On the *Morning of Christ's Nativity*

To G. N. Shuster (*The English Ode from Milton to Keats*, 1940, 67–70) the *Nativity* suggests 'Tasso and Giles Fletcher in particular.' It was 'a step forward, a long step forward, in the history of the English ode.' Although it did not attract attention for a long time, 'it established the religious ode as a permanent art form.' The stanza of the prelude is that of Spenser's *Hymnes*, but with a final Alexandrine. 'The form of the "hymn" proper is, however, in no sense Spenserian but resembles Jonsonian ode stanzas so closely (for all the added subtlety of thought and structure) that a common or cognate source is evident. Jonson also used the final Alexandrine (in *An Ode to Himselfe*). Above all the resemblance lies in the shifting line length and the swift movement achieved by the introduction of trimeter lines (cf. Jonson's Pindaric ode). The hard ring of masculine rhymes is heard throughout, too, though Milton also makes striking use of feminine rhymes upon occasion.' Shuster sees 'the prosodic germ of Milton's poem' in Sir John Beaumont's *Ode on the Blessed Trinitie* (included in his volume of 1629), a poem on a lofty religious theme with 'the combination of three, five and six stress lines.'

The first full, precise, and coherent analysis of the *Nativity* was given by Arthur Barker ('The Pattern of Milton's *Nativity Ode*,' *UTQ* 10, 1940–1, 167–81; repr. in *Milton: Modern Judgements*, ed. A. Rudrum, London, 1968). With Hanford, Barker sees Milton's conscious sense of his calling as a poet-prophet first embodied in this poem, an experience, though strongly aesthetic as well as religious, akin to the Puritan's sense of conversion or election. 'This poem strikes a note altogether new in his poetry, includes an implied rejection of his earlier manner, and records a vision which produced a confident and harmonious purposefulness by overcoming the forces of gloom and confusion' (169). Barker's thesis is 'that the recognition of the significance of Christ's incarnation and sacrifice recorded in the *Ode* was coupled with a recognition of the potentialities of a peculiarly complex poetical symbol, and that these recognitions together bestowed a new unity of feeling upon both Milton's thought and his art' (170). Using the triple pattern of *Lycidas* as criterion and contrast (his brief but fruitful analysis of that poem is quoted in its appropriate place), Barker finds, not the pressing problems of the elegy, yet 'profound feeling and calm determination' expressed 'in much the same way'; the *Nativity* is unified, though less strictly, 'because it is built upon another kind of design.' Apart from the prelude and the brief conclusion, 'it too consists of three equal movements, held in relation, not by the repetition of a structural pattern, but by the variation of a basic pattern of imagery. The first eight stanzas of the "Hymn" describe the setting of the Nativity, the next nine the angelic choir, the next nine the flight of the heathen gods.... A brief analysis will show that the three movements each present a single modification of the simple contrast, preserved throughout the poem, between images suggesting light and harmony and images of gloom and discord.' (173)

In the first movement 'The Nativity setting is described in a series of negatives whose effect is to reduce light and sound to a minimum while subduing all discordant elements.' 'The eighth stanza completes this peacefully hushed and faintly illuminated scene by introducing the shepherds,' and 'also serves as a link with the second movement,' since the angelic music breaks in upon them 'with a suddenness for which the poet has carefully prepared.' The second movement is dominated by ideas and images of harmonious sound and brilliant colour. The music of the spheres, 'representing the order of nature,' is linked with the angelic symphony of heaven, which recalls the music of the Creation. The vision of a new golden age 'is dissipated by the thought of the Cross, and the movement comes to an end with a reference to the last judgment which prepares for the third movement by introducing ideas of dissonance and gloom in sharp contrast with the harmony and order of the second.' 'The last movement is full of discordant sounds, distorted forms, and shadows.' But toward the end light and order return (unhappily in 'the sun in bed') and prepare for the picture in the last stanza. This stanza 'catches up the pattern underlying the preceding movements, bringing order after confusion and reflecting the peaceful hush and the brilliant harmony of the first two movements. It is pervaded by the clear and steady brilliance of the new star's "handmaid lamp," and enclosed by the "order serviceable" of the "bright-harness'd angels." Its static quality fixes with appropriate firmness the pattern of light and harmony on which the poem has been composed.' (173–5)

'The effect of the *Nativity Ode* is thus produced by its reiteration of a pattern of imagery, variously presented in the three movements, and impressed with finality in the concluding verse. The balanced contrast between the first and third movements serves to throw the central movement into sharp relief. This emphasis defines the poem's significance for Milton.' 'The *Nativity Ode* is his first achievement of composition and pattern in the full Miltonic sense, and it is so because it expresses his achievement of composition and pattern in himself through the harmonious illumination resulting from his recognition of the significance of the Incarnation. It is the first of Milton's inspired poems; and the angelic choir is the symbol of his inspiration.' (175)

However traditional the imagery of the angelic choir, none of Milton's contemporaries—Giles Fletcher, Herbert, Vaughan, Crashaw—'developed the idea and its varied associations with anything like the controlled complexity of the central passage of the *Ode*' (176–7). 'It is thus the symbol of illumination and harmony provided by the choir and the spheres which fuses the heterogeneous particles of the *Ode* and gives it its controlled power. It does so because it enables the poet to draw on a vast reservoir of pagan and Christian suggestion while transcending the conflict between the two traditions, and consequently to express something approaching the totality of his literary experience. The fruit of this experience is his sense of divine inspiration.' (177–8)

'It is significant that there is no reference to the celestial music in Milton's poetry before 1629' [angelic music is heard in *El* 3.59–60, 65]. 'His attention seems to have been drawn to it when he had to compose his second academic prolusion,' a discourse which suggests the germ of the ode's pattern. 'The force with which this idea struck Milton's imagination is indicated by the fact that from the *Ode* to *Lycidas* he was almost incapable of writing on a serious subject without introducing the music.' The beauty of the *Nativity* 'surpassed anything Milton had hitherto written because it expressed with perfect adequacy and complete control a new and profound religious emotion....It was this experience, at once aesthetic and religious, which crystallized Milton's conviction of special poetical calling and provided him with a definition of his function.' The experience involved 'a recognition, not only of the personal significance of the Incarnation, but also of its relationship to the classical and humanistic doctrine of harmonious perfection symbolized by the music of the spheres. Of this perfection divinely inspired poetry seemed to him the supreme expression.' (178–81)

Woodhouse's 'Notes on Milton's Early Development' (*UTQ* 13, 1943–4, 66–101) included a discussion of the *Nativity* (73–7) which added valuable insights to those of Barker. One was the distinction drawn between the music of the spheres as the ode's '*aesthetic* centre' and the banishment of the pagan gods, which is 'in some sort its *intellectual* core.' (This idea is utilized by L. Stapleton, below, under 1953–4.) But Woodhouse's discussion is not summarized here because its elements, along with many other materials, are distributed through the copious annotation in IV below; see also above, Chronological Survey III. A summary comment, including a contrast with Crashaw's *Nativity*, appears in Woodhouse's posthumous volume of lectures, *The Poet and his Faith: Religion and Poetry in England from Spenser to Eliot and Auden* (Chicago, 1965), 51–4.

Malcolm M. Ross ('Milton and the Protestant Aesthetic: The Early Poems,' *UTQ* 17, 1947–8, 346–60; *Poetry & Dogma*, New Brunswick, 1954, 183–204), writing from the Anglo-Catholic standpoint, finds in the *Nativity* the first poetic evidence of Milton's Protestantism, his loss of the fullness and depth of Catholic tradition. The Christ of the *Nativity* is not a Person but an abstract symbol (188). While Milton of course believed in the Incarnation, he 'was unable to imagine poetically the humanity of God,' and his poetry 'nowhere expresses the incarnational and operative sense of Christ' that belongs to the full Christian tradition. In the *Nativity* Christ is 'Son of God but never Son of Man.' As for redemption, 'Man is the passive spectator (and astonished beneficiary) of an abstract and remote performance....There is, therefore, no poetic continuity—no "character"—in the representation of Christ, but rather a series of separate symbolizations of the might and goodness of God' (191). 'The form and strength of the poem, as...Arthur Barker has shown, derive from the active images of harmony and light. To these the Person of Christ is subordinated, and from these man is excluded.' Thus there is here 'a significant reversal of value.' Christ, in typical Catholic art the all-inclusive and constant symbol, 'has become a variable symbol dependent for meaning upon superior and controlling ideas' (191).

Rex Warner (*John Milton*, London and New York, 1949, 1950, 50–1), after outlining the poem, remarks: 'Thus at the very beginning of his life we find themes and a style which will develop, but remain essentially the same till the end. There is the possibility of the return of Truth and Justice; there is the ambiguous position of Greek divinities, sometimes being exalted, as "the mighty Pan" is equated with Jesus Himself, sometimes being, rather regretfully, assigned to Hell; there is the orderly, serene and majestic company of angels; there is confusion to be dealt out to the enemies of God; there is a higher harmony which, but for sin, would be audible to us all; there is a longing for innocence and for perfection. And in the style there is not only an English magic and a Vergilian grace and pathos; there is also a strange majesty, a virile robustness. This double response, to what is sensuous and to what is supernaturally dignified, can be observed in many of the early poems.'

Maynard Mack (*Milton*, New York, 1950, 5–7), going on from Woodhouse and Barker, sees the *Nativity* as 'an enactment of the fusion, in which nature is not repudiated but transformed by grace.' The first movement (stanzas 1–8) 'presents the natural order' in its hushed expectancy. The second movement (9–17) turns to the order of grace. 'The half light and the hush of the first section give place to images of intense light and especially of music—the harmony of the angels and the spheres. As in Milton's poetry generally, this harmony is used as a symbol of the concord, felicity, and perfect union to be found in a world in which nature has been completed by grace and restored to it.' The third section (18–26) turns back to the order of nature. The description of the rout of the pagan deities 'serves two purposes. It images the purgation that the order of nature must undergo as a condition of its restoration to grace. The false gods,...in addition to being the pagan deities of history, symbolize the elements in nature that are alien to grace, especially the tendency of man to deify his own natural powers and those of his environment. Milton's attitude toward this purgation is by no means simple-minded; the poem rejoices at the flight of a brutal deity like Moloch, but there is an air of wistfulness in its farewell to some of the more innocent manifestations of nature worship.' 'The rout serves also to depict the triumphant might of the new dispensation.' The power that justifies the image of Christ as an infant Hercules 'is not hostile to nature as such. Rather, its operation is such that it can be likened to the natural progress of the dawn—the Sun of the opening section brought back now in a metaphor of the Son (st. 26)—driving away the shadows of the night.' Mack's comment on the final stanza is quoted in the note on 237–44 below.

C. Brooks and J. E. Hardy (*Poems of Mr. John Milton*, New York, 1951, 95–104) see in the 'Hymn,' not the clear tripartite division shown by Barker, but two parts: 'a morning scene' 'filled with sun and star imagery' (stanzas 1–15) and a second part (stanzas 16 f.) dealing 'with what may be called the negative aspects of the occasion.' Such a division seems to blur and attenuate, if it does not quite destroy, Milton's organic development of his theme and symbolic contrasts, and the ensuing explication, while more or less in agreement with Barker, cannot altogether repair the damage. This explication contains numerous suggestive comments—e.g. on the 'aesthetic distance' Milton maintains throughout—though not all are valid (see below, 74 n.).

Laurence Stapleton ('Milton and the New Music,' *UTQ* 23, 1953–4, 217–26; repr. in *Milton: Modern Essays in Criticism*, ed. A. Barker, New York, 1965) starts from Barker and Woodhouse, especially the latter's distinction between the aesthetic centre of the poem (the music of the spheres) and its intellectual core (the routing of the pagan gods). She asks how these two poles are related, and finds an analogy, not necessarily a source, in the *Exhortation to the Greeks* (L.C.L.) of the Platonist church father, Clement of Alexandria. Clement's 'new music' is the truth to be found in Christ, who is not a deceiver like Orpheus and the rest (p. 9). The new faith in Christ, the Logos, stands for reason, order, and harmony in both the macrocosm and man the microcosm (p. 13). 'The act of creation, the bringing of order out of chaos, began, indeed constituted, the music of the spheres, and to Milton, as to Clement, was the work of the Logos. As Clement put it, "this pure song, the stay of the universe and the harmony of all things, stretching from the centre to the circumference and from the extremities to the centre, reduced this whole to harmony...." (p. 13).' 'This symbol of the music of the spheres allows Milton to achieve in the centre of his composition a masterly focus, making the present moment both revive man's lost capacity for perfection and prophesy its future realization.' 'But to guard the poem and the realization itself from the vacuity of mere wish, Milton turns from a cosmic vision of the future to the decisiveness of its immediate effect on human history,' the banishing of false gods. As Clement had said to the Greeks, 'worship of these gods represented an inferior stage in human existence; confronted by a religion of love and mercy, they could not survive (pp. 19, 27, 243).'

Don C. Allen deals with the *Nativity* and *Comus* in a chapter called 'The Higher Compromise' (*The Harmonious Vision*, Baltimore and London, 1954, 24–9: cited hereafter as *Vision*). While the ode is seen as Milton's 'most perfect early work,' its power 'does not spring from a true reconciliation of its intellectual and emotional disunities, but rather from the fact that they are not reconciled at all, or, better still, that they are erased in a unity of a higher order.' 'In the "Hymn" there are two central contentions: the minor dissonance between the two aspects of Nature, and the major dissonance between the two kinds of harmony.' In the first section (stanzas 1–7), reconciliation 'takes the form of Redemption. Nature, whose biography is that of the Magdalene—an intrinsically baroque identification—is redeemed by the greater Sun. Hence the redemption that arises from this conflict looks forward to the redemption of man in the latter stanzas....' 'The conflict between Christian and pagan harmony that governs the second and third sections makes the "Hymn" an artistic wonder.' 'Milton succeeds in effecting an artistic harmony while describing a spiritual disharmony. When he contemplates the difference between the pagan and the Christian world, he finds, like Plato's friend Archytas, a musical explanation.' The 'description of Christian harmony begins with a heraldic blending of clearly recognizable emblems: the circle, the globe, light,' but 'they all become music.' 'To this is joined the intermediate music of the spheres and the lower chant that the poet is composing. For Milton realized, as did the authors of the Psalms, that the music of the creatures was a required melody for the bass of Heaven's organ; and he knew, too, that at the moment of the Incarnation, the harmony was without flaw for the first time since the springtime of Creation. Distemperature comes again with the death of God and then the full music cannot be heard until after the Day of Wrath. This is the meaning of this section.' In the third section, from the conflict 'between the limited music of the Church Militant and the discordant melodies of pagan theology, Milton anticipates the multitoned yet perfectly matched harmony of the Church Triumphant. This is the third and greatest compromise.

'The "Ode" has, then, three series of poetically expressed contrasts, and from each of them Milton draws a compromise that is far more splendid than the parts conflicting. From the variance between past and the present, he extracts the solution of timelessness; from that between Nature abandoned and Nature redeemed, he creates a Nature as immutable and untarnished as Faith, Hope, and Peace; from the disagreement between pagan and Christian harmony, he derives the harmony of God. Underlying all of this is the conventional modulation of the universal and the particular which is signified by the movement from the abstract character of Peace to her concrete manifestations, a modulation that is also orchestrated by the epodic contraction and expansion of the metrical line. The result of this artistic procedure is a magnificent unity that greatly affects us.

'This method of displaying the opposed unrealities and of drawing from the opposition a high poetic reality is a basic Miltonic technique.' Louis L. Martz (*The Poetry of Meditation: A Study in English Reli-*

gious Literature of the Seventeenth Century, New Haven and London, 1954, 164–7) contrasts Milton with Crashaw. Milton deals mainly 'with all the world except the manger scene, briefly mentioned in the first stanza, and almost visualized in the last....Milton puts last the concrete scene which would normally begin a Catholic meditation on this subject. The Incarnation is not the essential point of his poem: it is the Redemption and its effects on the future course of human history. Even the briefest comparison with Crashaw's hymn on the Nativity, "Sung as by the Shepherds," provides us with a significant contrast between the spirituality of English Puritanism and the spirituality of the Counter Reformation. Crashaw, through the shepherds, makes himself intimately present at the manger-scene....At the same time, the theological emphasis lies on God's Love; though the paradoxical Power of this "Mighty Babe" is fully recognized, it is overpowered by the stress on "love's Noon" in the second line, on "Love's architecture" in the middle, and on the gentleness of his Kingship at the close....The eucharistic reference, occurring in a passage that echoes the motifs of popular love-poetry, reminds us forcibly that this poem is centered on the Incarnation....But Milton's poem in its opening lines announces the difference in theme....The Love of God is never mentioned in Milton's poem; it celebrates instead his wondrous Power, displayed throughout the universe, from the moment of its Creation to the moment of its ultimate Doom....With the theme of Redemption comes an emphasis on the need for redemption: the "leprous sin" of man, the "scaly Horrour" of the Dragon, and the worship of false gods: an emphasis announced in the opening images of nature's depravity [37–44]. But in Crashaw's poem the snowflakes move toward the manger in an effort to assist and pay tribute to the Infant....Crashaw, then, produces a ritual love-song; Milton, a hymn in praise of the Power and Glory.' (See also the essay by Martz summarized below under 1965.)

Lowry Nelson ('Góngora and Milton: Toward a Definition of the Baroque,' *CL* 6, 1954, 53–64; *Baroque Lyric Poetry*, New Haven and London, 1961, 32–52) stresses Milton's 'baroque' shifting of tenses and the significance of this procedure. The first two stanzas of the prelude take us into the remote past of the first Christmas; in the last two the poet places himself in that time and place. The first line of the 'Hymn' says 'It *was* the Winter wilde,' but in line 3 the divine child 'in the rude manger *lies*.' Throughout the poem tenses continue to shift as the poet shifts his focus from the actual event to the whole panorama of time between the Creation and the Judgment. 'The poem ends in as precise a present as possible:

> And all about the Courtly Stable,
> Bright-harness'd Angels sit in order serviceable.

'While the past tense has been left far behind, we cannot think that the poem merely emerges into a historical present; in terms of structure and in terms of the central paradox...the tense has helped to identify the birth of Christ with Christmas as it has been celebrated ever since. So we see how much the time structure depends upon special uses of tense, and how closely tense is linked to meaning. All the main elements of the poem work together remarkably well to achieve the almost ecstatic joy, and, by transforming it, the final serenity.'

F. T. Prince (*The Italian Element in Milton's Verse*, Oxford, 1954) sees Milton's English verse up to 1638 as written mainly in discipleship to Spenser and Jonson, but as already revealing some technical lessons learned from Italian poetry. The *Nativity* 'illustrates this reflection of Italian form in the Spenserian tradition' (59). The Italianisms in this and some other early poems 'may be ascribed almost wholly to Milton's following of Spenser. The Spenserian quality of the language and the rhythms of the hymn is a commonplace of criticism. It appears in nothing more clearly than in the management of adjectives; and such usages as "dark foundations deep", "flowre-inwov'n tresses torn", and "Timbrel'd Anthems dark", which Spenser derived from the Italians, Milton accepts as proven elements in English poetic diction. The stanza itself reveals the same origins. The concluding alexandrine seals its Spenserian character, and both this and the preceding octosyllable would be impossible in any strict adherence to the methods of the Italian *canzone*. Yet the pattern and movement of the stanza, and the very notion of employing such a stanza for a solemn ode of this sort, could only derive from the tradition of the *canzone*' (60).

K. Muir (*John Milton*, London, 1955, 1960, 24–7) outlines 'Milton's first masterpiece,' accepting his youthful 'baroque images' without qualms, and praises what Tillyard called his 'architectonic grasp,' his skill in manipulating stanzas and easy transitions from stanza to stanza and topic to topic. The poem's 'bright colouring and vivid pictorial effects are as remarkable as its varied music. It is not surprising that it was Dylan Thomas's favourite poem, or that Keats admired the lovely nineteenth stanza, and remembered it when he wrote his "Ode to Psyche." ' 'The poem uses classical mythology and subsumes it to a Christian purpose; in its brilliance and its occasional tenderness it reveals the Renaissance Milton unspoilt and unequalled.'

D. Daiches (*Milton*, London, 1957, 38–48) notes many evidences of Milton's growing imaginative and artistic power, though he rather slights his structural instinct. The last stanza of the prelude 'brings in a sense of movement which provides the external framework of the poem.' The Hymn, as a set piece, is 'more stylized, more deliberately artful,' in its ornate and somewhat baroque conceits. Of the early part of the Hymn

The whole effect is, one might say, theatrical. First, the hushing into silence. Then a brief look at the audience. Then, suddenly, the ravishing music. Finally, after the music has been playing for some time, the curtain slowly rises and we actually see the angelic choir singing. (42)

'Music symbolizes the divine order.' 'Milton finds it hard to tear himself away from the contemplation of this divine concert'; his imagination was haunted 'by thoughts of prelapsarian bliss in Paradise, and its return in a new Golden Age.' When he comes to banish the false gods, 'It is remarkable how effectively Milton manages to suggest the different evils of different kinds of pagan religion.' In regard to the classical divinities 'he cannot restrain an occasional elegiac note.' His animosity is directed mainly 'against the gods of ancient Palestine against whom the Chosen People had fought' and who were always represented as 'false and cruel misleaders of men or at best as empty names.' His feeling 'is clearly one of fascinated repulsion.' 'Images of order, degree, stability' in the last stanza attest 'the divine harmony.' 'As a piece of deliberate craftsmanship' the ode

is a most remarkable achievement. It is, of course, limited in range and complexity, but it achieves its effects with admirable success, showing a precision in the handling of imagery and a virtuosity in the manipulation of rhythms that mark the self-conscious artist. Nevertheless, the ode is not a fair indication of the road Milton was to travel as a poet. He never wrote anything quite like this again. He was to develop a poetic style less Spenserian, less coyly artful in its manipulation of conceits, less exhibitionist, one might almost say, though this is perhaps unfair to the ode, which remains an impressive but isolated example of Milton's virtuosity. (48)

Rosemond Tuve (*Images & Themes in Five Poems by Milton*, Cambridge, Mass., and London, 1957, 37–72) begins with the central fact that Milton's 'subject is the Incarnation not the Nativity,' a fact which 'controls the imagery.' The poem 'exists to celebrate a mystery rather than to describe and comment upon an event'; it 'celebrates the meaning of the Incarnation not only in history but after history is over, an event both in and not within created nature, a peace both in and not within created time.' As Milton himself had indicated at the end of his sixth *Elegy*, his theme is 'our peace.' All this implies and foreordains the use of a body of traditional ideas and symbols that belong to Christian and classical traditions. There is no conflict between these realms of reference 'because the power of Milton's basic theme of the redemptive promise of the Incarnation had centuries before him Christianized these and other classical images' (41). So we have, handled with a mixture of traditionalism and active originality, the age-old concepts and images of Nature, Peace, Harmony, the Golden Age, the 'old Dragon,' and, above all, Light and Music—and the opposites of all these, which are overcome or transformed. As Miss Tuve's readers know, her learnedly perceptive pages continually enrich our understanding, but they cannot be squeezed into an outline, so that this paragraph can only emphasize the value of her interpretative commentary.

J. B. Broadbent ('The Nativity Ode,' *The Living Milton*, ed. F. Kermode, London, 1960, 12–31) makes his temperamental antipathies into an arraignment of the poem. He has got 'no help' from any studies later than Cook's except those of Allen and Miss Tuve, and he writes mainly to confute the latter. 'The language of Milton's poetry is notoriously deficient in "body"' [the basis of 'notoriously' is not revealed], and his use of traditional beliefs, ideas, and symbols is stunted and warped by both abstract Platonism and ascetic Puritanism. Milton could not accept and feel the fullness and variety of sensuous life; 'he is indifferent to most of the traditions that expressed joy in the perfecting of nature' (17). 'Milton alone, even among classical and patristic authors, ignores the central naturalness of motherhood' (26). 'Milton associated the animal with sin' (31). The false gods are defeated by Milton's art rather than by Christ; 'the sanction of the poem's action is not divine power but Miltonic art and intellect' (28–9). 'As the superb pomp of the induction's organ shows, it isn't really any less egotistical than Milton's other poems' (30). The critic applies a remarkable adverb to Milton's last stanza: 'the babe is cleverly restored to the courts of everlasting day' (20). Much of the discourse, for all its modernity of costume (including the author's inevitable bits of Freudianism) is only a restatement of the old complaint (punctured by various critics from Hanford to Miss Tuve) that Milton should have written about the human story of the Nativity instead of the Incarnation—and, we may infer, he needed the Dionysian vitality of, say, D. H. Lawrence. In this connection one might refer to the more general view, expressed by other critics cited here and in particular by M. M. Mahood (*Poetry and Humanism*, 203: see also II above), of Milton's exuberant 'sense of fertility, which gives a Swinburnian sensuousness to the fifth Latin Elegy, *In adventum veris*, and a bounding energy to the Nativity Ode,' and 'was undiminished at the time when Milton wrote his major poems, and it is apparent in every book of *Paradise Lost*. Much Puritanism of the seventeenth century decried the pleasure of the senses, but Milton was too thorough a humanist to have any part in such a negation.' A concluding summary complaint of Broadbent's is that 'we can't "do" anything with the art, only experience it'—which might seem, for most readers of this and other poems, to be a good deal.

In a monograph of over 100 pages (*The Hidden Sense and Other Essays*, Norwegian Studies in English, No. 9, 1963), Miss M.-S. Røstvig applies to Milton (chiefly to the *Nativity* and *Comus*) and some other poets of the age the new method of occult arithmology. Citing medieval and Renaissance authorities, Miss Røstvig outlines the traditional science of numbers [the tradition itself of course is quite substantial], tries, with natural difficulty, to show that Milton was not unreceptive toward the tradition, and turns to an analysis of the *Nativity*. She builds (43 f.) on 'the Platonic exposition of creation in numerical terms, according to which all numbers proceed from the One until we reach the cube of the first odd and the first even number. This may be diagrammed as follows:

Miss Røstvig believes 'that the structure of Milton's Nativity Ode is patterned after this Platonic *lambda*, its 27 8-line stanzas representing the two impulses proceeding from the One.' The prelude has four 7-line stanzas and 28 lines, the 'Hymn' twenty-seven 8-line stanzas and 216 lines. The numbers of the prelude (4, 7, 28) point to the world of time, the sequence of weeks, months, and seasons, etc. The number 4 is pre-eminently the number of the created universe, so the 4-stanza prelude suitably symbolized Christ's becoming flesh. 'If we count the number of feet and syllables in each stanza, we arrive at 36—the great tetractys—and 72, which denotes the complete cycle of years attributed to the life of man from birth to death.' The change to 8-line stanzas 'means that we leave the world of time (the cosmic week of 7 ages within which the history of fallen man is acted out) for the eighth age of the reign of Christ' (56). 'The number of heavy stresses in each stanza is 32, the number of syllables 64—numbers which represent justice according to Pythagoras' (58). The unreliable statistics somewhat weaken the concluding summary (even if the pyramid of cubes had any significance): 'Finally it may be mentioned that the product of the two cubes, 8 and 27, is 216—which in its turn is the cube of 6. The total number of lines therefore forms a number signifying perfection kept steady in three-dimensional security. We have, then, cubed figures everywhere—the cube of 2 in the number of lines per stanza, the cube of 3 in the number of stanzas, the cube of 4 in the number of syllables in each stanza, and the cube of 6 in the total number of lines; everywhere perfection is in this manner made permanent and lasting' (58). The monograph needs to be read in full; these bits are excerpted from my comment, 'Calculus Racked Him' (*SEL* 6, 1966, 1–6; repr. in *Engaged & Disengaged*, Cambridge, Mass., 1966); Miss Røstvig's reply (*SEL* 7, 1967, 191–4) may be thought an ineffectual defence of her method.

Harriet Frazier ('Time as Structure in Milton's "Nativity Ode," ' *Universitas* [Detroit], 3, 1, 1965, 8–14) sees as a central and unifying idea the Christian and especially the Boethian contrast between time and eternity. Christ's birth is the only event that occurs both in and out of time, an event that can have no ending. 'Christ must subdue three separate elements of the temporal before it may be at one with the eternal, and these are Nature, man, and the pagan gods.' Milton begins with Nature, 'the oldest aspect of the temporal'; though she has shared in man's fall, she 'is instantly aware of and sympathetic to the birth of Christ.' For the moment, with the cessation of sound and motion, Nature is taken out of time and linked with the eternal. But man, represented by the shepherds, is wholly unaware; Milton makes 'a sharp separation between the preparedness of Nature and that of man.' Yet the shepherds are enraptured by the angelic music of eternity, which carries us back to the golden age and forward to the greater golden age when time shall cease. Satan is now curbed and the evicted pagan gods will not, like Nature, regain sound and motion. Thus Christ's birth bridges the gulf between earth and heaven, time and eternity; it is a continuing event which transforms Nature and man.

L. L. Martz ('The Rising Poet, 1645,' *The Lyric and Dramatic Milton*, ed. J. H. Summers, New York and London, 1965, 22–33) stresses the technique of naïveté, enrichment of 'the mode of the nativity ballad.' The stanza form of the prelude, rhyme royal with a final alexandrine, declares Milton's allegiance to the Spenserian tradition. 'The stanza of the Hymn proper is even more significant, for its first six lines suggest the movement of a popular song or carol.' But the alexandrine draws the poem out of the popular into a larger world. 'In stanza after stanza we may feel this change from the simple language and steady beat of the ballad into the realms of a more ambitious art.' 'This decorum of an ancient and traditional simplicity pervades every aspect of the poem, versification, language, scene painting, imagery, and theme' (28). Unlike the false gods catalogued in *Paradise Lost*, the vanquished gods here 'are not devils in disguise; they are the supernatural beings of antique folklore, who exist in their own right as a part of nature....' The last two stanzas 'sum up the basic techniques and attitudes of the poem.' Now, 'attuned to the poem's peculiar decorum, we can perhaps accept...as a youthful excess' the poem's 'most extravagantly naïve image,' that of the sun in bed. Then come 'the ghosts and fairies of folklore, treated with sympathy and even affection,' and lastly 'the manger scene upon which this technique of the naïve has been based.' 'That is not to say that the poem is simple-minded in the range of its implications, but that the chosen mode of simplicity creates a world in which theological problems are pushed beyond the fringe of our vision.' What we have is 'a song of praise for the peace and harmony that the divine child has brought to earth....'

Isabel G. MacCaffrey (*John Milton: Samson Agonistes and the Shorter Poems*, New York, 1966) emphasizes the quality of vision in Milton's religious imagination and poetic method. In the *Nativity* 'The development of the theme is heroic, not only in the attitude it seeks to evoke, but in the inclusiveness of the vision.' 'The temporal range...is coextensive with human history itself,' and the spatial range embraces heaven and hell and all between. Starting from the 'rude manger,' 'the vision rays out in a great burst of centrifugal power to touch and illuminate the major concepts of the Christian faith as they have been embodied in the myths of scripture and tradition.' And 'it comes to rest in the "Courtly Stable" of the King of Kings, whose Kingdom has just been surveyed.' The subject is shaped 'in vision rather than sequacious narrative. In this poetic mode, the meaning of the whole work is made visible in each of its parts.' 'The pattern of redemption is...established in the opening movement. Thereafter, Milton renders a series of dazzlingly imagined "scenes," grouped around their center like the panels of an altarpiece.' Thus we see Peace and Mercy (stanzas 3 and 15), both from Psalm 85, as two figures in a diptych, 'inhabiting the same space, the temporal distance between them miraculously annihilated by the power assumed by the poem's maker.' Milton's symbolic imagination works on a colossal scale, in a wide focus; 'details are subdued to an over-all clarity of outline and movement, brilliantly accurate to both eye and mind.' So here 'the imagery is focused upon the two poles of Sun and Dragon': 'ancient and traditional symbols of divine and demonic power...spring forth to embody the basic struggle at the roots of the world and of history.'

C. A. Patrides (*Milton and the Christian Tradition*, Oxford, 1966, 258: cited hereafter as *Milton*), surveying 'The Christian View of History,' comments on the total difference between Milton and Crashaw and their poems on the Nativity. 'Crashaw approaches the Nativity "vertically", focusing attention on the manger and dwelling upon the directly perpendicular relationship between God and man. Milton, by contrast, concentrates on the "horizontal" significance of "the rude manger" as it affected the relationship not between God and man but between God and all mankind, the totality of all human beings. The devotional Crashaw concentrated on the one specific moment in history that witnessed the union of God and man. Milton chose to go much further, affirming the birth of Jesus as an event affecting the whole universe. Milton's far-ranging references to the idols and deities of Assyria and Egypt, Greece and Rome, were imperative, and collectively they argue that the Atonement was all-embracing in its effect, that the infant Jesus achieved not merely peace but, in Milton's words, "a *universal* Peace" (l. 52). Nor did Milton forget to observe that, although mankind's bliss began upon the birth of the Saviour, its consummation cannot be until after the Second Coming....' Patrides goes on to say that only one critic, R. Tuve, has recognized that Milton 'celebrates the meaning of the Incarnation not only in history but after history is over....' (Tuve, *Images*, 39); but this idea—made very clear in the poem—seems to have been recognized by some of the critics noticed above. See also Patrides, 143.

F. S. Kastor ('Miltonic Narration: "Christ's Nativity," ' *Anglia* 86, 1968, 339–52) thinks that critics have been preoccupied with patterns of imagery and have neglected narrative, which was an integral part of the ode from Pindar onward and of English odes from Drayton to Keats. Moreover, the story of the Nativity had long been told in various ways, notably by Prudentius, as a central part of the panorama of Christian world history, from Creation to the Judgment Day. In the ode, as in *PL* and *PR*, Milton relates the Nativity to Christ's redemptive mission, his lyrical treatment being conditioned by his form and occasion. Kastor finds difficulties in his handling of tenses, of time past, present, and future [on this point see L. Nelson above, under 1954], but the method does allow 'for both immediacy and scope.' Like *PL*, the poem is a network of contrasts, some pointed out by Barker [above, under 1940–1], and others as well (pure heaven and fallen world, Christ and Satan, and so on).

Jon S. Lawry (*The Shadow of Heaven: Matter and Stance in Milton's Poetry*, Ithaca, 1968, 27–41: this book is cited hereafter as *Shadow*) is concerned with Milton's devoutly Christian and poetic belief that 'the individual man and the individual poem derive their existence and value from union with God, the source of being and meaning and beauty' (1); and he studies the various manifestations of that belief in the major poems. Although his book is addressed to the general reader, the exposition does not lend itself to summary. In regard to the *Nativity*, he accepts Barker's division of the Hymn into three movements (see above, under 1940–1) but would emphasize the prelude and the end of the poem so as to have 'five interconnected sections.' Milton's 'matter' supplies 'an objective recognition and celebration' of the harmony of eternity, which here, as in most of his early works, is 'relatively static.' 'Milton's resolution of the apparently changeless with the seemingly change-bound, of the sense of God's will with the sense of man, supplies the significant action of the ode. The stance expertly accommodates itself to that chosen matter.' A running commentary develops the pattern of harmony and discord, eternity and time, and Milton's control of the reader's imaginative participation.

B. Rajan ('In Order Serviceable,' *MLR* 63, 1968, 13–22; repr. in *The Lofty Rhyme*, London, 1970) enriches established ideas in an essay concerned both with the *Nativity* itself and with its anticipations of *Paradise Lost*; Milton's characteristic religious conceptions take on an altered weight and focus in the epic of human responsibility. The suggested models do not go very far toward explaining the young poet's very individual achievement in substance, form, tone, and rhythms. The traditional paradoxes that invest the Incarnation mean comparatively little to him; his Christ 'is a Christ of creative power and unifying energy, who looks forward to the Christ of *Paradise Lost*, vanquishing Satan and creating the world out of chaos.' The Logos 'enters history as the irresistible champion of the light' (14). 'We, like the shepherds, cannot anticipate the onset of significance; but when the truth shines forth we are profoundly aware of the pattern' (15). Rajan elaborates Barker's account of the poem's three movements (above, under 1940–1), noting that the third, on the rout of the pagan gods, is three stanzas longer than the first and second. This designed asymmetry—which is reflected in the designed asymmetry of the stanza—directs our attention to the poem's 'imaginative centre of gravity' (17): 'The deepest affirmation of the *Ode* is its sense of the power and glory of God, of the inevitable victory of the light when it elects to shine forth in its radiance' (16). 'Darkness...is uniformly embodied in images of constraint and confinement...' (20). Milton is concerned, not with the inward significance of the Incarnation, but with 'a decisive event in the structure of events without which the other events are incapable of forming a structure. It is an intervention transforming the nature of history and the destiny of man' (21). The young poet's joyous optimism—as in stanza 18—is far from Michael's bleak prophecies in *Paradise Lost* (21).

'The quiet close of a Milton poem sets it in shape, bringing the higher mood into consonance with the everyday. So the *Nativity Ode*, after its movement through space and history, comes back to a local habitation both humble and resplendent. The imagery of light endures but the lesser lights are subordinate and attentive to the prince of light.... Finally, the order which the last lines invoke is not directed to any climax of contemplation. It is "order serviceable" designed for an active purpose, the intervention in history which is itself the decisive renewal of the hope of order. In this context the bright-harnessed angels are the energy of light, mobilized and held ready for a creative purpose.... For Milton too, a serviceable order has been created and the instruments are at hand for the greater work ahead.' (22)

John Carey (*Milton*, London, 1969: cited hereafter as *Milton*, to be distinguished from 'Carey,' which refers to the Carey–Fowler edition of Milton's *Poems*) seems to find something more or less discreditable almost anywhere in Milton's character and writings. His account of the *Nativity* elaborates the old-fashioned and wrong-headed notion that the poem is cold, inhuman, and unreligious in contrast with Crashaw's warm, human, and devout treatment of the theme. A sufficient sample of critical understanding and manner might be this (33–4):

'But wisest Fate says no' (149). God clamps down on wishful thinking. The plan must grind to its horrible climax.

> The Babe lies yet in smiling Infancy,
> That on the bitter cross
> Must redeem our loss.

By locating 'Babe', 'smiling' and 'cross' in consecutive lines Milton transforms the act of redemption from an adult sacrifice to the impaling of an unsuspecting baby. Nothing so savage is laid to the account of the heathen gods. The poem's cruellest moment drives home the iron will of 'wisest Fate'.

P. Cullen ('Imitation and Metamorphosis: The Golden-Age Eclogue in Spenser, Milton, and Marvell,' *PMLA* 84, 1969, 1559–70) compares Spenser's *April* eclogue, the *Nativity*, and *The Picture of little T.C.* with Virgil and with the Renaissance emphasis on uninhibited love (Tasso, Guarini, et al.). Queen Elizabeth becomes an idealized symbol of the golden age. The *Nativity* is distinguished by its religious theme, its Christianizing of pagan motifs: the true Messiah was foretold by the

Old Testament prophets; the wondrous child is no other than the Son of God, the sovereign of nature, the agent of man's redemption. And the golden age is not, as in Virgil's cyclical view of time, a return to or recovery of an ideal past, but—since 'wisest Fate sayes no, / This must not yet be so'—will come only with the end of the world and time and the beginning of eternity.

So far, of course, we agree, but we may be surprised by such comments as these:

The meditator, misinterpreting nature and the music, accepts the old pagan conception of cyclical time, believing that the lost golden age will return...[But he] suddenly understands that this is not so...Seen in this perspective, the meditation falls into two parts...In the first part, the meditator, possessing only a partial knowledge of Christian truth, misrepresents and misinterprets nature, the celestial music, and the meaning of the Nativity itself. In the second part, the meditator, abandoning pagan illusion, comes to a full Christian understanding of the Nativity and the true golden age.

This is surely a distortion of the poem. From the first line onward the poet proclaims his full Christian understanding; he is nowhere for a moment the real or imagined victim of 'partial knowledge' and 'pagan illusion' and 'darkness'; his reference to the pagan golden age is not 'a focal point for the conversion of the meditator's inner vision,' it is merely a brief, conscious, half-wishful fancy invoked for contrast with the delayed fulfilment of Christian truth.

IV. NOTES

In addition to general influences, probable or possible, noticed in II above, the details of Milton's richly allusive texture suggest countless other probable or possible sources or analogues. Of special value for annotation is A. S. Cook's 'Notes on Milton's Ode on the Morning of Christ's Nativity,' *Trans. Connecticut Acad. of Arts and Sciences* 15 (1909), 307–68 (hereafter cited as Cook).

1–28 The prelude fixes the time and the occasion, invokes the Heavenly Muse, and suggests the poet's pressing forward to Bethlehem to offer his birthday gift to Christ. The idea furnishes an unobtrusive principle of progression for the

Hymn, if we think of its successive sections as representing the phases of the Christmas story on which the poet reflects in his imaginary journey. The mission here undertaken is concluded in the final stanza of the Hymn (see 237–44 and n.).

The first four stanzas, constituting the prelude, are in a different metre, an adaptation of the traditional rhyme royal (*ababbcc*) with an alexandrine instead of the final pentameter. [This pattern Milton had already used in the *Fair Infant*: see below.]

1 *this the happy morn.* Cook compares 'This is that happie Morne' (*Phoebus arise* 15, W. Drummond, *Poetical Works*, ed. L. E. Kastner, Edinburgh, 1913, 1, 32), and Spenser: 'Borne at one burden in one happie morne, / Thrise happie mother, and thrise happie morne' (*F.Q.* 4. 2. 41: Variorum Ed., ed. E. Greenlaw et al., 10 v., Baltimore, 1932–57).

3 *wedded Maid, and Virgin Mother.* Cf. Matt. 1. 18, 21–5.

5 *holy Sages*: the Old Testament prophets who foretold the coming of Christ, e.g. Isa. 7. 14, 9. 6–7, Jer. 23. 5–6.

6 Should cancel the penalty of death under which we lie (*OED*: deadly 4b; forfeit 4; release *v.* 1), i.e. the penalty of death pronounced upon all mankind for Adam's disobedience and remitted through the obedience and death of Christ (Gen. 2. 16–17, 3. 3; Rom. 5. 12, 19; 1 Cor. 15. 21–2). [Cf. *PL* 3. 227–65, 274–343, 403–11, 12. 395–410.]

7 *work*: make, as in 'work the peace of the present,' Shakespeare, *Temp.* 1. 1. 24 (*Complete Works*, ed. G. L. Kittredge, Boston, 1936): cited by A. W. Verity, ed., *Milton's Ode on the Morning of Christ's Nativity*, etc. (Cambridge, 1924: 1st ed., 1891). Cf. Col. 1. 19–20: 'For it pleased the Father...having made peace through the blood of his cross, by him to reconcile all things unto himself.'

8–14 [The contrast between Christ's divine power and glory and his humble earthly life and human suffering was a traditional paradox. Cf. Phil. 2. 6–8; Tasso's *Canzone* (cited above in 11); Spenser, *Hymne of Heavenly Love* 134–40; G. Fletcher, *Christs Victorie, and Triumph* 1. 1 (cited hereafter as *C.V.* 1 and 2, *C.T.* 1 and 2: *Poetical Works of Giles and Phineas Fletcher*, ed. F. S. Boas, 2 v., Cambridge, 1908–9); Milton, *PR* 4. 596–9. W. J. Roscelli ('The Metaphysical Milton (1625–1631),' *TSLL* 8, 1966, 478–9) quotes George Herbert's *Christmas* 9–12 (*Works of George Herbert*, ed. F. E. Hutchinson, Oxford, 1945) along with Fletcher and remarks: 'Unlike Fletcher, Milton and Herbert describe the Nativity in terms of light wholly enveloped by darkness, a complete reversal of the traditional Christian representation of Christ's birth as a sudden illumination of a world which had been darkened by sin since Eden'; both 'produce an unusual effect that is wholly absent in Fletcher: the telescoping of time.' Milton and Herbert (15–16: cf. 16 n. below) both imagine themselves present at the first Christmas; cf. 23 n. below.]

8–9 This association of *Form* and *Light* with Christ introduces a symbol important in the pattern of imagery in the Hymn.

8 *unsufferable*: unbearable by human sight. [Cf. George Sandys, *Ovid's Metamorphosis Englished* (London, 1626: cited hereafter as *Ovid*), p. 2: 'I'th' midst unsufferable beames reside.']

10 *wont*. [Editors note that the past participle is used as a preterite, meaning 'was accustomed.' Carey cites 'wonned' in Spenser, *S.C.*, *February* 119, and 'did won' in *F.Q.* 3. 9. 21, used in this sense.]

10–11 Cf. 'O Trinal-one, one God and Persons three' (Patrick Hannay, *Songs and Sonnets*, 1622, *Sonn.* 20, p. 250; *Minor Poets of the Caroline Period*, ed. G. Saintsbury, 1, Oxford, 1905, 726). Cook compares 'that Trine-one with himself in councell sits' (P. Fletcher, *Purple Island* 1. 44: cited hereafter as *P.I.*); although this poem was not printed until 1633, Milton may possibly have known it in a manuscript copy [not that he needed a source].

13 *Courts*. Originally used of the enclosures surrounding the Tabernacle and forming the Temple (Ps. 65. 4, 84. 2, 100. 4, 116. 19), the word was readily transferred to God's heavenly dwelling place. Cf. P. Fletcher (*P. I.* 1.43): 'To store heav'ns courts.' *everlasting Day*. Cook cites Rev. 21. 23, 25; 22. 5. ['The word "forsook" (a *negative* one) is, if I am not mistaken, the very key to the amplitude of the image—while making the "courts" and the "everlasting day" less *objectively* and more *potentially* present' (L. Vivante, *English Poetry*, London, 1950, 72: from *La poesia inglese*, Firenze, 1947).]

14 *darksom House of mortal Clay*. C. Dunster (*Considerations on Milton's Early Reading, and the Prima Stamina of his Paradise Lost*, London, 1800) cited 'this house of clay' (Sylvester, *D.W.W.* 2. 1. 1. 763, Grosart, 1, 106). H. J. Todd (*Poetical Works*, 5th ed., 4 v., London, 1852) compared 'smoakie house of mortall clay' (Marston, *Scourge of Villanie* 3. 8. 194: *Poems of John Marston*, ed. A. Davenport, Liverpool, 1961). [The religious idea (as applied to Christ or man) and kindred phrases were common; cf. Shakespeare, 'this muddy vesture of decay' (*Merch.* 5. 1. 64).]

15 *Heav'nly Muse*: Milton's first reference to this source of his inspiration, to be much elaborated in *PL* 1. 6 f., 7. 1 f., 9. 20 f. (see notes on these passages). [Urania, the classical Muse of Astronomy, became the Christian or Heavenly Muse chiefly through the influence of Du Bartas' *L'Uranie* (published in his *La Muse Chrestiene*, 1574); see Lily B. Campbell, 'The Christian Muse,' *Huntington Library Bulletin* 8 (1935), 29–70, and her *Divine Poetry and Drama in Sixteenth-Century England* (Berkeley and Cambridge, 1959).]

sacred vein: special talent or aptitude for religious verse (*OED*: vein 11) or, possibly, special or characteristic style (ibid. 12) [or religious and poetic power beyond the poet's own? 'The gift is not given by him but through him.... Milton used classical figures for the life that was in them, and this of the muse is no tag of adornment but a necessary help to say that he could of himself have no offering to bring' (R. Tuve, *Images*, 43).]

16 *Afford*: furnish (*OED* 7). *Present to the Infant God.* Cf. *Dona quidem dedimus Christi natalibus illa* (*El* 6. 87). Cook was inclined to hear an echo of George Herbert's 'The shepherds sing; and shall I silent be? / My God, no hymne for thee?' (*Christmas* 15–16), arguing that the poem, though unprinted, was written before 1629 and possibly known to Milton. [Cf. Roscelli in 8–14 n. above.]

19–20 The Sun's chariot has not yet started its diurnal course across the sky, which has taken no imprint of light from the feet of its horses. The phrasing exemplifies the play of fancy, characteristic of this poem, which has led commentators to talk loosely of Milton's temporary addiction to conceits. The classical image recurs at 79–84. Todd and Dunster collected allusions to the Sun's and other celestial teams from Shakespeare (*1 H. IV* 3. 1. 220), Kyd (*Cornelia* 3. 1. 70, *Works*, ed. F. S. Boas, Oxford, 1891), John Fletcher (*Faithful Shepherdess* 4. 4. 3, *Beaumont and Fletcher*, ed. F. E. Schelling, New York, 1912), and Sylvester (*D.W.W.* 1. 4. 597, 2. 1. 4. 344, Grosart, 1, 57 and 125).

21 The stars, glittering as if adorned with spangles [cf. below, *Ps* 136. 27 n.], keep watch, drawn up in formation. Cook notes that, though elsewhere the phrase is applied to the angels, the stars are called 'the host of heaven' in Deut. 4. 19 [and in Spenser, *Epithalamion* 289], and Milton speaks of 'the starrie Host' (*PL* 4. 606); also that they are referred to as drawn up in order and never fainting in their watches (Ecclus. 43. 10: *Apocrypha*, v. 4 in *The Authorised Version of the English Bible 1611*, ed. W. A. Wright, Cambridge, 1909). Todd cited 'The starres shined in their watches' (Baruch 3. 34) and noted from Dunster (as applied, however, to angels) 'Heav'ns glorious Hoast in nimble squadrons' (Sylvester, *D.W.W.* 1. 1. 599, Grosart, 1, 24); also 'their bright Squadrons round about us plant' (Spenser, *F.Q.* 2. 8. 2) and 'archt in Squadrons bright' (Drummond, 2, 25, *Hymn of the Ascension* 103; [cf. 2, 43, 'Starres, Hoste of heaven']. It would appear that *squadron* was commonly used of the angels, not the stars (cf. 'embatteld Squadrons bright,' *PL* 6. 16), but that the phrase *host of heaven* was applied indifferently to either [Hughes cites it in Neh. 9. 6; cf. Shakespeare, *Ham.* 1. 5. 92]. Milton himself refers to the watchful heavens (*Vac* 40, *Comus* 112–13). See further Cook's notes, pp. 311–14. [The ambiguity of the language accomplishes a remarkable effect in what appears to be a simple pictorial line. The words telescope time and space: the stars still shining over London become the stars over Bethlehem, and the poet is transported to ancient Palestine.]

22 *Eastern rode*: leading, that is, from the east to Bethlehem.

23 For the wise men see Matt. 2. 1–2, 7–12. It is needless to question, with Cook, Milton's orthodoxy here (and in *PL* 12. 360–2, *PR* 1. 249–50) in bringing the Magi to Christ's cradle instead of placing the event two years later. Calvin, commenting on these verses (*Harmonie upon the Three Evangelistes, Matthewe, Marke, and Luke*, London, 1610, 79–81; *Commentary on a Harmony of the Evangelists*, tr. W. Pringle, 3 v., Edinburgh, 1845–6, 1, 127–30), takes precisely the same view as Milton and does not even mention the problem of time.

Wisards. *OED* and Cook cite Sir John Cheke's translation of Matt. 2. 1 (*The Gospel according to Saint Matthew*, ed. J. Goodwin, Cambridge and London, 1843): '...lo, then ye wisards cam from th'est parties...' The word was the equivalent of 'wise man,' with the sense of special and often—though not always—of occult or astrological learning. Calvin assumes that the Magi were astrologers. Cf. 'Ægyptian wisards old, / Which in Star-read were wont have best insight' (Spenser, *F.Q.* 5, proem 8; and ibid. 3. 1. 16, 4. 12. 2). The increasingly pejorative sense appears in the context of *F.Q.* 1. 4. 12 and (according to Verity) is always present in Shakespeare. In Milton that sense is always absent except in *Comus* 570; in his prose (*Works* 3, 60, 342; 5, 73) the word is used in the sense of wise men, the contexts only rendering it ironical.

[M. M. Ross ('Milton and Sir John Stradling,' *HLQ* 14, 1950–1, 129–46) notes parallels with, and the possible influence of, the *Divine Poemes* (1625) of Stradling, a versifier in the Du Bartas–Sylvester line (and translator of Lipsius' *Two Bookes of Constancie*). Ross, while concerned chiefly with *PL* and its opening, quotes two stanzas, from pages 43 and 41, for the similarity of the personal offering and the idea of hastening to Bethlehem:

So here I vow, in singleness of heart
(Sith better gifts to offer I have none)
With those three pious Kings to bear a part
And, most unworthy, yet I'll make up one
My self and all I have to dedicate
To Thee, whose sacred story I relate.

Here leave I now these Isra'lites awhile
And hasten forward towards Bethlehem,
Poetick liscense, must your thoughts beguile:
Conceaue we iourney from Ierusalem
To see that Virgin-Mother, blessed Dame,
Her Sonne whom shee Immanuel should name.

Cf. 8–14 n. and Carey's comment on Tasso near the end of II above.]

23 *odours*: [perfumes, spices (*OED* 2).]

24 *prevent*: come before, anticipate (Lat. *praevenire*); cf. 26. *OED* 2 gives examples. [E. W. cites E. Fairfax, *Godfrey of Bulloigne, or The Recoverie of Jerusalem* (1600: cited hereafter as *Jerusalem*) 3. 1. 7, where the word means 'foreruns,' and also Milton, *Ps* 88. 56 and *PL* 3. 231, 11. 3. W. McQueen (*MiltonN* 2, 1968, 63–4) quotes Wisd. of Sol. 16. 28: 'That it might bee knowen, that wee must prevent the Sunne, to give thee thanks, and at the day-spring pray unto thee'—a verse partly quoted by Donne (*Sermons*, ed. G. R. Potter and E. M. Simpson, 10 v., Berkeley, 1953–62, 5, 281). *Prevent* in this sense also recurs in the Book of Common Prayer.]

25 *blessed feet*: in Shakespeare, *1 H. IV* 1. 1. 25 (Cook).

27 *the Angel Quire*. See 93–172 and n., 115 n., and Luke 2. 13. *Quire*: the older phonetic spelling of choir (never altered in the *Book of Common Prayer*): a band of singers (cf. Latin *chorus*) of ritualistic religious song (*OED* 1).

28 *From out his secret Altar toucht with hallow'd fire.* A very significant allusion to Isa. 6. 6–7, where one of the Seraphim takes a burning coal from the altar and touches the prophet's lips. This becomes for Milton the symbol of the purification, dedication, and inspiration of the Christian poet, which can be attained only 'by devout prayer to that eternall Spirit who can enrich with all utterance and knowledge, and sends out his Seraphim with the hallow'd fire of his Altar to touch and purify the lips of whom he pleases' (*RCG, Works* 3, 241). One part of the symbolism of the angelic orders which Milton seems to have known and accepted is that which pertains to the Seraphim, Cherubim, and Thrones, here to the first as representing the love of God. [Cf. D. *Dionysii Areopagitae Opera* (Cologne, 1557), c. 7, *De Seraphim, Cherubim, et Thronis*, pp. 14–18.] Bacon,

citing Dionysius, says that 'the angels of love...are termed Seraphim' (*Advancement of Learning, Works*, ed. J. Spedding, R. L. Ellis, and D. D. Heath, 7 v., London, 1870–5, 3, 296). See *IlPen* 45–54 n. [Cf. Drummond, 2, 50: 'Here doe Seraphines / Burne with immortall love, there Cherubines / ... delight their Sight' (*Shadow of the Judgement* 15–18).] Thus, unobtrusively but unmistakably, Milton avows love to be the motive of his birthday gift for Christ.
    secret: set apart, Lat. *secretus* (Verity).

The Hymn. The term covers any sacred song, differing only from the *ode* (24) in implying a religious theme and purpose. For this, the body of the poem, Milton appears to have invented his own stanza form. [F. T. Prince (*Comus and other Poems*, London, 1968, 107: cited hereafter as *Comus*) remarks that the stanzas—in addition to the concluding Spenserian alexandrine—'are also shaped by Italian example: the combination and the grouping of three-stressed and five-stressed lines, in the first six lines of the stanzas, derive from the *canzone* tradition, and may have been suggested by the openings of many of Tasso's lyrics...; but the English stanza is shorter and swings along more quickly than is usual in Italian.' The prosody of the *Nativity* will be fully analysed in the separate volume of the *Commentary* being prepared by E. Weismiller.]

29–92 The subject of the first movement of the Hymn [on the structural divisions see A. Barker, summarized above in III, under 1940–1] is the peace of the first Christmas [and Nature's awareness, on the eve of her Creator's coming, of her imperfection, the imperfection brought about by the Fall; cf. 39–44 n.]. The note of the imagery is subdued light and colour and subdued, though harmonious, sound.

29–31 [For Milton's use throughout of past and present tenses (already operating in the prelude), see L. Nelson and H. Frazier in III above, under 1954 and 1965. F. T. Prince (*Comus*, 108) remarks that, while the present tense 'can be described as "the historic present", the effect is to make the Nativity an event both "in and out of time"—an act of God continually renewed.']

29 In a poem written in northern latitudes it is hardly necessary to account for the winter setting, as Cook is at pains to do. The elaborate precedent he quotes from Mantuan (*Parthenice, Opera*, Paris, 1513, 1, 70^{r-v}) shows that the winter scene was as clearly a feature of the Nativity for the Italian as for the English poet.

32–44 [D. Daiches ('Some Aspects of Milton's Pastoral Imagery,' *More Literary Essays*, Edinburgh and London, 1968, 96–114) observes that Milton has moved far from the classical imagery of nature in his Latin verse, 'in spite of the almost pagan personification of Nature.' Lines 37–44 are 'a baroque pathetic fallacy which is at the same time primitive and sophisticated.' Cf. 37–44 n. below.]

32 *Nature*: here virtually a synonym for Earth (Cook). [John G. Demaray (*Milton and the Masque Tradition*, Cambridge, Mass., 1968, 31–40: cited hereafter as *Masque Tradition*) illustrates from masques of the period Milton's masque-like figures of 'Nature, the Sun, Peace, Truth, and Justice,' and other images.]

33 *doff't*. Verity quoted Robert Sherwood's appendix to Randle Cotgrave's *Dictionary of the French and English Tongues* (1650): 'To doff, *c'est à dire*, to Doe off, to put off' [also in 1632 ed. *gawdy*: gay, showy (cf. *IlPen* 6 and n.)].

34 *so to sympathize*: be in accord with (*OED* 2b), i.e. by divesting herself of her glory, as Christ of his (Cook).

35 *no season then* refers both to the time of year and to a proper or fitting occasion (*OED* 14).

35-6 The contrast with *El* 5. 55–60 can hardly have been unintentional: *Exuit invisam Tellus rediviva senectam,* | *Et cupit amplexus Phoebe subire tuos*, etc. For examples of the sun as the earth's lover, and of earth adorned for or by him, see Cook on *Nat* 36 and the Variorum note on *El* 5. 55–60. *wanton*: sport amorously, play sportively, heedlessly, or idly (*OED* 1, 1b). [*OED* 1c cites Shakespeare, *Shrew*, Ind. 2. 54: 'seem to move and wanton with her breath.']

37-44 carry the personification of Nature (Earth) into the poem's most fanciful conceit. [The animistic conceit has been likened to a common mode of description in Sidney's *Arcadia*, but the idea introduces the theme of stanzas 1–8, the imperfection of earth, here stripped of her summer foliage. Apropos of these lines, Grierson remarks that the young Milton's conceits are not metaphysical but 'belong to the older Petrarchan, Spenserian, Sidneian tradition,' to which Drummond also adhered (*Cross Currents in English Literature of the XVIIth Century*, London, 1929, 240–1). Cf. G. R. Potter, *PQ* 6 (1927), 396–400. W. J. Roscelli (*TSLL* 8, 1966, 463–84) slightly modifies this orthodox view. On this particular passage, he follows Tillyard. He finds occasional somewhat metaphysical images in half a dozen of Milton's poems of 1628–31, chiefly in poems concerned with death. In general, his early conceits—compared especially with George Herbert's (cf. 8–14 n. above)—lack particularity and dramatic personal tensions, and they do not show the influence of any metaphysical poets.]

37 *fair*: courteous(ly) (*OED* 2). Verity cites: 'Go seek him out; speak fair' (Shakespeare, *Ham.* 4. 1. 36).

38 *woo's*: entreats, as in *Sonn* 13. 13 [but here continuing the erotic imagery of 35–6]. Todd compared: 'Nature's Mantle fair, / When in the Sunne,... / She seems with smiles to woo the gawdie Spring' (Sylvester, *D.W.W.* 2. 1. 4. 163–5, Grosart, 1, 123). *gentle*: of wind and weather, mild, not stormy (*OED* 6); of persons, mild in disposition, kind (ibid. 8): here combined as applied to the personified *Air*.

39–44 Nature (Earth) shared in the results of the fall (cf. *PL* 9. 782–4, 1000–4, 10. 651–719) and, as is here implied, in its *blame*, i.e. guilt (*OED* 3). Verity notes Shakespeare's play on the two meanings: 'Wrong hath but wrong, and blame the due of blame' (*R. III* 5. 1. 29).

39 *front*: face (*OED* 1), described as *guilty* because manifesting shame arising from the consciousness of guilt: *OED* has no example of this use. The phrase *innocent Snow* reflects the association of snow (both for its whiteness and cold-ness) with purity and innocence, a literary commonplace rooted in the Bible as regards colour (Ps. 51. 7; Isa. 1. 18; Matt. 28. 3), and used repeatedly by Shakespeare with both references (*Cym.* 2. 5. 13; *Macb.* 4. 3. 53–4; *Ham.* 3. 1. 141; *Cor.* 5. 3. 66; *Temp.* 4. 1. 55; *Tim.* 4. 3. 386): citations from Cook.

40 *naked shame*. The phrase is scriptural; cf. Mic. 1. 11, 'having thy shame naked'; and Rev. 3. 18, quoted under 42 below. Cook has further less relevant citations.

41 *Pollute*: polluted (*Lat. pollutus*): *OED*. 'Milton often uses these contracted participles of Latin origin,' e.g. in *PL* 3. 6, 208, 6. 641; *PR* 2. 399 (W. J. Rolfe, ed., *Minor Poems of John Milton*, New York, 1887). *blame*: see 39–44 n.

42 Cook (on 40) cites: 'I counsel thee to buy of me... white raiment, that thou mayest be clothed, and that the shame of thy nakedness do not appear' (Rev. 3. 18). *Saintly*. [*OED*'s earliest example of this word (used also in *IlPen* 13) is of 1660 (W. B. Hunter, 'New Words in Milton's English Poems,' *Essays in Honor of Walter Clyde Curry*, Nashville, 1955, 243, 256).]

43–4 *Confounded*: abashed, put to shame or mental confusion (*OED* 1). Cook cites Ps. 83. 17, but there 'confounded' is coupled with 'put to shame, and perish.' *deformities*: moral disfigurements (*OED* 4).

45 *cease*: put a stop to (*OED* 5). Cook compares (rather remotely) *solve metus* (Virgil, *A.* 1. 463). [Cf. W. Browne, *Brit. Past.* 1. 4. 611–12: 'send some servant ... / To cease their clamour' (*Poems*, ed. G. Goodwin, 2 v., London, 1894).]

46–52 The scene is strongly reminiscent of court masques [cf. 32 n. above], where mythological or allegorical figures often descended from the heavens, as Pallas does in *The Golden Age Restor'd* (*Ben Jonson*, ed. C. H. Herford and P. and E. M. Simpson, 11 v., Oxford, 1925–52, 7, 421), and as the Attendant Spirit may in *Comus* (see first Direction and n.). Irene or Peace in *Part of the Kings Entertainment* (*Ben Jonson* 7, 97) does not so descend; but Verity noted that she bore 'a wreathe of olive on her head, on her shoulder a silver dove: in her left hand, shee held forth an olive branch. . . .' The association of the olive with peace is a commonplace: 'Olives bene for peace' (Spenser, *S.C.*, *April* 124). E. K.'s Gloss has several explanations: that olive trees cannot be properly tended except in time of peace; that they will not grow near to fir, dedicated to Mars; and that, when Neptune and Minerva strove for the naming of Athens, there sprang up at her behest an olive 'to note that it should be a nurse of learning, and such peaceable studies.' In this symbolism Christian and classical traditions meet. Cook cites Ps. 52. 8: 'But I am like a green olive tree in the house of God: I trust in the mercy of God for ever and ever' [see also Gen. 8. 11]; Aeschylus, *Eumen.* 44; Virgil, *G.* 2. 425 (*placitam Paci nutritor olivam*); etc. For *crown'd with Olive green* cf. Jonson's Irene above. Cook cites 'Eirene, that a garland wears / Of guilded olive, on her fairer hears' (G. Fletcher, *C.V.* 1. 69) and recalls that Beatrice appears to Dante *cinta d'uliva* (*Purg.* 30. 31: *Divina Commedia*, ed. G. Vandelli, Milan, 1946). Cook errs slightly in citing Prudentius: it is not Concordia but Discordia who, in 'the counterfeit shape of a friend,' displays 'her hair wreathed with leafy olive' (*Psych.* 684, 687).

47–8 *came softly sliding* | *. . .turning sphear.* Cook compares 'But peace straight from above gan softly slide' (*To the Prince*, st. 11, dedication of William L'isle's *A Saxon Treatise*, 1623). Verity cites 'turning Sphears' (Sylvester, *D.W.W.* 1. 4. 142, Grosart, 1, 53) and 'Walk'st on the rowling Sphear' (Milton, *HistBr*, *Works* 10, 11). [Hughes defines *sphear* as 'the visible Diurnal Spheare' (*PL* 7. 22), 'the starry globe of the heavens turning daily about the earth.'] Cf. 125–32 n. For *sliding* (gliding) Rolfe compares *Vac* 4, *Lyc* 86, Shakespeare, *Sonn.* 45. 4.

49 *Harbinger*: one who goes before to provide lodging (harbourage) for his lord (*OED* 2); hence one who announces the coming, a forerunner (*OED* 3; Milton, *May* 1).

50 *Turtle*: turtle-dove. 'At once suggestive of. . .purity (cf. Pliny, *Hist. Nat.* 10. 52), peacefulness (Horace, *Od.* 4. 4. 27–8 [error for 31–2]), harmlessness (Matt. 10. 16). . .lovingness, holiness (Tibullus 1. 7. 18), and the presence of the

Holy Spirit (Matt. 3. 16; John 1. 32)': Cook. These suggestions are carried by *dove* generally; specifically, the turtle-dove suggests constancy in love; [Verity cites Song of Sol. 2. 12 and Shakespeare, *Phoenix*]. But it has also some association with peace; cf. 'The throat of warre be stopt.../ And turtle-footed peace dance' (Jonson, *E. M. out of his Humour*, Epilogue 27–8). *amorous*: i.e. of Peace, and surrounding her. Cook notes Mercury (whose numerous descents that of Peace somewhat resembles): *turbida tranat | nubila* (Virgil, *A.* 4. 245–6).

51 *mirtle wand*. The wand is doubly appropriate, as a wand of office in the hands of Peace as harbinger or herald, and as an instrument of her magic power. Perhaps, as Cook suggests, Milton remembered the wand of Hermes (Mercury), herald of the gods (Homer, *Od.* 5. 47, 24. 1 f.) and pacifier (Ovid, *M.* 14. 291). *Myrtle* is sacred to Venus and symbolic of love (*Lyc* 2 n.). The combination fortifies the interdependence of peace and love already suggested (50 n.).

52 *strikes*: produces instantaneously, at a stroke, rather than produces with sudden force, as L. E. Lockwood assumes (*Lexicon to the English Poetical Works of John Milton*, New York, 1907). This meaning is not recorded in *OED*, which treats the verb under 88 headings, but it is confirmed, e.g. by 'Descend with all the gods.../ To strike a calm' (Beaumont and Fletcher, *Maid's Tragedy* 1. 2. 263–4, reported by Todd from Dunster), and 'Dark Night, / Strike a full silence' (ibid. 212–13). Newton interpreted Milton's line in the light of the Latin *ferire foedus* (*OED* 69, 70), but Warton rightly opposed him: 'It is not a league, or agreement of peace between two parties....A quick and universal diffusion is the idea. It was done as with a stroke' (*Poems upon Several Occasions...by John Milton*, 2nd ed., rev. and enlarged, London, 1791). *a universal peace through Sea and Land*. 'Milton must have been aware that this was a classic formula in relation to the establishment of peace by the Romans, especially under Augustus' (Cook). Cook notes the use of *terra marique* by Suetonius, *Augustus* 22, and Livy 1. 19.

53–60 'The currency of the conception that the peace of Augustus prevailed at the birth of Christ is perhaps due as much to Orosius [*Historiarum adversus paganos libri vii*]...as to anyone' (Cook). Christian commentary saw this Augustan peace as fulfilling the prophecy of Isa. 2. 4. Cook cites St Jerome on that text (Migne, *Pat. Lat.* 24, 46–7):

Veteres revolvamus historias, et inveniemus usque ad vicesimum octavum annum Caesaris Augusti (cujus quadragesimo primo anno Christus natus est in Judaea) in toto orbe terrarum fuisse discordiam, et singulas nationes contra vicinas gentes arsisse studio praeliandi, ita ut caederent et caederentur. Orto autem Domino Salvatore, quando sub praeside Syriae Cyrino prima est in orbe terrarum facta descriptio, et Evangelicae doctrinae pax Romani imperii [pace] praeparata; tunc omnia bella cessaverunt, et nequaquam per oppida et vicos exercebantur ad praelia; sed ad agrorum cultum, militibus tantum legionibusque Romanis contra barbaras nationes bellandi studio delegato: quando impletus est angelorum ille concentus: *Gloria in excelsis Deo, et in terra pax hominibus bonae voluntatis* (*Luc.* II, 14); et in diebus ejus orta est justitia et multitudo pacis.

Cook also quotes, *inter alia*, Dante, *Parad.* 6. 55–7, 80–1, *Convivio* 4. 5 (ed. M. Simonelli, Bologna, 1966, 141–2; tr. W. W. Jackson, Oxford, 1909, 206), and Mantuan, *Parthen.* 3. 1 f. [(*Opera*, Paris, 1513, 1, 67ᵛ: extracts from Mantuan, while checked with the 1513 *Opera*, are given in Cook's modernized form)]: *Iam mare, iam tellus Italo deterrita Marte, | Caesaris imperium Romanaque iura ferebat. | Pax erat, et domitum late placaverat orbem | Tuta quies; nusquam litui, non arma sonabant, | Et sua bifrontem ducebant limina Janum.* [Cf. Augustine, *City of God* 18. 46, and Tasso's *Canzone* (cited in II above), 58 f.] Even Lyly refers to the traditional idea that 'Christ would not be borne, untill there were peace through-out the whole worlde' (*Euphues*, ed. E. Arber, London, 1868, 456). [Cf. Patrides, *Milton*, 143, 258 (the latter passage quoted in III above, under 1966).]

53   Cook cites: 'No warre was knowne, no dreadfull trompets sound' (Spenser, *F.Q.* 5, proem 9).

55   *The idle Spear...up hung.* Warton cited *et vetus in templo bellica parma vacat* (Propertius 2. 25. 8), but thought that 'chivalry and Gothic manners were here in Milton's mind.' Todd compared Tasso, *Gerusalemme Liberata* 20. 144: *viene al tempio con gli altri il sommo duce: | e qui l'arme sospende* (*Poesie*, ed. F. Flora, Milan, 1952).

56   *hooked Chariot.* Bowle (reported by Todd) cited Livy 37. 41 on Antiochus' use of *falcatae quadrigae*, which terrified his own men. Keightley (*Poems*, 2 v., London, 1859) quoted Spenser (*F.Q.* 5. 8. 28): 'a charret hye, / With yron wheeles and hookes arm'd dreadfully.' Cook adds 'three hundred chariots armed with hooks' (2 Macc. 13. 2), and notes that this type of war chariot is attributed sometimes to the Persians (Xenophon, *Cyr.* 6. 1. 30, 50; *Anab.* 1. 7. 10, 1. 8. 10), sometimes to the northern barbarians (Silius Italicus 17. 416–17). [Cf. *falcatus currus* (with varying case and number) in Q. Curtius 4. 13. 33; Statius, *Theb.* 10. 544; Val. Flacc. 6. 105 (also *falcatos axes*, ibid. 387), and *falciferos currus* in Lucretius 3. 642, 5. 1301.]

59   *awfull*: 'filled with awe' (*OED* 5). Cook cites Marlowe, *Faustus* 991–2 (*Works*, ed. C. F. T. Brooke, Oxford, 1910): 'Monarch of hel, under whose blacke survey / Great Potentates do kneele with awful feare.' The contrasting context, if Milton remembered those lines, is piquant. But the meaning, not very sharply distinguished from the above, may be 'reverential'; *OED* 6 cites 'how dare thy joints forget / To pay their awful duty to our presence?' (Shakespeare, *R. II* 3. 3. 75–6).

60 *sovran*. Rolfe noted that Milton's spelling of 'sovereign' is 'etymologically the more correct' (Ital. *sovrano*, from Lat. *superanus*), the common form being 'due to a fancied connection with *reign*.'

61–3 Cook suggests that Milton may have remembered Wisd. of Sol. 18. 14–15: 'For while all things were in quiet silence, and that night was in the midst of her swift course, Thine almighty word leapt downe from heaven, out of thy royall throne.' Cook also compares Mantuan, *Parthen.* 3 (*Opera*, 1513, 1, 70ᵛ): *Attulerat medio nox alta silentia cursu, / Astraque per tenebras tremulis ardentia flammis / Lustrabant dubio frigentem lumine terram.* Milton combines light with peace: cf. 'For unto us a child is born...; and his name shall be called...The Prince of Peace' (Isa. 9. 6), and 'I am the light of the world' (John 8. 12).

64–5 *whist*: hushed (pf. participle). Commentators have cited the same rhyme in Shakespeare, *Temp.* 1. 2. 377–8: 'kiss'd, / The wild waves whist'; and other examples of the word: 'So was the Titaness put downe and whist' (Spenser, *F.Q.* 7. 7. 59); 'Southerne windes are whist' (Marlowe and Nashe, *Dido* 1084, or 4. 1. 25). [Warton mistakenly said that Stanyhurst translated *intentique ora tenebant* (Virgil, *A.* 2. 1) as 'They whisted all'; the phrase is Surrey's.]

66 *Ocean*: trisyllabic also in Shakespeare, *John* 2. 1. 340, *Merch.* 1. 1. 8, *2 H. IV* 3. 1. 50. Cf. below, *union* (108), *session* (163): (Rolfe).

68 *Birds of Calm*: halcyons. Ceyx and Alcyone, transformed to halcyons (kingfishers) by the gods' pity, continued as husband and wife to produce their offspring upon the sea in seven—other writers give other numbers up to fourteen—days of calm in midwinter (Ovid, *M.* 11. 745–8), i.e. at the winter solstice, *c.* 22 December. Cook assembled many references to these days of calm in classical, patristic, and later writers, e.g. the *Hexaemera* of Basil (8. 5: Migne, *Pat. Gr.* 29, 175–8) and Ambrose (5. 13: Migne, *Pat. Lat.* 14, 224), Sylvester (*D.W.W.* 1. 5. 777–89, Grosart, 1, 68), and, most relevantly, Mantuan, *Parthen.* 3 (*Opera* 1, 70ᵛ): *Halcyonis foetae variis nova pignora pennis / Iam tolli audebant, primosque efferre volatus. brooding*: 'Literally, as in *P.L.* 1. 21' (Cook).

   charmed: under a spell or charm (*OED* 1), but here used figuratively. [Rajan (*MLR* 63, 18: see III above, under 1968) notes 'the manner in which the link between "calm" and "charm" preserves the sense of bewitchment and how the potentially disturbing effect of "wave" is arrested by its metrical placing and smoothed out by the spreading of the *a* sound into it.']

69–70 *The Stars...gaze.* Cook cites: 'The starres that strayed in the midest of heaven, desired to stay, to see that great, and new marvaile' (A. Villegas, *Flos Sanctorum, The Lives of the Saints*, tr. Kinsman, 3rd ed. [1630], 1025). Brooks and Hardy (97), noting that the regular procession of the heavenly bodies marks the time for man, observe: 'Time itself thus almost misses a step in token of this foretaste of eternity.' *amaze*: amazement (cf. *PR* 2. 38, *SA* 1645).

71 *Bending...influence.* *influence*: the astrological term for power emanating from the stars and affecting nature and man for good or ill (*OED* 2). Here the stars direct their influence all *one way*, i.e. toward Bethlehem (perhaps also wholly to good). Cf. *PL* 9. 105–7: 'for thee alone, as seems, / In thee concentring all thir precious beams / Of sacred influence.' Verity cites 'the sweet influences of Pleiades' (Job 38. 31), which Milton adapts in *PL* 7. 374–5 [cf. also *PL* 4. 668–73].

72–3 Cook assembles many examples of the delay of dawn, a few religious (e.g. Sannazaro, *De Partu Virginis* 1. 369 f., *Poemata*, ed. J. A. Vulpius, Padua, 1731), but mostly amatory.

73 *For all*: in spite of, notwithstanding (*OED*: for 23).

74 *Lucifer*: the morning star. [The allusion could not here be to the sun, as some have taken it, since 'The Sun himself' is introduced as a new figure in stanza 7.] Verity quotes: 'Venus starre otherwise called Hesperus...and Lucifer, both because he seemeth to be one of the brightest starres, and also first ryseth and setteth last' (Spenser, *S.C., December* Gloss). No doubt his being the last to set caused Lucifer to be thought of as the marshaller of the other stars; cf. *diffugiunt stellae, quarum agmina cogit / Lucifer et caeli statione novissimus exit* (Ovid, *M.* 2. 114–15); Cook also cites ibid. 11. 97–8 and other examples. Brooks and Hardy (98) find a trace of irony in the fact that Lucifer 'was also another name for Satan,' who would wish 'that stars and men pay as little attention to the great event as possible.' The reviewer of Brooks and Hardy in *TLS* (12 July 1957, 428) raised a critical question of some importance: 'Now, poetically, the intrusion of Lucifer-Satan into this part of the "Nativity Ode" is just what is not wanted; it detracts from the charmed air of peace the poet is in the act of creating. And it is hard on a poet if critics, in their eagerness for an ambiguity at all costs, thrust on him a secondary meaning which, though possible theoretically, he never intended.' [The fallacious idea is repeated by W. Empson: 'Lucifer, though Satan, cannot lead them away; their *influence* may even have caused the appearance of Christ, but his order must destroy them' (*Some Versions of Pastoral*, London, 1935, 1950, 182); and Carey (*Milton*, 32): 'the choice of name designedly connects the figure with the sun and Satan as well.']

75 *glimmering Orbs.* There seem to be two possible meanings of *Orb* in this context: (1) 'The space on the celestial sphere within which the influence of a planet [or] star...is supposed to act' (*OED* 2); (2) 'Each of the concentric hollow spheres supposed ⟨in the Ptolemaic scheme⟩ to surround the earth and carry the planets and stars with them in their revolution' (*OED* 7). The former would hark back to *influence* (71), the latter look on to *Crystall sphears* (125). *OED* does not cite this example; Cook reports editors' doubts and, like Verity, offers no explanation. R. C. Browne (*English Poems by John Milton*, 2 v., rev. ed. Oxford, 1894) explains as 'orbit' and compares 'Venus in her glimmering sphere' (Shakespeare, *Dream* 3. 2. 61), which seems to confirm (2). [Hughes also seems to favour this and cites the stars 'fixt in thir Orb that flies' (*PL* 5. 176); in his other citations (*PL* 1. 287, 3. 668, 8. 30) *Orb* seems to mean the heavenly body itself.]

76 *bespake*: spoke out, perhaps 'with some notion of...remonstrance' (*OED* 2); cf. *Lyc* 112.

77–84 Warton compared Phoebus' retreat before Elizabeth in Spenser, *S.C.*, *April* 75–8: 'But when he sawe, how broade her beames did spredde, / it did him amaze. / He blusht to see another Sunne belowe, / Ne durst againe his fyrye face out showe'; and G. Fletcher, *C.V.* 1. 78: 'heav'n awaked all his eyes, / To see another Sunne, at midnight rise.' [Cf. an example of the Spenserian conceit from a poetaster of 1613, quoted in Bush, *Mythology and the Renaissance Tradition* (rev. ed., New York, 1963), 204.] Cook cited Mal. 4. 2: 'But unto you that fear my name shall the Sun of righteousness arise with healing in his wings'; Prudentius, *Apoth.* 626–7: *rota lurida solis / haeret, et excidium sentit iam iamque futurum*; G. Herbert, *Miserie* 33–4 [not yet published]: 'The sunne holds down his head for shame, / Dead with eclipses, when we speak of thee'; etc. In Milton the Sun-god as viewed in pagan literature—as the earth's lover (cf. above, 36 n.) and as driving his chariot across the sky (cf. 19–20, 84)—is contrasted with and subordinated to the Sun of righteousness, the 'Prince of light' (62). [W. J. Roscelli (*TSLL* 8, 1966, 481–2) finds that Milton gives to the conventional conceit a paradoxical twist that 'closely approximates the metaphysical manner': the sun is mistaken in regard to a change in the physical, cosmic order but not in regard to the inauguration of a new order of peace and harmony.]

77 *gloom*. [Ants Oras, in an elaborate gloss on this word (used also in *IlPen* 80, *Comus* 132, etc.), takes the noun 'in the sense of "darkness," to have been coined by Milton' ('Notes on Some Miltonic Usages, their Background and Later Development,' 61–6, *Acta et Commentationes*, B XLIII, 3, Tartu, 1939).]

78 *her room*: her space, place. Cook, asking whether *her* refers to *gloom* which yields the *room*, or to *day* which now rightfully possesses it, inclines to the former. The masculine *his* would seem more natural for *day*, especially perhaps to the classicist Milton. [Another point in favour of Cook's first alternative is that Milton may be echoing Spenser's phrase about night: 'And yeeld her roome to day' (*F.Q.* 3. 4. 60).]

80–3 See 77–84 n.

81 *As*: as if: 'introducing a supposition, expressed by the subjunctive mood' (*OED* 9).

84 Phoebus Apollo (identified with Helios and Roman Sol) is described by Ovid as dwelling in a sumptuous palace (*M.* 2. 1 f.) and at dawn, when Lucifer has marshalled the departing stars (ibid. 114–15), as issuing forth in his chariot to drive across the sky *ignifero...in axe* (ibid. 59), where *axis* means *currus*. [Cf. Milton, *El* 5. 31–2.] Cook adds other phrases for a fiery *axis*, e.g. Seneca, *Herc. Oet.* 1386–7, 1524. [Cf. *candentem...axem* (Ovid, *M.* 2. 297), rendered by Sandys (*Ovid*, 1626, 29) as 'the glowing Axeltree' (by L. C. L. as 'the white-hot vault'). Carey cites 'The burning axletree' in Chapman, *Bussy D'Ambois* 5. 3. 152 (5. 4. 105 in Chapman's *Tragedies*, ed. T. M. Parrott, London and New York, 1910). See the fuller note on *Comus* 95–101.] *Then*: a variant form of *than*.

85–92 The shepherd is common to Christian story and to the pastoral tradition, a fact Milton exploits by presenting the shepherds of the first Christmas in terms of the classical tradition, as he elsewhere combines the two traditions to different purpose (cf. *Lyc* 64–8 n.). [Daiches (103: see above, 32–44 n.) sees 'a kind of wilful pictorial naïveté that is worlds apart from anything in the portraits of shepherds by Theocritus or Virgil,' in spite of *Pan* and the 'almost throw-away reference to classical pastoral' in 91–2. 'There is a deliberate demoting of the shepherds here, to emphasise the contrast between these simple characters and the mighty revelation that is to be made to them.']

85 *Lawn*. See *Lyc* 25 n. and *Comus* 567 n.

86 *Or ere*: before. The two forms are variants of the same word, O.E. *ær* [*OED*: ere: B. 1, C. 1 d; or: B. 1 b]. The phrase in Shakespeare et al. is thus tautological, possibly because *ere* was confused with *e'er*; Milton's use is peculiar only in being prepositional instead of conjunctive (Verity). *point of dawn*: daybreak (Fr. *point du jour*: *OED* 23); point, in reference to time, might also mean, not a moment, but the fourth (or possibly fifth) part of an hour (*OED* 10).

87 *simply*: unaffectedly, perhaps innocently [or unaware of the great event?]. Cook cites 'To simple Shepherds, keeping watch by night' (*PL* 12. 365).

89 *the mighty Pan*: Originally a local deity, born in Arcadia, the son of Hermes and a nymph; his grotesque appearance at birth amused all the gods, who 'called the boy Pan because he delighted all their hearts' (*Homeric Hymn to Pan*). He became the guardian of shepherds and their flocks (Virgil, *E.* 2. 33, 10. 26; *G.* 1. 17). His worship spread throughout Greece and, according to Ovid (*F.* 2. 277–9, 5. 91–102), was carried by Evander to Italy, where he was identified with the Roman Faunus. In the Orphic *Hymn to Pan* he is a symbol of the sun or even the universe. Cook, who notes that this and other references which assume a connection of the name with *pan* ('all') depend on a false etymology, finds in his association with the sun another invitation to identify Pan with God or Christ. It is from his central role of shepherds' god, however, that Christian humanism chiefly developed whatever equation it could make of Pan with Christ; this of course involved the ignoring of those licentious traits added to his character and mentioned by Christians only to be condemned (e.g. Prudentius, *Perist.* 10. 241–2).

Milton's phrase *mighty Pan* occurs (as Warton noted) in Spenser: 'The brethren twelve, that kept yfere / the flockes of mighty Pan' (*S.C.*, *July* 143–4); [and in Browne, *Brit. Past.* 1. 4. 246, 2. 4. 791, 2. 5. 758]. The Gloss in *S.C.* explains merely as a reference to the twelve shepherd sons of Jacob, leaving the reader to detect any larger symbolic reference to God's chosen people, and through it to Christ's Apostles and Church. Cf. further: 'For Pan himselfe was their ⟨the faithful shepherds'⟩ inheritaunce' (ibid. *May* 111); the Gloss explains 'Pan himselfe) God,' the reference being to the tribe of Levi. Elsewhere in the *S.C.* the identification of Pan and Christ is clear: 'And wonned not the great God Pan, / upon mount Olivet?' (*July* 49–50): 'When great Pan account of shepeherdes shall aske' (*May* 54). On this last the Gloss comments: 'Great pan) is Christ, the very God of all shepheards, which calleth himselfe the greate and good shepherd. The name is most rightly (me thinkes) applyed to him, for Pan signifieth all or omnipotent, which is onely the Lord Jesus. And by that name (as I remember) he is called of Eusebius in his fifte booke de Preparat. Evang; who thereof telleth a proper storye to that purpose'—the story, from Plutarch, remembered by Milton at 181–3 (see note). Though the editors of the Variorum Spenser do not note the fact, the Gloss is in error: Eusebius regards Pan as a demon and his death as an example of Christ's destruction of such. The interpretation given in the Gloss is recorded in Lavater's *Of ghostes and spirites walking by nyght* (1572; ed. J. D. Wilson and M. Yardley, Oxford, 1929, pp. 94–5 in both). After referring correctly to Eusebius, it notes that other Christian writers interpret the words as concerning Christ's crucifixion: 'by the whiche voice being uttered in a wildernesse of solitarie rockes, it was declared that our Lorde and God had suffred for us. For the word *Pan* in Greeke signifieth all; and then the Lord of al the world was Crucified.' This interpretation of the death of Pan is also given by Rabelais (4. 28), with the usual appeal to the name as signifying 'our All,' and Rabelais' characteristic insistence that Christ was slain by the envy and injustice of the priests, monks, and pontiffs of the Mosaic law. Milton had, then, abundant precedent for identifying Pan and Christ; and Cook adds other references. The important point is that here, as again at 226–8 (see note), Milton is content to relate the classical and the Christian, while in the poem generally (and especially 173–96) he repudiates the classical in favour of the Christian and by implication Pan among the rest (181–3 and n.). [I. L. Myhr (*Explic.* 4, 1945–6, Item 16) suggested that the idea of Pan the musician might lead up to the celestial music. On the whole literary and allegorical history of Pan see Patricia Merivale, *Pan the Goat-God* (Cambridge, Mass., 1969), 1–34; C. A. Patrides, cited under 173 below; and Helga Spevack-Husmann, *The Mighty Pan: Miltons Mythologische Vergleiche* (Münster, 1963, 88–98, on 'Christus-Pan.')]

90 *kindly*. Cook noted the double meaning: 'In accordance with his nature; by natural disposition' (*OED* 1a); 'benevolently, lovingly' (ibid. 2).

91 The preoccupations of the shepherds of classical pastoral. See below, *L'All* 67–8 n.

92 *silly*: 'simple, rustic' (*OED* 3c); cf. *simply* and *rustick* (87 above). Like *simple*, *silly* often, and no doubt here, connotes harmless, innocent; *OED* fails to record this meaning, but Verity recognizes it. The shepherds of classical pastoral dwelt commonly in a state of innocence, naturalistically conceived; and while in the Christian view primal innocence was of course lost, the shepherd remained relatively natural and innocent. Milton does not make use of the tradition that contrasted the simple, unlettered shepherds of the Christmas story with the Magi, as in Sidney Godolphin's 'Lord when the wise men came from Farr' (*Poems*, ed. W. Dighton, Oxford, 1931, 28). [Cf. W. Browne, *Shepherd's Pipe*, 5, Arg., 'silly shepherds,' *Poems*, 2, 143; *Brit. Past.* I. I. 19–20: 'A shepherd...rich / With all the gifts that silly men bewitch.' Cf. the lines from Shakespeare, *3 H. VI* 2. 5. 42–5, quoted near the end of the note on *L'All* 67–8.]

93–172 The subject of the second movement of the Hymn is the song of the angelic choir. The note of the imagery changes to bright light and colour and clearly defined forms, and, above all, to fully articulated harmonious sound.

93–100 'And suddenly there was with the angel a multitude of the heavenly host praising God, and saying, Glory to God in the highest, and on earth peace, good will toward men' (Luke 2. 13–14).

93–4 Cook compares: 'Sweete Musique heavenly rare, / Mine eares...dooth grecte' (E[dmund] B[olton?], *The Sheepheards Song: a Caroll or Himne for Christmas, England's Helicon*, ed. H. E. Rollins, Cambridge, Mass., 1935, 1, 131).

95 *strook.* [For the past participle of *strike* Milton uses *strook*, *struck* and *struck'n*, the first chiefly.]

96–7 For several of the words used Verity compares: 'most heavenly noyse was heard / Of the strings, stirred with the warbling wind' (Spenser, *Ruines of Time* 612–13). *warbl'd*: melodiously sung or sounded (*OED* 1; *Comus* 853).

97 *Answering*: making a responsive sound or echoing (*OED* 18), or perhaps coming in antiphonally (ibid. 17).
  stringed noise. Noise could mean melodious sound or music (*OED*: noise 5) of the voice (cf. Spenser, *F.Q.* 1. 12. 39) or instruments or both (cf. *SolMus* 18); here of course produced by stringed instruments. [Cf. Ps. 98. 4–5, under 115 below.]

98 *took*: captivated, put under a spell. Verity cited R. Cotgrave, *Dictionarie of the French and English Tongues* (1611): 'Fée...taken, bewitched.' Editors quote Shakespeare: 'No fairy takes, nor witch hath power to charm' (*Ham.* 1. 1. 163); and 'daffodils, / That come before the swallow dares and take / The winds of March with beauty' (*W. Tale* 4. 4. 118–20). [Cf. *Comus* 255 and n. and 557.] *OED* oddly overlooks this well established though now archaic meaning, which was perhaps connected with the pervasive idea in the verb of seizure, capture.
  all their souls: the whole soul of each of them, rather than the souls of them all (Cook).

99–100 A conceit similar in kind to those of 37–44, 69–70 [cf. *Comus* 556–9].

100 *close*: 'conclusion of a musical phrase, theme or movement; a cadence' (*OED: sb.*² 2); cf. *Comus* 547.

101–8 The ideas and assumptions underlying this stanza are: (1) the music of the spheres, though inaudible to man, is, or symbolizes, the power that keeps the whole realm of nature, the earth, planets, and stars, in their ordered and harmonious motion, the music thus connoting the highest perfection attainable on the natural level; (2) that, distinct from this, is the higher music of the angelic choir, connoting the perfection of the heavenly order; (3) that, were this higher music to continue to penetrate the natural order, even to its lowest sublunar level, the music of the spheres would become superfluous, since the heavenly music would not only fulfil the former function of the spheres' music but unite earth and heaven, the natural and the supernatural. See further 125–32 n. [and *Arc* 68–73 and n. and *SolMus* and notes. The stanza further reminds us of the widely familiar Aristotelian-Christian idea that the part of the world below the moon was the realm of change and decay, while all beyond the moon was pure and changeless. One might add a strained fancy from W. Empson (*Some Versions of Pastoral*, 182): 'Cynthia too...feels that the music at Christ's birth means that "her part was don"; Elizabeth and her age counted as another paganism.']

102–3 *hollow round | Of Cynthia's seat*: the sphere of the moon.   *Airy region*. For the three regions of the air see *FInf* 16 n. Here the three seem to be taken collectively. Cook notes 'airy region' in Shakespeare, *Romeo* 2. 2. 21, and Virgil's *aetheria plaga* (*A.* 1. 394).

104 *won*: allured, induced (*OED* 9c).

106 The word *its* occurs only three times in Milton's verse, here and at *PL* 1. 254, 4. 813. [Normally he uses 'his' or 'her.']

108 See note on 101–8.

109–16 At first appears only a globe of light which seems to surround them (*Globe* may have both its literal meaning of a spherical body and its figurative, of a perfect body: *OED* 1, 1 b); then the angelic forms, armed *Seraphim* and *Cherubim* (the two highest orders in the angelic hierarchy), define themselves. Verity cites 'him round / A Globe of fierie Seraphim inclos'd' (*PL* 2. 511–12) and 'no sooner did the force of so much united excellence meet in one globe of brightnesse and efficacy' (*Apol, Works* 3, 337). Cook adds: 'strait a fiery Globe / Of Angels on full sail of wing flew nigh' (*PR* 4. 581–2); and 'A globe of winged

Angels' (G. Fletcher, *C.T.* 2. 13); and finds a suggestion of Lat. *globus*, a troop, as in Virgil, *A.* 10. 373.

111 *shame-fac't. Shamefaced* is an etymological misinterpretation of *shamefast* (*OED*), modest, bashful (ibid. 1), modesty being a virtue; but *shamefast* could also mean ashamed, abashed (ibid. 2), though the only examples of *shamefaced* in this sense are from the nineteenth century. The former meaning suits well the image conveyed by *array'd*; the latter meaning recalls nature's shame (32–44) and the sun's (80–2). [Cf. Spenser, *F.Q.* 2. 9. 43.] *array'd*: adorned, decked (*OED*: array 9b); [or simply 'clothed' (ibid. 9a)? Could Milton intend a play on 'ray' ('beam')?]

112–13 Scripture speaks only of 'a multitude of the heavenly host' (see 93–100 n.). Milton accepted and used the traditional idea that the Seraphim symbolized love of God and the Cherubim rational contemplation of God's perfection (see 28 n. and *IlPen* 45–54 n.).

114 *displaid*: unfolded, opened to view (*OED* 1); in heraldry, having limbs or wings extended (ibid. 2).

115 *Harping*. Cook cites 'and I heard the voice of harpers harping with their harps' (Rev. 14. 2). *loud and solemn*. Cook compares: 'Make a joyful noise unto the Lord...; make a loud noise, and rejoice...Sing unto the Lord with the harp' (Ps. 98. 4–5); and: 'It is a good thing to give thanks unto the Lord... upon the harp with a solemn sound' (Ps. 92. 1, 3). *quire*. Besides the general sense exemplified in 27 above (see n.), the word has a special one, being applied to each of the nine orders of angels (see 125–32 n.); *OED* 4 quotes Richard Carpenter, *Experience, Historie, and Divinitie* (1642), 3. 4, p. 17: 'there are nine Orders, or Quires of Angels'; and 'the Quires of Cherubim' (*PL* 3. 666). The preceding reference to two of the orders suggests that this specialized meaning was also in Milton's mind. Finally, since the adjectives *loud and solemn* refer primarily to the hymn, we may remember that the related *chorus* could also mean anything sung by a number of singers together (*OED*: chorus 4), a meaning Milton may transfer to *quire*.

116 *unexpressive*: inexpressible, indescribable. Editors cite 'the unexpressive nuptial Song' (*Lyc* 176). Warton quoted 'The fair, the chaste, and unexpressive she' (Shakespeare, *A.Y.L.* 3. 2. 10). 'In the English of Shakespeare and Milton the force of participial and adjectival terminations is not rigidly fixed' (Verity); he cites 'innumerous' (*Comus* 348), 'uncomprehensive' (Shakespeare, *Troi.* 3. 3. 198), etc.

117–24 [The music attending the birth of Christ, the second supreme event in world history, recalls the first, the creation.] The highly stylized account of creation is characteristic of the poem [and in substance seems to be mainly a blending of the Bible and Ovid].

119 Verity cites: 'When the morning stars sang together, and all the sons of God shouted for joy' (Job 38. 7), and 'son of the morning,' used of Lucifer, the day star (Isa. 14. 12 and margin). *when of old*. Cook cites 'Of old hast thou laid the foundation of the earth' (Ps. 102. 25).

122 Cook quotes Ovid, *M*. 1. 12–13: *nec circumfuso pendebat in aere tellus | ponderibus librata suis*. [Hughes quotes Job 26. 7: 'He...hangeth the earth upon nothing'; and *PL* 7. 242: 'And Earth self ballanc't on her Center hung.']

hinges. Hinge is a derivative of *hang*; hence (among its other meanings, by transference), 'the axis of the earth; the two poles about which the earth revolves' (*OED* 3, which quotes the Countess of Pembroke, Ps. 89. 4: 'the Earth.../ The unseene hinge of North and South sustaineth.' Hales (reported by Verity) cited 'To move the world from off his stedfast henge' (Spenser, *F.Q*. 1. 11. 21). [Cf. Manilius, *Astronomicon*, ed. J. Scaliger, Leyden, 1600, p. 9, line 28: *Libratumque gerit diverso cardine mundum*; Housman (*M. Manilii Astronomica*, Editio Minor, Cambridge, 1932, 1. 280) reads *regit* for *gerit*.]

123 *cast*. The precise meaning is uncertain (witness Verity's misapplication of 2 Kings 19. 32). What seems to be required is a synonym for *laid*; possibly Milton's idea was of throwing down to a great depth, *cast* being reinforced by *deep*. Two other possibilities are: (1) that *cast* refers to moulding (as in casting metal: *OED* 49, 50, 51); or (2) that no physical action is intended, *cast* meaning to determine, devise, or arrange (ibid. 43, 44, 45), as in 'appointed' (Prov. 8. 29, quoted in 123–4 n.).

123–4 Cook cited: 'Where wast thou when I laid the foundations of the earth?' (Job 38. 4). But yet more relevant are: 'Who laid the foundations of the earth, that it should not be removed for ever' (Ps. 104. 5); 'Whereupon are the foundations thereof fastened?' (Job 38. 6); 'the Lord thy maker, that hath...laid the foundations of the earth...that divided the sea, whose waves roared' (Isa. 51. 13, 15); and especially: 'When he gave to the sea his decree, that the waters should not pass his commandment: when he appointed the foundations of the earth' (Prov. 8. 29). Verity compares *positi late fundamina mundi* (*Patrem* 47) and 'Fate had cast too deep / Her dark foundations' (*PL* 6. 869–70). [Cf. Ovid, *M*. 1. 29–31, 36 f.]

124 Cook cites: 'Or who shut up the sea...?' 'And said, Hitherto shalt thou come, but no further: and here shall thy proud waves be stayed' (Job 38. 8, 11).

weltring waves: apparently a common phrase. *OED* quotes George Turbervile, *Tragical Tales*, ed. Edinburgh, 1837, 342 [see also 293]; Verity cites W. Painter, *Palace of Pleasure*, Novel 28, epitaph on Timon (ed. J. Jacobs, 3 v., London, 1890, 1, 113). *weltring*: tumbling, tossing. Cf. *Lyc* 13 n. [and *PL* 1. 78].

oozy. The adjective is formed from the noun meaning slimy mud, especially that of the sea bottom or the bed of an estuary or river. *OED* (ooze: *sb.*[2] 1) cites *oous* in Nashe (*Works*, ed R. B. McKerrow, 5 v., London, 1904-10, 2, 36) and *ose* in R. Carew, *Survey of Cornwall* (1602), 27. Cook compares 'the ooze and bottom of the sea' (Shakespeare, *H. V* 1. 2. 164) and 'mudded in that oozy bed' (*Temp.* 5. 1. 151); [cf. *Lyc* 175].

channel. *OED* notes the extension of the meaning from 'the hollow bed of running waters' to 'the bed of the sea'; the latter is obviously the meaning here, though *OED* gives no example so early. Perhaps the extension was furthered by the ancient conception of the Ocean stream. Milton uses the word because he is emphasizing the confining of the sea. Cook quotes: 'And the channels of the sea appeared, the foundations of the world were discovered, at the rebuking of the Lord' (2 Sam. 22. 16).

125-32 References to the music of the spheres were common and widely understood, as Shakespeare's use of them indicates; editors regularly quote *Merch.* 5. 1. 60 f., and Rolfe adds *A. Y. L.* 2. 7. 6, *Twel.* 3. 1. 121, *Antony* 5. 2. 84. The idea appealed strongly to Milton, especially the young Milton: it provided the theme of *Prol* 2 and figures in *Arc* 62-73, *SolMus* 19-24, *Comus* 1019-20 (see notes on these passages). In the Pythagorean tradition the transparent spheres surrounding the earth, and containing the heavenly bodies, produced music as they turned; the idea was taken over by Plato, with his own modifications (see *Arc* 62-73 n.), and reported by Cicero (*Somnium Scipionis*, in *Rep.* 6. 18; *N.D.* 3. 11). The music was, or symbolized, the force that preserved the order and harmony of the natural world, though inaudible to mortal ears. [This pattern of mathematical and musical harmony developed potent implications during the centuries from Plato through the seventeenth. Some discussions of varying focus and length are, or are in: Cook, 342-3; Spaeth, *Music* (passim); Leo Spitzer, *Classical and Christian Ideas of World Harmony*, ed. A. G. Hatcher (Baltimore, 1963; rev. from *Traditio* 2-3, 1944-5); Gretchen L. Finney, articles of 1940 f. collected in *Musical Backgrounds for English Literature: 1580-1650* (New Brunswick, 1962); James Hutton, 'Some

English Poems in Praise of Music' (*English Miscellany*, ed. M. Praz, 2, 1951); J. Hollander, *The Untuning of the Sky: Ideas of Music in English Poetry* (Princeton, 1961); C. A. Patrides, *Milton*, 41–5.]

The number of spheres, increasing as the Ptolemaic system was elaborated, varied in poetic reference. Milton here assumes nine [in *PL* 3. 481–3 there are ten, those of the moon, Mercury, Venus, the sun, Mars, Jupiter, Saturn, the sphere of fixed stars, the crystalline sphere, and the *primum mobile*]. The number nine corresponds to the nine orders of angels [Seraphim, Cherubim, Thrones; Dominations, Virtues, Powers; Principalities, Archangels, Angels]. Tillyard (*Milton* 377–8, on *SolMus*) says that Milton identifies the music of the spheres with the song of the angels [so also, e.g., Hanford, Prince], but Milton always distinguishes between the two, and nowhere more emphatically than here: the spheres with their *ninefold harmony* are bidden to complement, 'Make up full consort to th'Angelike symphony.' To repeat from 101–8 n., the sphere music represents harmony in the natural order, the angels' song the higher harmony of heaven; they are parallel, but on different levels, as in *PL* 5. 616–27, where the angels' dance 'Resembles' the movements of planet and star; cf. *SolMus* 17–24 n., *Comus* 1019–20 n. The parallel and the distinction are traditional. Thus Donne speaks of 'All, three Quires, heaven, earth ⟨ i.e. man ⟩, and sphears' (*Upon the Translation of the Psalmes* 23: *Poems of John Donne*, ed. H. J. C. Grierson, 2 v., Oxford, 1912). Thomas Heywood, telling how the various orders of God's angels 'all / Resound his praise in accents musicall,' adds 'So doe the Heav'ns and Planets, much below them' (*Hierarchie of the blessed Angells*, 1635, p. 582). The confusion, which Milton and these poets scrupulously avoid, perhaps arose from the Christian idea of angels assigned to guard and rule the heavenly bodies (as Uriel is 'Regent of the Sun,' *PL* 3. 690), and ultimately from the notion that each sphere 'is kept in rotation by a special intelligence,' which Cook traces to Aristotle (*Meta.* 12. 8). Dante, who seems to be using an already accepted idea (Hutton, 23 [cf. Spaeth, *Music*, 103, n. 1, 144–8]), preserves the distinction in referring to 'the song of them who always sing following the notes of the eternal spheres' (*Purg.* 30. 92–3, tr. C. E. Norton). Without impairing it, Heywood asks 'what reference the Seraphim / Hath with the Primum Mobile. Then, what kin / The Cherub from the Starry Heav'n doth claime' (272). Again without confusing the two kinds of music, Heywood (who published too late to influence Milton) illustrates the still current idea of correspondence in this summary (283: quoted by Hutton, 26):

The Primum Mobile doth first begin
To chime unto the holy Seraphim.

> The Cherubim doth make concordance even
> With the eighth Sphere, namely, The Starry Heaven.
> The Thrones, with Saturne. The like modulations
> Hath Jupiter with the high Dominations.
> The Vertues have with Mars a consonance sweet:
> The Potestates, with Sol in symptores meet.
> The Principates with Venus best agree:
> Th' Arch-Angels, with the Planet Mercurie.
> The Angels with the Moone, which melody
> Hosanna sings to Him that sits on high.

For the sources of such elaborate parallels, see writers cited earlier in this note, e.g. Hutton, 14–28.

128 *silver chime. silver*: 'Having a clear gentle resonance like that of silver; ...melodious' (*OED* 13). *chime*: 'sequence of harmonious sounds,' by transference from that given forth by a set of bells (*OED* 5). Cf. 'Spheary chime' (*Comus* 1020); 'If Musicke did not merit endlesse prayse, / Would heav'nly Spheres delight in silver round?' (I[ohn] D[avies], *Hymne in prayse of Musicke*, F. Davison's *A Poetical Rhapsody*, ed. H. E. Rollins, Cambridge, Mass., 1931, 1, 201). Todd compared G. Markham, *The Dumb Knight* (*Dodsley's Old English Plays*, ed. W. C. Hazlitt, 10, 1875, 148): 'It was as silver, as the chime of spheres' (the preceding words being 'in his words / Found I more music than in choirs of angels'). Verity cited 'Of fayre Elisa be your silver song' (Spenser, *S.C.*, *April* 46; the Gloss says *silver song* is from Hesiod's *argureon melos* [a phrase not in Hesiod]). The epithet, especially in the alliterative 'silver sound,' seems to have been a commonplace, e.g. N. Breton, *Countess of Pembroke's Love*, st. 7 (in *The Pilgrimage to Paradise* 21, *Works*, ed. Grosart, 2 v., 1879, 1); Shakespeare, *Romeo* 4. 5. 130.

130 Cook notes that Dorylaeus, quoted by the third-century Censorinus (*De Die Natali* 13), called the planetary system God's organ, *organum Dei*; and that the lowest note in the scale played by the spheres was assigned by Cicero (*Rep.* 6. 18) to the moon, by Servius (on Virgil, *A.* 2. 255) to Saturn. This suggests one possible meaning of Milton's *Base*. Another is suggested by the frequent use in the sixteenth and seventeenth centuries of a 'ground bass,' often played on the organ, while other instruments erected their 'varied harmonies...over it' (P. A. Scholes, *Oxford Companion to Music*, ed. 1950, 385–6). ⟨This note contributed by Miss C. A. Balter.⟩ [Spaeth (*Music*, 102) remarks that *the Base* 'may possibly be taken literally, as Burnet would have it (*Early Greek Philosophy*, London, 1908, p. 351, n. 3), but it would seem that the bass is here not a following part but a leading one'; that Milton 'seems to be thinking of the fundamental or most important tones as much as of actual bass notes.' Cf. Spenser, *F.Q.* 2. 12. 71: 'The silver sounding instruments did meet / With the base murmure of the waters fall.']

131 Verity (from Dunster) cited: 'Her ⟨ Urania's ⟩ Nine-fold Voice did choicely imitate / Th'Harmonious Musik of Heavens nimble Dance' (Sylvester, *Urania*, st. 9, Grosart, 2, 3).

132 See 125–32 n. *consort*: 'accord or harmony of several instruments or voices...in tune' (*OED* 3: from Lat. *consortium*, fellowship). Cf. 'That wonder was to heare their trim consort' (Spenser, *F.Q.* 3. 1. 40); 'Visit by night your lady's chamber window / With some sweet consort' (Shakespeare, *T.G.V.* 3. 2. 83–4); *IlPen* 145, *SolMus* 27 (Rolfe). The word is distinct from the slightly later *concert* but often replaced it; *OED* (concert *sb.*) quotes R. Cotgrave, *Dict.* (1611): '*Concert de Musique.* A Consort of Musicke.'

133–48 As the first effect of the *Angelike symphony* was to suggest that Nature's responsibility was at an end, and that the heavenly music might sustain the order of all things in place of the music of the spheres, the second effect is to suggest a return of the golden age, the reign of Cronos or Saturn, a partial parallel in classic myth to the state of innocence in Hebrew–Christian story (Hesiod, *Works and Days* 109–26; Ovid, *M.* 1. 89–112). In *Prol 2* (*De Sphaerarum Concentu*) Milton had suggested that to hear the music of the spheres would be to bring back the golden age: if we were as pure in mind as Pythagoras, *tum quidem suavissima illa stellarum circumeuntium musica personarent aures nostrae, & opplerentur; atque dein cuncta illico tanquam in aureum illud saeculum redirent* (*Works* 12, 156). Hutton ('Praise of Music,' 45) comments: 'We know that now the *musica mundana*, primarily sphere-music, holds the universe together; but it is itself an imperfect copy of the music of the angels...At the moment of Christ's birth, the true music seems about to replace the copy. And the physical sphere-music is summoned (Stanza 13) to be heard and to be in perfect accord with the *prima musica*...If this perfection is attained...both the physical universe and human nature...[133–5] will have returned to their primitive accord with heaven.' As we saw above, the return of the golden age is the central theme of Virgil's Messianic Eclogue, and this enters the tradition in which the *Nativity* stands. After the golden age, when men no longer obeyed the behests of natural justice, its goddess Astraea fled to the heavens and became the constellation Virgo (Ovid, *M.* 1. 149–50). In Spenser, *F.Q.* 5. 1. 11, Astraea is said to have fled because 'Mongst wicked men...no truth she found,' which Milton perhaps remembered in restoring them together (see *El* 4. 81–2 n., *FInf* 50–2 n.).

But with the return of the golden age she will return: *iam redit et Virgo* (Virgil, *E.* 4. 6). The return of the golden age was a favourite theme in Jonson's masques, *The Golden Age Restor'd*, *Pleasure reconcild to Vertue*, etc. [C. G. Osgood remarked (*AJP* 41, 1920, 79): 'Various sources of details in this passage [133–53] from the Psalms, the *Iliad*, the Fourth Eclogue of Virgil, and Horace, have been noted by the editors. But the thought as a whole is that in the Fifth Book of the *Divine Institutes* of Lactantius.' As Michael Fixler says (*Milton and the Kingdoms of God* (London and Evanston, 1964, 55), 'The central prophetic vision of the poem...is that of the restoration through Christ of the Golden Age....No utopian image is suggested here by the Golden Age. It is principally the divine harmony restored as a law of life....' Cf. W. J. Grace, *Ideas in Milton* (Notre Dame and London, 1968), 39–44. For the general theme and tradition, see A. O. Lovejoy and G. Boas, *Primitivism and Related Ideas in Antiquity* (Baltimore, 1935); A. B. Giamatti, *The Earthly Paradise and the Renaissance Epic* (Princeton, 1966); H. Levin, 'The Golden Age and the Renaissance,' *Literary Views*, ed. C. Camden (Chicago, 1964), and *The Myth of The Golden Age in the Renaissance* (Bloomington and London, 1969). Cf. P. Cullen at the end of III above.]

136 *speckl'd*: used figuratively of the mortal blemishes of sin, vanity. *OED* 2c quotes 'Before my soule looke black with speckled sinne' (Dekker et al., *Patient Grissil* 1. 2. 71 [and cf. 2. 2. 53]: *Dramatic Works of Thomas Dekker*, ed. F. T. Bowers, 4 v., Cambridge, 1953–61, 1). Joseph Warton (quoted by Thomas) compared *mos et lex maculosum edomuit nefas* (Horace, *C.* 4. 5. 22). T. Warton explained: 'Vanity ⟨is⟩ dressed in a variety of gaudy colours' or perhaps '*spots*, the marks of disease and corruption.' The latter idea is followed by Rolfe: 'Covered with plague-spots; a figure in keeping with... *leprous Sin*' (138), and by Cook, who quotes: 'walk not as other Gentiles walk, in the vanity of their mind, Having the understanding darkened, being alienated from the life of God' (Eph. 4. 17–18). *OED* 1 quotes: 'He is no better then a leper in Gods eyes,... outwardly spotted and speckled' (Thomas Taylor, *Commentarie upon the Epistle ...to Titus*, Cambridge, 1612, 1. 15, p. 308).

138 *leprous*. See 136 n. Both leprosy (*OED* 1b) and leprous (ibid. 1d) were used figuratively for the contamination of sin. Todd compared 'The Leprosie of our contagious sin' (Sylvester, *D.W.W.* 2. 3. 2. 529, Grosart, 1, 182) and 'My whole life is so leprous' (Beaumont and Fletcher, *Maid's Tragedy* 4. 1. 201). Cook cited: 'For sin is a leprosy, various and multiform' (Chrysostom, *Homilies ...Timothy*, etc., Oxford, 1843, 298). [Cf. Drummond, 2, 23, *Hymn of the*

Ascension 42, 'Edens leprous Prince.'] Cook illustrates *melt from* by 'Authority melts from me' (Shakespeare, *Antony* 3. 13. 90). *earthly mould*. Verity says that *mould* seems 'in Milton to signify "material"' and cites 'none.../ Of human mould' (*Arc* 72–3) and 'Ethereal mould' (*PL* 2. 139, 7. 356), and adds that 'The metaphor is that of casting metals.' Cook explains: 'Either from humanity (cf. *Arc.* 72–3...) or from the earth (cf. *Com.* 17..."this sin-worn mould")'; see notes on these passages. *OED* (mould: *sb.*[1] 4) cites the present example under 'Earth regarded as the material of the human body,' together with more literal and unquestionable examples. None of these explanations seems quite satisfactory or conclusive. That the basic image is indeed from the casting of metal is confirmed by the verb *melt*; *earthly mould* refers, then, neither to the earth as a whole nor to the dust from which man was made, but to the 'imparted form,' conferring the 'distinctive nature' (*OED*: *sb.*[3] 9) of earthly things, and especially of man, whose imparted form is in the image of God (Gen. 1. 27). Sin entering has impaired this form and from it the corrupting element must be melted away. The rejected meanings, of course, may still supply secondary suggestions.

140 Warton compared Virgil, *A.* 8. 243–6: *si qua penitus vi terra dehiscens | infernas reseret sedes et regna recludat | pallida, dis invisa, superque immane barathrum | cernatur, trepident immisso lumine Manes.* Hales (quoted by Verity) added Homer, *Il.* 20. 61–4 (L.C.L.): 'And seized with fear in the world below was Aïdoneus, lord of the shades, and in fear leapt he from his throne and cried aloud, lest above him the earth be cloven by Poseidon, the Shaker of Earth, and his abode be made plain to view for mortals and immortals....' Cook added Mantuan, *Georgius* (*Opera* 1, 236ʳ): *fuit tremor usque in Tartara, et umbrae | Tartareae timuere omnes ne terra dehiscens | Concideret, Stygiasque domos ostenderet astris.* [Cf. *Naturam* 30–2 and n. (*V.C.* 1, 217).]

peering. Warton interpreted as prying (*OED*: peer 1 b). There seems no reason to question this, or to adopt Dunster's 'to make its first appearance' (recorded by Todd). That meaning of the word is possible (*OED* 2, 3); but his reason for advancing it (that the primary reference is to the rising of the Sun of Righteousness) is not consonant with 149–72 (see below, 149–50 n.). And the passages cited from Virgil and Homer (in 140 n. above) support Warton. [I do not see that the sense 'appearing' is less consonant than the rest of 135–48 with 149–72, or that the Virgilian and Homeric passages support Warton, since neither has the idea of 'prying day,' and that idea may seem decidedly out of key in the Miltonic context. For the meaning 'appear' *OED* 3 cites Shakespeare,

Venus 86 ('a divedapper peering through a wave'), *H. V* 4. 7. 88 ('a many of your horsemen peer / And gallop o'er the field'), and *W. Tale* 4. 4. 3 ('Flora / Peering in April's front'). William Bell (*Comus; Nativity Ode*, etc., London, 1921–9; first pub. 1889–90), supporting 'appear,' cites *Shrew* 4. 3. 176: 'So honour peereth in the meanest habit.' Prince says that '"Peering" was used by the Elizabethans to mean "overlooking."']

141–6 To *Justice* (Astraea), whose return will mark the restoration of the golden age (see 133–48 n.), Milton adds *Truth* and *Mercy*; Peace he had already introduced at 45–52. Editors cite Ps. 85. 10: 'Mercy and truth are met together; righteousness and peace have kissed each other.' Justice, Truth, Mercy, and Peace are the four Daughters of God (see H. Traver, *The Four Daughters of God*, Bryn Mawr, 1907, and S. C. Chew, *The Virtues Reconciled: An Iconographic Study*, Toronto, 1947). In a long tradition extending from Hugo of St Victor and Bernard of Clairvaux to Milton's own century, and expressed in prose, verse, and pictorial art, these four allegorical figures are found, 'ranged in opposing pairs..., engaged in their debate on the high problem of fallen Man and the Atonement, and reconciled with one another when the Son of God offers Himself as a vicarious Sacrifice' (Chew, 5). Although here Milton makes no mention of the debate, his grouping of Truth and Mercy with Justice recalls the tradition and thereby transforms a classical into a Christian reference. His lines remind us of and balance those describing the descent of Peace, and they have the same masque-like quality. But there is a significant difference: in place of the subdued note and colour characteristic of the first movement, we have the more rapid and confident rhythm and the bright colour characteristic of the second. Dunster (in Todd) conjectured that the whole picture might have been suggested by a frontispiece to Sylvester's translation of Du Bartas' *Triumph of Faith*, which represented Christ descending to judgment, amidst a blaze of light and completely encircled by a rainbow, and beneath his feet wreathed clouds which he may be imagined as propelling or directing. [See *FInf* 50–2 and n.]

143–4 In 1645 the lines read: *Th'enameld Arras of the Rainbow wearing, / And Mercy set between....*(*Works* I, 416; *Facs.* 160). The later reading Cook explains by reference to paintings of the Virgin Mary 'completely surrounded by the aureole, or glory'; here the 'glory' is of the colours of the rainbow, which gives special point to the *like glories* attributed to Mercy [see also the latter part of the note on 141–6]. Cook cites 'and there was a rainbow round about the throne' (Rev. 4. 3). Verity thinks of the heads only as thus orbed and compares 'a rainbow was upon his head' (Rev. 10. 1). Brooks and Hardy (99) note that the rainbow has Christian associations (God's covenant with Noah: Gen. 9. 13) and classical (Iris: cf. *Comus* 991 and n.).

146 This line suggests figures of the masques, who so often come down on a cloud; cf. 46–52 n., and, e.g., the descriptions in Carew's *Coelum Britannicum* (1634: *Poems*, ed. R. Dunlap, Oxford, 1949, 154, 182). *With radiant feet.* Dunster (in Todd) compared: 'How beautiful...are the feet of him that bringeth good tidings, that publisheth peace' (Isa. 52. 7). *tissued*: woven, especially in the form of 'tissue,' a cloth in which gold or silver threads were introduced (*OED*). Verity compared *plighted clouds* (*Comus* 300).

148 *the Gates of her high Palace Hall.* Keightley cited Virgil, *A.* 10. 1: *Panditur interea domus omnipotentis Olympi.* Cook compared *magni...Palatia caeli* (Ovid, *M.* 1. 176) and 'this is the gate of heaven' (Gen. 28. 17).

149–50 Like the first impression given by the heavenly music, the second, that the golden age is about to be restored, proves premature. [It has been only a brief wishful vision entertained by the Christian poet, who knows the divine plan for man's redemption and had proclaimed it in his opening stanza.]

149 *wisest Fate*: here a synonym for God's will; cf. 'what I will is Fate' (*PL* 7. 173). Virgil ends his prophecy of a new age with a reference to fate: '*Talia saecla*' suis dixerunt '*currite*' fusis | concordes stabili fatorum numine Parcae (*E.* 4. 46–7).

151 The word *Infancy*, after *Babe*, is not redundant, but presumably, as Brooks and Hardy remark (100), carries its literal Latin sense, 'not speaking.'

152–3 Rolfe cited 'nail'd / For our advantage on the bitter cross' (Shakespeare, *1 H. IV* 1. 1. 26–7).

154 Cf. John 17. 4–5: 'I have finished the work which thou gavest me to do. And now, O Father, glorify thou me with thine own self, with the glory which I had with thee before the world was.' Keightley cited: 'And the glory which thou gavest me I have given them' (ibid. 22).

155 *ychain'd.* 'Y, is a poeticall addition' (Gloss on Spenser, *S.C., April* 155). Historically, it is a relic of O.E. *ge*, the prefix for past participles.

155–6 *in sleep*: i.e. of death. *wakeful*: awakening (*OED* 6: no other example given). *trump*: trumpet. Rolfe cites: '...we which are alive...shall not prevent ⟨ go before ⟩ them which are asleep. For the Lord himself shall descend from heaven...with the trump of God: and the dead in Christ shall rise first'

(1 Thess. 4. 15–16). [Hughes quotes Dan. 12. 2: 'And many of them that sleep in the dust of the earth shall awake....']

156–64 [Having glanced back at the first supreme event, the creation, and the music that accompanied it (117–24), Milton now looks forward to the third. The day of judgment will be announced with the kind of harsh sounds that attended God's giving of the ten commandments to Moses.] Cook quotes Exod. 19. 16 f.: '...there were thunders and lightnings, and a thick cloud upon the mount, and the voice of the trumpet exceeding loud; so that all the people...trembled.... And mount Sinai was altogether on a smoke, because the Lord descended upon it in fire; and the smoke thereof ascended as the smoke of a furnace, and the whole mount quaked greatly.'

159 *smouldring*: stifling, as in Spenser, *F.Q*. 2. 5. 3: 'The smouldring dust did round about him smoke' (*OED*: *ppl. a.* 1). The association with smoke was natural enough and early (ibid. 2); the idea of burning slowly with smoke but without flame was an early but apparently not common meaning of the verb (ibid. *v.* 2). Warton assembles several illustrations: Spenser, *F.Q*. 1. 7. 13, 1. 8. 9; Fairfax, *Jerusalem* 13. 61, 'a smouldring fire.'

160–2 *The aged Earth agast | With terrour of that blast, | Shall...shake.* [Cf. Milton's youthful *Ps* 114. 15: 'Shake earth, and at the presence be agast'; and Spenser, *F.Q*. 1. 8. 4: 'Might once abide the terror of that blast.' *center*: see *Comus* 381 n.]

164 *middle Air*: the clouds of heaven (Dan. 7. 13; Matt. 24. 30). [For the traditional meteorological significance see *FInf* 16 n.] Browne cited: 'Then we ...shall be caught up...in the clouds, to meet the Lord in the air' (1 Thess. 4. 17). *spread his throne*: expand or display it (Verity). Cook cites Jer. 43. 10: '...set his throne upon these stones...and...spread his royal pavilion over them.'

165–7 After the Last Judgment the true golden age will return. 'Our glorification will be accompanied by the renovation of heaven and earth, and of all things therein adapted to our service or delight, to be possessed by us in perpetuity' (*DocCh* 1. 33, *Works* 16, 379). Cf. Isa. 65. 17; 2 Pet. 3. 13; Rev. 21. 1–2. But the movement of history which leads to this consummation begins with Christ's birth: 'His kingdom of grace, indeed, which is also called "the kingdom of heaven," began with his first advent...; but his kingdom of glory will not commence till his second advent' (*DocCh* 1. 33, *Works* 16, 359).

168–72 'And I saw an angel come down from heaven, having the key of the bottomless pit and a great chain in his hand. And he laid hold on the dragon, that old serpent, which is the Devil, and Satan, and bound him a thousand years, And cast him into the bottomless pit, and shut him up, and set a seal upon him, that he should deceive the nations no more, till the thousand years should be fulfilled: and after that he must be loosed a little season' (Rev. 20. 1–3; cf. 12. 3–4 and 9). The passage quoted is one of those taken to refer to the Millennium, a thousand years of rule on earth by Christ and his saints, which is variously placed and interpreted, but by Milton, at least in *DocCh* (1. 33, *Works* 16, 358–9), is regarded as coincident with the period of the Judgment. Here, however, he applies the imagery of the binding of the dragon to the partial limiting of his sway effected by the advent of Christ. On the Dragon, Cook cites also Mantuan, *Parthen.* 3 (*Opera* 1, 72ʳ).

169 *straiter*: narrower (*OED* 2).

170 *casts*: 'the metaphor of casting a net' (Verity). Perhaps rather, in the simplest sense, to throw, but figuratively, in order to suggest his throwing out, extending, of his power to its utmost limit.

171 *wroth*: [*wrath* in 1645. The variant adjectives mean 'stirred to wrath,... very angry' (*OED*).] Cf. 'Whereat the Prince full wrath....' (Spenser, *F.Q.* 4. 8. 43).

172 *Swindges*: lashes (*OED*: swinge v.¹ 4). Warton quoted: 'Then often swindging, with his sinnewy train, / Somtimes his sides, somtimes the dusty Plain' (Sylvester, *D.W.W.* 1. 6. 410–11, Grosart, 1, 75). [Cf. Lucan 1. 208: *ubi se saevae stimulavit verbere caudae*; Seneca, *Herc. Fur.* 812: *utrumque cauda pulsat anguifera latus.*] *Horrour.* The quality of exciting horror is used concretely of the thing possessing this quality (*OED* 5); the word retains the Latin connotation of rough or bristling (*OED* 1). Verity cites 'this drear Wood, / The nodding horror of whose shady brows' (*Comus* 37–8) and Milton's use of 'horrid,' e.g. *Comus* 428. A 'scaly tayle'—one feature of Spenser's 'Dragon'— 'the crest...did enfold' of Arthur's helmet, evoking 'suddeine horror' (*F.Q.* 1. 7. 31). *foulded*: coiled, twisted (*OED*).

173–236 The third movement of the Hymn describes the effect of the Nativity in accomplishing the first stage in the process of man's salvation—'it being,' as Ralph Cudworth said in 1678, 'not only agreeable to the sense of ancient doctors, but also expressly declared in the scripture, that one design of Christianity was to abolish and extirpate the Pagan polytheism and idolatry' (*True Intellectual*

System of the Universe, ed. J. Harrison, 3 v., London, 1845, 1, xxxvii). Milton takes in the divinities of Greece and Rome (173–96), Phoenicia and Canaan (197–210), and Egypt (211–28), ending with 'all the Gods beside.' Browne cites Hooker, *Eccles. Pol.* 1. 4. 3: 'These wicked spirits ⟨ i.e. the fallen angels ⟩ the heathens honoured instead of gods…; …some in oracles, some in idols, some as household gods, some as nymphs: in a word, no foul and wicked spirit which was not one way or other honoured of men as God, till such time as light appeared in the world and dissolved the works of the devil' (*Works*, ed. Keble, Church, and Paget, 7th ed., Oxford, 1888, 1, 215). Sir Walter Ralegh in his *History of the World* (1614) gave a number of such particulars as Milton uses (1. 6. 8: cited by Bush in *SP* 28, 1931, 260): 'The houses and sumptuous buildings erected to Baal ⟨cf. lines 197–8⟩, can no where bee found upon the earth.…There are none now in Phoenicia, that lament the death of Adonis ⟨cf. 204⟩; nor any in Lybia…that can aske counsaile or helpe from Jupiter ⟨cf. 203⟩. The great God Pan hath broken his Pipes ⟨cf. 182–3 and n.⟩, Apolloes Priests are become speechlesse ⟨cf. 176–80⟩; and the Trade of riddles in Oracles ⟨cf. 173–5⟩, with the Devils telling mens fortunes therein, is taken up by counterfait Ægyptians, and cousening Astrologers.' [On the whole theme of 'the retreat of the false gods,' R. Tuve (*Images*, 66 n.) cites especially Augustine, *City of God* (bks. 6, 11, 18), Lactantius, *Divine Institutes* (Bk. 2, cc. 1, 3, 15–19, and 4. 27: Migne, *Pat. Lat.* 6, *Works of Lactantius*, tr. W. Fletcher, 2 v., Edinburgh, 1871), Prudentius, *Apoth. c.* verses 400–500. Citing various lines in the whole passage 173–220, T. Kranidas (*The Fierce Equation*, The Hague, 1965, 116–17) remarks that 'we see in contrast to the resonant music of the Word, the pagan sound released into an unresponsive landscape.…The heavenly music is heard, it effects a response, it affects and inspires. The moaning sounds of departure affect nothing, get no response, they expire; like air from a punctured balloon, they simply vanish.' Rajan (*MLR* 63, 20–1: see III above, under 1968) observes that the false gods are shadows easily scattered by the light, while in the roll call in *PL* they are fully described as potent forces of evil and denounced with the voice of moral outrage.]

173 *The Oracles are dum.* The widespread tradition that at the time of Christ's early ministry the pagan oracles fell silent goes back chiefly to Plutarch's *The Obsolescence of Oracles* (L.C.L. 5). The fact, thus vouched for by a pagan author, was taken up, e.g. by Eusebius, *Preparation for the Gospel* 5. 16 (tr. E. H. Gifford, Oxford, 1903, 1, 224); Jerome, *In Isaiam Prophetam* 41. 21 f. (Migne, *Pat. Lat.* 24, 418). Prudentius writes: *torquetur Apollo | nomine percussus*

Christi, nec fulmina Verbi | ferre potest (*Apoth.* 402–4); and declares (438–43) that, since the Incarnation,

> Delphica damnatis tacuerunt sortibus antra,
> non tripodas cortina regit, non spumat anhelus
> fata Sibyllinis fanaticus edita libris.
> perdidit insanos mendax Dodona vapores,
> mortua iam mutae lugent oracula Cumae,
> nec responsa refert Libycis in Syrtibus Hammon.

(Cook cites this and some passages from Prudentius and others quoted below.) Among passages readily accessible to Milton was the Gloss to Spenser's *S.C.*, *May*, which, however, associates the cessation of oracles with the Crucifixion. Citing Plutarch (*Obsolescence* 17, quoted in full by Eusebius, 5. 17) and Lavater (89 n. above), the Gloss tells how the pilot of a ship sailing from Italy to Cyprus 'was bidden, when he came to Palodes, to tel, that the great Pan was dead.' When he did so, 'there was heard suche piteous outcryes and dreadfull shriking, as hath not bene the like. By whych Pan, though of some be understoode the great Satanas, whose kingdome at that time was by Christ conquered...(for at that time, as he sayth, all Oracles surceased, and enchaunted spirits, that were wont to delude the people, thenceforth held theyr peace)...yet I think it more properly meant of the death of Christ, the onely and very Pan, then suffering for his flock.' Though Milton used the not uncommon identification of Christ with Pan (above, 89 n.), he adopts the wailing from the shore (181–3) as pagan lamentation and associates the cessation of oracles (and, by implication, the death of Pan) with Christ's triumph over Satan, not in the Crucifixion but in the Incarnation—as G. Fletcher does: 'The Angells caroll'd lowd their song of peace, | The cursed Oracles wear strucken dumb' (*C.V.* 1. 82). See, in addition to 89 n. above, Cook's list of classical references on 173 and MacKellar's Variorum note on *PR* 1. 456, which lists other classical writers besides Plutarch who commented on the failing of the oracles: Cicero (*Div.* 1. 19, 2. 57, on the declining fame of Delphi); Strabo (7. 7. 9, 9. 3. 2 f., on the virtual silence of Delphi, as of the rest); Lucan (5. 69–70, 102 f., 111–14, on the silence of Delphi); Juvenal 6. 553–6. Philippe du Plessis-Mornay (*Trunesse of Christian Religion*, tr. Sir Philip Sidney and A. Golding, 1604, pp. 552–4) assembles testimony to the effect that the 'miracles and Oracles of Divels' had ceased 'ever since Christ was borne and preached.' Among his particulars is Apollo's answer to the Emperor Augustus: 'An Hebrew Child, which daunteth with his power | The blessed Gods, doth straightly me commaund | To get me hence to Hell this present howre; | Therefore of mee no Counsell now demaund.' On Plutarch's conjecture that the oracular spirits were mortal, Mornay observes that 'hee should rather have said that they were shut up as in a Jaile' (cf. *Nat* 233). He associates the cry, 'Pan is dead,' not with the Nativity but with the Crucifixion, placing it in Tiberius' reign, but he still makes it refer to the destruction of the pagan deities and not to the death of Christ. [In Reginald Scot's *The discoverie of witchcraft* (1584), c. 3 of book 8 is headed 'That Oracles are ceased' (160 f.) and in c. 4 he tells the story of 'Great Pan' from Plutarch and Eusebius.

In 'The Cessation of the Oracles: The History of a Legend' (*MLR* 60, 1965, 500–7) C. A. Patrides, with many references, shows traditional agreement on the linking of the death of the oracles with the death of Pan (504): 'This idea is directly related to the widespread Christian belief that the pagan gods were fallen angels and the oracles their instruments of delusion. Justin Martyr was the first, but certainly not the last, to propound this theory; thereafter the notion appears in such divers thinkers as Tertullian, Origen, and Lactantius, and continues uninterruptedly until the Renaissance.' Patrides also says, citing some of our witnesses and others, that the cessation of oracles 'was most often' associated with the Nativity, not with the Passion (he slips, p. 501, in having Spenser's E.K. link the end of oracles with 'the Incarnation'). See also P. Merivale (cited under 89 above) and M. Y. Hughes, '"Devils to Adore for Deities,"' *Studies in Honor of DeWitt T. Starnes*, ed. James Sledd, T. P. Harrison et al. (Austin, 1967), 241–58; also L. W. Hyman, 'Christ's Nativity and the Pagan Deities,' *Milton Studies II*, ed. J. D. Simmonds (Pittsburgh, 1970), 103–12.]

178 *hollow*: sepulchral (*OED* 4). Verity cites 'how hollow the fiend speaks' (Shakespeare, *Twel.* 3. 4. 101). [See 173–236 n. above.] *steep of Delphos*. Cook cites 'the Delphian cliff' (*PL* 1. 517) and explains as a reference to the high terraces on which Delphi stands, though overshadowed by the perpendicular cliffs of Parnassus. *Delphos* is 'Not an uncommon form; cf. *P.R.* 1. 458' (Verity).

179 *nightly*: nocturnal; cf. *Arc* 48 (Verity). [*trance*: state of 'exaltation, rapture, ecstasy' (*OED* 3b).] *breathed*. It would seem evident that the words are breathed, i.e. uttered (*OED*: *v.* 12), by the priest; but Cook seems to take them as issuing from the earth and cites Lucan 5. 82–5 on Apollo's taking possession of Delphi when he perceived *vastos telluris hiatus | Divinam spirare fidem ventosque loquaces | Exhalare solum.* [Milton's use of *Inspires* might seem to support Cook: the priest would not be inspired by his own utterance but by a power outside himself, as the word *trance* also suggests. Cf. the Virgilian priestess' frenzy: *adflata est numine quando | iam propiore dei* (*A.* 6. 50–1).]

180 *pale-ey'd Priest.* B. A. Wright (*Shorter Poems of John Milton*, London and New York, 1961: first pub. 1938) explains as a necessity for divination 'that the soul should be freed from the body, whether in ecstasy or sleep or by bodily weakness' produced by fasting, sickness, etc. Cook traced the phrase to Prudentius' account of the priest's turning pale in the midst of his rites and exclaiming that a greater power was intervening: *exclamat media inter sacra sacerdos / pallidus* (*Apoth.* 469–70). [Cf. Shakespeare, *R. II* 2. 4. 10–11: 'The pale-fac'd moon looks bloody on the earth, / And lean-look'd prophets whisper fearful change.'] *prophetic cell.* Lat. *cella* designated the shrine, that part of the temple where the god's image was placed (cf. [Cicero, *Phil.* 2. 8. 19, 5. 7. 18]; Livy 5. 50. 6, 6. 29. 9); here, whence the oracles were given (Browne). The *arched roof* (175) is that of the cell or temple.

181–8 [A stanza notably touched by the feeling, here almost nostalgic, that animates *El 5*, on the coming of spring. As R. Tuve says (*Images*, 70), 'the kind of allegiance he here gives to pagan myth and thought and imagery was a kind he never had to repudiate. To the end of his life he distinguishes thus between loveliness and sacredness.']

181–3 Milton remembers the 'piteous outcryes' from the shore of Palodes (above, 173 n.), but also (as Warton noted) the phrasing of Matt. 2. 18: 'In Rama was there a voice heard, lamentation, and weeping, and great mourning'; and (as Cook added) of Ps. 6. 8: 'the Lord hath heard the voice of my weeping.' [Browne cited 'voice of weeping' in Isa. 65. 19.]

181 *lonely.* [To the idea of solitude Milton (cf. *IlPen* 86, *Comus* 199) adds suggestions of 'melancholy or solemn scenery' (A. Oras, 'Notes,' 49).]

182 *the resounding shore.* [Cf. *resonantia longe / litora* (Virgil, *G.* 1. 358–9).]

184 *haunted*: in one of its two earliest meanings, 'frequented' (*OED*: haunt *v.*[3] and haunted 2), but with a secondary suggestion, 'frequented by spirits' (ibid. haunted 3). [Cook cites *IlPen* 137–8; cf. *PR* 2. 296–7.]

185 *poplar pale.* Verity cites *quo pinus ingens albaque populus* (Horace, *C.* 2. 3. 9). Cook adds *candida populus* (Virgil, *E.* 9. 41). For the ancient association of poplars and springs Cook cites Homer, *Od.* 6. 291–2, Theocritus 7. 135–7, Ovid, *M.* 5. 590; etc.

186 *Genius*: the *genius loci* of Roman myth, the guardian spirit of a locality; see *Arc* 26 n., *Lyc* 183 n. [The word *parting* combines the senses of 'departing' and 'parted, separated from' (*OED*).]

187 *flowre-inwov'n tresses torn.* The image of the Nymphs crowned with wreaths is repeated in *Comus* 120, 861–2; [and cf. Milton, *El* 5. 63 (of the Earth in spring): *vario madidos intexit flore capillos*]. C. G. Osgood (*Classical Mythology of Milton's English Poems*, New York, 1900 [hereafter cited as *C.M.*], 65) finds suggestions in Hesiod, *Theog.* 255, and Claudian 22. 345 (2, 26), and notes offers of wreaths to them in Horace, *C.* 3. 27. 29–30, and Ovid, *M.* 9. 337. Ovid speaks of the Graces (often associated with the Nymphs) as thus adorning themselves (*F.* 5. 219–20). In Rome the wearing of garlands was associated with feasts, with relaxation and enjoyment (Tibullus 3. 6. 63–4). The Nymphs are here overtaken in their pagan gaiety by the birth of Christ, which turns it to mourning and reduces them to the appropriately scriptural [and also classical] sign of lamentation, the tearing of the hair (Ezra 9. 3). Citations are given, without comment, by Cook. [Todd quoted Fairfax, *Jerusalem* 3. 75: 'The weeping Nymphes fled from their bowres exilde.']

188 *twilight.* [A. Oras, citing also *IlPen* 133, *Arc* 99, *Comus* 843, etc., finds that the young Milton was original in using the word as an adjective (cf. *OED* 4) and in exploiting its descriptive, visual quality ('Notes,' 57–8).]

189–96 *Lars* (Lat. *Lares*) were tutelary deities, guardians of the family and home, and sometimes identified with the spirits of ancestors, whose altars were called *lararia* (Ovid, *F.* 2. 631 f.), and whose worship centred about the hearth, *focus Larum quo familia convenit* (Pliny, *N.H.* 28. 81. 267). There were public as well as family Lares, whose office was likewise protective (ibid. 3. 5. 66; Ovid, *F.* 5. 129 f.). It is to the family Lares that *holy Hearth* applies; it is perhaps in the service of the public Lares that the *Flamins* (Lat. *flamines*, official order of priests) are engaged. *Lemures* are the shades of the departed, called *nocturnos lemures* by Horace (*Ep.* 2. 2. 209). Ovid (*F.* 5. 421 f.) describes the feast of the Lemures, at which gifts were offered to the spirits of the dead (hence Milton's reference to *Urns* as well as *Altars*); at midnight the ghosts were exorcized from the dwelling (hence the idea that they *moan with midnight plaint*—a plaint intensified by their final eviction at the coming of Christ). Both Lares and Lemures are peculiar to Roman religion and are not always clearly distinguished; Milton seems to be using them with precision. Keightley objected that consecrated earth for burial of the dead is not Roman but Christian and has no connection with Lares or Lemures; but Cook observes that ceremonies of consecration certainly existed and included sacrifices to the Lares (Cicero, *Leg.* 2. 21–2). (Some of these references are drawn from Osgood, *C.M.*, and Cook.) Prudentius (*Apoth.* 460–502; cf. above, 180 n.) tells of a priest struck powerless at a service of sacrifice to Hecate and crying in terror that the spirits he had summoned were scattered: this not at the Incarnation, but because of the presence of one follower of Christ in their midst.

193 *drear.* [The adjective—used in *F.Q.* 2. 11. 8, 3. 11. 55—appears in the Spenserian context of *IlPen* 119 and in *Comus* 37, where it is associated with 'monotonous, dismal wildernesses.' In *Nat* 193 it suggests a melancholy sound akin to that of *F.Q.* 1. 8. 38, 'an hollow, dreary, murmuring voyce' (Oras, 'Notes,' 40–3).]

194 *quaint*: 'strange..., curious' (*OED* 7). See *Comus* 156–7 n. and cf. 'his uncouth guise and usage quaint' (Spenser, *F.Q.* 4. 7. 45).

195 *the chill Marble seems to sweat.* W. P. Mustard (*AJP* 29, 1908, 4) cites: 'The marble pillers and images echeone,/ Swet all for sorowe' (Alex. Barclay, *Ecl.* 3. 487–8: *Eclogues*, ed. B. White, E.E.T.S., 1928). Cook refers to sweating statues of Apollo and Victory mentioned by Cicero (*Div.* 1. 43. 98) and, for association with the Lares, Lucan 1. 556–7: *Indigetes flevisse deos urbisque laborem / Testatos sudore Lares.* Cf. Virgil, *G.* 1. 480, Ovid, *M.* 15. 792.

196 Richardson (reported by Cook) cited *excessere omnes adytis arisque relictis / di* (Virgil, *A.* 2. 351–2). Cook adds a number of citations, e.g.: Augustine observes that the crimes of the ancient Roman kings did not induce the gods to abandon their altars (*City of God* 3. 15); Tacitus, in his account of the Jewish wars, tells how the doors of an inner shrine were suddenly thrown open and a voice of more than mortal tone cried that the gods were departing (*Hist.* 5. 13); a similar tale in Josephus (*Jewish War* 6. 300); and Mantuan, *Dionysii Areop.* (*Opera* 1, 193ʳ):

> Iam nova progenies coelo descenderat alto
> Et prodire alius saeclorum incoeperat ordo;
> Dii Phlegethontaei, regnata tyrannide longa,
> Et maria et terras animis coelestibus aegre
> Cedere compulsi, errabant deserta latentes
> Per nemora extremi gelido sub cardine mundi.

197–220 Cf. *PL* 1. 381–505 and notes. [F. Berry (*Poetry and the Physical Voice*, London, 1962, 98–101; see partial summary in 'L'Allegro and Il Penseroso' III, under 1962) observes that no English poet makes such habitual and pervasive use of the sounds *n* and *ng* as Milton, and not only in such pure invective as *Lyc* 110–31 but in such passages as *Nat* 157–64, 197–212.]

197 *Peor, and Baalim.* Baal, the chief male divinity of the Phoenicians and Canaanites, was their god of the sun, which links these lines with earlier allusions to the sun (36, 79–84), although mythologists equate him with Priapus (cf. Selden, *De Dis Syris*, London, 1617, 65 f.; [Sandys, *Ovid*, Oxford, 1632, 331; Alexander Ross, *Mystagogus Poeticus*, ed. 1648, 346]); his rites were marked by licence (Num. 25. 1–3, Hos. 2. 13). Baal was worshipped in various localities and under particular names: *Baalim* is the Hebrew plural (Judges 2. 11). One principal locality was the mountain Peor (Num. 23. 28); hence the name Baal-Peor (Ps. 106. 28). Cook cites references to temples of Baal in 1 Kings 16. 32, 2 Kings 11. 18. Verity quotes: 'to draw them ⟨the Israelites⟩ from the Sanctuary of God to the luxurious, and ribald feasts of Baal-peor' (Milton, *Ref*, *Works* 3, 53–4).

199 *that twice batter'd god of Palestine*: Dagon. The Philistines set the ark of God beside the image of Dagon, but the next day they found Dagon 'fallen upon his face to the earth before the ark of the Lord.' He was set up again and fell again, and his head and the palms of his hands were cut off upon the threshold (1 Sam. 5. 2–4). Cf. *PL* 1. 457–66.

200 *mooned Ashtaroth*. Ashtoreth is the Hebrew name for the Syrian goddess known to the Greeks as Astarte (see Selden reference in 201 n. below; *PL* 1. 438–46). Milton uses the plural form (Judges 2. 13, 10. 6, 1 Sam. 7. 4, 12. 10) signifying the various local manifestations (cf. *Baalim*, 197). Astarte or Ashtoreth, for whom Solomon built a temple (2 Kings 23. 13; *PL* 1. 442–6), was a fertility goddess, associated (according to Lucian, *De Syria Dea* 4, L.C.L. 4) with the moon (hence *mooned* and *Heav'ns Queen*), as Baal was with the sun. Baalim and Ashtaroth are paired in the preceding citations from Judges and 1 Samuel. Milton explains in *PL* 1. 421–3 the 'general Names / Of Baalim and Ashtaroth, those male, / These Feminine.' Ashtoreth (Astarte) was the equivalent of Aphrodite or Venus and the lover of Thammuz (Adonis). (References from Verity, Cook, Hughes.)

201 Selden (cited by Newton, Keightley, and Cook) says that Ashtoreth (pl. Ashtaroth) was called *regina caeli* and *mater deum* (*De Dis Syris*, 141 f., 159, 166). Verity remarks that the former phrase is transferred (he thinks by Milton) from Juno, the latter from Cybele (cf. *Arc* 21–2); but *Heav'ns Queen* is clearly from Jer. 7. 18, 44. 17–19, 25, where 'queen of heaven' is applied, almost certainly, to Ashtoreth (Cook). The Protestant Milton may intend us to remember titles bestowed on, and honours paid to, the Virgin Mary. [Cf. Erasmus' *The Shipwreck* (*The Colloquies of Erasmus*, tr. C. R. Thompson, Chicago, 1965, 141.)]

202 *shine*: radiance (*OED*: sb.¹ 1).

203 The god Ammon, whose name signifies the unrevealed divinity, was represented as a ram with massive horns, symbolic of power (surely a more probable explanation of *shrinks his horn* than Cook's suggested 'allusion to snails'). Of Egyptian origin, he was later worshipped in the desert of Libya, where his oracle was visited by Alexander the Great. By the Greeks he was identified with Zeus, by the Romans with Jove. Ovid (*M.* 5. 321–8) tells how in fear of Typhoeus the gods fled to Egypt and concealed themselves in lying shapes: *duxque gregis...fit Iuppiter: unde recurvis | nunc quoque formatus Libys est cum cornibus Ammon.* Classical references to the god abound, e.g. Ovid, *M.* 15. 309, Lucan 9. 512–16, Sil. Ital. 13. 767–8. [*Corniger Hammon* was a stock phrase: Ovid, loc. cit.; Sil. Ital. 3. 10, 14. 572; Val. Flacc. 2. 482.] The oracle of Hammon is mentioned by Prudentius among those silenced by the birth of Christ (above, 173 n.).

204 *Tham(m)uz* was the lover of Astarte (Ashtoreth) and the Phoenician original of the Greek Adonis, whose slaying by the wild boar (hence *wounded*) represented the succession of winter to summer, and whose annual revival the return of summer [Sandys, *Ovid*, 1632, 366–7]. At the festival of Thammuz his death was lamented ('and, behold, there sat women weeping for Tammuz': Ezek. 8. 14) and then his revival celebrated; see Theocritus 15 [and *PL* 1. 446–57]. *Tyrian* stands for Phoenician generally, as in *Comus* 341 (Verity).

205–10 *Moloch* or Molech (meaning 'king') was a god of the Ammonites (1 Kings 11. 7) whose cruel rites of child sacrifice are much condemned in the O.T. (Lev. 18. 21; Ps. 106. 37–8; 2 Kings 23. 10). Warton noticed what Milton might have learned from George Sandys' *Relation of a Journey* (London, 1615, 186): 'wherein ⟨i.e. in the valley of 'Gehinnon'⟩ the Hebrews sacrificed their children to Molech, an Idoll of brasse, having the head of a calfe, the rest of a kingly figure, with armes extended to receive the miserable sacrifice, seared to death with his burning embracements. For the Idoll was hollow within, and filled with fire. And lest their lamentable shreeks should sad the hearts of their parents, the Priests of Molech did deafe their ears with the continuall clangs of trumpets and timbrels....' Warton remarked on the vividness of Milton's scene, which, avoiding the actual rites, presents the god as fled and the priests striving to recall him by the sounds with which they drowned the cries of his victims.

211–26 Osgood (*C.M.* 84) finds the list of Egyptian gods based on Plutarch's *Isis and Osiris* (L.C.L. 5); but much of that Platonist account is foreign to Milton's purpose and some of his material is derived from other sources. The gods are *brutish* because worshipped under the form of animals [cf. *PL* 1. 481]. On the religious veneration of animals in Egypt, Herodotus (2. 66–76) and Diodorus Siculus (1. 83–90) give more than Plutarch. The chief Egyptian divinities, the creators of all things, were Osiris, god of the sun, representing light and the masculine principle, and Isis, his sister and wife, goddess of the moon, representing moisture and the feminine principle. Horus (Milton's Orus), also sometimes represented as sun god, was their child. Anubis was the offspring of Osiris and his sister Nephthys and was found and brought up by Isis. Set (whom the Greeks called Typhon) was the impious brother and violent enemy of Osiris. The story of the life and death of Osiris and the vanquishing of Typhon is told by Plutarch (12–20) and by Diod. Sic. (1. 14–21). As a bringer of civilization to the Egyptians and other peoples, Osiris was identified by the Greeks with Dionysus (Diod. Sic. 1. 11. 3–4, etc.; Herodotus 2. 144). On his return from travel, Typhon formed a plot against him, induced him to enter a handsome chest, closed the lid, and cast the chest into the Nile to be carried out to sea. The grief-stricken Isis at last found it and hid it with great care. But Typhon discovered it and this time dismembered the body and scattered the parts far and wide. When after long search Isis found them (cf. *Areop, Works* 4, 338), she fashioned over each an image of Osiris and bestowed them in various cities for burial, setting up the worship of Osiris in each place (Diod. Sic. 1. 21. 5–6). Then, with the aid of Horus, she defeated Typhon, who was finally slain.

The cow was sacred to Isis, the hawk to Horus, the bull to Osiris. Anubis was represented with the head of a jackal, which the Greeks and Romans took to be that of a dog (Diod. Sic. 1. 87. 2; Virgil, *A.* 8. 698; Ovid, *M.* 9. 690; Juvenal 15. 8). Isis was represented as a woman, but with horns like a cow's (Herodotus 2. 41), or with a head-dress bearing a crescent in token of either the cow or the moon (Diod. Sic. 1. 11. 4). (References from Cook, supplemented by Verity, Hughes, Wright.) In a vision recounted by Ovid (*M.* 9. 686–94) these gods are assembled.

213–15 At Memphis Osiris was worshipped under the form of a bull, called Apis, which—as Isis had instructed—was luxuriously tended and, when he died, was given a sumptuous funeral (Diod. Sic. 1. 21. 9–10, 1. 84).

215 *unshowr'd*: 'There being no rain in Egypt' (Richardson, reported by Todd).

216–17 Wright, taking *he* and *his* to refer to Apis, explains *sacred chest* as that in which Apis was buried, representing the chest in which Osiris was confined. More probably *he* and *his* refer to Osiris himself and the *sacred chest* to a coffin containing the image of the god, the *worshipt Ark* (220 and n.); cf. 211–26 n. Plutarch (17) speaks of the image of a corpse carried about in a chest, but this, he says, is not a memorial of Osiris, as some have assumed. [Plutarch (39), describing a rite of Isis and Osiris, has the image of a cow covered with a black linen vestment and 'the sacred chest' (τὴν ἱερὰν κίστην) brought forth by *stolistai* ('keepers of the robes') and priests.]

218 *shroud*: place of shelter or retreat (*OED*: *sb.*¹ 3; *Comus* 147). To this primary sense the context might well add two secondary suggestions: shroud as winding sheet (ibid. 2) and shroud as crypt (usually in plural, as in 'A church under the ground, like to the shrouds in Pauls': Hakluyt, quoted, ibid. 4), since the service described is no doubt in his temple.

219–20 Herodotus says that each god was served by a college of priests (2. 37) and that the Egyptians first introduced 'solemn assemblies, and processions, and services' (2. 58). He also describes (2. 63) a ceremony in which the priests move a small shrine containing a god's image from one sacred edifice to another, the entrance to the second being resisted by another band. But this can hardly have given Milton any suggestion, as has been assumed; for the details are all different and the celebration is not in honour of Osiris but of some Egyptian equivalent of Ares. See above, 216–17 n.

219 *Timbrel'd*: accompanied by the timbrel, an instrument like a tambourine (*OED*), but here no doubt standing for the *sistrum*, a metal rattle used at the rites of Isis and Osiris and mentioned by Ovid (*M.* 9. 693) [and Propertius 3. 11. 43; Lucan 8. 832]. *dark*: of doubtful or mysterious import (*OED* 6), or, perhaps, evil (ibid. 4) or secret (ibid. 7).

220 *sable-stoled.* Verity explains as 'robed in black,' and compares (after Todd) 'Sable-vested' (*PL* 2. 962), on the ground that *stole* meant a long robe (*OED*: *sb.*¹ 1); and Cook, noting that Plutarch (52) and Apuleius (*Met.* 11. 3) have Isis robed in black, infers the same of her priests. But the special meaning of sacerdotal scarf was already long established (*OED* 2); cf. *IlPen* 35 n. [The meaning 'scarf' may be correct, but it may be noted that Sandys at least twice seems to use the word for 'robe': Ovid, 1626, 114: 'in long stoles of black array'd' (*M.* 6. 288, *cum vestibus atris*); 206: 'whome long linnen stoles invest' (*M.* 10. 432, *nivea velatae corpora veste*).]

Sorcerers: so called on account of the reputation of Egypt and its religion for the practice of magic [cf. *PL* 1. 479]. *worshipt Ark*: presumably the *sacred chest* of 217 (see 216–17 n.). The word could also mean a boat or other floating vessel (*OED* 4), and Cook gives some indication that the statue of Osiris may have been placed in such a vessel in his temples.

221–6 Perhaps, as Cook suggests, Milton remembered O.T. prophecies of the destruction of the Egyptian gods (Isa. 19. 1; etc.), and N.T. emphasis on the power resident in Bethlehem in the land of Juda (Matt. 2. 6, referring to Mic. 5. 2).

223 'An allusion to Osiris as a god of light; one of the symbols of Osiris was a sceptre with an eye in the head, indicating that the god surveys and rules the universe as does the sun' (Wright). *The rayes of Bethlehem* suggest the star.

224–5 Cook quotes Mantuan, *Parthen.* 3 (*Opera* 1, 79ʳ⁻ᵛ):

> Parthenices primo ingressu simulachra per omnem
> Legimus Ægyptum subita cecidisse ruina,
> Et collisa solo. Iacuit resupinus Anubis,
> Cornibus auratis solio ruit Isis ab alto,
> Occidit extemplo luctu quaesitus Osiris;
> Sicut cum trepidi per caeca silentia fures
> Noctis eunt taciti, vigilantque ad furta repente,
> Si densas abigat lux improvisa tenebras,
> Diffugiunt, lucemque timent, ceduntque diei.
> Attoniti vates illis responsa diebus
> Nulla dabant, stabatque oculos immotus aruspex.
> Sparsa sacerdotes timido legere deorum
> Frusta ministerio; coepit tunc perdere vires
> Caeca superstitio, verique exurgere Patris
> Cultus, et occulto superum latrea favore.

226 *Typhon* has occasioned disagreement among commentators. Osgood says that it is 'to Typhon of Egypt ⟨i.e. Set⟩ that Milton refers'; Hughes sees either the Egyptian Typhon or the monster of Greek myth. Milton's description suggests the latter, who was huge and wore great folds of serpents about his lower parts (Apollodorus 1. 6. 3); for *snaky twine* Cook cites *anguipedem alatos umeros Typhona ferentem* (Manilius 4. 581). But the context requires a reference to Egyptian myth, or rather, in view of 227–8, a transition from Egyptian to Greek; and this Milton finds in the fact that the Greeks identified the Egyptian Set with their own Typhon. Probably, then, he intends an allusion to both the Egyptian and the Greek Typhon. By it he effects the needed transition to Heracles (227–8); for, according to Virgil, Hercules was undaunted by the Greek Typhon (also called Typhoeus): *nec te ullae facies, non terruit ipse Typhoeus* (*A.* 8. 298). [Milton's phrasing (*Not Typhon huge*) suggests an echo of Virgil.]

227–8 A clear allusion to the infant Heracles' strangling the serpents sent by Hera to attack him in his cradle. It is perhaps significant that the scene is described by Philostratus the Younger in one of his *Imagines* (5) entitled *Heracles in Swaddling Clothes* (L.C.L.). Milton is probably recalling the story as told by Pindar (*Nem.* 1. 33–50), which is followed by the prophecy of Tiresias (60–72) concerning Heracles' labours and his glorification by Zeus after his death. Cook cites also Theocritus 24, but here the prophecy does not, as in Pindar, invite a parallel between Heracles and Christ. In this detail—as in the overt reference to Pan (88–90)—Milton departs from the repudiation of pagan myth that characterizes the poem and, in Christian-humanist fashion, says in effect: 'Christ is our Heracles' [cf. *Passion* 13–14]. It is perhaps needless to speculate, with Cook, whether there is here a further allusion to the idea that the star of Bethlehem blotted out the constellation of the Serpent (and others), thus figuring the downfall of the Dragon and the coming of Christ (Prudentius, *Apoth.* 615–18). [D. C. Allen ('Milton and the Descent to Light,' *JEGP* 60, 1961, 620–1) gives some references for the Christian view of Hercules as a 'type' of Christ, e.g. Alexander Ross: 'Our blessed Saviour is the true Hercules' (*Mystagogus Poeticus*, 1648, 169). See also F. M. Krouse, *Milton's Samson and the Christian Tradition* (Princeton, 1949), 44–5, etc.; M. Y. Hughes, *Études Anglaises* 6 (1953), 205 f.; E. M. Waith, *The Herculean Hero in Marlowe, Chapman, Shakespeare and Dryden* (New York, 1962); H. Spevack-Husmann (89 n. above), 81–8. Marcel Simon (*Hercule et le Christianisme*, Paris, 1955) deals mainly with the early Christian centuries.]

229–31 [What has seemed quaint or grotesque to many readers is of course the sun's *chin*, and *Pillows* (the earliest use of the verb recorded in *OED*) seems more suggestive of the sun's going to bed than of his rising. Coleridge (*Coleridge on the Seventeenth Century*, ed. R. F. Brinkley, Durham, N.C., 1955, 569: this work is henceforth cited as 'Brinkley'), who might be said to speak with special authority on personifications of the sun, remarked: 'I have tried in vain to imagine, in what other way the Image could be given. I rather think, that it is one of the Hardinesses permitted to a great Poet. Dante would have written it: tho' it is most in the Spirit of Donne.' Daiches (*Milton*, 47) observes that the image 'is curiously precise and domestic for its cosmic context; yet it is effective in its odd way, and helps to modulate the poem into a new key.' L. Stapleton (*UTQ* 23, 225) suggests that Milton was perhaps 'pleasing himself by a bit of humour.' R. Tuve gives a more ample explanation: 'The conceited element here does not lie in the chin-pillowing. To contemporaries the single adjunct of the curtaining clouds would recall the whole dignified tradition of awakening Phoebus, and iconographical associations (even if only through astronomical diagrams) with the round and rosy-faced planet would provide an effect markedly different from that which some commentators seem to think Milton intended. There is no flavor of old-Gaffer-Sun-in-his-nightcap, bedtime-story style, in the image itself. The conceit lies in the parallel between the light-bringer and Christ as *Sun*:*Son*, and in the hyperbolical amplification in the parallel between the fleeing of the dispersed spirits or "shades" and the sullen flight of the false gods, who are darkness even as Christ is light. These are traditional Christian conceits.' (*Elizabethan and Metaphysical Imagery*, Chicago, 1947, 315). Carey (99) refers to 'the beautiful baroque image of the sun in bed'; in his *Milton* (30) his comment is: 'The "Sun-in-bed" image deftly removes the manger, and substitutes a four-poster with red curtains.']

Cf. Spenser, *Epith.* 75–7: 'The Rosy Morne long since left Tithones bed,/ ...And Phoebus gins to shew his glorious hed.' Todd cited: 'All the purple pride that laces / The crimson curtains of thy bed' (Crashaw, *New Year's Day*: *Poems*, ed. L. C. Martin, 2nd ed., Oxford, 1957). Cook cited: 'when farre in the East yee doe behold / Foorth from his Christall Bed the Sunne to rise, / With rosie Robes and Crowne of flaming Gold' (Drummond, 2, 14); and Chapman's 'And from Apollos bed the vaile doth twine' (*Amorous Zodiack* 24, *Poems*, ed. P. B. Bartlett, New York, 1941).

231 *Orient*: 'adj. Situated in or belonging to the east' (*OED* B. 1). The adjectival use depends on the substantive, which designates the quarter in which the sun rises (ibid. A. 1) or the sunrise itself (ibid. A. 3) with its connotation of light and colour. Although some editors and L. Lockwood gloss as eastern, Keightley, Verity, Bell, and others rightly observe Milton's use of the adjective as a synonym for bright (which L. Lockwood accepts as possible), e.g. *Comus* 65, *PL* 1. 546. [In some contexts, as here, the original sense, eastern, may remain, secondary to bright.] Cf. A. Townshend, *Tempe Restord* (1632): 'Then the Scene is changed into an orientall skye, such as appeares at the Sun rising' (*Poems and Masks*, ed. E. K. Chambers, Oxford, 1912, 90).

232-6 While these lines form part of a simile describing the retreat of the pagan deities before the rising Sun of Righteousness, they also serve to introduce the figures of native myth and superstition, to balance those of classical (173–96). Though here the two are separated, it is relevant to recall the association of fairies and nymphs. Cook quotes: 'frendly Faeries, met with many Graces, / And lightfote Nymphes can chace the lingring night' (Spenser, *S.C.*,

June 25–6); and (after E. K. Chambers): 'Elfes, Fairies…of our latter age, which…the fantasticall world of Greece ycleaped…Dryades, & Hamadryades' (T. Nashe, *Works*, ed. McKerrow, 1, 347). [Cf. Robert Burton's *Anatomy of Melancholy* 1. 2. 1. 2, 'Digression of the Nature of Spirits' (ed. H. Jackson, 3 v., London, 1932, 1, 180–202).]

232–4 Editors refer to the widespread belief that ghosts and other spirits flee before the dawn, citing Shakespeare, *Ham.* 1. 1. 152–5, 1. 5. 89–91, and *Dream* 3. 2. 379–84, especially 'At whose approach ghosts, wand'ring here and there, / Troop home to churchyards.' [Eleanor Prosser, in her elaborate account of Elizabethan demonology, notes 'the popular belief that only hellish spirits were banished by the light of the sun,' whereas 'Good spirits…can appear at any time' (*Hamlet and Revenge*, Stanford, 1967, 109, 121–2).]

232 *shadows pale.* Cook cites, among Latin examples, *ad umbras, / pallentis umbras Erebi* (Virgil, *A.* 4. 25–6).

233 *Troop to th'infernal Jail.* Cf. Shakespeare's 'Troop home' in 232–4 n. For the idea of a prison Cook cites, e.g., Virgil, *A.* 6. 548–58; Seneca, *Herc. Fur.* 1222, *inferorum carcer*; 'spirits in prison' (1 Pet. 3. 19); 'the secrets of my prison house' (Shakespeare, *Ham.* 1. 5. 14); P. Fletcher: 'Breaks ope the jayl, & brings the prisoners thence' (*P.I.* 7. 12).

234 *fetter'd Ghost.* Rolfe explains *fetter'd* as 'bound to return.' Verity compares 'unlaid ghost, / That breaks his magick chains at *curfeu* time' (*Comus* 433–4).
    several: separate or respective; cf. *Comus* 25: 'commits to several government' (Verity).

235 *yellow-skirted Fayes.* No precedent has been found for this fancy. Cook notes that the sea-nymph Telesto is so adorned (Hesiod, *Theog.* 358). [Carey remarks: 'Selden 163 associates the "fays" with Lucina and Eileithyia, the Roman and Greek goddesses of childbirth. Their flight is particularly significant in this nativity poem and is therefore placed last.' This idea seems far-fetched; and would Milton, even in a comparison, associate with the birth of Christ fairies whom he is linking with the banished gods of paganism?]

236 *Night-steeds.* [Night had a chariot and horses analogous to those of the Sun; cf. Aeschylus, *Choeph.* 660; Virgil, *Cul.* 202: *Iam quatit et biiugis oriens Erebois equos Nox*; *A.* 5. 721, 738; Milton, *QNov* 69–70 and n.] *Moon-lov'd maze.* Verity defines *maze* here as a labyrinth (*OED*: *sb.* 4) and cites 'the quaint mazes in the wanton green' (Shakespeare, *Dream* 2. 1. 99); Cook identifies *maze* with 'the blind mazes of this tangl'd Wood' (*Comus* 180). But the reference here would seem to be rather to the movements of the fairies' dance (*OED* 4c), or perhaps to the marks of this dance on the turf, as in the case of 'fairy-rings.' Milton's coined epithet is designed simply to associate the fairies' dance with moonlight, and may mean loved by the moon, or loved by the fairies when the moon shines, or both [cf. *PL* 1. 781–7]. Verity compares 'dance in our round / And see our moonlight revels' (Shakespeare, *Dream* 2. 1. 140–1). Cook sees an allusion to Diana, goddess of the moon, with whom Titania, queen of the fairies, was sometimes identified.

237–44   This final stanza, though part of the Hymn, is disjoined from the three movements and balances the prelude, marking the completion of the mission of praise there undertaken (see 1–28 n.). The scene is now completely static, in contrast to the movement in the body of the Hymn, and the static quality is heightened by a certain formality in the description. [The simply pictorial stanza is also a final and oblique statement of the theme of order, of the new bond between heaven and earth. 'The last stanza is a kind of coda, replacing the third movement's atmosphere of darkness, discord, conflict, and might with a reminder of the harmonious brightness found at the center of the poem in the predicted reunion of grace and nature. Hence the number of allusions in this stanza which carry the mind back to earlier symbols—this "tedious song" to the music of the spheres and angels (stas. 9–14); this "youngest teemèd star" to the constellations of the first Creation (stas. 6, 12); these bright-harnessed angels to those who sang and shone (sta. 11)—culminating in the Christ-child himself, emblem of grace incarnate in nature, nature fulfilled in grace.' (Mack, *Milton*, 7.) See also Rajan in III, under 1968.]

239   *our tedious Song should here have ending.* [Cf. Browne (*Brit. Past.* 2. 3. 482): 'grow so tedious in so rude a song.']

240   *youngest teemed*: youngest or latest born. Chrysostom discusses the question whether this was one of the original stars or a new creation (*Homilies...on... St. Matthew*, 3 v., Oxford, 1843–51, Hom. 6, 1, 80 f.). [Calvin (*Harmonie*, 1610, 79–80; tr. Pringle, 1, 127–30: see 23 n. above) thinks a knowledge of astrology probably helped to bring the Magi to Bethlehem, though 'it was not a naturall starre.']

241   *polisht Car*: gleaming chariot, by analogy with those given to the sun and other moving luminaries.

242   *with Handmaid Lamp attending.* Chrysostom dwells on the star's pausing above and, as he suggests, descending to stand over the stable (*Homilies*, loc. cit. under 240 above).

243 *Courtly Stable*. Milton makes singularly little use of the paradoxes of Christianity which are the basis of what W. J. Courthope called 'theological "wit"' (*History of English Poetry*, 6 v., London and New York, 1895–1910, 3, 118). This is an exception [and cf. 8–14 and n.]. Chrysostom, considering the coming of the Magi to worship the newborn king, asks: 'And what sign at all of royalty did they behold, when they saw a shed, and a manger, and a Child in swaddling clothes, and a poor Mother?' (*Homilies* [see 240 above] 1, 79).

244 Angels clad in bright armour (cf. 112–14) and ready for service. Newton (reported by Todd) cited Exod. 13. 18: 'And the children of Israel went up harnessed out of the land of Egypt.'

A Paraphrase on Psalm 114
and Psalm 136

※

I. DATE AND CIRCUMSTANCES [D.B.]

These two paraphrases, Milton's earliest extant pieces of English verse, were included in his *Poems* of 1645, although he did not then print his next two English poems, the *Fair Infant* and *Vacation Exercise*. In both editions, 1645 and 1673, he indicated that the paraphrases were to be judged as juvenilia: 'This and the following *Psalm* were done by the Author at fifteen years old,' i.e. between 9 December 1623 and 8 December 1624, near the end of his attendance at St Paul's School. As Hanford says (*Poems*, 29), 'They may be school exercises, but one is tempted to believe that his father's interest had something to do with their composition, for the elder Milton had written some tunes for Ravenscroft's Psalter of 1621.'

The Reformation stimulated many efforts to provide metrical versions of the Psalms suitable for congregational and family singing. According to Philip von Rohr-Sauer (*English Metrical Psalms from 1600 to 1660*, Freiburg, 1938, 10), the version of the pedestrian pioneers, Sternhold and Hopkins, had 78 editions from 1562 until the opening of the seventeenth century [the British Museum Catalogue lists, by my count, some 72], and, in spite of multiplying rivals, countless editions after that. 'Although between 1600 and 1660 some thirty writers entered the race for a new version suitable for church services, they produced only one version of value, Wither's [1623]; and that was not accepted,' because the Stationers' Company was able to block the authorization of both James I and Charles I (ibid. 9, 16, 17). Motives for the versification of the Psalms, as a whole or in selections, might be pious or literary or both, and were shared by Anglicans as well as Puritans; and some poets of repute, even the courtly amorist Thomas Carew, contributed their quota. Further data and references are given below under Psalms 1–8, 80–8.[1]

II. CRITICISM [D.B.]

G. Saintsbury ('Milton,' *Cambridge Hist. Eng. Lit.*, 7, 1911, 124) says that Milton's juvenilia 'exhibited nothing that almost any good versifier of that fertile time might not have written. Of the two boyish Psalm-paraphrases, 114 has absolutely nothing distinctive; the other, a good metre, but nothing more.'

John Bailey (*Milton*, London, 1915, 95–7) notes signs of the later Milton. For example, two of his 'life-long themes,' the power and the splendour of God, appear in the lines, 'Who by his all-commanding might, / Did fill the new-made world with light,' a very Miltonic transformation of the biblical phrase 'him that made great lights' (Ps. 136. 7).

Hanford ('Youth,' 1925, 94–6): While Milton's later versions of two groups of Psalms 'are severely plain in language, and the first set, at least, as nearly literal as Milton could make them,' 'The early versions ...are independent poems. They are characterized by a freedom of rhythm which marks them as the products of a genuine though immature poetical enthusiasm, and their original Hebrew substance is all but

---

[1] E. S. Le Comte ('Milton as Satirist and Wit,' *Th'Upright Heart and Pure*, ed. A. P. Fiore, Pittsburgh, 1967, 53–4) sees it as 'just possible that Milton made his debut as a polemicist with his "Paraphrase on *Psalm* 114," "done...at fifteen years old." One wonders why, of the 150 psalms, it was No. 114 that was chosen. (Given 114, 136 will follow, for its similar theme.) True, it characteristically, prophetically, gratifyingly, sounds the note of "liberty." ' Le Comte finds a possible clue in John Chamberlain's account (*Letters*, ed. N. E. McClure, Philadelphia, 1939, 2, 516) of rejoicing in London when Prince Charles, in October 1623, returned from Spain without a Roman Catholic bride: '...there beeing solemne service in Powles the singing of a new antheme was specially observed, the 114th psalme, when Israell came out of Egipt and the house of Jacob from among the barbarous people.' 'Thus, from the St. Paul's schoolboy, we could be getting something of a political allegory, like *Absalom and Achitophel*, with "Israel" meaning England in both heroic-couplet poems.' This, as its author indicates, is an interesting but very dubious suggestion.

lost in the ornamental phraseology which Milton adopts from the religious verse of seventeenth century England. More specifically their stylistic inspiration is Sylvester, whose rich and elaborate though somewhat undignified language apparently satisfied Milton's youthful sense of verbal beauty. The choice of the 114th and 136th Psalms and the manifest enthusiasm which Milton puts into the compositions is evidence also of a deeper sympathy with the poetic substance of Sylvester, whose broad and pious sense of the greatness and goodness of God as witnessed by the excellence of created nature Milton reproduces not ineffectively. We have here the beginning of a strain in Milton's poetry the importance of which, far more than any mere consideration of style, justifies the claim of Sylvester's *Du Bartas* to be counted among the permanent sources of his inspiration, a strain which reaches its culmination and full Miltonic glory in the morning hymn of Adam and Eve in the fifth book of *Paradise Lost.*'

Tillyard (*Milton*, 1930, 9) notes that Psalm 114 'is in the metre and manner of Sylvester,' as the 'violence' of the last two lines especially indicates. Psalm 136, 'though still reminiscent of Sylvester, is different. It is simple and it is dignified,' e.g. 29–30. 'And it is in places original: there is nothing in the Psalm to suggest the image in "The floods stood still like Walls of Glass, / While the Hebrew Bands did pass." Milton at fifteen had already gone beyond Sylvester.' Yet 'Sylvester's fame as a noble didactic poet probably worked on his imagination and guided his ambition.'

W. B. Hunter ('The Sources of Milton's Prosody,' *PQ* 28, 1949, 141) remarks that 'the outstanding fact about Ps. 136 is that the lines (not including the regular refrain) vary in length. They are normally iambic tetrameter, but they frequently show truncation; that is, they often lose their first syllable. Now while this became Milton's regular practice in *L'Allegro* and *Il Penseroso*, it could never do for a psalm meant to be sung, since the melody would be broken by omission of the syllable for its first note. There are no comparable examples in the psalters, and I am thus forced to conclude either that the young Milton was writing this psalm as a literary exercise or that if it were meant to be sung its music would have been of quite an individual kind which cannot be matched elsewhere. Interestingly enough, this is the only one of Milton's psalms to be found in the usual hymnal today....'

Brooks and Hardy (1951: 105–6) see in both Psalms a 'rather wooden conventionality,' 'in most essentials' an adherence to the original too close 'to achieve any considerable freshness in the adaptation. The principal changes are made in the interest of meter and rhyme,' and 'the meter in both Psalms is poorly managed.' But a glance at the two Psalms in the Bible shows how freely the boy elaborated; and the critics ignore the common purpose of such paraphrases, to produce versions for singing, not for students of poetic technique. On the other hand the critics, looking for hints of the mature Milton, make much of the rhetorical antitheses of the last couplet of 114 ('That glassy flouds from rugged rocks can crush, / And make soft rills from fiery flint-stones gush'), and see in the same lines a more intricate 'comparison of the water to molten glass,' 'a picture of the rock being with the one blow crushed, melted, and fused by its own fire into glass'—'what amounts to still another miracle'. [Hanford (*Poems*, 29) sees no such matter]. Brooks and Hardy also note in 'Erythraean' an anticipation of Milton's use of 'classical names of geographic features, for their evocative sense of remoteness and grandeur.'

Fletcher (*Intell. Dev.*, 1, 1956, 187–98, 291–2) makes a full comparison of Milton's paraphrases with Hebrew, Latin, and English versions. Speaking of Psalm 114, he concludes (192): 'This...was not based on any standard English version. It represented what Milton produced from his "double translation" after much polishing and in a particular verse form. He had begun by memorizing the Psalm in English from the 1611 version, and in Latin, from Vulgate or Tremellius-Junius. Then he had turned these into each other, probably into Greek and perhaps into Hebrew. Starting with his Hebrew text he may have paraphrased it, probably first in Greek, next in Latin, and finally in English. Then he compared each of these renderings with their originals, his Latin with the Vulgate or Tremellius-Junius, his English with the 1611 version. However he did it, he had produced a poem, not merely a school exercise.' We may perhaps doubt if the process of composition was quite so elaborate. Fletcher sees Milton following a similar method with Psalm 136, although this poem of praise invited a simpler form.

Daiches (*Milton*, 1957, 14) remarks, like others, on the young poet's expanding Psalm 114 'with Sylvester-like epithets,' and on the 'quite different' Psalm 136, which 'is not great poetry, but...has assurance, cogency, and technical control.'

H. Darbishire (*Essays and Studies 1957*, 34–5), speaking of Milton's apparently inborn sense of poetic decorum, imagines him—apropos of Psalm 136—asking 'himself what is wanted in an English Hymn? Answer—simplicity and exaltation—that is all. And how extraordinarily difficult for a schoolboy poet! Pomp and elaboration would be much easier. But Milton sets to work to meet the difficult demands, and the result is a hymn which has just those qualities a hymn should have. It sings well; the language is crystal clear, *simple* and *sensuous*; the words move in their natural order, phrase by phrase; there is no involution, no elaboration.'

III. NOTES [D.B.]
Psalm 114

Here, as elsewhere, quotations from Sylvester are cited according to the line numbers in Grosart's edition of his *Works* (2 vols., 1880); the text of the quotations is taken from Sylvester's *Du Bartas, His Divine Weekes and Workes* (London, 1621), which includes the translator's minor pieces. Phrases from George Buchanan's Latin version of the Psalms are quoted from his *Opera*, ed. T. Ruddiman (Leyden, 1725, v. 2).

1 *Terah's faithful Son*: Abraham (Gen. 11. 27; Heb. 11. 8). In the prose of the Bible (A.V.) the phrase is 'Israel...the house of Jacob'; cf. *PL* 12. 151–2. 'Milton altered the reading of his original...for the sake of the allusion to Abraham's faith in God,' his father Terah being an idolater (Hughes, *Paradise Regained, The Minor Poems and Samson Agonistes*, New York, 1937).

3 *Pharian Fields*: i.e. Egypt, from the small island, Pharus or Pharos, with a lighthouse tower, near Alexandria. Hanford ('Youth,' 94 n.) cites Buchanan's *arva Phari*. Cf. Sylvester, 'high Pharian-Tower' (*D.W.W.* 1. 1. 500, Grosart, 1, 23).

4–6 *Led...known*: Milton's elaboration.

8–9 *to hide his froth becurled head | ...Jordans clear streams recoil.* Dunster cited Sylvester, *Bethulians Rescue* 1. 51–2: 'Cleer Jordan's Selfe, in his dry oazie Bed, / Blushing for shame, was fain to hide his head' (Grosart, 2, 177). Cf. Bible: 'The sea saw it, and fled: Jordan was driven back.'

9–10 *recoil, | ...foil.* Dunster cited the same rhyme in Sylvester, *D.W.W.* 2. 3. 2. 44–5 (Grosart, 1, 178).

11 *high, huge-bellied Mountains skip.* Dunster cited Sylvester, *Triumph of Faith* 4. 17: 'Compels the Mountains burly sides to shake' (Grosart, 2, 18). Cf. Bible: 'The mountains skipped like rams, and the little hills like lambs.'

12 *Amongst their Ews.* Hanford (loc. cit.) cites Buchanan's *Ut...dux gregis inter oves.* Cf. Bible, quoted in 11 n.

14 *Why turned Jordan toward his Chrystal Fountains?* Dunster cited Sylvester, *D.W.W.* 1. 3. 78–9: 'And toward the Crystall of his double source / Compelled Jordan to retreat his course' (Grosart, 1, 41). H. C. H. Candy (*N&Q* 158, 1930, 93–5) cited 'crystal fountain's' and 'crystal founts' in Browne, *Brit. Past.* 1. 4. 729, 1. 5. 160.

17–18 *glassy flouds...crush, | ...gush.* Dunster found *glassy* 'not unfrequent' in Sylvester, e.g. *D.W.W.* 1. 3. 24, 'glassie Plains' (Grosart, 1, 40). For the *crush–gush* rhyme, cf. ibid. 1. 2. 549–50 (Grosart, 1, 32). Dunster noted the recurrence of *gush* in the Bible, e.g. Ps. 78. 20; 105. 41.

Psalm 136

3 *ay endure.* Dunster noted the frequency of *ay* in Sylvester, *D.W.W.* 1. 1. 39, 86, 99, etc.

5 *blaze.* See *Arc* 74–80 n.

9 *Who doth...tyrants quell.* The biblical 'Lord of lords' (Ps. 136. 3) Buchanan renders as *Cui domini rerum submittunt sceptra tyranni*, and Milton, says Hanford (loc. cit.), gives 'a similar republican touch'; but Milton was to be a good monarchist for many years to come.

9 f. In 1673 *Who* replaced the recurrent *That.*

18 *watry plain.* Todd cited the phrase in Spenser, *F.Q.* 4. 11. 24; Browne, *Brit. Past.* 2. 3. 677; etc.

23 *Golden-tressed Sun.* Dunster cited Sylvester's phrases about the sun: 'With golden tresses, and attractive grace' (*D.W.W.* 1. 4. 603, Grosart, 1, 57); 'his golden tress' (*D.W.W.* 2. 3. 3. 597, Grosart, 1, 189). Hanford (loc. cit., after Todd) cited Buchanan's *solem auricomum*.

26 *horned Moon.* The epithet was a commonplace; Todd noted the phrase in Spenser, *F.Q.* 4. 6. 43, and Shakespeare, *Dream* 5. 1. 244.

27 *spangled.* Dunster noted the frequency of the word, applied to the stars (and spheres), in Sylvester, e.g. *D.W.W.* 1. 1. 603 (Grosart, 1, 24).

29 *thunder-clasping hand.* Dunster noted Sylvester's use of 'thunder' in other compound epithets, e.g. 'mighty Thunder-darter' (*D.W.W.* 1. 1. 272, Grosart, 1, 21).

32-3 *Pharao fell,* | *...his Israel.* Dunster noted 'Pharaoh's fell hands' in Sylvester, *D.W.W.* 2. 3. 3. 645 (Grosart, 1, 190), and four examples of the *fell–Israel* rhyme (*D.W.W.* 2. 3. 3. 440–1, Grosart, 1, 188; etc.).

35-6 *The ruddy waves...* | *Of the Erythraean main.* The Red Sea. Dunster cited 'th' Erithraean Deep' (Sylvester, *D.W.W.* 1. 3. 77, Grosart, 1, 41), and 'the Erythraean ruddy Billowes rore' (Sylvester, *Bethulians Rescue* 2. 232, Grosart, 2, 183).

38-9 *The flouds stood still like Walls of Glass,* | *While the Hebrew Bands did pass.* Commentators have cited Sylvester (*D.W.W.* 2. 3. 3. 701–8, Grosart, 1, 190): 'With wals of crystall, beautifull and strong. | This flood-less Foord the Faith-full Legions pass, | ... Two Wals of Glass....' J. M. Steadman ('Milton's "Walls of Glass" (Psalm 136),' *Archiv* 198, 1961, 34–7) notes that the simile is not biblical and that commentators have seen Sylvester's influence. He observes hints in the Bible (Exod. 14. 22 and 29, 15. 8), which were developed by patristic commentators; and he cites also the Geneva version of Ps. 136. 13: 'which divided the red Sea into two parts.' Cf. the reference in *PL* 12. 197: 'As on drie land between two christal walls.'

41-2 *devour* | *...power.* Dunster noted the same rhyme in the account of Pharaoh's overthrow in T. Hudson's *Judith*, which was included in the 1621 edition of Sylvester (p. 704). *Tawny King.* Todd cited Fairfax, *Jerusalem* 3. 38: 'tawnie kings.'

50-1 *He foild...* | *...the Amorrean coast.* Dunster cited 'th' Amorrean Hare, | Foyl'd' (Sylvester, *D.W.W.* 2. 2. 4. 556, Grosart, 1, 159). *Seon*: Sihon, an Amorite king (Num. 21. 21 f., etc.). Todd cited Buchanan: *Stravit Amorrhaeum valida virtute Seonem.*

53 *large-limb'd Og*: king of Bashan (Num. 21. 33–5; Deut. 3. 1–4, 11).

Dunster cited 'a large and mighty limbed Steed' (Sylvester, *D.W.W.* 1. 5. 346, Grosart, 1, 64). Todd cited 'large-limb'd Oke' (*Owle* 1105: Drayton, 2, 509). Hanford (loc. cit.) quoted Buchanan's *confisum viribus Ogum*.

56   *his Servant Israel*: Jacob (Gen. 32. 28, 35. 10–12).

68   *warble forth*. Dunster cited the phrase in Sylvester, *D.W.W.* 1. 1. 18 (Grosart, 1, 19). H. C. H. Candy (*N&Q* 158, 1930, 93–5) cited 'warbled forth' in Browne, *Brit. Past.* 1. 5. 47.

72   *Above the reach of mortal eye*. Dunster cited 'With mortall eyes, under Nights horned Queen' (Sylvester, *D.W.W.* 1. 2. 1036, Grosart, 1, 36). Cf. 'mortall eyes' (*D.W.W.* 1. 4. 313, Grosart, 1, 55). Todd cited other examples of *mortal eye* in Sylvester, Spenser, *F.Q.* 1. 7. 33, 2. 2. 41; etc.

On the Death of a fair Infant
dying of a Cough

🦋

I. DATE AND CIRCUMSTANCES

This poem was omitted from the *Poems* of 1645 and first printed in the second edition of 1673. The caption *Anno aetatis 17* would place composition between 9 December 1625 and 8 December 1626. But W. R. Parker (*TLS*, 17 Dec. 1938, 802; cf. *Milton*, 738, n. 46) reported the discovery of the burial of Anne Phillips on 22 January 1628, and argued persuasively that this was the infant commemorated. (Milton had also made a slip in dating *In obitum Procancellarii* in the 1645 *Poems*.) Edward Phillips, in his biography of his uncle (H. Darbishire, *Early Lives of Milton*, London, 1932, 62), accepting *Anno aetatis 17* without demur, says that the baby was the daughter of Milton's sister Anne, and therefore Phillips' own sister, dead before he was born. Parker found in the parish register of St Martin's in the Fields the records of the baptism and burial of three children of Edward Phillips the elder and his wife Anne, who were married on 22 November 1623: John (16 Jan. 1625–15 March 1629); Anne (12 Jan. 1626–22 Jan. 1628); Elizabeth (9 April 1628–19 Feb. 1631). If we assume that Phillips was right in identifying the child as his own sister, the facts adduced would seem to be decisive. Parker concludes that 'the poem was evidently written after January 22 and probably before April 9, 1628—in other words, during the Lent term of his fourth year at Cambridge, the year in which he wrote his "Vacation Exercise" and first turned from Latin to English verse. The "Fair Infant" elegy thus fits nicely into its new place in the chronology....' Further, the complexity and virtuosity of the poem, which some recent critics have made a good deal of, and the note of

119

religious fervour which the artistry does not entirely conceal, favour the later date, a date nearer Milton's first great religious poem, the *Nativity*.

[Carey goes back to the older dating, the winter of 1625–6, following Milton's caption and Edward Phillips and internal evidence. But he has no evidence for a Phillips child that died at that time (see Parker's list above); Milton, as we saw, can make a mistake; and Phillips is not always reliable. Carey thinks that the two-year-old Anne cannot have been Milton's subject, since his infant 'did not outlast even a single winter (*3–4*)'; but Milton might naturally think of the child's not having survived the winter just passing or passed. Carey finds further support for 1625–6 in the reference to the plague (64–70), since 1625 was the great plague year; but Milton might have thought of the child's being born in time to drive away the plague (Parker, 738, n. 46). What knowledge we have seems to favour Parker's date.]

II. CRITICISM [D.B.]

Hanford ('Youth,' 1925, 96–9) remarks: 'The piece was conceived in a mood of tender grief and sympathy, not untouched with a larger sense of the mystery of death and immortality, motives toward which his mind had naturally been drawn by the ravages of the plague in London, even before they were brought home to him in a domestic sorrow. The literary influence under which his emotion characteristically shapes itself is the seventeenth century poetry of death. In style it belongs, as is evident both from its meter and its language, to the Spenserian tradition as represented particularly by Giles and Phineas Fletcher. The verbal conceits which chill the feeling in all but a few stanzas show Milton in the toils of a fashion which he was later to repudiate.' However, Hanford notes phrases 'which suggest the beginnings of a more individual style,' and references to Astraea and other figures, and to a guardian spirit, which anticipate the *Nativity* and later poems. In the fifth stanza, in his rejection of death, the young poet is for a moment borne 'on the wings of the great tradition of Elizabethan and Jacobean song.' Hanford's similar remarks in *Poems* (1953) include these: 'There is no trace of the influence of John Donne and his seventeenth-century imitators, though this has sometimes been affirmed. He is seeking elevation rather than forcefulness of expression, and he as yet knows of no way to attain it save by abounding in the aureate rhetoric of the age.'

Tillyard (*Milton*, 1930, 19–20): This poem, 'though often said to imitate Spenser, is rather in the tradition of the Ovidising Elizabethans, of poems like *Hero and Leander* and *Venus and Adonis*....But the effect of the poem is individual. The bright staccato quality of the Elizabethan conceits has been resolved into something slower, more hesitating, but more gravely sonorous. Once at least the verse breaks into stateliness'— 'Yet art thou not inglorious in thy fate' (22). 'The assurance of tone is very marked in the last stanza. He orders the child's mother to cease grieving,...with the instinctive certainty of a commanding nature, but forgetful that the lady he addresses may have more experience of life than himself. But against this tactlessness may be set the line (so prophetic of the *Nativity Ode*)—"Let down in clowdie throne to do the world some good" (56)—which exhibits a touch of the engaging innocence that often redeems Milton's less amiable qualities.'

Brooks and Hardy (1951: 241–3), taking the poem as conventional, object to Hanford's 'tender grief' as a mood hardly achieved or even intended. What the apprentice poet has attempted 'is a sort of formal statement in which the appropriate sentiments on such a death can be controlled and unified. And the matters of most legitimate critical interest are, therefore, formal problems: his handling of metaphor, and his choice of Phineas Fletcher's stanza.' The various analogies (a flower, the 'Athenian damsel,' a fallen star) 'find their justification in the conception of a tender, beautiful, and helpless being whose beauty and tenderness has attracted a force which destroys it in attempting to possess it. And this doubtless was all that Milton could make of the occasion, whatever personal meaning the death of his little niece may possibly have had for him. In this poem, however, the metaphors, unlike those of the metaphysicals, do not work to enforce a paradox: they seem to be used primarily for their decorative quality, for their function in making large and magnificent an occasion that would ordinarily seem trivial and unimportant.'

Daiches (*Milton*, 1957, 21–5) speaks of the Elizabethan rhetorical style, echoes of Ovid and Phineas Fletcher, and conceits that are not really functional. 'The poem is indeed a mass of separate conceits, obviously the work of a young poet indulging in an exhibitionist use of language.' Thus the 'not ineffective rhetorical formality' of the first line is followed by descriptive variations which do not rise to a climax and suggest the ingenuity of an exercise. The third stanza has an impressive rhythmic ease. 'The rest of the poem is largely taken up with ingenious mythological speculations intended to provide comfort.' Only in the fifth stanza 'does the imagery begin, in however slight a degree, to be Christian rather than classical,' and the sixth 'develops the Christian implications'; the seventh returns to the 'purely pagan.'

This first full-dress English poem of Milton's is not, taken as a whole, successful, but it has many features of interest. It shows him as yet unable to integrate pagan classical imagery into a Christian theme; each element exists in the poem separately. It shows Spenserian and post-Spenserian influences, together with an occasional line which rings out with a new kind of gravity and eloquence. It has echoes of Ovid and of Ovid's way of handling mythological stories. It reveals an experimental ear for rhetorical and decorative devices and at the same time a 'sage and serious' temperament. (24–5)

Several critics have given the poem more detailed analysis. In a chapter on the poetic treatment of death D. C. Allen (*Vision*, 1954, 47–52) finds in it 'a vivid indication of the poet's mature technique.' Confronted with the special problem of an infant too young to have shown any real character, Milton, after a traditional opening, 'invents the fiction that he can converse with the dead.... To make the achievement of the poem still more difficult, he refrains from blending pagan and Christian myths, separating them by a poetic barrier that is central to the poem.... By neither blending nor apologizing for these intrusions, Milton gives to his poem a horizontal movement of three tenses, the past, the present, and the future and a vertical movement from heaven to earth, from *here* to *there*.' 'Since the infant has no mythology, she must be made a myth by simile; hence the illusion of the antique is further extended by two familiar myths that are associated with the

legend of the rose'; the child becomes the bride of Winter and an innocent victim like Hyacinthus (see comments in notes on 8–11 and 22–8).
'At this point the structure of the poem changes'; the opening *lamen-
tatio* 'becomes an epicedium with the proclamatory line: "Yet can I not
perswade me thou art dead." ' Milton then follows the classical tradition
of a picture of immortal life (Ovid, *Am.* 3. 9. 59–66; etc.), as he had done
already in his Latin elegies on two bishops; but he does so through a
series of mythological allusions—the war of the giants and gods, a
fallen star, the flight of Astraea. 'Pagan myth, with Christian undertones,
leads to universal philosophical abstractions that open the door to
Christian legend.... The remaining stanzas are an epitome of the traditional *consolatio*,' although Milton, 'caught in his own mythical web,'
lapses into a commonplace and incoherent conclusion.

H. N. Maclean ('Milton's *Fair Infant*,' ELH 24, 1957, 296–305;
repr. in A. Barker, *Milton*, 1965) recognizes the *Fair Infant* as 'an
occasional poem, celebrating, in accordance with the conventions of
a tradition, a relatively unimportant event in terms designed to enhance
and magnify the significance of that occasion'; and, as such, it belongs
to the tradition that runs from Donne's *Anniversaries* to Dryden's ode
on Anne Killigrew. But, starting from Allen, Maclean is chiefly concerned to show 'that the structure and imagery...reveal a greater degree
of unity and progression than has so far been proposed.' (He notes,
incidentally, as one evidence of Milton's relative lack of emotional
involvement, the complete absence of references to sound; here 'all is
visual.') In the Latin elegies on Bishops Andrewes and Felton 'Christian
images supersede the classical vision, but do not banish' classical
images; and 'in neither poem is the central figure (once received into
heaven) considered to be *acting* further in man's behalf.' But here the
combination of classical and Christian is more complex and the child
becomes 'an active agent' in the Christian scheme.

'In a general way...the poem reflects the characteristic movement of
Christian elegy,' from grief through amplified meditation to consolation
and hope based on recognition of the true meaning of death. There are
four structural divisions. The first three stanzas emphasize the idea of

'incompleteness and mistake,' 'negation and futility.' From stanza IV, with its significant word 'transform'd,' myth moves toward new life, though still in an atmosphere of uncertainty and error. But stanza V reaches 'Above mortalitie,' with no hint of error; 'Death is *really* transcended.' The questions in VI 'allow the re-entrance and fuller flowering of classical imagery.' In VII–IX Milton moves through tentative conjectures to the triumphant celebration of heaven's purpose. Stanza X, in returning to the problem of early death, provides a larger answer than that of IX: the infant becomes 'nothing less than a mediatrix for all men,' 'virtually a Redeemer.' But 'Such a figure, in this poem, is beyond Milton's intentions and powers,' and he ends 'with a stanza balancing the suggestion of a wrathful God...by an admonition to await the pleasure of a merciful God.' The mood of Christian elegy is restored, though at the cost of a hasty anticlimax. Thus the poem represents 'an intermediate stage in Milton's early development'; it stands between the relatively simple juxtapositions of classical and Christian ideas and images in the two Latin elegies and the assured strength, complexity, and coherence of the *Nativity*.

W. M. Jones ('Immortality in Two of Milton's Elegies,' *Myth and Symbol*, ed. B. Slote, Lincoln, Neb., 1963, 133–40), so far as he deals with the *Fair Infant*, gives a generalized restatement of Allen and Maclean, but with his own emphasis on parallels and contrasts between this poem and the *Epitaphium Damonis*. In both Milton 'reveals the same basic attitude toward death. In spite of the promise of heavenly reward the individual man accepts the reality of death and works within that reality toward fulfillment of earthly possibilities. Anne Phillips must accept the essentially irreconcilable loss of one child in the hope of future children. Milton must accept the loss of a friend and meditate patiently upon the fertility which he, as a bearer of heavenly power, has received. True fame may have its root in heavenly soil, but it is achieved in this world. The Christian promise, like the classical metamorphosis, remains too unreal and illusory for Milton's own practical needs. In "The Fair Infant" Milton began his search for the meaning of death in the reality of the dead child, moved through the natural world and the classical to the Christian and returned finally to the only consolation that he could find emotionally satisfying: productivity is assurance of fame to the world's end....' (139–40).

It is hard to relate Milton to such a view of the poems and its emphasis on earthly motives and the 'illusory' promise of religion, an emphasis which rests heavily upon a literal reading of the last two lines: 'The fertility of nature is the earthly hope that Milton holds out to Anne Phillips who was already pregnant with another child' (135). See below, 76–7 n.

J. I. Cope ('Fortunate Falls as Form in Milton's "Fair Infant," ' *JEGP* 63, 1964, 660–74) argues that the *Fair Infant* 'was scarcely less rigorous in its own mode [than the *Nativity*], and no less dedicated to annunciating the resurrection promise....' In it 'Milton employed that physical structure of rising and falling which later was to give pattern to *Paradise Lost*,' though the concept of the fortunate fall is embodied in images from classical myth. The 'often elusive, unfocused' allusions 'spur the reader's recollection of multiple narratives' and 'the quint-essential sameness of their promise.' The rape of the infant by Winter (Aquilo-Boreas) is motivated by pride and thus linked with Satan's revenge on man. In stanza IV 'the first resurrection figure, Hyacinthus, emerges as partial analogue to the child,' and the poet's first reaction is despair; but evil is 'turned to good as Hyacinthus' death becomes itself the instrument through which Apollo works the boy's immortality.' 'The infant's fate recapitulates the infancy of mankind' in Eden. Stanzas V and VI reformulate the resurrection theme in a new Christian dimension, and Christian ideas are adumbrated in VII–IX in 'compressed repetitions of the ascent–descent pattern.' The figure of Astraea is especially suggestive in relation to Virgil's Messianic eclogue and the allegorical–typological tradition of mythographers. 'Satanic Winter's violence' gives way to the conception of 'Astraea the redeemer,' 'of an ultimate redemption and resurrection for mankind.' Stanza IX 'repeats the pattern of descent and reascension...as it abandons classical for Christian phraseology.' But the ordinary infant lamented can appear 'only as shadow, as figure for the redemption, not as its instrument.'

The last stanza is a 'culmination rather than the tired surrender to hyperbole' commonly seen. The address to the mother of the child goes beyond the conclusion of the Messianic eclogue to sum up in Christian terms the reiterated pattern of the fortunate fall, to translate the child's wintry death into the promise of spring.

Cope's analysis is much too learned and complex for brief summary; and some readers may ask if the poem contains or suggests all that he finds in it.

Isabel G. MacCaffrey, in a discussion of *Lycidas* (*The Lyric and Dramatic Milton*, ed. J. H. Summers, New York, 1965, 68–9) illustrates the 'importance of a firmly established spatial foreground' by glancing at the *Fair Infant*. 'This poem foreshadows *Lycidas* in the immediacy of its opening and in its reference to vegetation untimely cropt.... This is, however, precisely a poem *without* a landscape. Despite references to the seasons, there is no country where their sequences can be observed. Nor is there any spot where the speaker can establish himself as chief actor. He speaks from no place, and so the range of effective eloquence is severely limited for him; though there is plenty of movement, it lacks focus and therefore point. The poet has also neglected to provide himself with a metaphorical base, a fictive geography enabling the reader to assess the figurative weight of the conceits. Lacking the feigned literalness of "Yet once more...I come," the opening metaphor fails to evoke a world in which Hyacinth, Astraea, Winter, and Truth can live together. The address at the end to "the mother of so sweet a child" is disconcertingly abrupt; such a sudden emergence from fiction to fact need not occur in pastoral because the fiction is the fact incarnate.'

J. T. Shawcross, in a general account of 'Milton's *Nectar:* Symbol of Immortality' (*English Miscellany* 16, 1965, 131–41), starts from lines 47–9, where Milton asks if 'earths Sonnes' attacked heaven and the infant was 'some goddess fled / Amongst us here below to hide thy nectar'd head.' 'Thus conceived of as immortal, it is no wonder that she had left earth to ascend again.... The equation of Olympus and Heaven, and thus of Jove and God, is easily discerned in the stanza in which the word ['nectar'd'] appears, but the Christian quality inherent in the word suggests more than only the next stanza (VIII) citing Justice (Astraea), Mercy, and Truth. The Giants' rebellion against Jove was identified, and here amidst such Christian symbolism and equation must be identified, with the revolt of Satan and his cohorts. The upshot of these identities, perhaps sacrilegious for some, is that Milton thinks of his niece symbolically as a kind of Christ whose kenosis was effected to bring salvation to man. Stanza VIII says as much by theorizing that she is one of the triad of attributes of God—Justice, Mercy, Truth—and by the line: "Let down in clowdie throne to do the world some good". She has personified in her short life the fourth daughter of God— Peace. Undoubtedly there is a temporal reference intended for the years 1626 through early 1628 (her lifetime). Indeed Milton is perhaps more concerned in the poem with temporal conditions and the decline of justice for God's true servants than with consolation for the girl's death.'

Shawcross—who ignores the fact that 'Mercy' is an editorial insertion (see 53-4 n. below), and who seems to imply that Milton is already an anti-monarchist—proceeds to sketch the friction growing in 1626-8 between Charles and parliament and people which led to the Petition of Right. 'The imminent birth alluded to in the last stanza becomes, therefore, a kind of second coming, a symbol of hope for all God's creatures, and the passage of the Petition of Right would confirm Milton's hope.' [The Petition of Right was read on 2 June 1628: Shaw- cross takes 17 March, when parliament was called, as 'perhaps then a *terminus ad quem*' for the date of the poem.] Shawcross cites a thesis by V. Mollenkott, who suggested that Milton had two biblical passages in mind. One is Wisd. of Sol. 4. 1-2: 'Better it is to have no children: and to have virtue: for the memoriall thereof is immortal.... When it is present, men take example at it, and when it is gone they desire it....' The other is Isa. 56. 5 [quoted by Hughes in 1957 in support of a dif- ferent interpretation: see below, 76-7 n.] For Shawcross 'These quota- tions help establish Milton's poem as a vehicle for his concern with political difficulties: the birth and death of his niece stood in Milton's mind like a parable of God. Anne's birth, coinciding with the overt resistance and partial success of parliament, became an epiphany of justice for Milton. Her decline and death at a time when the Commons were unable to manifest their will paralleled Justice's forsaking the world. But the second coming (the imminently expected millennium of the seventeenth century, which would establish good government, freedom from wickedness, etc.) would bring immortality to God's chosen.'

All this seems highly imaginative.

III. NOTES

[For detailed interpretations of the significance of the mythological allusions, see the full texts of the discussions of Allen, Maclean, and Cope, which are briefly summarized above.

The metrical pattern of the stanza is an adaptation of the traditional rhyme royal (*ababbcc*), with an alexandrine instead of the final pentameter. This scheme had been used by Phineas Fletcher in some of his miscellaneous pieces (*P.W.* 2, 227–9, 261 f.), but his poems were not published until 1633. It has been assumed that Milton—who used the stanza again in the prelude to the *Nativity*—saw them in manuscript, and possibly he did, but we do not need to assume that Phineas Fletcher could invent what Milton could not. They were both disciples of Spenser, as the final alexandrine reminds us.]

1–2 *O fairest flower...timelesslie*. Todd and later editors compare: 'Sweet rose, fair flower, untimely pluck'd, soon vaded, / Pluck'd in the bud, and vaded in the spring!' (Shakespeare, *Pass. Pil.* 10). Allen (*Vision*, 48) notes that the allusion (which looks forward to 'the rathe Primrose' of *Lyc* 142) belongs to a tradition that goes back to the Greek pastoral elegists: 'The quickly fading rose is a symbol that dominates epitaphic verse, and the primrose that sprung from the blood of the young Adonis as the anemone that grew from Aphrodite's tears ...is a perpetual emblem of those who died before their time.' *timelesslie*: unseasonably, out of due time (*OED*), commoner in adjectival form, as in Shakespeare, *Romeo* 5. 3. 162 (cited by Browne).

3 *honour*: glory, that for which it is honoured, as in Shakespeare, *H. V* 1. 1. 12–13, *All's W.* 4. 2. 42.

4 *made…drie*: withered. [Lines 3–4 are appropriate for the child's death in January (Parker, 738, n. 46).]

5 *amorous on*: in love with. The now obsolete form with *on* (*Much* 2. 1. 161) and the surviving form with *of* can both be illustrated from Shakespeare.

6–7 *thought to kiss | But kill'd*. Newton (reported by Todd) and later editors cite Shakespeare, *Venus* 1109–10: 'If he did see his face, why then I know / He thought to kiss him, and hath kill'd him so.' [The conceit was a commonplace of the Adonis story (Bush, *Mythol.* 138; *The Dead Adonis*, in *Greek Bucolic Poets*, L.C.L., 480–3). It was used of Boreas (along with Milton's *boisterous*, line 9) by Sylvester: 'Comming to kiss her, makes her lips afeard; / …in a fury with his boystrous wings' (*D.W.W.* 1. 4. 709–12, Grosart, 1, 58).]

6 *envermeil*: tinge with vermilion (*OED*). [Cf. 'vermeil-tinctur'd lip' (*Comus* 751).]

8–11 *since grim Aquilo…wedded not*. Boreas (*Aquilo*), the North Wind, long wooed in vain Orithyia, daughter of Erechtheus, king of Athens, but was rejected because of his Thracian domicile. Resolving to be himself, he changed his tactics and snatched her away over the mountains in storm and darkness (Ovid, *M.* 6. 682–713). For this allusion and *kiss* (line 6), Dunster cited Sylvester: 'the cold frozen Scythia / Too-often kist by th'husband of Orithya' (*D.W.W.* 1. 2. 483–4, Grosart, 1, 31). [See references in S. K. Heninger, *Handbook of Renaissance Meteorology*, Durham, N.C., 1960, 123–4.] Milton, who can invent myth as well as adapt it, makes Aquilo the charioteer of Winter (*Hiems*) and his exploit the incentive of his master's action.

12–14 *Thereby to wipe…was held*. Newton (reported by Todd) cited Claudian 33. 32–6 (2, 294–6) for the same motive attributed to Pluto's abduction of Proserpine. [Cope (*JEGP* 63, 661) links Winter's motive, pride, and the action of stanza 3, with Satan's.]

13 *eld*: old age (*OED* 3).

14 *wanton gods*: the lustful and promiscuous Olympian deities.

15 *ycie-pearled*. Dunster (reported by Todd) noted 'Ice-pearl(s)' in Sylvester (*D.W.W.* 2. 3. 1. 293, Grosart, 1, 166; *Battail of Ivry* 133, ibid. 2, 248). *carr*: chariot.

16 *middle empire of the freezing aire*: the middle one of the three regions or layers of air above the earth. [It was cold and stormy because the top layer cut it off from the sphere of fire and the bottom layer blanketed it against the rays of the sun rebounding from the earth: K. Svendsen, *Milton and Science*, Cambridge, Mass., 1956, 88 (cited hereafter as *Science*); Heninger, *Meteorology*, 37–46. Cf. *Vac* 41–2, *Nat* 164, *PL* 1. 515–17, *PR* 1. 39–42, 2. 117–26. E. W. compares Spenser, *F.Q.* 5. 4. 42: 'Soaring through his wide Empire of the aire.']

19 *Snow-soft chaire*: chariot (*OED*: *sb.*²), i.e. the *carr* of 15, now described as cushioned with snow.

20–1 *But all unwares...fair biding place*. Cf. 6–7 and n. *cold-kind*: kind in intention but chilling, indeed death-dealing, in effect; Milton compounds the epithets to heighten the oxymoron. *Unhous'd thy Virgin Soul*. The periphrasis brings into relief the soul or spiritual essence, the *thou* which is to be the subject of the queries and speculations of stanzas 6–10. Dunster noted Sylvester's 'For, her owne Father, Nature had un-hous'd' (*Funeral Elegie* 79, Grosart, 2, 292).

22–8 *Yet art thou...no power*. Milton is clearly following Ovid (*M.* 10. 162–219), who tells how the discus hurled by Apollo accidentally killed his beloved Hyacinthus, who associates the incident with the river Eurotas (169), speaks of Sparta's pride in her son (217), and emphasizes Apollo's grief and innocence of guilt unless in having loved. From Hyacinthus' blood Apollo produced the purple flower (209–13) which confers, as the flower blooms every spring, a sort of immortality (164–6). Winter, Milton laments, had no such power; but Ovid notices a limitation on the power of Apollo, who, if grim fate had given him time, would have set the youth in the sky (162–3); this Milton does not mention, but it may have had some indirect influence on 37–8 and 43 (see notes). [In some versions (not in Ovid's) the fatal accident was caused by the jealous Zephyr, the West Wind, or (as in Servius on Virgil, *E.* 3. 63) by Boreas (Aquilo). Allen (*Vision*, 49) suggests that Milton was reminded of Hyacinth by his preceding allusion to Aquilo.]

23 *unweeting*: a variant of *unwitting*. [Cf. Spenser, *F.Q.* 1. 2. 40, etc.; Browne, *Brit. Past.* 2. 5. 419, 'with unweeting hand.']

25–6 [The repetition is especially Spenserian; cf. *F.Q.* 3. 6. 45, which includes a reference to Hyacinthus and Milton's word *transform'd*.]

29–35 [W. J. Roscelli (*TSLL* 8, 1966, 472) finds this stanza similar to 'metaphysical invocations of death' (e.g. George Herbert's *Death*) in its use of 'a favorite metaphysical paradox, simultaneously predicating of the child beauty and decay, corruption and immortality.' He recognizes that this is a universal paradox, illustrated in Nashe's famous stanza, though Nashe is general, Herbert concrete.]

30–1 *Or that thy coarse corrupts...in wormie bed.* Warton (for phrasing merely) compared: 'Already to their wormy beds are gone' (Shakespeare, *Dream* 3. 2. 384). Hughes (for content) compares: 'Neither wilt thou suffer thine Holy One to see corruption' (Ps. 16. 10; Acts 2. 27).

35 *Above mortalitie.* There seem to be two possible interpretations: 'above what is seen in *mortals*' (*OED* 1 b), or 'above the reach of *death*' (ibid. 2c). [The total context may appear to favour the second.]

38–40 *where e're thou...(if such there were).* Warton cited as the original of this and such other poetic questionings: *anne novum tardis sidus te mensibus addas,* | *qua locus Erigonen inter Chelasque sequentis* | *panditur...* | *quidquid eris* (Virgil, *G.* 1. 32–6). Hughes cites *IlPen* 88–92. Browne notes the passage of the soul through the spheres in *PL* 3. 481–2; not less significant is the adjacent allusion to 'Plato's Elysium' (ibid. 472). Unlike Homer's Elysian fields, a region in the far west near the stream Ocean (*Od.* 4. 561–9), and unlike the underworld Elysium of Virgil (*A.* 6. 637 f.) and Ovid (*M.* 14. 110 f.), the Platonic Elysium is 'in the pure heaven,' in that elaborate metaphysical and mythical cosmology outlined in the *Phaedo* (109–14; summarized in *Comus* 975 n.); clearly it is to this that Milton alludes in *the Elisian fields.* The addition, *if such there were,* is 'the first of those conscientious reservations with which Milton checks himself in his instinctive use of classical mythology' (Hanford, 'Youth,' 97), but one may observe that a note of hesitancy is struck in Plato's own description.

39 *high first-moving Spheare:* the outermost sphere, the *primum mobile,* which in the Ptolemaic system communicated motion to the inner spheres. [Cf. *PL* 3. 483, 'that first mov'd,' and n.]

43–6 *Wert thou some Starr...reinstall?* The fancy is based (as Wright [on *Comus* 1] observes) on the notion that Olympus, rising above the clouds, penetrated the sky; here the stars are placed, not at the 'threshold of Joves Court' (*Comus* 1), but in its roof. Presumably Olympus is *shak't* by the war of the gods and Titans, in which 'wide Heaven was shaken and groaned, and high Olympus reeled from its foundation' (Hesiod, *Theog.* 680). The star is dislodged and falls, but Jove restores it for *natures true behoofe,* advantage or benefit (*OED* 1). [This and other classical allusions in *FInf* are more or less paralleled in the Latin poem *Naturam non pati senium* (written probably some months later in 1628), where they are used against the doctrine of Nature's decay: see *V.C.* 1, 211.]

47–9 *Or did of late...nectar'd head.* Despite early and late confusing of the war of the giants on the gods with the war of the gods and Titans, there seems no reason to assume, with Browne and others, that Milton is confusing them here. The giants as well as the Titans were *earths Sonnes*, conceived by her from the blood of Uranus when he was mutilated by Cronos (Hesiod, *Theog.* 183–5). It may be that, having glanced at the war of the gods and Titans in 43–6 (see n.), Milton now alludes by way of analogy to the war of the giants against the gods, and specifically to the story of the gods' fleeing [from the monster Typhon to Egypt (Apollodorus 1. 6. 3; Ovid, *M.* 5. 321–31; cf. Milton, *Naturam* 21 f.)].

48 With *sheenie Heav'n* Warton compared 'shinie firmament' (Spenser, *M. Hubberds Tale* 1269). [Hunter ('New Words,' 256) lists *sheeny* as a Miltonic coinage.]

49 *nectar'd head.* See *Lyc* 175 and n. [and Shawcross's article partly summarized in *FInf* II above]. The epithet occurs in *Comus* 478. Todd gives examples from John Davies of Hereford.

50–2 *Or wert thou...us once more?* The *just Maid* is Astraea, goddess of Justice, who, when corruption followed the golden age, quitted the earth, the last of the divinities to go (Ovid, *M.* 1. 149–50). Milton's *Maid* and Ovid's *virgo* alike refer to her being identified with the constellation Virgo. Browne compares: 'the righteous Maide, / That for disdaine of sinfull worlds upbraide, / Fled back to heaven, whence she was first conceived' (Spenser, *M. Hubberds Tale* 1–3). [For Astraea's return, cf. Virgil, *E.* 4. 6, Milton, *Nat* 141–6 and n. Cope (*JEGP* 63, 665 f.: see II above) has much to say of the allusion in *FInf*.]

53–4 *Or wert thou that sweet smiling Youth! / Or...truth?* [The printer, as sometimes elsewhere, used an exclamation mark instead of a question mark.] [E. W.: 'In the first of these verses, a dissyllable word is wanting, which probably fell out at press' (Warton, quoted in Todd). The likelihood of this conjecture is increased by the fact that lines 53–4 are the first two on their page (p. 20) in the 1673 *Poems*, and that there is a typographical disturbance (*cown'd* for *crown'd*) in the second line as well; see Fletcher, *Facs.* 24. That the error was not caught in proof may be owing to the fact that *FInf* 50 begins *Or wert thou that*, which renders the impaired reading of 53 superficially plausible.] Newton (*Poetical Works*, 3 v., London, 1761–2) and later editors have inserted *Mercy* after *thou*, the proposal made by John Heskin (identified by Warton). [R. L. Ramsay ('Morality Themes in Milton's Poetry,' *SP* 15, 1918, 137–8) commented: 'As emended, the line involves the absurdity of making Mercy masculine, or else supposing that the poet uses "youth" here to mean a young woman. Masson accepts the former alternative, explaining that we have in "the three personages of the stanza Justice (the maiden), Mercy (the young man), and Truth (the matron)." But, not to mention the fact that the conception of Mercy as masculine is unexampled in literature, Milton is here addressing his niece, and could hardly ask her if she had been a young man. On the other hand, the word "youth" is never feminine elsewhere in Milton, in Spenser, or in Shakspere; nor have I been able to find any instance of such a use of the word in its concrete application, at least in the singular. Heskin's reason for supposing that Mercy is the missing word is the use together of Truth, Justice, and Mercy again in stanza 15 of the *Ode on the Nativity*. But Milton is not wont to repeat himself so exactly; and I should like to suggest instead that the line originally read: "Or wert thou that sweet [Peace, in] smiling youth?" The substitution of Peace for Mercy would enable us to explain the entire stanza from classical mythology alone, as is every other allusion in the poem. Furthermore, the epithet "sweet" is used of Peace in Milton's translation of the psalm, and was the favorite epithet for that divinity of Milton's master Spenser.' 'J. A. Himes, *MLN* xxxv (1920) 441–2 and xxxvi (1921) 414–19, opposes any emendation and reads the line as a reference to Ganymede. The sex of the child ("Her" 72) is against this' (Carey).]

Allen (*Vision*, 51 n.) suggests '"Virtue," whom the pagans considered the child of Truth; see Gyraldus, *Syntagma deorum*, in *Opera* (Leyden, 1696), I, 27–28.' In a letter to Woodhouse (29 Sept. 1960) Allen further supported 'Virtue.' He quoted Cartari, *Imagini* (Padua, 1615, 329): *Et Filostrato, dicendo che la Verità era dipinta nel sacro antro di Anfiarao, la fa vestita di bianchissimi panni, & in altro luogo la chiama poi madre della Virtù*; and he added: 'It seems to me that the abstract goddess Truth might naturally be followed by her daughter, the abstract goddess Virtue.' H. Maclean (*ELH* 24, 1957, 302 n.) quoted Milton's *Prol* 4, where he questioned 'whether, for instance, Astraea was the last of the goddesses to leave the earth; for I suspect that Peace and Truth would not have abandoned even hostile mortals many ages after her' (*Works* 12, 175), and argued that Peace rather than Mercy is the appropriate emendation. [Cope (*JEGP* 63, 670) supports Mercy.] The difficulty with all these conjectures is that 'Youth' implies a male figure, as Allen admitted in his letter. Mercy and Peace are universally recognized in Christian iconography as two of the Four Daughters of God (*Nat* 141–6 n.). In classical Latin *Pax* is inevitably a female figure or deity (as in Ovid, *F.* 1. 709–12), and Peace is female in *Nat* 45–52; and Peace provides only one syllable. One of the few eligible personifications which is or may be masculine is Honour (Allen, letter), which also provides the required two syllables. [Woodhouse's notes indicate an inclination toward Temperance (pronounced Temp'rance) as a very Miltonic virtue (cf. *Epistol* 19, *Works* 12, 81, where Milton exhorted Richard Jones to judge of true greatness by justice and temperance; and his many earlier utterances); as a virtue most difficult to achieve in youth and yet in Aristotle a virtue exercised without struggle. Woodhouse also entertained the possibility of a Platonic Eros or Amor. It may be added that Drummond's *Hymne of the Fairest Faire* (2, 38–9) includes, among figures near God's throne, Youth (lines 35–9), Truth (57–61), and Love with 'sweete-smiling Face' (81–4).]

54 *white-robed truth.* Osgood (*C.M.* 51) noted that Truth (Aletheia) is white-robed in Philostratus, *Imagines* 1. 27; cf. the excerpt from Cartari in the preceding note. Todd quoted Cesare Ripa, *Iconologia* (Rome, 1603, p. 501; 1625, p. 712): *Verità. Donna risplendente, di nobile aspetto, vestita di color bianco, pomposamente....*

55–6 The image of a figure *Let down in clowdie throne* inevitably suggests the court masque, where personified virtues or other classical figures, the *heav'nly brood*, were often given this mode of entry. Cf. *Nat.* 45–8 and n. [R. L. Ramsay (see 53–4 n.) suggests (136) that the allusion may be to 'Hesiod's statement that "upon the bounteous earth Zeus has thrice ten thousand spirits, watchers of mortal men, and these keep watch on judgements and deeds of wrong as they roam, clothed in mist, all over the earth" (*Works and Days*, ll. 252–55).']

57 *the golden-winged hoast*: the angels, who (especially the Cherubim) were portrayed with golden wings; cf. *Comus* 213, *IlPen* 52–4. Bowle (reported by Todd) cited: 'Yet farre more faire be those bright Cherubins, / Which all with golden wings are overdight' (Spenser, *Hymne of Heavenly Beautie* 92–3).

58 *humane weed*: human body (*OED*: *sb.²* 3). See *Comus* 16 and n.

59 *praefixed*: preordained (*OED* 1). *poast*: post, hasten (*OED*: *v.¹* 2).

66 *whom sin hath made our foe*: i.e. death. [But several expressions—*his wrath whom*, *our deserved smart*, and line 70—may seem to mean God. The phrase was evidently so read by Todd, who printed *His wrath*. Spenser speaks of a loving God who sends angels 'To serve to wicked man, to serve his wicked foe' (*F.Q.* 2. 8. 1); and Quarles, closely echoing this Spenserian passage, speaks of the love of God whose angels 'fly to and fro, / Assisting wretched man, their deadly foe' (*Feast for Wormes*, 1620, *Medit.* 1, sig. C3: *Works*, ed. Grosart, 3 v., 1880–1, 2, 10, lines 131–2). Cf. *PL* 2. 721–2, where Death and Satan will 'never but once more... / ...meet so great a foe,' i.e. the Son; and especially ibid. 10. 219, where the Son, pitying Adam and Eve, 'thought not much to cloath his Enemies.']

67 *perdition*: ruin (*OED* 1); not damnation but some temporal ill comparable to pestilence and death; otherwise the effect of 68 would be anticlimax.

68 *pestilence*. [The last great outbreak of the plague was in 1625-6 (cf. *El* 3. 1 f.). This line, and line 70, have been an argument for dating the poem at that time (see headnote); but in both lines Milton might be anticipating another visitation of the plague (such as came in 1630). See Parker's suggestion, cited at the end of 1 above.]

75 *render*: give back, restore (*OED* 3); cf. *PL* 10. 749.

76-7 [Some editors (e.g. Masson, Hanford, Shawcross; and W. M. Jones in II above) have taken these lines as a literal assurance that Anne Phillips would have another child (and one was baptized on 9 April 1628). But it seems most unlikely that Milton would make such a private allusion to his sister's pregnancy and still more so that, if he did, he would utter such a wildly extravagant prophecy as that the child *till the worlds last-end shall make thy name to live*. Moreover, the birth of a child does not depend upon the mother's showing patience under bereavement, as Milton says the *off-spring* does (see the *if* of 76). Hughes is much more persuasive in hearing an echo of Isaiah's promise (56. 5) to the childless (though the Phillipses had one child): 'Even unto them will I give...a name better than of sons and of daughters: I will give them an everlasting name, that shall not be cut off.' (See also Wisd. of Sol. 4. 1-2, quoted under Shawcross in II above, under 1965.) But Milton's idea seems to be broader than the promise in Isaiah: the figurative *off-spring* is the earthly peace and strength and the heavenly life coupled in the Bible with exhortations to patience and promised to all the faithful (e.g. Heb. 6. 12). The appeal to Isaiah was perhaps first made by J. A. Himes (*MLN* 36, 1921, 417; *Miltonic Enigmas*, Gettysburg, 1921, p. 6).]

At a Vacation Exercise
in the Colledge

I. DATE AND CIRCUMSTANCES

This poem, which Milton dated *Anno Aetatis 19* (i.e. at the age of 19), was written in 1628, presumably in the weeks preceding its public recital some time, it would appear, in July. It formed an appendage to the two Latin speeches that make up his sixth *Prolusion*. [Milton's doings during this summer involve some puzzles. On 2 July he wrote to Alexander Gill from Cambridge that he expected to spend the summer there (*Works* 12, 13; *C.P.W.* 1, 313–14). On 21 July, writing from Cambridge, he accepted an invitation from his old tutor, Thomas Young, to visit him shortly at Stowmarket (*Works* 12, 15; *C.P.W.* 1, 315–16); we may assume that the visit was paid, though we do not know. In neither letter did Milton refer to the Vacation Exercise. In the opening of *Prolusion* 6 (*Works* 12, 205) he says that he had lately returned to Cambridge from London but that his promised private studies had been suddenly interrupted by the invitation to speak. (Cf. Parker, 44, 49, 739–41, notes 55, 60, 61.)]

Milton concludes the *Prolusion* by announcing the innovation of adding English verses to the usual Latin discourse (*Works* 12, 247; *C.P.W.* 1, 286). [He had been called upon to be 'Father' or 'Dictator' at this College assembly, which, set as it was near the beginning of the long vacation, had a festive as well as academic character. Milton's Latin speeches carried on this double vein. 'The nature of the occasion and his office for the day—an evidence of his growing popularity—prompted a genially urbane discourse; the latter half of it was a less happy effort in the kind of humor expected at such a time. Then followed these English verses, in which Milton took his hearers into his confidence. His poetry hitherto had been almost wholly in Latin. Now he salutes his native language, avows his distaste for the trifling themes and eccentric style of some student poets, and goes on, in couplets of more smoothness and eloquence, to sketch the "graver" subjects that attract him—nature and the cosmos and "kings and queens and heroes old" ' (D. Bush, ed., *Complete Poetical Works*, Boston, 1965; London, 1966).]

The *Vacation Exercise*, like the *Fair Infant*, was omitted from the *Poems* of 1645 and first printed in the 1673 edition, where it was misplaced. It stood, with the translation from Horace, between the numbered sonnets and *On the new forcers of Conscience*; the Errata directed its removal to a position immediately after the *Fair Infant* [which had apparently been written a few months earlier. This misplacing and related questions have been discussed by J. T. Shawcross (*SEL* 3, 1963–4, 77–84; cf. Parker, 739–40, n. 55).]

II. CRITICISM [D.B.]

Hanford ('Youth,' 1925, 93–4, 117–18) remarks that Milton's 'feeling for English is a home-felt delight, implying a still closer discrimination of the harmonies and ornaments of speech.' After quoting the *Vacation Exercise* 1–6, 17–22, he says: 'There is no reason to suppose that these enthusiasms do not go back to the early years of Milton's schooling. They are, like the born artist's love of color, his initial gift as a poet, and they antedate the need which he later felt to find an expressive medium for those "naked thoughts that rove about / And loudly knock to have their passage out." ' (93–4)

'Milton seems in his second academic year to have abandoned for the time being his early experimentation in English verse, presumably as a result of the humanistic tendency to undervalue the vernacular as a source of serious culture. There were additional reasons why he should have employed the learned medium.... To give rein to sensuousness in the vernacular was to range oneself with a group of unacceptable licentious rhymesters. To do so in Latin was to follow the tradition of the honored classics and of the eminently respectable learned moderns, like Buchanan, who had imitated them. Against this somewhat pedantic attitude stood Milton's patriotism and his natural instinct for expression in his mother tongue, and ultimately these forces triumphed over his humanistic predispositions and freed him to pour himself out in English. His feelings on the subject are recorded in the enthusiastic apostrophe to his native language...composed...a year earlier than the fifth Latin elegy, and it is natural to associate Milton's renewed consciousness of the claims of English verse with the access of creative power which he describes in the latter poem. We may connect it also with more mature and serious meditation on his vocation as a poet, clear evidence of which appears in these pieces for the first time.' (117)

In *Poems* (1953) Hanford remarks: 'Milton's use of English and his proud praising of his native tongue is an expression of his feeling that this after all was his true medium. It is characteristic of him that he should thus advertise his calling before his tutors and fellow students. The poem suggests his fastidious interest in words and style. He eschews "new-fangled toys and trimming slight," and declares his allegiance to the luxuriant Renaissance expression of poets like Spenser. His characterization of the type of subject which calls him points forward to his epic aspirations....Except for Psalm 114, this is Milton's first and only use of the heroic couplet.'

Tillyard (*Milton*, 1930, 30–2): 'This poem has a double interest: it contains the earliest passage of Milton's verse in which the rhythm is sustained with the peculiar Miltonic sublimity; and it shows Milton critically aware of contemporary English poetry. Marking his contrast with the word *yet*, he turns from describing the task for which he must now use his native language to describing that to which his genius prompts him. And the verse that has kept the ground now takes wing.' After quoting lines 29–53, Tillyard proceeds: 'If Milton had not already in his eighteenth year decided to become a poet, this passage makes it tolerably plain that by now he had decided; and in his native tongue. But if the poem shows Milton decided to be a poet, it shows him undecided how to write. The passage quoted may be individual, but in the rest he falls into whatever current style he thinks best suits his subject. In writing of the rivers he imitates Spenser through Browne [lines 95–8]. But when discussing the way he means to write he falls into the contemporary extravagance of sustained metaphor, too loosely named metaphysical. He speaks of his native language as "Driving dum silence from the portal dore, / Where he had mutely sate two years before." And later he says: "I have some naked thoughts that rove about, / . . . aray." Those passages show Milton, as I said, critically aware of the different modes of contemporary verse: as too does another passage in which he disclaims a certain literary mode' [see below, 19–20 n.].

Tillyard returned to the poem in 'Milton and the English Epic Tradition' (*Seventeenth Century Studies Presented to Sir Herbert Grierson*, Oxford, 1938; repr. as 'The Growth of Milton's Epic Plans,' *The Miltonic Setting* [cited hereafter as *M. Set.*], Cambridge, 1938, 168–204). Milton's active awareness of contemporary poetic theory and practice shows itself in his 'attacking (even while partly practising) a contemporary mode of extravagance.' On the positive side he indicates three types of poetry he would like to give his mind to: 'some kind of exalted lyric' (lines 33–9), such as the odes and hymns of Pindar and Callimachus which he later cited (*RCG*, *Works* 3, 238); a 'second type, dealing with natural philosophy and the creation of the world,' like Hesiod's *Theogony*, Ovid's *Metamorphoses* (bk. 1), and especially Du Bartas or Sylvester; and, thirdly, 'the straightforward heroic.' 'Now it is remarkable that at the early age of nineteen Milton should already have been weighing in his mind two kinds of "epic,"' both popular in the Renaissance. Another connection with the contemporary epic appears in the concluding lines, 'Rivers arise' (91–100), 'the most masterly in the whole poem, being free from the slight sense of strain that pervades those already quoted. And they are entirely Miltonic, uttering a music that issues from the very core of Milton's being and yet fastidiously precise, full, and appropriate in thought. Further they suggest big tracts of poetry then popular and they look forward to more than one of Milton's later ventures' (173). Tillyard cites Browne's *Britannia's*

Pastorals, Drayton, Spenser, and the whole store of 'British myth and its Tudor connections.'

Brooks and Hardy (1951, 238–40) see Milton, 'facing explicitly the problems presented by his native language,' as 'characteristically fastidious.' They go along with Tillyard in rejecting the notion that lines 19–21 are 'a thrust at metaphysical poetry,' and observe that 'the very figure in which Milton disparages the "late fantasticks" is itself an example, though a humble one, of the witty extended figure dear to the metaphysicals.' Also, the clash between 'gay'st attire' and 'deepest Spirits' has at least a 'mildly "metaphysical" effect.' The poem as a whole points up 'the fact that by the end of his twentieth year Milton is acutely aware of the problem of style. He has felt the attraction of the Ovidizing Elizabethans, of the Spenserians, and of the witty poets of the metaphysical school. But the important thing is that he is entirely satisfied with none of them: he is preoccupied with the task of picking and choosing, and of making a style for himself. And perhaps it is precisely this dissatisfaction of Milton's that is of first importance in our consideration of the significance of these influences.'

Daiches (*Milton*, 1957, 32–4) remarks that 'It is typical of Milton that he should proclaim his resolution to devote himself to English rather than Latin poetry in a public oration to his fellow-students. The resolution itself was not so obvious as it may seem to us,' since Latin was still the international language and modern Latin verse was important. Milton seems to feel 'that he could express his "naked thoughts" more fully and immediately' in his native language than in 'a foreign tongue, however well mastered.' 'There is clearly more here than a careerist resolve to be an English rather than a Latin poet: deep emotional factors are involved. Those who accuse Milton of forcing English into a Latin mould should at least realize that he expressed the sense of the *nativeness* of his native English more forcefully than any English poet has ever done.' The 'new fangled toys' that Milton dismisses may be the Metaphysical style or the verbal ingenuities of some Cambridge students. It is large themes that attract him, and, when he refers to the *Odyssey* (lines 48–52), 'The verse sings out in quiet eloquence...; Milton's imagination is now really involved. He is thinking in terms of cosmic imagery involving the whole created universe, and the origin of things; but he wants not only to impress but also to move to tears....It seems that he wants to be Homer and Lucretius and Ovid all in one. So far, it is worth noting, he is content to express his poetic ambitions in images that are at least outwardly wholly classical and pagan.'

III. NOTES

1–58 *Hail native Language...resign my Roome.* The announced innovation of adding English verses to the Latin oration (see 1 above) gives occasion for this address to the English language. This in turn carries Milton far from the present scene, to which he recalls himself at 58.

1 *by sinews weak*: i.e. the tongue was not yet strengthened by exercise.

5 *dum silence.* Dunster noted the phrase in Sylvester, *D.W.W.* 1. 1. 560 (Grosart, 1, 24). Todd cited 'the mute Silence' (*IlPen* 55).

8 *latter task*: perhaps 'later,' i.e. present (Hughes, 1937; cf. *OED* 2), as contrasted with the earliest, i.e. his first essays in speech (1–6); but probably the phrase refers to the English verses as contrasted with the former task, the Latin speech, the meaning supported by 11–14.

10 *little Grace can do thee*: can reflect little credit upon thee (*OED* 1 d).

12 *thither packt the worst*: have put the inferior language, or perhaps the most unskilful expressions, in the first part, the Latin speech. Milton either contrasts Latin unfavourably with English, or his skill in Latin unfavourably with his skill in English.

13 *happen as I did forecast*: turn out as I planned (*OED*: forecast 1).

14 *daintiest dishes...last*: an adaptation of the traditional phrase about keeping the good wine till the end of the feast (John 2. 10). [To quote E.W. in advance of his volume, 'The spelling in 1673 is *daintest*, which editors have often taken as a misprint. But Spenser uses the word *daint* in *F.Q.* 1. 10. 2. 7 and 3. Pr. 2. 7; *dayntest* appears in *F.Q.* 2. 12. 42. 7 (1590 only; the 1596 spelling is *dayntiest*). Of *daint* the *OED* says that it "appears to be merely a shortened form [of *dainty*], or perh. a misreading of the old spelling *dainte*, *deynte*, etc."']

16 *small neglect*: i.e. of having given English the second place.

17 *strait*: straightway, immediately (*OED*: straight c. 2); [cf. *L'All* 69]. *Pleasure*: favour (*OED* 5c).

18 *wardrope*: a room for the storing of apparel (*OED* 1); Milton uses a spelling frequent in and before his time (cf. *Lyc* 47 n.). In this and the following lines he adopts the conventional notion Pope was to sum up in 'Expression is the dress of thought' (*Essay on Criticism* 318: *Poems* 1, ed. E. Audra and A. Williams, London and New Haven, 1961).

19–20 *Not those new fangled toys...delight*. Warton, followed by Todd, assumed that Milton is censuring Euphuism, but this is unduly remote for *late fantasticks* if *late* means recent (cf. *PL* 5. 113, 'deeds long past or late'; and *OED*: *a.*¹ 6), as the context seems to demand; [and Euphuism, though it appeared in verse, was identified with prose]. Wright sees a probable reference to the metaphysical 'school' of Donne, whose conceits were admired and imitated by the young courtiers; and suggests that the opening stanzas of Milton's *FInf* 'provide a mild example of the metaphysical conceit' here condemned. But those stanzas are in the fanciful, mythological, 'Elizabethan' vein rather than the metaphysical. [Tillyard, evidently taking *late* as 'former,' asks why *late* when the metaphysical movement was in its first vigour: had a Cambridge group clustered around George Herbert? (*Milton*, 31–2).] Browne, seeking to bring the reference nearer home, had seen an allusion to those in his audience whom Milton had described as marked by a 'quite laughable froth of words, from whom if you take away the medley begged from modern authors...you will find them even more empty than a bean pod' (*Prol* 1, *Works* 12, 121); but there Milton is referring to the style and matter of his fellow students' Latin prolusions, here to the style of recent practitioners (whether courtiers or students) in English verse. [W. J. Harvey (*N&Q* 4, 1957, 523–4) sees Milton opposing Spenserian opulence to bare wit, the kind of thing Carew praised in Donne, and glancing at the cult of 'strong lines' within the context of Cambridge culture.] Perhaps, despite the appearance of particularity, the lines are no more than a general condemnation of conceits [though lines 23–8 might come under such a ban]. The phrasing of 19–20 obviously indicates contempt.

19 *new fangled toys*: idle fancies, odd conceits, appealing in their novelty (*OED*; cf. Spenser, *F.Q.* 1. 4. 25; 'Full of vaine follies, and new fanglenesse'). *triming slight*: ornamental additions of no substance or worth (*OED*: trimming 1 b, 2 a). [The Columbia *flight* is a misprint.]

20 *takes...fantasticks*: captivates, puts a spell upon (cf. *Nat* 98 n.) those who indulge in fanciful ideas; *OED* B. 1 quotes Marston, *Certaine Satyres* 3. 39–40: 'thou art Bedlam mad... / And glori'st to be counted a fantastick.'

21–32 What follows indicates no addiction to a plain style, no prejudice against poetic ornament as such. The poet's first desire is general: for the *richest Robes, and gay'st* (finest: *OED* 4, but here without the usual suggestion of showy) *attire* (21), i.e. the richest utterance adapted to the subject. The principle of decorum is plainly implied in the phrases *deepest Spirits*, persons possessing the most profound and searching minds, and *choicest Wits*, those possessing either the most discriminating (*OED*: choice *a*. 3) or the most exquisite (ibid. 1) minds (*wit* here being a virtual synonym for *spirit* and pertaining, as Wright notes, to the whole mind: *OED* 1 and 2). Cf. Shakespeare, *Caesar* 3. 1. 163: 'The choice and master spirits of this age.'

The poet's second desire is for the best *aray* (26) of the *naked thoughts* (23) which he is eager to utter (24–5) on the present occasion, and again the principle of decorum is implied in the hope that his words may be fitted to his audience, that without *suspect* (i.e. suspicion: *OED*: sb.¹ 1) *or fears* as to their fitness, they may come to this *fair Assembly's ears* (27–8). His third desire is for, in the future, *some graver subject* (30), specifically a heroic theme (33–52), such as will require the highest effort of language (31) in order to *cloath* the *fancy*, i.e. invention (*OED* 5), *in fit sound* (32), appropriate language—again the principle of decorum. In all these references the emphasis falls on the solid worth of appropriate adornment, as, e.g., in the use of the word *coffers* (31), whose primary meaning is a chest in which treasure is stored (*OED* 1). [A. Oras ('Notes,' 20) observes that the earliest example in *OED* (8b) of this figurative use of *clothe* is the much less elaborate 'in sighs thus clad' of *PR* 2. 65.]

29–52 [D. C. Allen (*Vision*, 13–16) quotes, as similar in idea, passages from the Hermetic *Poimander*, *IlPen* 161–6, and Milton's *Prol* 3 (*Works* 12, 169–71). Cf. J. Carey, *RES* 15 (1964), 184 n.]

33–52 *Such where...sweet captivitie.* In his ambition to attempt ultimately the epic form, the highest in the hierarchy of genres, Milton conforms to the traditional pattern of the Renaissance poet. We need not question the reality of his ambition; cf. the picture of the heroic poet in *El* 6. 55 f. But we may question Warton's notion that Milton is here 'anticipating the subject of the Paradise Lost, if we substitute christian for pagan ideas'; actually, the successive subjects and regions mentioned are those dealt with in the classical epic. For the idea of the poet *transported* in mind and viewing the various regions, cf. *El* 5. 15–20, although there they include the nether world, of which Milton here stops short.

33-9 *the deep transported mind...Kingly Sire.* Dunster thought these and following lines owed part of their inspiration to Sylvester, *Urania* 14 (Grosart, 2, 3): 'I am Urania (then a-loud said she) / Who humane-kind above the Poles transport, / Teaching their hands to touch, and eyes to see / All th' enter-course of the Celestiall Court'; Dunster admitted Milton's 'heathenising' the subject 'with some fine classical touches.' Browne noted that *deep* is used for high 'as Latin *altus* has both meanings.' Milton refers first to Olympus or Heaven, the seat of the gods, the highest region represented in the epic, as in Homer.

34 *wheeling poles*: the revolving heavens or skies. *Polus* was used in Latin poetry of the sky or vault of heaven. [Svendsen (*Science*, 62–3) defines as 'the imaginary axle of the universe which was thought to coincide with the Pole or North star,' and cites *gemini poli* (*Patrem* 34).] Perhaps Milton remembered Horace's use of the word in a passage which refers to the home of the gods: *nec quicquam tibi prodest | aërias temptasse domos animoque rotundum | percurrisse polum morituro* (*C.* 1. 28. 4–6).

35-6 *each blissful Deitie*: *blissful* adds to happy (*OED* 1) the idea of blessed, sacred (ibid. 3).

36 *thunderous.* Jove, wielder of the thunderbolt, is called by Ovid (e.g. *M.* 1. 170) *Tonans*, the Thunderer [also in Milton, *QNov* 204. Cf. above, *Ps* 136. 29 n.].

37-9 Osgood (*C.M.* 11) refers the singing and playing of Apollo before the gods to Homer, *Il.* 1. 603 f. It is also depicted on the shield of Heracles: 'And there was the holy company of the deathless gods: and in the midst the son of Zeus and Leto played sweetly on a golden lyre' (Hesiod, *Shield of Heracles* 201–3, L.C.L.).

37 *unshorn*: a stock epithet for Apollo, e.g.: Homer, *Il.* 20. 39; *Homeric Hymns* 3. 134; Pindar, *Pyth.* 3. 14, *Isth.* 1. 7; Horace, *C.* 1. 21. 2, *Epod.* 15. 9; Ovid, *M.* 12. 585.

38 *Hebe*: Zeus's daughter and cup-bearer; see below, *L'All* 29 n. Osgood notes that Hebe is not present in the scene on Olympus (*Il.* 1. 584 f.) to which he traces Milton's lines, her place being taken by Hephaestus, the focus of comedy unsuitable for Milton's purpose.

Immortal Nectar. Hughes (1937) explains the epithet, applied to the drink of the gods, as 'immortality-conferring,' and cites 'immortal streams' (*Sonn* 14. 14) and 'Nectar' (*PL* 5. 633), the drink of angels, who 'Quaff immortalitie and joy' (ibid. 638). This meaning (if the interpretation is correct) seems to be peculiar to Milton; but *immortal* was used in his day in the vaguer sense of divine, pertaining to immortal beings (*OED* 1 b; cf. *SolMus* 13: 'Touch their immortal Harps of golden wires'), and enduring, as in 'that immortall garland' (*Areop*, *Works* 4, 311; *OED* 2).

40–6 *Then...in her cradle was.* In his descent to earth and the deeds of heroes, the poet thinks of himself as *passing through* the heavens, and glances at the cosmological elements and implications that might enter the traditionally encyclopaedic epic and loosely related forms. Beyond the strictly epic form were other poetic treatments of cosmology, such as those of Lucretius, Ovid (*M.* 1), [Tasso's *Mondo Creato*], and Milton's early favourite, Sylvester's translation of Du Bartas. [Svendsen (*Science*, 46) quotes the similar but fuller catalogue in Milton's *Prol* 3 (*Works* 12, 169–71).]

40 *Spheres of watchful fire.* [This phrase has been interpreted in different ways; Woodhouse's note is given as (1).] (1) The spheres of the Ptolemaic system containing the heavenly bodies (stars, planets, sun, and moon); this was the aethereal region or region of fire, which entered into the composition of these bodies. Cf. *Nat* 21: 'And all the spangled host keep watch in squadrons bright.' The actual phrase *watchful fire* is approximated in the Latin poets: *vigilemque sacraverat ignem, | excubias divum aeternas* (Virgil, *A.* 4. 200–1); and *vigil flamma* (Ovid, *Tr.* 4. 5. 4; cf. *A.A.* 3. 463) (Warton). Possibly *watchful* means no more than wakeful, unsleeping (*OED* 1), as *vigil* does in the lines quoted above. [Cf. 'those faire Brands, | Which blaze in Heavens high Vault, Nights watchfull eyes' (*Hymne of the Passion* 5–6, Drummond, 2, 14).] But Hughes suggests that Milton remembered the office of the sun, moon, and five planets which, in Plato, 'came into existence for the determining and preserving of the numbers of Time' (*Timaeus* 38 c). [(2) Svendsen (*Science* 87) explains the phrase as a reference to the theoretical layer of fire directly under the sphere of the moon (Donne's 'Element of fire'), described here as *watchful* in protecting the supralunar vault from contamination by a 'corruptible,' an exhalation drawn or driven upward. This layer or sphere is shown, e.g. in the 'Figure of the Heavens and Elements' which formed the frontispiece in Robert Fage's *Description of the Whole World* (1658) and is reproduced in Svendsen, 49.]

41 *mistie Regions of wide air next under*: i.e. the region of air next under that of fire (see 40 n.). Ovid tells how the 'air hung over all, which is as much heavier than fire ⟨the substance of the first region⟩ as the weight of water ⟨the substance of the third region⟩ is lighter than the weight of earth ⟨the substance of the fourth⟩'; and how in the region of air the creator bade 'the mists and clouds to

take their place, and thunder, that should shake the hearts of men, and winds.
. . .' (*M.* 1. 52–6, L.C.L.). Warton quoted Du Bartas' account of how the soul,
though imprisoned in the body, often springs aloft into the airy regions, and
'learns to knowe / Th' Originals of Winde, and Hail, and Snowe, / Of Lightning,
Thunder, Blazing-Stars and storms' (Sylvester, *D.W.W.* 1. 6. 850–2, Grosart,
1, 79). The word *loft* originally signified the sky, air, or upper region (*OED* 1):
lofts of piled Thunder presumably means (as Browne suggests) thunderbolts piled,
amid the clouds, in the upper air (*OED*: thunder 1). [Cf. *El* 5. 136. On all these
matters see Svendsen, *Science*, and Heninger, *Meteorology*.]

43–4 *May tell. . .all his waves.* The poet now reaches the third region, that of
water, ruled by Neptune (cf. *Comus* 18 and n.). For *green-ey'd* Warton cited
Virgil on Proteus: *ardentis oculos intorsit lumine glauco* (*G.* 4. 451).

45–6 *Then sing. . .in her cradle was*: tell of the creation of the world as it was
told by such writers as those mentioned above in 40–6 n., and was to be by
Milton himself. Editors suggest that *Beldam* here means grandmother: *OED* 1;
Browne, Hughes (1937), Wright, et al. Possibly the phrase suggested itself as an
adaptation of the common 'Dame Nature.' In any case the word *Beldam* may
contain two added suggestions: a still-living ancestress more remote than grandmother (*OED* 1b), which would extend the remoteness of the time when she
herself *in her cradle was*; and, secondly, the common use of beldame for a nurse
(*OED* 2; cf. Spenser, *F.Q.* 3. 2. 43), with the idea here of *Nature* as the nourisher
and protector of life. Rolfe cites 'old beldame earth' (Shakespeare, *1 H. IV*
3. 1. 32). In *secret things* Milton may remember Spenser's 'sawst the secrets of
the world unmade' (*F.Q.* 1. 5. 22) [and Virgil, *G.* 2. 490 f.: *Felix, qui potuit
rerum cognoscere causas....*].

47–52 *And last of Kings. . .sweet captivitie.* The poet comes at last to the chief
subject of epic, illustrating it from the song of the minstrel Demodocus, who
sang of the fall of Troy when Odysseus was entertained at the court of Alcinous,
king of the Phaeacians; the song, while it pleased the others, moved Odysseus to
tears (*Od.* 8. 487–543). In both effects it showed the power of *melodious harmonie* over the *soul*. With the last line Todd compared 'The willing Chaines of
my Captivitie' (Sylvester, *Bethulians Rescue* 5. 66, Grosart, 2, 196). [Warton
cited Tasso, *G.L.* 6. 84: *giogo di servitù dolce e leggiero*.]

53–8 *But fie. . .my Roome.* Milton now returns to his task as 'Father,' the
introduction of his 'Sons'; for this is what is expected of him, and not the digression into which his *wandring Muse* has led him (53–4). The Muse's *bent*,

aim (*OED*: *sb.*² 7) must now be *To keep in compass*, within the limits (*OED*: *sb.*¹ 9), of her *Predicament*, present situation—probably without the somewhat later suggestion of an unpleasant or hazardous situation (*OED* 3), but with a play on the technical meaning of the word (ibid. 1; 'Direction' below). Thus Milton may fulfil his office and retire (57–8). [With 53 cf. Horace, *C.* 3. 3. 70–2: *quo, Musa, tendis? desine pervicax | referre sermones deorum....*]

⟨Direction⟩ *Then Ens...explains.* In parody of the Aristotelian logic Milton as 'Father' represents *Ens* or absolute Being, while his 'Sons' are the ten 'Categories': 'Substance' (particular entity) and its nine 'Accidents,' Quantity, Quality, Relation, Place, Time, Position, Possession, Action, and Passion. In scholastic logic, still taught at Cambridge in Milton's day (and the object of his attack in *Prol* 3), the 'accidents' were called 'predicaments': i.e. they were the classes into which fell whatever could be 'predicated' of any particular entity, and this supplied the general rules, what Milton calls the *Canons* (*OED*: canon¹ 2 b) of such predication.

59–90 *Good luck befriend thee...Gordian knot. Ens* thus addresses Substance. Warton remarked that this is the only instance in which 'the system of the Fairies was ever introduced to illustrate the doctrine of Aristotle's ten categories,' and added, with a pleasant touch of malice, that 'they both were in fashion, and both exploded, at the same time.' The bestowal of gifts on a child at its birth, and the prophesying of its future fortunes, are common features of fairytales. (With the fairies' *tripping to the Room* Todd compared Shakespeare, *1 H. IV* 1. 1. 87, 'some night-tripping fairy'; but there the purpose is theft of the child.) Here the gift of invisibility is bestowed (65–6), since Substance is a mere abstraction and cannot be seen.

69–72 The *Sybil* (Lat. *Sibylla*) is here a hag or witch with prophetic powers, symbolized by a *Prospective Glass*, a crystal in which future events could be seen (*OED* 1); the phrase was already beginning to be used of the telescope (ibid. 2: earliest example 1626), a fact which may have influenced the description *long and dark*. [Cf. Browne, *Brit. Past.* 2. 1. 859–60: '...a glass prospective good and true, | By which things most remote are full in view.']

73–90 The warning of the *Sybil* plays on the popular meaning of *Accident* and its technical meaning in logic (see note on Direction above), and also (as Warton noted) on the word *subject*: the Substance is the *subjectum* of the Accidents. The prophetic description of the relation of Substance to its Accidents continues (75–88) and assumes increasingly the form of a paradox or enigma which is proposed to the audience in the final lines (89–90). Though the Accidents all pertain to Substance, which is thus superior to them, the Substance underlies the Accidents; the Substance is still Substance with or without Accidents, while Accidents have no existence without Substance. 'But what is most characteristic of substance appears to be this: that, although it remains, notwithstanding, numerically one and the same, it is capable of being the recipient of contrary qualifications' (Aristotle, *Categories* 5. 4a, *Organon* 1, L.C.L., p. 33).

90 [The proverbial phrase, 'cut the Gordian knot,' refers to the summary solution or evasion of a difficult problem, from Alexander the Great's cutting with his sword the inextricable knot on the chariot of the Phrygian king Gordius. Here the reference is rather to the difficulty.]

⟨Direction⟩ *Relation* (see above, note on previous Direction) *was call'd by his Name*, i.e. by the surname of the person representing *Relation*. W. G. Clark (reported by Masson) found from the Admission Book of Christ's College that George and Nizell Rivers, sons of Sir John Rivers, were admitted on 10 May 1628. It is evidently to one of these two freshmen that the following lines refer.

91–100 *Rivers arise...Towred Thame.* Milton offers a parody of the poetic catalogues of rivers found in Spenser and Drayton. Warton noted the marriage of the Thames and the Medway, attended by a host of other rivers, in *F.Q.* 4. 11, and added: 'I rather think he consulted Drayton's *Polyolbion*.' [D. Daiches (*More Literary Essays*, 103), apropos of Milton's transition from the classical imagery of his Latin verse to the English scene, finds here—in accordance with the praise of his native language—'something more than a Draytonian exercise in patriotic topography...; it suggests, however faintly, a deliberate desire to pit the English landscape against the classical.' Geographical and literary details about the rivers are supplied by A. H. Gilbert, *A Geographical Dictionary of Milton* (New Haven, 1919).]

91–2 *the Son, | Of utmost Tweed.* The Tweed marked the boundary between England and Scotland (cf. *F.Q.* 4. 11. 36); hence *utmost*. *Oose*: no doubt the Ouse, a principal river of the Eastern Midlands (*F.Q.* 4. 11. 34; *Poly.* 22. 1 f.), not 'The Ouze, whom men doe Isis rightly name' (*F.Q.* 4. 11. 24). *gulphie Dun*: the Don in Yorkshire. *OED* 1 defines *gulphie* as full of eddies. Drayton speaks of 'my lively Don' and 'her lusty course' (*Poly.* 28. 47–8).

93–4 The *thirty Armes* of *Trent* are [the 'thirty sundry streames' of *F.Q.* 4. 11. 35], 'those thirtie Floods, that wayt the Trent upon' (*Poly.* 26. 171), from which it is conjectured the river takes its name (*Poly.* 26. 187–8, 12. 553–4). Among various examples of the indenting of land by water Warton, Dunster, and Todd noted several in Sylvester, e.g.: 'There, silver Torrents rush; / Indenting Meads' (*Little Bartas* 480–1, Grosart, 2, 89). [*like some earth-born Giant spreads* / ...*Meads*. Cf. Virgil's picture of Tityos, *Terrae omniparentis alumnum,* / ...*per tota novem cui iugera corpus* / *porrigitur* (*A.* 6. 595–7).]

95 Drayton tells how the *Mole*, for love of the Thames, digs for herself a channel underground to escape parental restraint and join him (*Poly.* 17. 49–64; [cf. *F.Q.* 4. 11. 32]). The word *sullen* (flowing sluggishly: *OED* 5 and *Poly.* 28. 91) suggests that Milton is not thinking of Drayton's fiction but simply of the underground stream (he has a later reference in *Animad, Works* 3, 149).

96 The *Maidens death* of which the *Severn* was *guilty* was Sabrina's. The story —see below, *Comus* 823–31 n.— was told, e.g. by Spenser (*F.Q.* 2. 10. 17–19; cf. 4. 11. 30) and Drayton (*Poly.* 6. 130–78), but with no suggestion of guilt in the river, which adopts her and her name.

97 *Rockie* would seem to identify the *Avon* intended, by its gorge at Bristol. Spenser (*F.Q.* 4. 11. 31) makes the Avon 'Proud of his Adamants' (which here apparently means diamonds and is used figuratively, but might easily be confused with its more general meaning of very hard rock). *Sedgie Lee.* Spenser speaks of 'The wanton Lee, that oft doth loose his way' (*F.Q.* 4. 11. 29), and Drayton of the Lee's 'winding course' (*Poly.* 16. 264) as it flows to join the Thames, but they offer no suggestion for *Sedgie* (overgrown with sedge).

98 *Coaly* is obvious for the Tyne. Drayton makes the river boast of the coal for which Newcastle is no less famous than India is for her mines (*Poly.* 29. 120–5). Cf. Spenser, *F.Q.* 4. 11. 36. *antient hollowed Dee.* [Most editors read *hallowed* without comment; H. Darbishire notes it as an emendation of 1720.] Spenser speaks of the Dee 'which Britons long ygone / Did call divine, that doth by Chester tend' (*F.Q.* 4. 11. 39). [Drayton uses the phrase 'the hallowed Dee' in *Poly.* 10. 215. Tillyard (*M. Set.*, 174) explains that 'The Dee is "hallowed"' because frequented by the Druids'; the accepted explanation—the river's prophetic power—is given below, *Lyc* 55 n.]

99 *Humber loud* is presumably the 'storming Humber' of *F.Q.* 4. 11. 30. The name was supposedly derived from the Scythian invader of Britain who was drowned in the river (*Poly.* 8. 45–6, 28. 465–71). [Spenser refers to the 'Scythian king' in *F.Q.* 4. 11. 37–8; cf. 2. 10. 16. Milton mentioned the story in *HistBr* (*Works* 10, 15).]

100 Warton noted that the smoothness of the *Medway* (unmentioned by Spenser or Drayton) is suggested by 'that wont so still to slide' (L. Bryskett,

Mourning Muse of Thestylis 157: in Spenser, *Poetical Works*, ed. J. C. Smith and E. de Selincourt, Oxford, 1912, 553). Warton also saw in *Royal Towred Thame* an allusion to Windsor. [Milton applied *Towred* to cities in *L'All* 117 and *Turrigerum* to London in *El* 1. 74. Tillyard (*M. Set.*, 174) remarks that 'the Thames is called royal-towered not only to recall Windsor and Hampton but also, probably, to connect the royal houses of Tudor and Stuart with the early British Kings.' E. W. cites Spenser, *F.Q.* 4. 11. 27, and perhaps Drayton, *Poly.* 15. 295–6 and 313–18.]

The Passion

꽃

I. DATE AND CIRCUMSTANCES [D.B.]

Hanford ('Youth', 1925, 127) remarks that Milton apparently proposed
to himself 'a series of lofty religious poems celebrating the successive
events in the life of Christ and the festivals of the Christian calendar.'
The *Nativity* 'was triumphantly completed,' and *The Passion* was
'earnestly begun' at the following Easter (1630). In that year Good
Friday fell on March 26. The year is not certainly indicated by the allusion to the *Nativity* in lines 1–4, but 1630 has been accepted with good
reason [Parker, 71, 753, n. 27]. If we did not have this evidence of succession, the quality of the poem would have led us to place it some time
earlier than Milton's first masterpiece. *The Passion* is indeed unique in the
Miltonic canon in being unfinished and in being an avowed failure. The
appended note said: 'This Subject the Author finding to be above the
yeers he had, when he wrote it, and nothing satisfi'd with what was
begun, left it unfinisht.'

Reasons for critical dissatisfaction appear in II below. If we ask why
Milton chose to print a fragment of which he himself had a poor opinion,
some speculative answers may be cited. Sirluck suggests that he did so
'because from the outset he had something of a conscience about his
decision not to take orders, and was unwilling to dispense with any bit
of the meager evidence that he had been God's servant in another guise'
(*JEGP* 60, 1961, 757–8). Martz (in Summers, *Lyric Milton*, 1965, 21)
thinks that 'the inclusion of the fragment has a clear function: to stress
the immaturity of these opening pieces, to suggest the ambitious young
man outreaching his powers, and achieving poetical success only when
he can subject his muse to some deliberate limitation'—as he was to do
in *On Time* and other poems. In *The Poet and his Faith* (1965, 93)

151

Woodhouse's answer is: 'Surely because it had a profound personal significance for him: one might almost call the printing an act of penance. All the rest of his verse till he leaves Cambridge is secular in subject'; but in an Italian sonnet (3), 'where he owns the absolute sway of love, ...the young poet unexpectedly adds: "O that this hard and sterile breast might be / To him who plants from Heaven a soil as free." ' Patrides (*Milton*, 145) asks if Milton's publishing an unsuccessful fragment was 'his way of warning the world not to expect devotional poetry from him? And was his lack of ardour for the Passion just personal idiosyncrasy or Protestant?...The comprehensive frame of reference of the *Nativity Ode*, the emphasis on obedience in *Upon the Circumcision*, the theme of temptation enunciated in *Comus*, all seem inevitably to propel Milton toward the one event in the life of Jesus which appealed to him, I mean the temptation in the wilderness set forth in *Paradise Regained*.' J. G. Demaray (*Masque Tradition*, 40–2) offers the rather strained suggestion that the poem, as a companion to the *Nativity*, was to depict 'Christ as the featured figure in a masque,' but that, since the pagan masques afforded no models, Milton fell into digression and frustration.

II. CRITICISM [D.B.]

Saintsbury (*Cambridge Hist. Eng. Lit.*, 7, 1911, 126): The *Nativity* showed the poet, the *Passion*, or rather the appended note, 'shows us the critic whom...every great poet must contain.' 'There have not been many poets who would have been "nothing satisfied" with such lines as "He sov'ran Priest stooping his regall head...His starry front low-rooft beneath the skies"; or, best of all, "See see the Chariot, and those rushing wheels, / That whirl'd the Prophet up at Chebar flood." But Milton felt this dissatisfaction: and Milton was right.' He had 'drifted into mere respectable Fletcherian *pastiche* with some better touches. And he knew this....There could be no doubt about him after the acquisition and demonstration of this double knowledge. The recognition of this is the most important thing in the study of the first stage of Milton's poetical career.'

The Passion

Hanford ('Youth,' 1925, 127): Milton's 'failure to complete this piece illustrates the breakdown of his higher inspiration when the theme found no responsive echo in his own experience. The crucifixion, neither now nor later, had the slightest hold on his emotions. That Milton did not fully recognize the conditions of the successful exercise of his poetic faculty is suggested by the character of the note appended to the *Passion*, and also, perhaps, by the fact that he appears still to have cherished the plan of a series of poems on the events [in the life of Christ] as late as the Horton period, when he wrote the complete but uninspired piece *On the Circumcision.*'

Tillyard (*Milton*, 1930, 44): 'In *The Passion* Milton attempts to recapture, and in accordance with the more tragic theme to deepen, the mood that prompted the *Nativity Ode*. The failure is complete. It is as full of conceits as the earlier poem: but these call a dreadful attention to themselves; puerility has supplanted youthfulness. Milton seems to have forsaken the Italians and in his poverty of invention to have resorted to the common stock of English seventeenth-century extravagance.' Later (*M. Set.*, 1938, 177–8), outlining the growth of Milton's epic ambitions, Tillyard noted that in the *Passion* 'he had the strict classical epic in his mind, though not a classical subject.... Christ is his theme, but though committed to lyric at the moment, he must needs mention Christ as an epic hero, while, partly to make it clear that he has not forgotten classical precedent, he hints that Christ is another Heracles' (lines 13–14). 'In the fourth stanza Milton speaks of his own lyric intentions in dealing with the Passion, but betrays his present interest in the epic by recalling how others have treated the life of Christ more largely,' and he refers to Vida's neoclassical *Christiad*.

Woodhouse ('Notes,' 1943–4, 80–1) goes along with Hanford in taking the *Passion* as an effort, following close upon the *Nativity*, toward the writing of 'further specifically Christian poems, a suggestion greatly strengthened by the probability that Milton had been reading in preparation for such an effort the *Christiad*, Vida's epic on the life and death of Christ [see below, notes on 13–14 and 24–8], and by the religious verse which three years later sprang from the renewed self-dedication of *How soon hath Time*.' Quoting Milton's note and the last stanza of the poem, Woodhouse proceeds: 'How beautiful the lines are —and how exquisitely inappropriate! It is not the touch of "wit" in the concluding couplet, that is alone at fault (there is as much wit in the *Nativity Ode*), but something more pervasive. It is the failure of the subject to take possession of Milton's imagination and at once to foster and express a religious and aesthetic experience, capable of subordinating everything to itself,' as in the *Nativity*. 'In *The Passion* it is absent, and Milton's imagination lies open to every wayward fancy. One of them comes straight from the rejected world of the *Elegies*. Unawares he finds himself once more in "The gentle neighbourhood of grove and spring." Where Echo is, Genius and the nymphs with flower-inwoven tresses, and all the gods of earth and heaven, may easily follow. Milton pauses just in time. The religious experience of the *Nativity Ode* has faded and is not now renewable, by this subject at least. And so the thoughts and images appropriate to Milton's years begin to reassert their sway, as in his note he partly divines.'

Brooks and Hardy (1951: 107–11): The poet's problem, more difficult than that of the *Nativity*, is 'to find appropriate forms for the presentation in terms of the senses of what is now a *spiritual* reality.' 'If God is now no longer incarnate in nature, the poet can put Him back into nature only by resorting to the "pathetic fallacy"....' He starts images and ideas (the comparison of Christ to a star, 18; 'my Phoebus,' 23) which are not developed or are overdeveloped. Stanza 5, the appeal to night, 'is stultifying,' and the effort toward an 'ecstatick fit' (41) is factitious. Stanza 7 brings 'complete collapse'; 'The overingenious conceit tries to accomplish too much, and ends in accomplishing nothing.' The poet's painful self-consciousness explains the failure of the whole. He 'is obviously the young poet struggling with the problems of form...presented by a religious subject,' problems which he could resolve in *Lycidas*. Here his conceits fail not so much because of any 'intrinsic lameness' but because they are 'decorative' rather than 'structural.'

L. L. Martz (*The Poetry of Meditation*, 1954, 167–8), asking why, after the superb *Nativity*, Milton failed with the *Passion*, quotes lines 27–8 and makes the initial suggestion that he failed because he 'tried to write a love-song.' But the lute and the viol 'are instruments for Herbert and Crashaw,' and 'Milton cannot handle them. He follows the traditional themes and methods: he calls for tears, he transports himself to the scene, he tries to visualize it: the devices of Catholic meditation struggle to find a home in Spenserian poetic.' Then Milton stops, 'with the worst line he ever wrote.' Failure may have had a deeper reason than age, 'perhaps the explanation provided by Haller, when he says that the Puritan preachers "made the atonement signify the appointment of the elect soul to join with Christ in the war against the eternal enemy. ...Thus the symbolism of the nativity and the passion came to mean little to the Puritan saints, and Christmas and Easter faded from their calendar...." ' [However true these remarks are of Puritans in general, their logic, applied to Milton, should make the *Nativity* a failure too; we may remember also that the Milton of 1629–30 still expected, so far as we know, to be a clergyman in the Church of England, and that he was not enough of a Puritan to refrain from writing love poems in Italian.]

N. Frye (*Milton's Lycidas*, ed. C. A. Patrides, New York, 1961, 208): 'Of all Milton's poems, the one obvious failure is...*The Passion*, and if we look at the imagery...we can see why. It is the only poem of Milton's in which he is preoccupied with himself in the process of writing it. "My muse," "my song," "my Harp," "my roving verse," "my Phoebus," and so on for eight stanzas until Milton abandons the poem in disgust. It is not a coincidence that Milton's one self-conscious poem should be the one that never gets off the ground.'

W. R. Parker (*Milton*, 1968, 71–2) also emphasizes Milton's fatal self-consciousness. His verses 'seemed laboured, and artificial, and empty of genuine feeling. His delight in the implications and details of the Christmas story had been real, but his professed grief at thoughts of the Crucifixion turned out to be literary. *He was writing a poem about himself writing a poem*; in every stanza except the third he had described himself in the process of composition. It was like making sorrowful faces at a mirror.'

155

III. NOTES

1–4 *Ere-while of Musick…divide to sing.* The reference is to the *Nativity*, which—with Psalms 114 and 136—preceded this piece in *Poems* (1645). The description emphasizes the centrality of musical imagery in *Nat.*

1 *Ere-while*: formerly.

Ethereal: heavenly, angelic. Raphael is called 'heavenly Guest, Ethereal Messenger' (*PL* 8. 646). In their literal senses Lat. *aether, aetherius* (or *aethereus*) referred to the upper and purer air as opposed to the lower (*aer, aerius, aereus*); but already in poetry *aether* (Virgil, *A.* 1. 379, 12. 140) and *aetherius* (Ovid, *M.* 15. 859) referred to heaven. In Milton the distinction between *ethereal* and *aerial* is maintained whether *aerial* is used of the region of air, *ethereal* of the region of fire (see above, *Vac* 40 n.), or *aerial* of everything below heaven and *ethereal* of everything therein (see below, *Comus* 1–4 n.).

mirth: rejoicing (*OED* 2; cf. Spenser, *F.Q.* 1. 12. 40: 'Great joy was made that day of young and old, / … That their exceeding merth may not be told'). *OED* 1 notes that *mirth* was often used of religious joy.

4 *did divide to sing.* There is a play on the verb *divide*. The primary meaning appears to be 'share' (*OED* 8b), as Milton clearly proposes to share with the angels in hymning the infant God (*Nat* 27); but *divide* has in music a technical meaning, to perform with divisions, descant (*OED* 11), i.e. to provide a variation on, or accompaniment to, a theme, which was originally conceived as the dividing of each of a succession of long notes with short ones (*OED*: division 7). Examples of *divide* in this sense occur in Spenser (*F.Q.* 1. 5. 17, 3. 1. 40) and of *division* in Shakespeare (*Romeo* 3. 5. 29–30), also with a play on two meanings of *divide*: 'Some say the lark makes sweet division; / This doth not so, for she divideth us'; cf. *1 H. IV* 3. 1. 210.

6 *In Wintry solstice like the shortn'd light*: like the shortened daylight at the winter solstice.

7 *long out-living night.* Wright explains as 'lasting inordinately' and compares 'livelong' (*Shak* 8); but the literal meaning seems quite satisfactory: night, which lasts far longer than day at the winter solstice.

10 *sease*: seize.

13–14 *Most perfect Heroe…human wight. Heros* is the term repeatedly used of Christ in Vida's *Christiad* (see below, 24–8 n.). Todd compared 'to make the captain of their salvation perfect through sufferings' (Heb. 2. 10). Editors see in the hero who assumes the *plight* (undertaking: *OED*: *sb.*[1] 3) | *Of labours huge and hard* an allusion to Hercules, to whom Milton had likewise alluded obliquely in *Nat* 227–8. See the note on those lines.

15–16 Though Milton is speaking here of the Incarnation, it is in anticipation of Christ's sacrifice and mediation: *sov'ran Priest* refers at once to Christ's office as Priest and as King (cf. *DocCh* 1. 15). *sov'ran.* See *Nat* 60 n.

16 *That dropt...his fair eyes*: recalling the anointing of the High Priest as the 'type' of Christ. Cf. 'Then shalt thou take the anointing oil, and pour it upon his head, and anoint him' (Exod. 29. 7); 'And the priest, whom he shall anoint, ...shall make the atonement....' (Lev. 16. 32); and more immediately the anointing of Christ himself just before the last Passover: 'There came unto him a woman having an alabaster box of very precious ointment, and poured it on his head....' (Matt. 26. 7). [Cf. also Ps. 45. 7, Heb. 1. 9.]

17 *fleshly Tabernacle*: a phrase repeated in *PR* 4. 599. Originally designating a tent or temporary dwelling (*OED* 1), *tabernacle* took on a religious association from its place in the history of Israel. Scriptural also is its figurative use as a synonym for the body, the temporary dwelling-place of the soul (2 Cor. 5. 1–4, 2 Pet. 1. 13–14). [Cf. Heb. 9. 11–12: 'But Christ being come an high priest of good things to come, by a greater and more perfect tabernacle, not made with hands, that is to say, not of this building; Neither by the blood of goats and calves, but by his own blood he entered in once into the holy place, having obtained eternal redemption for us.']

18 *His starry front...the skies.* Milton may be thinking of the *front* (forehead: *OED* 1) of the Son as surmounted by a 'crown of twelve stars' like that of the symbolic woman of Rev. 12. 1.

19 *O what a mask...disguise.* The literal sense is that God is here masked and disguised in human form. The image is taken from the early form of the entertainment that developed into the masque, namely the arrival at banquet or ball of a company concealing their identity under masks, as in Shakespeare, *Romeo* 1. 5. George Cavendish (*Life and Death of Cardinal Wolsey*, Temple Classics, 32 f.; ed. R. S. Sylvester, E.E.T.S., 1959, 25) described the arrival at the Cardinal's of Henry VIII and a group of courtiers masked and dressed as shepherds. Bacon speaks of 'masks (which they then called disguises)' (*Henry VII, Works* 6, 244). Cf. *Masque of Augures* (*Ben Jonson* 7, 631): 'Disguise was the old English word for a Masque, sir, before you were an implement belonging to the Revels.' Todd suggests that Milton was thinking of 'diverse plots did frame, to maske in strange disguise' (Spenser, *F.Q.* 3. 3. 51); but the idea of a masque or play is carried through the opening stanzas (cf. 2, 'the stage of Ayr and Earth'; 22, 'These latest scenes').

21 *Then lies...by his Brethrens side.* Hughes quotes Heb. 2. 16–17: 'For verily he took not on him the nature of angels; but he took on him the seed of Abraham. Wherefore in all things it behoved him to be made like unto his brethren, that he might be a merciful and faithful high priest in things pertaining to God, to make reconciliation for the sins of the people.'

22 *latest*: 1645, *latter*. This is the only significant textual change in 1673.

23 *To this Horizon...bound.* The name of Phoebus (Apollo), the Olympian god of the sun, was early used in poetry for the sun itself. This is primary in Milton's image (Phoebus moving toward the horizon), but the meaning demands the identification of Phoebus with poetry or poetic inspiration; *OED* misses this use of Phoebus and gives its earliest example from 1776. The play in the word *bound* is obvious: the course of *my Phoebus* is directed to *this Horizon* (*OED*: bound, *ppl. a.*[1] 2) and confined to it (ibid. *ppl. a.*[2] 1; and 22 above, *confine*, etc.).

24–8 *His Godlike acts...apt for mournful things.* Others have described the earlier scenes of Christ's earthly ministry, including the Temptation in the wilderness (the theme, many years later, of *PR*). Milton had evidently been reading the Neo-Latin *Christiad* (1535) of Marco Girolamo Vida (1485–1566), born in Cremona in Italy; cf. above, 13–14 n. [The *Christiad* and other poems of Vida's are often quoted in *V.C.* 1 in illustration of Milton's Latin verse.] *Trump* prepares for the contrast in *softer strings*, i.e. softer music of stringed instruments: the *Lute, or Viol still*, i.e. quiet, as in 'still small voice' (1 Kings 19. 12); see *IlPen* 127 n.

29–30 *night best Patroness...mantle throw.* Todd cited: 'Night with his mantel, that is derk and rude, / Gan oversprede the hemysperie aboute' (Chaucer, *Merch. T.* 1798–9: *Works*, ed. F. N. Robinson, 2nd ed., Boston, 1957) [and also (as E.W. notes): 'And o're the dark her Silver Mantle threw' (*PL* 4. 609).]

Pole: sky (see above, *Vac* 34 n.). [Apropos of this stanza Grierson remarks that the conceits 'are not those of Donne and Cowley. They are those of Marino and Southwell and Crashaw' (*Cross Currents*, 241).]

31 *flatter'd*: courted (*OED*: *v.*[1] 2), with the suggestion of a deviation from truth common to many uses of the word *flatter*; *fancy* itself in most contexts carried the same suggestion. Milton here recognized the literary attitude that Ruskin was to call the pathetic fallacy.

34-5 *The leaves...a wannish white.* Warton reported a volume of elegies, in the possession of George Steevens, with white printing on black pages. [Dunster (reported by Todd) described Sylvester's *Lachrimae Lachrimarum* (1612) which had a black title page with white letters;] and Todd added citations from Thomas Heywood, W. Browne, and Crashaw which give some support to—though they do not prove—his belief that black pages with white letters were 'the general fashion of the times' for funereal verse. [Carey remarks that Milton may 'have in mind the more common practice of edging the page on which a funeral elegy was printed with a thick band of black, and thus be distinguishing between his page, which should be "all" black, and the usual page, which is only edged.' One of Todd's citations has a further interest in regard to Milton's lines 48-9 below: 'My blubb'ring pen her sable tears lets fall / In characters right hieroglyphical, / And mixing with my tears are ready turning / My late white paper to a weed of mourning' (Browne, *Brit. Past.* 1. 5. 75-8).]

36-40 *See see the Chariot...guiltless blood.* The lines are based on a series of passages in Ezekiel: 'Now it came to pass..., as I was among the captives by the river of Chebar, that the heavens were opened, and I saw visions of God' (1. 1), The first vision was of 'a whirlwind...out of the north, a great cloud, and a fire....Also out of the midst thereof came the likeness of four living creatures ...' (1. 4-5), to which was presently added the appearance of wheels (1. 15 f.). 'And above the firmament that was over their heads was the likeness of a throne. ...' (1. 26). Later the vision of the throne and the wheels is repeated (10. 1 f.), but now the living creatures are recognized as cherubim: 'And the cherubims lifted up their wings, and mounted up from the earth in my sight; when they went out, the wheels also were beside them....This is the living creature that I saw under the God of Israel by the river of Chebar; and I knew that they were the cherubims' (10. 19-20). 'Moreover the spirit lifted me up, and brought me unto the east gate of the Lord's house...' (11. 1). The *transporting Cherub* anticipates the 'Cherub Contemplation,' based on the same vision (*IlPen* 45-54 n.). *Salem*: the ancient name for Jerusalem, signifying peace. The poet is borne by a Cherub (i.e. by contemplation) to Jerusalem as the locale of the Passion, and perhaps also because Jerusalem is the 'seat of sacred poetry' (Hughes, Wright), as Milton later makes specific (*PL* 1. 10-12, 3. 29-31). Jerusalem is here called Salem because of the association with Melchizedek, king of Salem, who met Abram and blessed him (Gen. 14. 18-19) and was regarded as the 'type' of Christ in his office of Priest (cf. Heb. 5. 6-10, 6. 20, 7. 1). Probably, as Warton noted, Milton's attention was directed to Salem and its fate by his reading of George Sandys' account of Jerusalem (*Relation*, 1615, 154–5): 'This Citie, once sacred and glorious,...was founded by Melchisedech...and called Salem...which signifieth Peace....' The city of a later day (A.D. 70) 'was destroyed by the wrath of God, and fury of Titus: wherein eleven hundred thousand by famine, pestilence, the enemies sword, and civill butcheries, most desperatly perished. Onely three towers...(built by Herod, and adjoining to his Pallace) he left unrazed, exceeding the rest in greatnesse and beauty;...But threescore and five years after, Ælius Adrianus inflicting on the rebelling Jewes a wonderfull slaughter, subverted those remainders....'

41–2 *There doth my soul in holy vision sit | In pensive trance, and anguish, and ecstatick fit.* Warton compared 'There held in holy passion' (*IlPen* 41). Dunster and Todd noted somewhat similar phrases in Sylvester: 'extased (as in a holy Transe)' (*Urania* 29, Grosart, 2, 4); 'rapt-up in sacred Transe' (*Urania* 84, Grosart, 2, 7); 'sweetly rapt in sacred Extasie' (*D.W.W.* 2. 4. 2. 1215, Grosart, 1, 237); and the soul's 'sweet Transe' is termed a 'holy Fit' (ibid. 2. 1. 1. 409–12, Grosart, 1, 103).

43 *that sad Sepulchral rock*: the 'sepulchre which was hewn out of a rock' (Mark 15. 46; cf. Matt. 27. 60). [Warton cited Sandys' description of the Holy Sepulchre at Jerusalem, and Carey notes his repeated use of the word 'rocke' (*Relation*, 1615, 166–7).]

46 *the softned Quarry*: the mass of rock from which the sepulchre was hewn (*OED*: *sb.*² 2), which the poet thinks of as being softened by grief (in analogy to the stony heart). [Cf. *Sonn* 3. 13.] *score*: cut (*OED* 1).

46–9 [Tillyard (*Milton*, 44–5) contrasts four lines from Crashaw's *Upon the Death of a Gentleman* (ed. Martin, 167), cited by Todd: 'Eyes are vocall, Teares have Tongues, / And there be words not made made with lungs; / Sententious showers, o let them fall, / Their cadence is Rhetoricall.' 'Crashaw's critical intelligence is all alert and we feel it: Milton's intelligence here seems confined to counting the feet and seeing that the grammar is right.' Cf. the quotation from W. Browne in 34–5 n. above.]

47 *plaining*: lamenting, mourning (sometimes distinguished from complaining: *OED*: *v.* 3 quotes Sidney's *Arcadia*, *Works*, ed. A. Feuillerat, Cambridge, 1, 1912, 181: 'Whereof though he plaine, he doth not complaine: for it is a harme, but no wrong, which he hath received'). *as lively as before*: as vividly as if I had been able to carve it with my hands (cf. 45).

48–9 Though later in date, the conclusion of Eldred Revett's *Elegie* on

Richard Lovelace (d. 1656/7), quoted by Todd, is so apposite that it deserves to be recalled. For the sake of clearer punctuation it is quoted here from *Poems of Richard Lovelace*, ed. C. H. Wilkinson (Oxford, 1930, 229) rather than from Revett's *Poems* (London, 1657, 49):

> Why should some rude hand carve thy sacred stone,
> And there incise a cheap inscription;
> When we can shed the tribute of our tears
> So long, till the relenting marble wears?
> Which shall such order in their cadence keep,
> That they a native Epitaph shall weep;
> Untill each Letter spelt distinctly lyes,
> Cut by the mystick droppings of our eyes.

49 *order'd Characters*: letters (*OED* 4, but originally a sign cut or engraved) so ordered as to spell the required words. [See the excerpt from W. Browne in 34–5 n. above.]

50 *viewles wing*: invisible wing (of the transporting Cherub, 38); cf. *Comus* 92: 'I must be viewles now,' and *OED* 1. [Browne cites 'viewless winds' in Shakespeare, *Meas.* 3. 1. 124.]

51 *Take up a weeping on the Mountains wilde.* Warton cited Jer. 9. 10: 'For the mountains will I take up a weeping....'

52 *The gentle neighbourhood of grove and spring.* Cf. 'where the Muses haunt / Cleer Spring, or shadie Grove' (*PL* 3. 27–8). For Milton, spring (cf. *Nat* 184, *PL* 4. 272–4) and grove (cf. *PL* 4. 272–3) connote the pagan world in its gentler aspects, the relevant association here (although *grove* can also take on, from the O.T., more sinister suggestions of idolatry and lust; cf. *PL* 1. 403, 416, 9. 388, *PR* 2. 184).

54 *beguild*: diverted, charmed away (*OED* 5).

55–6 *th' infection...on som pregnant cloud*: that the poet's lament had so infected and transformed the cloud's yet unborn offspring that he might be said to have begotten them (as Ixion begot the Centaurs on a cloud fashioned by Zeus in the shape of Hera—an association Milton is careful not to invoke). [The same myth, also disguised, appears in Christ's speech in *PR* 4. 318–21.]

On Time

※

I. DATE, CIRCUMSTANCES, AND THE CAMBRIDGE MANUSCRIPT

[As Grierson (*Poems*, 1, x), Parker (*RES* 11, 1935, 279–80), and others have recognized, in the editions of 1645 and 1673 Milton arranged his poems in groups (the most obvious groups being religious and secular), and in chronological order within groups. There were some exceptions to these general rules. The *Nativity* was placed first, for more than one reason, and it was followed by the youthful versions of two Psalms. The next two, the religious *Fair Infant* and the secular *Vacation Exercise*, not printed in 1645, were intended for insertion here as being both early (1628); the printer's misplacing of the *Exercise* was corrected in the Errata. Then, in both 1645 and 1673, came a group of four religious poems, *The Passion, On Time, Upon the Circumcision*, and *At a solemn Musick*, presumably in chronological order; *The Passion*, of 1630, is not in the MS., the other three poems are. See the quotations from Shawcross and Parker on page 13, above.]

The MS. contains, in this order: (1) *Arcades*, a much-revised version used in the later process of composition; (2) two drafts of the *Solemn Musick*, without title, and the resulting fair copy with title; (3) two drafts of the 'Letter to a Friend,' both referring to *Sonnet* 7 (December 1632) and one containing a fair copy of it; (4) *On Time*, a fair copy with title, and with a subtitle, *To be set on a clock case* (deleted); (5) *Upon the Circumcision*, a fair copy with title, but with lining corrected at two points in the margin. Thus we can infer that, while the MS. contains in one form or another all the early poems known to have been written after *Arcades*, these versions belong to different stages of composition, ranging from first or early draft to final copy. That (2), (4), and (5) constitute a group composed within a fairly short time of one another is suggested by their common religious themes and their common (and peculiar) metrical form; and this is confirmed by their appearing together in 1645 and 1673, though in the order noted in the first paragraph above, i.e. (4), (5), (2). *On Time*, despite its occasional character indicated by the cancelled subtitle, is linked by the religious treatment of its subject with *Sonnet* 7 ('How soon hath time'). The appropriate date for the *Circumcision* is January 1, the day in the church's calendar commemorating the event; [and such a poem links itself with the *Nativity* of 1629 and the *Passion* of 1630]. Thus, in conformity with all the known evidence, we have the series: *Sonnet* 7 (December 1632), *On Time* (later in December), *Upon the Circumcision* (1 January 1633), *At a solemn Musick* (not long after; say January–February 1633); and the drafts of the 'Letter', with the Sonnet copied or referred to (perhaps February–March 1633).

[The scheme just given embodies what may be called the orthodox chronology; see also above, Chronological Survey, III.] An entirely different reading of the evidence is put forward by J. T. Shawcross ('Speculations on the Dating of the Trinity MS. of Milton's Poems,' *MLN* 75, 1960, 11–17). He would date the first part of the MS., *Arcades* to *Lycidas* inclusive, in 1637. He argues that Milton's letter to Diodati of 23 September 1637 (*Works* 12, 22–9: [probably of 23 November: Milton, *C.P.W.* 1, 325–8]) indicates a rekindling of ambition and a determination to go forward as a poet, and that the careful revision of *Arcades* (see Shawcross, 'The Manuscript of *Arcades*,' *N&Q* 6, 1959, 359–64) and of *Comus* (see Shawcross under *Comus* I below), the making of fair copies of *Sonnet* 7, *Time*, *Circumcision*, and the composing of *Solemn Musick* (as also of *Ad Patrem*, not in MS.) all depend on this ambition and resolve. Accepting Parker's date of 1632 for *Sonnet* 7, he yet argues that the 'Letter to a Friend' need not have been (or, in plain terms, was not) drafted until the latter half of 1637, and that 'some while since' may (or must) be taken as referring to that much extended period of over four and a half years. This leap, if it were taken, would entail or facilitate the re-dating of other items. It would move *Solemn Musick* forward from an earliest possible February–March 1633 to

September–October 1637, and create a probability that the metrically similar *Time* and *Circumcision* should likewise be advanced by some four and a half years. Without necessarily altering the date of the inception or performance of *Arcades*, it would reserve the final revision till the second half of 1637. Only if the whole argument could be established would it radically alter the orthodox conception of Milton's development as that is presented in this volume; by Shawcross and some others we are asked to believe that Milton's poetic career was without direction until after the composition or even the publication of *Comus*. [Parker (757) thinks Milton's use of the MS. 'may well have begun in 1629 or 1630.']

[Parker assigns *On Time* to Christmas 1630 or early 1631 (85, 761, n. 49), the *Circumcision* to 1 January 1631 (87, 762, n. 51), and *Solemn Musick* apparently to early 1631 (88–9, 762, n. 53); see also his comments summarized below at the end of *Arcades* 1. It is hard, on this dating, to imagine Milton turning immediately from this group of deeply religious poems to write the jocose pieces on Hobson the Cambridge carrier. Carey dates all three poems '1633?']

II. CRITICISM [D.B.]

Hanford ('Youth,' 1925, 134) feels that, in place of the 'disturbed self-searching' of *Sonnet* 7 and the Letter to a Friend, *On Time* expresses a 'deep religious and contemplative joy, the chords of which Milton had already touched in the *Nativity*....Similar imagery and an identical emotion pervade the poem *At a Solemn Music*. Both works are dignified and noble compositions, deeply felt and phrased in beauty. They are more mature in style than the *Nativity*, but come short of it in metrical felicity and in poetic fervor. The more vital forces of Milton's personality are not engaged in them.'

Tillyard (*Milton*, 1930, 60–3) sees *On Time* and its two companion pieces as a new departure in both technique and idea, 'experiments on high themes and in novel metres,' and 'they are the work of a master.' *On Time* and *At a solemn Musick* 'are more evenly good' than the

Circumcision. Metrically, the former two seem to show the influence of the Italian canzone and Spenser's *Epithalamion*, although Milton's 'slow concentrated stateliness ...is utterly different from the ample swell' of Spenser. 'The skill shown in the two pieces is consummate and suggests a greater mental power in the author than perhaps is found, except for a passage or two in *Comus*, till the writing of *Lycidas*.' The first paragraph (1–8) of the first poem deals with Time, the second (9–22) with Eternity. 'The rhythm of the first is slow, and dwindles grudgingly till the short last lines. The second paragraph, in superbly simple contrast, swells, after cunning little temporary ebbings, to the magnificent final Alexandrine.'

Woodhouse ('Notes,' 1943–4, 97–8): 'The effect of Milton's renewed dedication of himself and his lifework to God's service' in the sonnet *How soon hath time* 'is seen in the character of the poems to which he at once turns.' The subject of *On Time* 'links it closely with the sonnet. There Milton has stayed by an act of Christian self-dedication the disquieting thought of Time, which has stolen youth without bringing assured maturity. Now he completes the triumph over it by pointing on to the Christian hope of immortality.'

Brooks and Hardy (1951: 112–14) explain metaphors and stress the manipulation of rhythm, on which 'a great deal of the effect depends.' The alliteration in 1–3, especially in 2, 'tends to accentuate the "leaden step" of the hours.' The short lines 6–8 'slow the reader for meditation; line 12 insists upon the adjective "individual"; line 15 focuses emphasis on "perfectly divine," an idea which, for this poem, is basic; and line 17 forces the reader, in compensating for the shorter line length, to read slowly and emphatically the phrase "supreme Throne."' The periodic structure of the last five lines is compelling, and 'the extra long last line...brings the poem to a triumphant close.' See also the note on *individual* in line 12 below.

F. T. Prince (*Italian Element*, 1954, 60–6), after diagnosing the relative failure of *Upon the Circumcision* (*q.v.*), remarks that *On Time* and *At a solemn Musick* 'take as their basis an Italian form, the madrigal, which is less exacting than the *canzone*, and which Milton can develop with characteristic power' (63). These two poems 'have a sonority, a sustained emphasis of statement, and a rhythmic weight which give an assurance that Milton is again on the right track, finding means of expression which will bring out his full powers' (63–4). '*On Time*…derives from a branch of Italian poetry much cultivated in the later sixteenth century by Tasso, Marino, and others: the madrigal, used to reproduce the Greek epigram. Like many of their originals, these madrigals drew their subjects from pictures or statues and preserved the link between epigram and inscription.' Milton far surpassed the only other British practitioner in this vein, William Drummond, 'Yet his own more ambitious use of the form follows its essential features. In both these poems he builds up a triumphant epigrammatic close, which is marked by an alexandrine; both have an element of "wit-writing", though this is outweighed by a religious gravity and fervour.

'The madrigal in its origin was as it were merely one stanza of a *canzone*—a stanza which was not repeated; and it shared with the *canzone* the metrical basis of hendecasyllables and heptasyllables which had proved useful in English verse. Milton preserves the general nature of the form, but modifies it significantly, not only in his concluding alexandrines, but in his handling of the shorter lines. The Italian heptasyllable had found its theoretic equivalent in English in a line of six syllables and three stresses. Milton experiments, not only with this accepted equivalent, but with lines of four stresses. These are slightly tentative in the lines *On Time*: "With an individual kiss," and "Then all this Earthy grosnes quit," but provide the first magnificent climax' of the *Solemn Musick*, lines 14–16.

'These modulations are indicative of a feeling on Milton's part that full sonority in these Italianate forms could not be attained by pedantic imitation, and that he for his part could achieve the effect he wanted rather by a certain disciplined improvisation. The significance of the two poems is increased when we notice how this disciplined improvisation has enabled Milton to develop the long and elaborate sentence which is to be a structural element in all his mature poetry.…The poet who can draw upon such a syntax and rhythm' as govern lines 17–24 of the *Solemn Musick* 'has little need of intricate rhyme or stanzaic form.... The importance of *On Time* and *At a Solemn Musick* is that they point forward to *Lycidas* and the choruses of *Samson Agonistes*, and foreshadow Milton's exploitation of syntax as a structural element both in those later lyrics and in his blank verse' (64–6).

Daiches (*Milton*, 1957, 58–61), following Prince and Tillyard, adds further tribute to Milton's masterly handling of long and short lines and changes of pace and tone. 'The soaring conclusion [of *On Time*] reveals the poet's genuine excitement at the thought of the soul's final triumph over earthly change. It is interesting that Milton does not hesitate to use abstract nouns conveying a large, elemental meaning. A phrase like "When every thing that is sincerely good / And perfectly divine" is deliberately both abstract and simple, as though the ultimate in virtue and divinity cannot be expressed in any other way. Attack on such abstractions on doctrinaire grounds is surely misguided. They are absolutely right for this kind of statement in this kind of verse.

' "At a Solemn Musick" is similarly constructed, with similarly cunning variations of line-length and an even more impressive modulation of tone until the final climax.'

'These two poems are more than exercises: they are small works of art, perfectly controlled and cunningly modulated. They have not the complexity of much of Milton's later poetry, where he exhibits greater range and variety in his syntactical and metrical devices. But they do show that control over verse movement and some aspects at least of that "architectonic" power which are such conspicuous qualities of Milton's greatest work.'

III. NOTES

Under the title MS. has *To be set on a clock case*, crossed out (*Facs.* 394).

1–3 *Fly envious Time...heavy Plummets pace.* The lines turn on the dual aspect of time as fast and slow, flying and dragging. In the former aspect it is *envious*, seizing and devouring all things (an image carried on in 4–10); in the latter it seems to move with leaden steps, at the *Plummets pace*. The plummet (*OED* 5b) was probably the weight whose slow descent impels the mechanism of the clock (and not, as Wright [and some earlier editors] suppose, the pendulum, since its general use in clocks appears to be somewhat later and since there is no recorded example of the word plummet as signifying pendulum). It was often made of lead (the name being derived from Lat. *plumbum*); hence the appropriateness of *leaden-stepping hours*, a conception which Osgood (*C.M.* 44) would trace to Theocritus' description of the Hours as 'slowest of the blessed' (15. 104), but it seems doubtful whether Milton here has the Hours of classic myth in mind at all.

4 Wright would make *womb* 'the grammatical object' of *devours* and explains: 'Time devours the Hours which themselves devour the offspring of Time, *i.e.*, temporal things.' But it seems simpler to take *womb* as stomach (*OED* 1 b) and the subject of *devours*, allowing if one chooses a play on the remembered phrase 'womb of Time,' to complete the gestation and destruction of temporal things. [Milton might be thinking of the myth of Cronos, who devoured his own offspring (Apollodorus 1. 1. 5) and who was sometimes linked with Chronos, Time; cf. Milton's allusion in *Naturam* 14–15.]

9 *when as*: when.

11 *long*: to emphasize by contrast the shortness of time despite its *leaden-stepping hours* (2), but also with a transferred application to *individual kiss* (12). *bliss*: beatitude (*OED* 2c).

12 *individual*: not to be divided, inseparable (*OED* 2; *PL* 4. 486; and Lat. *individuus*). [Cf. Brooks and Hardy (112): 'Most editors gloss *individual* as meaning "indivisible": that is,…everlasting. This interpretation is certainly defensible, but the word may also mean "distinguished from others by attributes of its own; marked by a peculiar and striking character" (see N.E.D., A. 4, first reference cited 1646). The poet is speaking of the joy of the unencumbered soul (see ll. 11 and 13); and he seems to be saying that this joy will be unique, unlike any other joy ever experienced.' These critics also suggest the modern meaning of individual, which had developed before Milton's day: the resurrected soul will retain its identity. O. B. Hardison focused on this phrase in an elaborate study, 'Milton's "On Time" and its Scholastic Background' (*TSLL* 3, 1961–2, 107–22). Lines 11–12 echo Rom. 16. 16, 1 Cor. 16. 20, 2 Cor. 13. 12, 1 Pet. 5. 14, but for the biblical *sanctus* Milton, probably with *proprius* in mind, substitutes *individual*, meaning 'greet individually with a kiss.' The phrase is seen as a kind of repudiation of the Averroistic doctrine of the absorption of individual souls into the world-soul.]

14 *sincerely*: wholly (*OED* 4b); [cf. Lat. *sincerus*, 'clean, pure, sound.']

18 *happy-making*: i.e. the beatific vision. Cf. 'Blessed are the pure in heart: for they shall see God' (Matt. 5. 8).

20 *quit*: left behind (*OED* 7).

21-2 [W. M. Evans (*Henry Lawes*, New York, 1941, 88–9) saw in these lines 'various details of the final scene of *Cœlum Britannicum*—the "long" robe of Eternity "attired with stars" and the allegorical characters Truth, Peace, Love (Aletheia, Homonoia, Eusebia), who with Eternity are singing triumphal hymns about the Supreme Throne, no longer the piece of furniture symbolic of the Stuart Monarchy, but the Throne of the Almighty.' Such resemblances illustrate common traditions, but it is doubtful if we can go beyond that, since Carew's masque was produced in February 1634 and *On Time* is commonly dated 1632–3.]

21 *Attir'd with Stars*: crowned with stars (Keightley, citing Rev. 12. 1, 'upon her head a crown of twelve stars'). While the general meaning of *attire* was to dress or equip, it was sometimes used of adorning the head, as in 'those her golden tresses, / She doth attyre under a net of gold' (Spenser, *Amoretti* 37. 1–2; *OED* 3c), and the noun could also have this specialized meaning (*OED* 4).

22 *Triumphing…O Time*. Todd compared 'triumph both on Time and Death' (Browne, *Brit. Past.* 1. 4. 221). R. C. Browne added: 'Gets above Death, and Sinne, / And, sure of Heaven, rides triumphing in' (*Elegie On the…Marchioness of Winton* 99–100, *Ben Jonson* 8, 268). [Brooks and Hardy, asking why Milton makes Chance share in the defeat of Time and Death, answer: 'Chance must also be shut out from the world of Eternity because Eternity is a realm of perfectly harmonious order.' Along with the general promise of eternal freedom from mortal insecurity, we remember that in Renaissance literature 'Chance' was the hallmark of Epicurean, libertine, atheistic thought: two elaborate treatments of the theme are the debate between Cecropia and Pamela in Sidney's *Arcadia* (*Works* 1, 402–10) and Spenser's *Cantos of Mutabilitie*.]

Upon the Circumcision

✣

I. DATE

The dating of this poem is discussed under *On Time* above; see also Chronological Survey III. It has been commonly dated in 1633, on or about 1 January, the day commemorating the event in the church's calendar. [Parker (87, 762, n. 51) would assign the poem to '1 January 1631 or very near this day.']

II. CRITICISM [D.B.]

Some comments on this poem are included in critics' remarks on the group of religious pieces to which it belongs; these appear above under *On Time* II.

Hanford ('Youth,' 1925, 134-5), comparing this poem with *On Time* and *At a solemn Musick*, says that 'Milton strives to frame his thoughts to sadness in remembrance of Christ's sacrifice, symbolically suggested according to religious convention by the event which he commemorates, but the Muse withholds her wonted blessing on his endeavor. Only in the opening, where the poet is dealing momentarily with his native theme of the celestial song which attended the birth of Christ, does he achieve real beauty of feeling and expression.'

Brooks and Hardy (1951: 115-16) find the poem 'less ambitious but more nearly finished and more successful than "The Passion." ' 'God is still alive' on earth, and 'the poet need not resort to the pathetic fallacy....' 'The paradox in the doctrine of the atonement is treated meaningfully and brilliantly in lines 21-22: we expect the poet to say that Christ "Intirely satisfi'd" the Covenant which men had transgressed, but he writes "which we still transgress." Christ's atonement is no mere historical act; it is given a present and immediate reference.'

Upon the Circumcision

Tillyard ('Theology and Emotion in Milton's Poetry,' *Studies in Milton*, London, 1951, 160–1) cites *Nativity* 149–53 ('But wisest Fate... Must redeem our loss') and notes the same doctrine, 'in greater and in legalistic detail,' in *Circumcision* 12–24. 'There is a genuine emotional kinship between *Intirely satisfi'd...full wrath* in this poem and the tremendous line, *The rigid satisfaction, death for death* [PL 3. 212]... We have to do with an early and persistent element in Milton's emotions.' 'Although the lines *Upon the Circumcision* show what a deep hold the rigid doctrine of redemption had on the youthful Milton they do not betray any strain in the act of acceptance.' (Cf. below, 15–16 n.)

A. Oras (*N&Q* 197, 1952, 314–15) cited as a model Tasso's *Alla beatissima Vergine di Loreto* (*Opere*, Milan, 4, 1824, 574–8), but, as Carey observes, the rhyme scheme of this poem is not quite so close to Milton's as Petrarch's *canzone* cited by Prince just below.

F. T. Prince (*Italian Element*, 1954, 61–3) shows that Milton's 'two stanzas, each of fourteen lines, reproduce as closely as possible the stanza used by Petrarch in his *canzone* to the Blessed Virgin' (No. 366: *Vergine bella, che di sol vestita*, p. 1550 in *Le Rime di Francesco Petrarca*, ed. N. Zingarelli, Bologna, 1963). Since Petrarch's poem has 137 lines, and Milton's short piece involves only one repetition of the complex pattern, it would appear 'that Milton's talent did not function easily on such a basis.' Prince observes that, whether through ignorance or choice, Milton does not in the first stanza follow the orthodox (though often neglected) division between the first six lines and the rest of the stanza.

III. NOTES

Though instituted before the promulgation of the Mosaic Law, as a token of God's covenant with Abraham and his seed (Gen. 17. 11), the rite of circumcision was by both Jew and Christian closely associated with the Law. For the Christian the Law, expressive of the Covenant of Works, was given in consequence of the Fall and in order that it might demonstrate, by fallen man's inability to fulfil that Covenant, the need of a Redeemer. Christ came to fulfil the Law (Matt. 5. 17) in man's behalf, and submitted to its rites. By his Atonement, he at once expressed God's love for man (John 3. 16) and fulfilled the requirements of his justice: he freed believers from sin and from the condemnation of the Law (Col. 2. 13–14), admitting them to the liberty of the Gospel. Already in the O.T., circumcision was on occasion thought of as betokening moral and religious dedication, 'the circumcision of the heart' (Deut. 10. 16, 30. 6; Lev. 26. 41; Jer. 4. 4). St Paul takes up the idea (Rom. 2. 28–9), but develops it chiefly in connection with the New Covenant of Faith in Christ and his Atonement and the attendant liberty of the Gospel (Phil. 3. 3; cf. Rom. 3. 30, 4. 8–16; Col. 2. 11–14; Gal. 5. 6, 6. 15). All these themes are implied in Milton's poem, though the liberty of the Gospel, which was to figure so strikingly in his later thought (*DocCh* 1. 26 and 27), receives no emphasis here. Wright's useful note on 12 f. fails to recognize the marked development Milton's thought had undergone by the time of the *DocCh*, and consequently overemphasizes the idea of the liberty of the Gospel in this poem. Intent (as it seems) on linking this poem with the fragment, *The Passion*, Milton here views the Circumcision, the first wounding of Christ, as the 'type' of his Crucifixion. [Cf. Patrides, *Milton*, 144–5.]

1–6 *Ye flaming Powers...Now mourn.* In thus referring back to the subject of the *Nativity*, Milton deliberately recalls the opening of *The Passion* (1–8). ['Powers' were one of the nine orders of angels (above, *Nat* 125–32 n.), but the name could be used loosely for angels.]

1 Gabriel is called *winged Warriour* in *PL* 4. 576. [Cf. *Eli* 47, *Volatilesque... milites*; Todd cited *guerrieri alati*, Tasso, *G.L.* 9. 60.] The epithet *flaming* is applied to angels in *PL* 6. 102, 9. 156, 11. 101 [Warton]. The reason is that the angels are ethereal, associated with the highest of the four regions, that of fire; cf. 'fiery essence' (7).

2 *erst*: formerly.

6 *sad share with us to bear*: 'in order to join in our sorrow' (Wright).

7 *fiery essence can distill no tear*: the 'ethereal nature...excluding water as a contrary' (Wright, after Warton). Browne observes that Shakespeare (having no such scruple) makes the angels weep (*Meas.* 2. 2. 122). Hughes (1937) notes that at the fall of man 'dim sadness did not spare / ...Celestial visages' (*PL* 10. 23–4); we may add 'Tears such as Angels weep, burst forth' (ibid. 1. 620).

8–9 *Burn in your sighs...our deep sorrow.* Wright explains as an allusion to the sun's drawing up vapour from the sea and adds 'a typical metaphysical conceit.' [M. M. Mahood (*Poetry and Humanism*, 170) also sees in 6–9 'the metaphysical imagination of Donne'—perhaps with special reference to *A Valediction of*

Weeping.] One may notice, however, that the allegorical use of tears, sighs, etc. is typically Petrarchan (cf. *Sonn* 5). [See, e.g., D. L. Guss's *John Donne, Petrarchist* (Detroit, 1966), 173 and his index, 'Tear-floods (and fountains).']

10 *Heav'ns heraldry*: the heraldic pomp (*OED* 4) of the angels' announcing of Christ's birth: [the first recorded example of the word in this sense (Hunter, 'New Words'; Carey). *whilear*: whilere, 'a while ago' (Wright).]

11–28 *Enter'd the world...near his heart.* See headnote.

11–14 *now bleeds...to sease.* Christ fulfils the law (in this instance submits to the rite of circumcision) in order to rescue us from the condemnation of sin, which is thus said to *sease* (seize) on his *Infancy*. The verb might carry more than one relevant suggestion: to take possession by force (*OED* 6) or in pursuance of a judicial order (ibid. 5b), but also (of a weapon) to wound, penetrate deeply (*OED* 9b: cf. Fairfax, *Jerusalem* 7. 41: 'The wicked steele seaz'd deepe in his right side').

12–14 *Alas...to sease*: First written in MS. in two lines: *alas how soone our sin | sore doth begin his infancie to sease*; replaced in margin by three, as in text (*Facs.* 394). A precisely similar record of first and second thoughts occurs at 26–8.

15–16 *O more exceeding...but more exceeding love.* Richardson (reported by Todd [and repeated by Browne]) traced the construction to Virgil, *E.* 8. 49–50; but the parallel is not exact, for there the two elements (the mother's cruelty, the boy's heartlessness) are left in equipoise, but here the scale tips in favour of *more exceeding love.* Cf. 'O unexampl'd love, / Love no where to be found less then Divine,' *PL* 3. 410–11 [and the closer parallel, though apparently ironical, in Eve's exclamation: 'O glorious trial of exceeding Love' (ibid. 9. 961)]. Hughes compares 'the antithesis of *law* with *love* in the prophecy of Christ's satisfaction of *high Justice* in *PL* XII, 401–404.' [On traditional conceptions of the Atonement, and Milton's, see Patrides, *Milton*, 130–42. Citing this poem, *DocCh*, and *PL*, Patrides remarks (141): 'There are few opinions that Milton held more sincerely or more consistently than his view of the Atonement.']

17 *For we...remediles*: For we, by just *doom*, judgment (*OED* 2; *PL* 10. 769), were left without remedy (cf. *PL* 9. 919; *SA* 648).

19 *thron'd in secret bliss.* Cf. 'Thron'd in highest bliss' (*PL* 3. 305); 'thron'd / In the bosom of bliss' (*PR* 4. 596–7). *bliss*: blessedness (cf. *Time* 11 and n.).

20 *Emptied his glory.* Newton (reported by Todd) noticed that Milton here translates literally ἑαυτὸν ἐκένωσε (Phil. 2. 7); so also in the Latin of *DocCh* (*Works* 14, 342; 15, 274, 314).

21 *that great Cov'nant*: i.e. the Covenant of Works, embodied in the Mosaic Law. *still*: continually (*OED* 3).

23 *wrath*. [Patrides (*Milton*, 144; cf. 15–16 n. above), speaking of *Circum*, remarks: 'Perhaps the most interesting parallel occurs in a short poem by Herbert's enthusiastic disciple, Christopher Harvey, who maintained likewise that the circumcision served to "asswage / The wrath of heaven"' (*The Circumcision*, in *The Synagogue*, 1640, 24 f.; *Complete Poems*, ed. Grosart, 1874, 47–8); and he cites other parallels.]

25 *seals obedience*. In his later thought Milton, without at all abating his belief in the Atonement, emphasizes the obedience of Christ, the second Adam, as regaining all and more than all that Adam through disobedience lost; and here also the Circumcision at once *seals obedience* and is a 'type' of the Crucifixion.

26 *ere long...pierce more near his heart*. Here the idea of the 'type' is crystallized. The immediate reference is to the spear thrust into Christ's side (John 19. 34); but Milton is also remembering the 'circumcision of the heart' (see headnote). [Brooks and Hardy (116) think that 'The physical accuracy of the phrase "more neer his heart"...perhaps unfortunately distracts the reader from the point of connection, and distinction, Milton is making between Christ's present "wounding smart" and the suffering he will endure on the Cross. The "conceit," again, does not quite come off.']

26–8 See above, 12–14 n. [Line 27 in the MS. (*huge...hart*) was divided in the margin as in the text (*Facs.* 394).]

28 *Will*. MS. indicates that Milton hesitated between *will* and *shall*.

At a solemn Musick

❧

I. DATE

At a solemn Musick, evidently following closely after *On Time* and *Upon the Circumcision*, was the last of this group of short religious poems. The MS. contains two drafts and a fair copy of the whole and a version of lines 17–28; these are reproduced in Fletcher, *Facs.* 390–3 (see Notes below). The poem was published in the *Poems* of 1645 and not altered in 1673 except for the correction of *content* (line 6) to *concent* (see note below). The question of dating is discussed above in *On Time* I. [There has of late been wide divergence. The orthodox conjectural date is early 1633 (Parker, *RES* II, 1935, 281; Hughes, 1633; Hanford, 1633–4). But Shawcross (above, *On Time* I) argues for 1637, while Parker (*Milton*, 88–9, 762, n. 53) seems to favour early 1631. Carey, as we saw, dates all three poems '1633?']

II. CRITICISM [D.B.]

Milton's title might be paraphrased in modern terms as 'At a Sacred Concert' or perhaps 'At a Religious Service' (cf. *Il Penseroso* 155–66). The poem, a single paragraph of lines of irregular length which rhyme mainly in pairs, is, like *On Time*, a modified form of an Italian madrigal (Prince, *Italian Element*, 63). While this poem works out a musical metaphor, the theme is much the same as that of *On Time*, but the two poles or scenes are viewed in reverse order. *On Time* begins on earth and moves to heaven; the *Solemn Musick* moves almost at once from earth to a prolonged vision of heaven, then to a prolonged account of earthly life, and in the last lines returns to heaven. The same essential contrast between 'heaven' and earth appears in the first paragraph of *Comus* (1634).

175

Since some critics discuss this poem in connection with *On Time*, some comments on the former are cited above under the latter.

Tillyard (*Milton*, 1930, 63–5): 'The poem consists of only two sentences, the first containing the first twenty-four lines, the second the last four. But the first sentence is divided into two by a change (though not an interruption) of rhythm corresponding to a change of sense. This change is almost the reverse of the change noted in *On Time*, for the first sixteen lines, beginning slowly, work up to the ecstatic description of the "Cherubick host" and their heavenly music and end with the trochaic beat of "Hymns devout and holy Psalms / Singing everlastingly." In contrast, but still within the same sentence and verse-paragraph, follows in sober couplets a description of the earthly answer to this heavenly music, spoiled by the entry of sin into the world. The last four lines, couplets also, are a prayer that heavenly and earthly music may once again be in harmony. The skill with which Milton sustains the verse of the first sixteen lines is remarkable and deliberate. The gradual quickening of rhythm to the final trochaics is managed with extreme skill: compare, for example, the slowness of line 4: "Dead things with inbreath'd sense able to pierce" with the impetus in line 10: "Where the bright Seraphim in burning row." Wherever there is any danger of the voice resting as if at the end of a verse-paragraph, Milton obviates it by some skilful means. For instance it would be possible, as far as the rhythm goes, to make a longish pause at the end of lines 6 and 9. But the word *that* in line 6—"That undisturbed Song of pure concent"— suggests that the song is to be further described; while the last word of line 9, *Jubily*, being a new rhyme-sound, impels us to go on to find its rhyme-fellow, which is carefully kept back till *everlastingly* in line 16.'

This poem is further discussed in Tillyard's Appendix C (374–83), 'The Doctrine of Chastity in Milton,' which is concerned mainly with *Comus*. In the *Solemn Musick*, Tillyard says, 'the doctrine of the planetary music takes a new and more complicated form with the entry of Biblical mythology into what had been mainly Platonic. Here we get a hint of the doctrine that chastity is the means of hearing the celestial music' because 'the Platonic music of the spheres is identified with the song sung before the throne' in Rev. 14. 1–5. [The notes to this and other poems show that Milton never 'identifies' those two kinds of music.]

Tillyard's 'hint' of a doctrine of chastity is challenged by E. Sirluck in the course of a larger argument (*JEGP* 60, 1961, 759 f.). He believes that this poem is 'now being very widely misinterpreted to antedate by about five years a very important development in Milton's thought and art.' He 'can find nothing in the text of "A Solemn Musick" to link the "undisturbed Song of pure concent" with the particular song of Revelation 14:1–5, or the "just Spirits that wear victorious Palms" with the hundred and forty and four thousand virgins' (761). 'On the contrary, it seems to me clear that the "just Spirits that wear victorious Palms" and everlastingly sing "Hymns devout and holy Psalms" are the "great multitude, which no man could number, of all nations," "clothed with white robes, and palms in their hands," who have come out of "great tribulation" and have been justified by the blood of the Lamb, and who, with the angels, sing before the throne day and night of salvation and blessing" ' (763: cf. Rev. 7. 9–15). ' "At a Solemn Musick" is certainly a religious poem in which the poet aspires rightly to answer the melodious noise made by the angels and the just spirits in heaven, but I cannot see that sacrificial celibacy has anything to do with hearing or answering this song.'

Woodhouse ('Notes,' 1943–4, 98), speaking of the group of religious poems that followed closely upon 'How soon hath time,' remarks: '*At a Solemn Music* returns to the kind of *On Time*, and to its triumphal note. Whenever music is his theme Milton's thought quickens to inspiration; but in this poem the controlling ideas and their attendant emotion are religious. Some of the ideas are adumbrated in the *Nativity Ode*, but here they reach a new clarification: first, there is the essential harmony, the "pure concent" of the angel choir; secondly, the voice with which nature and man answered its strains "till disproportioned sin / Jarred against nature's chime"; finally, the faith that in the regenerate this harmony of nature and grace is restored and crowned at last by their union with the "celestial consort." Much of Milton's subsequent thought is implicit in this ideal of a harmony between nature and grace, and in the sense, so much more acute than in the *Nativity Ode*, that in order to restore it sin must be recognized and eradicated. These are the ideas embodied in *At a Solemn Music*; but, as in the *Nativity Ode*, and all other great poems, ideas become the basis of an aesthetic pattern and by its aid are realized, not as ideas merely, but as an experience at once religious and aesthetic. The two facts of the likeness of *At a Solemn Music* to the *Nativity Ode* and its immediate dependence on *How soon hath Time* are, taken together, highly significant: it is the clarification of Milton's own position in the sonnet that permits the clarification of the ideas adumbrated in the ode.'

Rex Warner (*John Milton*, 1949, 52–3) contrasts lines 6–13 with the lines on music in *L'Allegro* (136–44) and remarks that it is 'the same man who writes and feels the two passages,' a man who is extraordinarily affected by both the delights of the senses and the musical vision of heavenly harmony.

Brooks and Hardy (1951: 117–19) remark that 'The poem attempts to suggest through its metrical pattern the effect of the harmony which it celebrates.' They link the incompatible Sirens of Homer and Plato. 'In this poem, as in others, Milton combines classical and Christian materials,' and 'the transition from the pagan opening...to its central Christian theme is fairly easily accomplished, since the idea of love as a principle of universal harmony is already implicit in the Platonic reference.' 'The poem is a tissue of Biblical allusions.' Unlike Tillyard (q.v.), they think 'Jubi*ly*' (9) and 'everlasting*ly*' (16) are too widely separated 'for the rhyme to be effective, and the inevitable impression that the two lines are not rhymed detracts from the effectiveness of the poem. Milton's touch is not yet quite sure—not so sure as in "Lycidas"....'

The valuable comments of F. T. Prince (*Italian Element*, 1954) on the technique of the *Solemn Musick* appear in the extracts from him under *On Time* II.

The religious, metaphysical, and musical tradition to which the poem belongs has been expounded in the studies by Spaeth, Hutton, G. L. Finney, Spitzer, and Hollander cited above in the note on the *Nativity*

125–32. That note touched on the Pythagorean music of the spheres, the mathematical-musical starting point for a conception of cosmic harmony which was developed by Plato and Neoplatonism and was readily assimilated into Christian thought and feeling. But for the history and the complexities of that long and rich tradition the reader must turn to the authorities mentioned; here there is room only for summaries of the same authorities' comments on Milton's poem.

Hutton is cited above (*Nat* 125–32 n.) and below (1–2 n.). G. L. Finney (*Musical Backgrounds*, [1962], 117–18) finds the poem 'The most imaginative piece of poetry based entirely on this conception of sphere-born influence which can refine the soul, reveal heaven, and give life to the dead.... This "solemn" music resembles the "soft and solemn" sounds of *Comus*, that could "create a soul / Under the ribs of Death." It is the "solemn music" that Prospero calls for in *The Tempest* to evoke spirits and to restore sense to the captive nobles whom he has bewitched. This music, too—music and poetry, born of the spheres—breathes life into the soul of the listener, in Orphic tradition.... "Voice, and Vers" not only carry the spirit of life; they also present to the phantasy an image of the regions from which they came, a heaven which is musical. ...The final accomplishment of music is to make the nature of man celestial, to restore man to original purity, to make him one with celestial music....Milton was more subtle than the occultists; he enriched Hermetic notions with more intellectual ones. But the idea is the same: music, "The Imitatrix of the starres," breathes in life, provokes "heavenly influxes," and makes man "wholly Celestial." '

'One of the many remarkable virtues of this poem...is that with the line, "And to our high-rais'd phantasie present," it may be interpreted, also, within the framework of Ficino's philosophy of love.' According to Ficino, man, having perceived beauty in the harmony of virtues, colours and lines, and tones, 'experiences one of three kinds of love': the contemplative are lifted from the physical to the spiritual; the voluptuous descend to 'desire to touch'; and the practical 'are content with the pleasure of seeing or hearing....By beauty man is led to understand divine love and is fired with desire to unite with it.

'Milton, born, indeed, with an inclination to the contemplative life, heard and saw in the wedded sound of voice and verse, by means of "high-rais'd phantasie," the image of divine concord (like earthly concord, but much purer), which is both love and music. He imagined the "Saintly shout" of seraphim, angels of love. But the intellect went beyond the image to the idea of the love of God and the inaudible "musick" of man that is also the concord of love.... In this music of perfect love Milton desired to become a part; he longed to be united with this "celestial consort," the "unexpressive nuptiall Song" of "Lycidas."

'Yet there is no naming of "beauty" and only at the end of the poem a mention of the "love" of God. The debt to Neoplatonic doctrine, fallen into disrepute in Milton's day, is well disguised.' The kinship, however, is made clear by the final stanza of Spenser's *Hymne of Heavenly Love*, 'where visible or spiritual beauty only, not audible, lifts thoughts to God.' (164–5)

In his *Classical and Christian Ideas of World Harmony* (1963) Leo Spitzer gives a very full account of the Pythagorean–Platonic–Christian tradition and (pp. 103–7) a commentary on Milton's poem. It 'is a true Christian hymn with Jewish and Platonic accents; its music is "solemn" because it has the primordial and primeval aim of all Christian music: religious elation; the poem itself is simply a translation into words of this music celebrating the music of the world.' In the proemium the combined power of 'Voice, and Vers,' music and poetry, lifts our hearts toward heaven. In the second stanza (Spitzer speaks throughout of stanzas, though there are none: he means lines 1–8, 9–16, 17–24, 25–8) we drink in the beauty of the heavenly court, the singing of the angels and the souls of the just; the third section describes our own response, once innocent and complete but now lost through sin; 'the final stanza looks forward to that eternal reunion with God—which once again, in time, we shall know.'

After comments on Milton's revisions (see below, notes on lines 4, 10–11, 14–16, 19–25), Spitzer observes that he uses a traditional vocabulary for world harmony, that his poem is ' "beautiful within a tradition" as is all great poetry, and is an epitome of this tradition; it welds together the voices of all the civilizations (Greco-Roman, Jewish, medieval Christian) whose religious cult involved music and which are component parts of our civilization.'

While Shakespeare and Milton write with a new Renaissance ardour, 'they are still links in the great chain. We are lifted, as is done by sublime music, from the oppression of time into timelessness, from the burden of sin toward communion with God; and our battle with time (once we lost paradise, once again we shall regain it) results in everlasting triumph. What, in the beginning, is a conscious effort on our part (hence the imperatives: "wed," "present") is achieved, in the end, as a supernatural reality ("to live with God").' A somewhat obtuse remark of Warton's (quoted under 6 below) Spitzer would formulate as 'the ancient spherical harmony...ingrafted into the Christian history of man: paradise, sin, and hope for redemption.' 'The distribution of tenses in the poem (presents in the first, perfects in the second, futures in the last two stanzas) corresponds to the rhythm of Christian thought. It is no accident that the syntactical division shows one long sentence, coming to a close at the third stanza,' which suggests man's response to primeval goodness; and that the somewhat parallel metrical division 'shows the scheme *a-b-b-a* when we are in suspense before the vision of God in His heaven, but rhymed couplets from the moment that the human voices answer with their undiscordant "respond." ' Likewise it is no accident that ancient reminiscences occur mainly in the first stanza (two Platonic Sirens; 'mixt power' = *temperatio*; etc.), O.T. allusions mainly in the second, and medieval Christian concepts in the last part: 'first...world harmony, in its Greek form; then the Jewish monotheistic God appears'; the conclusion is 'a picture of the Christian life of the soul, in the well-known musicological terms of Boethius.' The Deity appears first as 'him that sits thereon,' then as 'their great Lord,' 'and finally, in the simplest and most touching part of the poem, as "God." ' The poem has 'a circular movement: a return to the beginning, to the harmony whence music comes,' and 'Colors are blended with tones from beginning to end.'

J. Hollander (324–31) remarks that the poem, while 'certainly a meditation,' does not have 'the set topic' required by L. L. Martz (*The Poetry of Meditation*, 1954); and since it is or purports to be occasional, its movement does not resemble 'the involved "symbolic action"' and its imagery does not embody the emblematic devices of the metaphysical poetry of religious contemplation. 'Instead, the contemplation moves from the consideration of a concrete, mundane event through a synthesized Classical-Christian account of the universal significance of that event, to a final supplication based on that account' (324). Or, as Hollander puts it later: 'Unlike the contemplative, solitary poetic treatment of personal prayer,' the poem 'starts out with the fact of a high musical service, moves from it to an account of its effects, . . . returns to the Biblical imagery of its immediate context (and of the text of an actual anthem?), and finally moves into the prayer for salvation. But it moves through the consciousness of a particular poet, for whom the concerns of the responsibilities of the poetic role and the poetic gifts were to become monumental' (330). Milton's brilliant technical achievement, indicated by Tillyard and others, was 'the product of arduous rewriting'; Hollander's comments on some main revisions are cited in the notes below.

Kurt Schlüter (*Die englische Ode: Studien zu ihrer Entwicklung unter dem Einfluss der antiken Hymne*, 1964, 59–66)—who omits the *Nativity* as less close to the classical hymn than several other early poems of Milton —argues in detail that the devoutly Christian *Solemn Musick* is akin to the Greek tradition in structure, language, and conception. The tripartite pattern consists of apostrophe, 'myth,' and prayer. Milton's Voice and Verse are not merely personifications invented by the poet but Platonic Sirens; they have an actuality like that of the Greek deities or Muses, and their exalted powers are set forth. In place of the Greek 'myth' Milton gives a concrete vision of the heavenly throne and angelic choir, a baroque tableau; then the concluding prayer. All three parts cohere through the sustained metaphors of harmony and discord, applied to celestial perfection and earthly sin, and the contrast is reflected in the language. Yet, with all the Christianizing of the theme, there remains something of the antique: the experience of festive music transcends the world of appearance, and the poet becomes the intermediary between heaven and earth, the priestly revealer of the divine.

P. L. Heyworth ('The Composition of Milton's *At a Solemn Musick*,' *Bulletin of The New York Public Library* 70, 1966, 450–8) attempts 'to reconstruct the textual pre-history' of the poem. He finds Spitzer's discussion (above, 1963) 'marred by inaccuracies' due partly to his using an unsatisfactory text and partly to carelessness and zeal for his case. Heyworth sees Milton's changes as guided by two main principles: the special avoidance, in a poem on music, of anything not euphonious, and the elimination of words and images inappropriate for an exalted religious theme. Some of his particular comments are cited in the notes below. He concludes: 'From the first draft it is clear that before he wrote it down the limits of the poem were fixed in his mind: the first four lines of the poem, the central *singing everlastingly*, and the last line, are all substantially the same' in MS. 1 [see below, the beginning of III, Notes] as in 1645. Milton's first concern was 'to get his individual images and lines "right," to find the exact word or phrase and the one appropriate in the context. This done, he turned to the task of making his poem into a coherent whole, rejecting superfluities...: he moves from a perfecting of the separate parts to the knitting of them into a self-consistent and interdependent unity.

'In this rigorous examination and correction of successive drafts of his poem there appear all the qualities of the mature Milton....'

J. S. Lawry (*Shadow*, 1968, 58–63) sees the poem as 'Milton's most perfect statement of the Renaissance idea of music,' which he had already used in the *Nativity*, *L'Allegro* and *Il Penseroso*, and *Arcades*. But in the *Solemn Musick* (as in a different way in *Ad Patrem*) there is a partial shift from ecstatic celebration of heavenly music to the idea of the preparation of fallen man through prayer (and poetry). This poem, unlike the *Nativity*, 'begins with the conviction of discord,' and, 'like *Comus*, it registers earth's attributes as dim and low.' Human sin jarred with the heavenly music, but the prayer asks 'that Voice and Verse may somehow restore man's place within that great harmony,' through 'the tempering and "tuning" of human wills toward concert with God's harmonious will, the achievement of an inner Paradise.' That process can be led by the inspired artist.

III. NOTES

Something of the process of composition may be traced in the Cambridge MS. The several versions are reproduced in Fletcher's *Facs.* 390–3, the variants in *Works* 1, 421–5. We designate the first (and unfortunately defective) copy MS. 1; the second, MS. 2; a third version of lines 17–28, MS. 2*a*; and the fair copy of the whole, MS. 3. In accordance with the principles of the Commentary we shall notice only changes of some critical importance and interest.

Title MS. 1 appears to have been headed simply *Song*. MS. 3 has the title *At a solemn Musick*. We may remember that the term *Musick* covers both vocal and instrumental music, that it means here 'a piece of music...performed' (*OED* 4), and, further, that *solemn* retains with full force its association with religion and means 'sacred' (*OED* 1).

1–2 *Blest pair of Sirens* ... / ...*Voice, and Vers.* Editors compare *Arc* 63; but Hutton (48–9) contends that the *Sirens* here are not to be confused with 'the "celestial Sirens" of *Arcades* 63, being not on the spheres but "sphere-born", just as Echo in *Comus* 241 is "daughter of the sphere".' ⟨A.S.P.W.: It should perhaps be noticed that MS. consistently spells *borne*, but 1645 and 1673 *born*. At a slightly earlier date the confusion of the two spellings was common (e.g. in the 1611 Bible, 'borne' in John 3. 3, 1 John 4. 7) but, if we may trust the printed texts of *PL* and *PR*, it seems not to have affected Milton (*PL* 1. 489, 2. 797; *PR* 1. 205) save in one instance (*PL* 4. 323) which might well be a printer's error. If Milton consistently distinguished between *born* and *borne*, then the spelling introduced in 1645 would represent a change in meaning, but we cannot be certain that he did.⟩ Hutton continues: 'They are earthly music. ...As such, however, they are "pledges of Heav'n's joy" because we return to heaven the source of music [Macrobius, Commentary 2. 3–4 on the *Somnium Scipionis* of Cicero, *Rep.* 6. 18: 'the soul brings to the body a memory of the celestial music': Hutton, 11–12], and penetrating us they may present as a true image to our high-rais'd phantasy the heavenly music of their ultimate origin.' It should be noted that *pledges* are at once securities given (*OED* 2) and children or offspring (*OED* 2d; *Lyc* 107 and n.; Spenser, *F.Q.* 1. 10. 4); so *Voice, and*

At a solemn Musick

Vers are at once the offspring of *Heav'ns joy* and given as a surety of our participation in it [cf. Hollander, 326]. The *Sisters* represent music and song on
earth; they are not earth-born, however, but *Sphear-born* because they echo the
music of the spheres, which in turn parallels the music of heaven. Milton seems
to distinguish carefully between the music of the spheres, which symbolizes
perfect harmony in the natural order, and the song of the angelic choir, which
represents the heavenly order (see notes on *Nat* 101–8, 125–32). On *Sisters,
Voice, and Vers*, Bowle (reported by Todd) quoted *Musica, e Poesia son due
sorelle* (Marino, *L'Adone*, Venice, 1623, 7. 1). *Voice, and Vers* stand for the two
respectively, and they are united to produce the full effect of music in the wider
Greek sense, in which music included poetry (Plato, *Rep.* 2. 376 E). [For French
efforts, in the Platonic tradition, to unite poetry and music, see Frances A.
Yates, *The French Academies of the Sixteenth Century* (London, 1947).]

3 *Wed your divine sounds.* Warton cited: 'the Mariage rites / Of two, the
choicest Paire of Mans delights / Musique and Poesie' (*Ben Jonson* 8, 401); cf
L'All 136–7. For *sounds, and mixt power employ*, MS. 1 had *power & joynt force
employ*. For the whole line (*Wed…employ*) MS. 2 had: *Mixe yo* *choise chords*,
& happiest sounds employ: deleted, and present text substituted. [Hollander
(326) remarks that revisions of the line show 'a movement from abstraction to
misplaced concrete imagery and then to a proper balance between the two,' and
'The redundancy of "power" and "force" is also removed.' Heyworth (452,
n. 9: see above, II, 1966) disagrees with the idea that *choise chords* was deleted as
too technical (L. Lockwood, 'Milton's Corrections to the *Minor Poems*,' *MLN*
25, 1910, 201–5; J. S. Diekhoff, 'Critical Activity of the Poetic Mind: John
Milton,' *PMLA* 55, 1940, 748–72). Heyworth points out the retention of *concent, disproportion'd*, and *Diapason*, and sees the motive for deletion in the im-
propriety of urging the Sirens 'to "mix choice chords" in the manner of a
country housewife making jam....']

4 *Dead things…to pierce.* Wright notes the reminiscence of the myth of
Orpheus (Ovid, *M.* 11. 1–2; Virgil, *G.* 4. 510; *PL* 7. 34–6). *pierce*: penetrate,
permeate (Lockwood); 'touch or move deeply' (*OED* 4); cf. 'Aires, / …Such
as the meeting soul may pierce' (*L'All* 136–8).

After 4 MS. 1 appears to have had the four additional lines, reproduced in
MS. 2 (*Facs.* 390) as follows (words deleted in favour of the preceding and final
expression are here enclosed in shaped brackets): *and as ⟨whilst⟩ yo* *equall
raptures temper'd sweet / in high misterious happie ⟨holie, but MS. 1 happie⟩
spousall meet / snatch us from earth a while / us of our selves & native ⟨home bred⟩*

woes beguile. [Spitzer (104) remarks that the *misterious spousall* 'would detract the attention from the main problem,' and that *a while* 'would emphasize the temporal aspect, which, in the final phrasing, would come in only later.' Hollander (327) observes that the four lines 'would have tended to hasten the conclusion of the poem, and somewhat to trivialize the import.' The lines 'reinforce the metaphor of wedding with an almost erotic image,' and 'Milton wanted to reserve the traditional figure of temperament and tuning for later expansion....But it was probably the premature supplication, not a prayer to God, but to the semi-deified Christian muses, which rang most false; and the "snatch us from earth"...had to go because of the almost hyperbolic quality of the image, when contrasted with the more staid, but more deeply believed, prayer at the end....' G. L. Finney (162) comments: 'Although Milton referred often to the ecstatic effects of music, he always avoided the literalism of lesser poets—a fault that he only narrowly escaped when he so fortunately eliminated ...the line "Snatch us from earth awhile."' Heyworth (452) notes the substitution of the subdued *native* for *home bred*, in the interest of decorum and unity of tone. He also (457) remarks that the lines *snatch...beguile*, which Milton deleted, are a petty and plaintive human bleat and 'detract from the sonorous vigour of the heavenly chorus.']

5 *our high-rais'd phantasie*: our imagination, the faculty of forming images of things not present (*OED* 4), as it is raised to new heights by the penetrating power referred to. MS. 1 had *fancies then*. [Milton deleted *high* and inserted *up* (probably because of *high lifted* in line 11), then wrote *loud uplifted* in 11 and restored *high* in 5 (Heyworth, 451).]

6 *undisturbed Song of pure concent*: uninterrupted song marked by pure harmony (the now obsolete *concent* is fairly frequent in the 16th–17th centuries, though often concealed by the misspelling *consent*). MSS. 1, 2, 3 have *concent*; 1645, *content*, a manifest misprint. Warton explains this *Song* (and that of *PL* 5. 625–7) as 'Plato's abstracted spherical harmony...ingrafted into the Song in the *Revelations* ⟨5. 11⟩'; properly understood, it is the song of the angels alone to which Milton here refers. [Cf. Spitzer's comment in 11 above.]

7 *Ay sung before the saphire-colour'd throne.* MS. 1 has *ay surrounds the saphire-colourd* ⟨*soveraigne*⟩ *throne*. The throne is [as Newton observed] the throne of God in Ezekiel's vision: 'And above the firmament...was the likeness of a throne, as the appearance of a sapphire stone' (Ezek. 1. 26; cf. 10. 1).

9 *Saintly shout, and solemn Jubily.* MS. 1 first had *sollemne crie*, corrected to *jubilie*. The juxtaposing of adjective and noun in each phrase is less for a deliberate effect of oxymoron than to harmonize two nouns with a religious context (since *Jubily* here means joyful shouting; cf. *PL* 3. 348 and *OED*: jubilee 5 b).

10–11 *bright Seraphim…Angel trumpets blow.* MS. 1, *princely row*; MS. 2 first had *tripled row*, corrected to *triple*; then *burning* substituted. [Heyworth (454) thinks *princely* supererogatory for the Seraphim; *tripled* suggests large numbers, but that idea was already given in line 12; hence the vivid and appropriate *burning*.] The angels generally were for Milton 'ethereal' beings, associated with fire (cf. *Circum* 7–8 n.; [Robert H. West, *Milton and the Angels*, Athens, Ga., 1955, 137]); and Seraph (which occurs only once in the Bible, Isa. 6. 2–6) is 'said to mean in Hebrew burning' (Wright); further, in the symbolic hierarchy of angels, the Seraphim burn with love of God (see *Nat* 112–13 n., *IlPen* 54 n.); hence perhaps *burning row.* *Their loud up-lifted Angel trumpets.* MS. 1 first had some word (or words) between *loud* and *trumpets* of which the first four letters, alone remaining, are read by the Columbia editors (*Works* 1, 423) and Fletcher (*Facs.* 390) as *unsa* but which Todd, reading (and guessing) in the torn but less impaired MS., thought was *immortal* [H. Darbishire reads [*th*]*ire loud unj*[*arring*] *trumpets blow*]; in any case it was deleted in favour of *loud symphonie of silver trumpets blow.* [Spitzer (105) remarks that *symphonie* 'would be too Grecian in a "Hebrew" stanza'—by which he means lines 9–16; see his comments in II above.] MS. 2 had first *high lifted loud arch-angell trumpets blow*, corrected to present reading [see Heyworth, 5 n. above]. In the Bible the only specific association of trumpets with angels appears to be in 'And the seven angels which had the seven trumpets prepared themselves to sound' (Rev. 8. 6), and in the passage that follows (8. 7–9. 21), where the context is one of menace, not rejoicing.

12–13 *Cherubick host…Harps of golden wires.* The O.T. has frequent references to the Cherubim, which perhaps lead Milton to describe them as a *host* grouped *in thousand quires*, i.e. bands of singers in church or temple (*OED*: choir 1 b, 1 c), though 'quire' was also applied to each of the nine orders of angels in the divine hierarchy (ibid. 4, which mistakenly quotes 'Hath brought me from the Quires of Cherubim / Alone thus wandring,' *PL* 3. 666–7; for there the use is identical with the present instance and the primary meaning must be groups within the order or quire of Cherubim). In the symbolic hierarchy the Cherubim represent the rational contemplation of God's perfection (see *Nat* 112–13 n.); and it is perhaps significant that Milton assigns to the Cherubim the *immortal Harps*, which (like the harp repeatedly mentioned in the Psalms) would be accompanying the words of a song (cf. *PL* 7. 594–9) [in *Nat* 112–16, however, both Cherubim and Seraphim are harping]. The association of the harp with angels, like that of the trumpet, is post-biblical; the only reference to harps in heaven seems to be Rev. 14. 2 [cf. ibid. 5. 8, 15. 2]. For *immortal* meaning either associated with divine beings or simply enduring see *Vac* 39 n. [With *golden wires* Todd compared *Vac* 38 and *PL* 7. 597.] An interesting step in the poem's composition seems to be obscured here by the impaired state of MS. 1 (*Facs.* 390), where the lines read: *and the *youthful* ⟨the asterisk indicating a correction, which is lacking⟩...*ubim sweet-winged squires | in ten thous*... *es* ⟨connected by a line to⟩ *Heavn's henshmen* ⟨in margin⟩. It seems possible that *Heavn's henshmen* was to stand in apposition to *squires* (since, as Todd notes, *henchman* could mean page or squire of honour: *OED* 1 b), and the *es* was probably the final letters of *quires* rhyming with *squires*.

14–16 *With those just Spirits...everlastingly.* Milton is thinking of those who 'stood before the throne, and before the Lamb, clothed with white robes, and palms in their hands' (Rev. 7. 9), and perhaps of the song of the hundred and forty and four thousand (ibid. 14. 3–4), as Tillyard, Hughes, and Wright suggest [cf. Sirluck, in II above; and cf. *Comus* 12–14.] MS. 1 has *beare* written in above *weare*, neither word deleted, which indicates that Milton hesitated between the two: *wear* could mean *bear* (as in 'wear arms,' *OED* 2). For *victorious Palms*, MS. 1 first had *fresh greene*, then *blooming*, then *victorious palmes*; MS. 2, *the blooming palmes*, but with a marginal note *blooming or victorious*; MS. 3, the final choice, *victorious* (*Works* I, 423; *Facs.* 390, 392). For *holy Psalms* MS. 1 has *sacred Psalmes*; MS. 2 the same, but with *holie* in margin. After 16, MSS. 1 and 2 add two lines which appear in MS. 2 as follows (words in square brackets are the rejected phrasing of MS. 1): *while all the starrie rounds* [MS. 1 had *that all the f...e of heaven*, changed to *whilst the whole frame of*, and finally to *while then all the starrie frame*] *& arches blue | resound and eccho Hallelu.* [Spitzer (104–5) suggests reasons for some of the changes: *Hallelu*, as an O.T. expression, would be in place only in stanza two (i.e. 9–16); *starrie rounds* would hardly be appropriate at the beginning of a third stanza (i.e. 17–24) which turns from heavenly music to earth; and *blue* is already in *saphire-colour'd*. Heyworth (451) notes the change from the unpleasant alliteration of *sacred Psalmes | singing* to *holie Psalmes*. He also suggests (453) that Milton found both *fresh greene* and *blooming* 'too verdant and colourful for the traditionally lustrous glories of heaven.' The two lines *while...Hallelu* were deleted presumably because they undercut the climax reached in *Singing everlastingly*; this short line 'is the heart of the poem, and that Milton intended it to be so from the beginning is clear from the fact that it is the one line certainly unchanged in all four drafts. To run on the sense into the resonantly hollow chorus of this couplet would be to dissipate the rhetorical impact of the first fifteen lines and Milton rightly cut it out.' (Heyworth, 456).]

17–24 *That we on Earth...their state of good.* Syntactically, *That* introduces a clause of purpose dependent on the imperatives, *Wed* and *employ* (3) and *present* (5); but the effect of the complicated construction is perhaps rather to anticipate the prayer *O may we* (25). In the beginning *all creatures* (everything God had created, angels, spheres, earth and all its inhabitants from man to the lower ranks of living things) joined in the *perfet Diapason*, complete harmony (a figurative use of the term originally signifying the harmony of the notes of the octave: *OED* 2), of their song to God, moved thereto by God's love and their *first obedience* in *their state of good*, the condition known to theology as 'original justice.' But all this was ended by the Fall, 'Mans First Disobedience' (*PL* 1. 1) with the entrance of *disproportion'd sin*; the epithet not only suggests the idea of deformity (cf. 'as disproportion'd in his manners / As in his shape': Shakespeare, *Temp.* 5. 1. 290–1), but emphasizes the contrast with the proportion that marks the relation of notes in the diapason. [Spaeth (*Music*, 109) remarks: '*Diapason* represents the harmony between Heaven and Earth as consisting of the interval of the octave, in other words, the most perfect concord excepting an actual unison.... Man's state of good consisted in an undeviating conformity to divine law.' Sylvester's birds teach the forests 'The Diapason of their Heav'nly Lay' (*D.W.W.* 1. 3. 1091; Grosart, 1, 49).]

19–25 *As once we did...renew that Song.* In place of these lines MS. 1 had: *by leaving out those harsh chromatick jarres / of sin that all our musick marres / & in our lives & in our song.* MS. 2 alters *chromatick* to *ill sounding* and adds *clamourous* before *sin*. MS. 2a (which commences here) had first, after *melodious noise, as once wee could* ⟨altered to *did*⟩ *till disproportion'd Sin / drown'd* ⟨altered to *jarr'd against*⟩ *natures chime & wth tumultuous* ⟨altered to *harsh*⟩ *din* (*Facs.* 392). ['The distinctive feature of the chromatic *genus* was its use of quarter tones. The resulting harmonies may well have "jarred" upon the simple combinations of the diatonic scale' (Spaeth, *Music*, 66). Spitzer (105) remarks that *chromatick* was too learnedly Greek, 'alluding as it does to an ancient theory no longer valid'; and that *clamourous* 'would really mar the solemn music of the poem, without suggesting the norm itself,' while *disproportion'd* reminds us of the proportion of *natures chime*. Hollander (328) accepts as possible this reason for the rejecting of *chromatick*, and suggests that *& in our lives & in our song* 'clearly differentiates...mundane existence from the special life of religious contemplation and prayer....' The final version 'includes a reference to Original Sin, and to...the prelapsarian audibility of the celestial music. "As once we did" introduces the historical dimension, and clearly outlines the reference of the final prayer's "O may we soon."']

20 *Jarr'd against natures chime*: broke the harmony of the natural order (since, though Milton does not here say so, all nature was impaired as a result of man's fall). Wright would connect the *Diapason* directly with the eight notes uttered by the Sirens seated on the eight spheres in Plato's vision of Er (see *Arc* 62–73 n.) and hence with *natures chime* interpreted as the music of the spheres. But the reference seems to be more inclusive, to the song of *all creatures*, while *natures chime* signifies that song on the natural level (of whose perfect harmony the music of the spheres was indeed for Milton the constant symbol). The young Christian humanist hopes that, despite the Fall, *we on Earth* may once more learn, *with undiscording voice* (i.e. a voice no longer out of tune with heaven on account of sin) to *rightly answer* (i.e. sing in harmony with, bear our part in response to) the *melodious noise*, the music of the angelic choir (cf. *Nat* 97 and n.) It is significant that in the first writing Milton recognized that fallen man must *learn* to answer the music of heaven. For 17–18, *That we on Earth with undiscording voice | May rightly answer*, MS. 1 first had *that wee below may learne w*[th] *hart & voice | rightly to answere*; then *below may learne w*[th] (*w*[th] no doubt in error) and *to* were deleted, and *may* was added before *rightly*, to read *that wee w*[th] *hart and voice | may rightly answere*. MS. 2 had *that wee w*[th] *undiscording hart & voice*, changed to present reading. Warton cited, with special reference to 19–20: 'Sin, that first / Distemperd all things' (*PL* 11. 55–6); 'To doe their Offices in Natures Chime' (*Ben Jonson* 8, 253). Todd added: 'A swete consent [i.e. concent; cf. above, 6 n.], of Musicks sacred sound, / Doth rayse our mindes (as rapt) al up on high, / But sweeter soundes of concorde, peace, and love, / Are out of tune, and jarre in every stoppe' (G. Gascoigne, *Steele Glas*, *Works*, ed. J. W. Cunliffe, 2 v., Cambridge, 1907–10, 2, 152); and: 'For Adams sin, all creatures else accurst: / Their Harmony distuned by His jar: / Yet all again concent....' (Sylvester, *D.W.W.* 2. 1. 3, Arg., Grosart, 1, 114). [As representative of the Renaissance use of musical terms, C. A. Patrides (*Milton*, 109) cites, among others, N. Culverwel (*Light of Nature*, 1654, 105): 'When God first tun'd the whole creation, every string, every creature praised him; but man was the sweetest and loudest of the rest, so that when that string apostatized, and fell from its first tuning, it set the whole creation a jarring.']

22 *whose love their motion sway'd.* [This may, as M. M. Mahood assumes (*Poetry and Humanism*, 194), echo 'a famous verse of the *Divine Comedy*' (presumably *Parad.* 33. 145), but the idea was a traditional commonplace.]

25–8 *O may we soon...endles morn of light.* The final consummation is not on earth, where we may indeed hope to *keep in tune with Heav'n* and *answer* the *celestial consort* (the heavenly choir), but in heaven, where God will *unite* us to it, make us one with it (*OED* 1) through an eternity of life and light. Cf. 'Lord place me in thy consort: give one strain / To my poore reed' (G. Herbert, *Employment* (1) 23–4); and 'Where, with thy Quire of Saints for evermore, / I shall be made thy Musique' (Donne, *Hymne to God my God* 2–3).

28 *To live with him, and sing in endles morn of light.* MS. 1 first had *To live & sing wth him in ever-endlesse light*; but this did not satisfy Milton and he tried, apparently in this order: *in ever-glorious light, in uneclipsed light, where day dwells w^{thout} night, in endlesse morne of light, in cloudlesse birth of light* (possibly also, for he brackets the last two: *cloudlesse morne of light* and *endlesse birth of light*), *in never parting light.* MS. 2 selects *in endlesse morne of light*, which MSS. 2a and 3 repeat; but the order of the phrase *To live & sing wth him* remains uncorrected in MSS. 2, 2a, and 3; it is given its present order in 1645.

An Epitaph on the
Marchioness of Winchester

❦

I. DATE AND CIRCUMSTANCES

Jane, Marchioness of Winchester, died in April 1631, at the age of twenty-three. The daughter of Thomas, Viscount Savage, by his wife Elizabeth (daughter and co-heir of Thomas Darcy, Earl Rivers), she was the first wife of John Paulet, fifth Marquis of Winchester, a Roman Catholic and an ardent Royalist (Cromwell's siege and destruction of his stronghold, Basing House, was one of the events of the Civil War). Masson in his introduction cites two accounts of her death. One (briefly noticed by Todd) is from a contemporary MS. copy of the poem in the British Museum, MS. Sloane 1446, which adds to the title 'whoe died in childbedd. Ap: 15. 1631' and ascribes the poem to 'Jo Milton of Chr: Coll Cambr' (*Works* 1, 425; Parker, below). The other account is from a newsletter of 21 April 1631, from John Pory to Sir Thomas Puckering (*Court and Times of Charles the First*, ed. R. F. Williams, London, 1848, 2, 106), which states that she 'had an imposthume upon her cheek lanced; the humour fell down into her throat, and quickly despatched her, being big with child, whose death is lamented as well in respect of other her virtues, as that she was inclining to become a protestant' (Masson, *P.W.* 1, 129; Parker, *Milton*, 767, n. 59). Though the MS. copy of the poem referred to above cannot be closely dated, it may have been made from a version earlier than that printed in Milton's *Poems* (1645); it differs significantly in one passage and introduces some quite appropriate paragraphing (see notes on 15–23, 47–8, 53, 70). W. R. Parker examined biographical and bibliographical data in 'Milton and the Marchioness of Winchester,' *MLR* 44 (1949), 547–50; among other

things he gave (n. 5) a third account of her death, from the Duchess of
Buckingham's letter of 16 April to her father; [see also his *Milton*, 766–8].

We have no information to suggest how Milton came to write on the
young Marchioness' death [or how he came to be, as Parker observes,
so well informed about her life]; we know of no connection with the
family or of common friends or associates. Warton suggested a connection through the Egertons, who must have known Lord Savage, their
estates lying in the same county, but that suggestion is highly speculative,
since Milton's acquaintance with the Egertons has itself to be explained
as through Henry Lawes. Warton was told that there was a Cambridge
collection of memorial verses in which Milton's poem appeared, but no
such volume is known, and Warton himself doubted the information
given him. Todd found support for such a collection in the MS. copy
and the terms of its ascription quoted above (see also the note on 55–9).
Whatever its origin, the poem is part of the young poet's apparently
deliberate practice in a wide variety of poetic forms, this time in the
Jonsonian lyric turned to the purpose of elegy. It reminds us at once of
William Browne's poem:

> Underneath this sable herse
> Lies the subject of all verse:
> Sidney's sister, Pembroke's mother...:

much more so indeed than of Jonson's own heavier and more laboured
effort on this same occasion, his *Elegie On the Lady Jane Pawlet,
Marchioness of Winton* (*Ben Jonson* 8, 268). It is significant that Milton
in his epitaph attempts a style as remote as possible from those practised
in his *On Shakespear* and his Hobson poems. His title, *An Epitaph*, is
significant also. The Latin *epitaphium* meant a funeral oration or eulogy.
The English *epitaph* from the fourteenth century onward was used for
the inscription on a tomb or for something written in commemoration
of the dead (*OED* 1B quotes a 1583 title, *A Booke of Epitaphes made
upon the Death of....*). Milton's poem belongs to this latter category,
but not without some influence from the former, since he starts by
recognizing—but casting into poetic form—the sort of information given
on a tomb: descent and relations, age, etc.

II. CRITICISM [D.B.]

Hanford ('Youth,' 1925, 125) observes that the elegy is Milton's 'first essay in octosyllabic couplets, a measure which carries with it the pure and classic style of the Jonsonian lyric.... The spirit of the earlier elegy on a Fair Infant finds an echo in the tender delicacy with which Milton celebrates this gentle mother's death in child-bed, likening her to the biblical Rachel,... but the poetic mode has changed.' Hanford cites the parallel openings of Milton's poem and Browne's epitaph *On the Countess Dowager of Pembroke*.

Brooks and Hardy (1951: 120–2): 'This poem is comprised of two parts: in the first the Marchioness is spoken of in the third person, and the story of her death is told; in the second, the lady herself is addressed and her present existence is described. The movement...is thus from the past to the present, and from a rather grave formality to a less reserved expression of grief, and finally of hope.' 'The irony of the situation is pointed up in several ways. The young mother, so soon to enter the tomb herself, became a living tomb for her child. Atropos...in destroying the fruit managed to destroy the tree as well. This last figure looks forward to the extended comparison...developed through lines 35–46': ...'the drooping of the uprooted plant is compared to the languishing of a human being,' so that we have 'a simile within a simile. The use of this human analogy within the plant metaphor and the fact that the plant is referred to as "she" tie the extended comparison very closely to the Marchioness' own case. She becomes a tender and beautiful doomed flower.' 'This section is probably the most successful part of the poem.' But even in the personal address (47 f.) 'the speaker keeps a certain reserve. He does not forget that she is of a "noble house" or that he is after all a stranger.' 'The last lines...turn from the tomb to the realms of light where the lady now is' (see below, 63–8 n.). 'It may be that Milton's failure to achieve complete success in this poem (and in several other of his witty exercises of this period) did much to estrange him from the explicitly "conceited" and witty poetry of Donne' [which, apart from the *Anniversaries*, was not yet published, and, in manuscript, was perhaps not likely to come Milton's way]. 'At any rate, a little later he developed for himself a kind of poem in which wit is not absent but is kept submerged and implicit, rather than dominant.'

III. NOTES

1–3 The Marchioness was *an Earls heir* through her mother (see 1 above).

4–6 *Her vertues fair*, also spoken of in the newsletter (1 above), were not to be attributed to her noble descent or to any earthly source, being the gift of heaven. Warton quoted the letter addressed to her 15 March 1626, by James Howell, who had taught her Spanish: Howell said that Nature, God's handmaid, and the Graces exhausted all their treasure and skill 'to frame an exact model of female perfection' (*Epistolae Ho-Elianae* 4. 14, Temple Classics ed., 1, 258–9).

7–8 *Summers...had told.* See 1 above.

11–14 Had her days been proportioned to her merits, her death would not have seemed, as it now does, unnatural, as if fate had intervened to destroy her prematurely.

15–22 The lines refer to her marriage to John Paulet. The bridesmaids (*The Virgin quire*) summoned Hymen (*The God that sits at marriage feast*), who came, but with his torch not well lighted, an ill omen (see *L'All* 125–6 n. and Ovid, *M.* 10. 6–7, there quoted), and with *a Cypress bud*, emblem of a funeral, intruding *in his Garland* (which Jonson describes as composed of roses and marjoram: *Hymenaei, Ben Jonson* 7, 210–11). For the funereal associations of cypress Newton (reported by Todd) cited Virgil, *A.* 6. 216, Horace, *Epod.* 5. 18, Spenser, *F.Q.* 1. 1. 8.

15–23 In place of these lines MS. Sloane 1446 has (see 1 above; *Works* 1, 426; H. Darbishire, 2, 312; Parker, *MLR* 44, 549; *Milton*, 767):

> Seaven times had the yeerlie starre
> in everie signe sett upp his carr
> Since for her they did request
> the god that sitts at marriage feast
> (when first the earlie Matrons runne
> to greete her of her lovelie sonne

23–6 The lines refer to the birth in 1629 of her first child, Charles, later the sixth Marquis and Duke of Bolton (Masson). The *Matrons* (contrasted with the *Virgin quire*) hasten (hence *early*) to congratulate her on having given birth to a son. (The sense of *greet*, to congratulate, though not the precise construction, appears several times in Spenser, *F.Q.*: *OED*: *v.*¹ 3e). And now with hope of a second happy delivery, she calls upon Lucina, the Roman goddess of childbirth, to aid her in her travail (Cicero, *N.D.* 2. 27; Ovid, *F.* 2. 449–52, 6. 39–40; Horace, *Epod.* 5. 5–6). [Milton's phrasing is close to G. Sandys' version of Ovid, *M.* 10. 507 (*nec Lucina potest parientis voce vocari*): 'Nor could she call Lucina to her throwes' (*Ovid*, 1626, 209). Cf. 'Lucina lent me not her aid, / But took me in my throes' (Shakespeare, *Cym.* 5. 4. 43–4).]

27 *blame*: fault (*OED* 3, and *Nat* 41 n.), as contrasted with *mischance*.

28 *Atropos*: the third of the Fates, who cut the thread of life (cf. *Arc* 62–73 n. and 65 n., and *Lyc* 75–6 n.).

30 *Spoil'd...fruit and tree*: slew at once the offspring and the parent. [An echo of the last line of Milton's *Apologus de Rustico & Hero*: *Nunc periere mihi & foetus & ipsa parens?*]

31–46 [W. J. Roscelli (*TSLL* 8, 1966, 475–6) finds the image in 31–4 'grotesque,' 'essentially metaphysical...deeply serious, structurally functional, and painfully specific'; 'It reconciles in distressing unity the apparent contraries of life and death.' It, joined with the following flower passage, produces 'an effect of chilling pathos' unique in Milton—although the tender image of the flower 'neutralizes the horror induced by the preceding figure.']

33–4 Todd noted examples of *living Tomb* in rhyming conjunction with *Womb* in Browne, *Brit. Past.* 2. 1. 67–8, and Sylvester, *D.W.W.* 2. 4. 3. 1008–9 (Grosart, 1, 249). *languisht*: reduced to languor, made languid (*OED*).

35–46 *So...some tender slip*, etc.: a slip or shoot (*OED*: slip, *sb.*² 1), carefully protected from winter's cold and now the pride of the other flowers (conceived as her attendants: *OED*: train, *sb.*¹ 9), plucked up by some careless rustic who thought to pick the flower, brought quickly to bloom by the showers of spring. The word *carnation* may refer to the kind of flower or merely to the colour from which it takes its name, as in *PL* 9. 429 (*OED*: carnation³ and carnation² 1). The homely and realistic simile then gives place to the happy conceit of the dying plant wept in advance (with *presaging tears*) by the morning dew, which parallels the premonitions of death in wedding and birth and strikes again the note of *funerall* (46). Hughes takes *funerall* as a synonym for death (*OED* 5 gives examples from Spenser, *F.Q.* 2. 5. 25, and Shakespeare, *Per.* 2. 4. 31–2), but the whole idea of *An Epitaph* suggests also the common meaning. [For morning dew as tears, cf. Ovid, *M.* 13. 621–2, and Milton, *QNov* 133–6. With Milton's

Pearls of dew (43), cf. the 'pearles of dew' which Sandys (*Ovid*, 1626, 183) added to his rendering of *M.* 9. 368–9. 'The plucked flower here is a highly stylised object derived from a long tradition of emblematic (rather than symbolic) use of such things' (Daiches, *More Literary Essays*, 104).]

47–8 *Gentle Lady...have.* MS. Sloane indents for a paragraph at 47. Warton compared 'Quiet consummation have, / And renowned be thy grave' (Shakespeare, *Cym.* 4. 2. 280–1).

50 *sease*: seize, take into one's possession (*OED* 5; cf. *Circum* 14 and n.), with at least a strong colouring from the legal sense of the term *seise*, which connotes lawful possession in perpetuity, or what was called *fee-simple* (ibid. 1, 2); whatever suggestion of violence the word *seize* might import is counteracted by this idea of lawful possession and by the very character of the subject, *Sweet rest.* [Brooks and Hardy take the word to mean *quiet, cease*, citing *Nat* 45, but this seems very strained.]

52 *lives lease.* The first word is the 'possessive case of *life*' (Darbishire). *lease*: the period during which possession is guaranteed (*OED*: *sb.*³ 2), here contrasting with the idea of perpetual possession (50 and n.).

53 MS. Sloane indents for a paragraph.

54 *House*: family, in the exalted sense with regard to descent and dignity, as in *Romeo* 3. 1. 111: 'a plague o' both your houses!'

55–9 Keightley took 55–6 to refer to the elegies by Jonson and other well-known poets on the Marchioness' death, and 57–9 to refer, in contrast, not to Milton's verses alone but to a collection of elegies sent from Cambridge (see 1 above [and H. Darbishire on 57–60; Hughes assumes such a collection]). Masson, evidently adopting this suggestion, thinks that *Helicon* is 'here used in its proper sense as the name of a mountain-range...in Boeotia,' one of the homes of the Muses, and not loosely for the spring Aganippe situated thereon. Thus we should have *tears*, i.e. mourning verses (cf. Spenser's *Teares of the Muses*, and see *Lyc* 14 n.) of *perfect*, i.e. fully articulated (*OED* B. 1: 'Thoroughly made, formed') *moan*, i.e. lamentation, produced *in Helicon*, the very home of the Muses, and in contrast with these the artless verses from *the banks of Came* [the river Cam at Cambridge], described not as worthy memorials to be pinned upon the hearse (see *Lyc* 151 n.), but as *som Flowers, and some Bays*, products of nature, not art, with *Bays*, sprigs of laurel, symbolizing however both victory and, as evergreen, immortality, and meet *to strew the ways* before the *Hears* (the bier) as it is carried to the grave. This interpretation, adopting Keightley's and

Masson's assumptions, but not worked out by them or their successors, seems to meet all the demands of the lines. It is of course not strictly necessary to assume a collection of verses from Cambridge (though the expression *som Flowers, and some Bays* suggests a collection): the image might refer to Milton's poem alone. Again, the general interpretation would survive the abandonment of Masson's explanation of *Helicon*. It may well be, as *OED* (Helicon 1) recognizes, that Milton here applies the name to one or both of the springs Aganippe and Hippocrene, so that 56, carrying on the image of *tears* as elegies, would suggest 'formed of drops from the fountains of the Muses.' For what it is worth, it may be noted that MS. Sloane has *helicon* without a capital. [Instead of the meaning of *perfect* given earlier in this note, one may prefer 'Entire, unqualified; pure, unmixed, unalloyed' (*OED* 5 d).]

61   *Saint*: one of the blessed dead (*OED* B. 1); [cf. *Sonn* 23. 1].

63–8   Rachel first appears as the keeper of her father's sheep (Gen. 29. 9). To Jacob, who had served for her fourteen years (29. 18–27), Rachel, after prolonged barrenness, bore Joseph (30. 22–4), destined to be *highly favour'd* in life (Gen. 40–50); she died in giving birth to a second son, Benjamin (Gen. 35. 16–20). [*That fair Syrian Shepherdess* illustrates Milton's as yet simple but effective accommodating of a biblical reference to the 'formalised imagery' of the whole poem; 'the individuality of the character is smoothed away to make her an emblematic pastoral figure,' but *That* 'suggests that of course we all know whom he is talking about' (Daiches, *More Literary Essays*, 104). With *That* cf. two famous examples, in *Lyc* 130 and *PL* 4. 271.]

70   *blazing Majesty and Light*. [Among differences or mistakes in the Sloane MS., Parker (*MLR* 44, 549, n. 2; cf. *Works* 1, 429) noted *might* for *Light*, which 'may represent Milton's original wording.' It may, no doubt, but *might* seems inappropriate here, and Milton is given to associating divine majesty and light, e.g. *Nat* 8–9, *Arc* 2, *PL* 7. 194–5.]

71–2   [The Marchioness and Rachel may become acquainted in heaven, since they have had the same fate, dying in giving birth to a second son (the Marchioness' was stillborn). Brooks and Hardy (122) think the connection between them 'is too accidental for what Milton tries to build upon it.' There is, if not positive support, at least much interest in the fact noted by Hanford (*Poems*, 79), that Dante (*Parad*. 32. 7–9) placed Rachel with Beatrice—'the first clear reference to Dante in Milton's poetry.']

74   *No Marchioness, but now a Queen*. To Todd *Marchioness* and *Queen*, read in relation to *Saint* (71), suggested a possible reminiscence of Anne Boleyn's last message to Henry VIII, 'thanking him for his advancing her, first to be a *Marchioness*; then to be a *Queen*; and now, when he could raise her no higher on earth, for sending her to be a *Saint in Heaven.*' But we could hardly think of a less appropriate allusion in an elegy on a Roman Catholic lady, however much 'inclining to become a Protestant' (see 1 above), and the wife of a presumably devoted and grief-stricken husband. Dunster (reported by Todd) deplored the anticlimax or, as he called it, bathos, of this last line [and many later critics have sighed or snorted. But the serious 'wit,' if not a complete success, is not a crass failure: taken along with line 3, 'A Vicounts daughter, an Earls heir,' the last line crowns an exemplary life translated from mundane to heavenly glory.]

Song. On May Morning

I. DATE

Since *Elegy* 5, *In adventum veris* (*Anno aetatis 20*), belongs to the spring of 1629, and since the *Song* says over again what is said in the *Elegy*, but reduced to simplicity and, as it were, set to an Elizabethan air, this may well have been an exercise in another mode undertaken at the same time. [Grierson (*Poems*, 1, xxi) and Tillyard (*Milton*, 43, 45, 372) assign the *Song* probably to May Day, 1630; Tillyard (373) finds it 'difficult to think that the style of the *May Song* and the *Nightingale Sonnet* is not maturer than that both of the *Fifth Elegy* and of the *Nativity Ode*. A new accent of certainty has entered in, for which I cannot account but by a fresh mental development.' Wright thinks 1 May 1629 'the likely date.' Hughes gives 1629–30, Hanford (*Poems*, 1953) '1631?'. In his *Milton Handbook* (New York, 1946, 145–6: repeated in rev. ed., 1970) Hanford had observed that in the *Poems* of 1645 Milton grouped his more serious religious pieces together, at the beginning: 'The lighter verse follows, arranged apparently in chronological order, with this poem at its head. Had it not been composed before the epigram *On Shakespeare* and the two pieces on the *University Carrier* I think he would have placed it after them, with *L'Allegro* and *Il Penseroso*.' Parker (96, 768, n. 60) agrees with Hanford's later date, 1631, and thinks the *Song* came soon after the *Epitaph on the Marchioness of Winchester*; his reasons are 'Its metre, its mood, and its position in the printed editions.' Carey dates 'Spring 1629?' but takes May 1631 as 'possible.']

Song. On *May Morning*

II. CRITICISM [D.B.]

Hanford ('Youth,' 1925, 119) describes the poem as 'a purified lyric comment on the theme of *Elegy V*, its contrast with the latter poem in style and mood being due to Milton's momentary reversion to the spirit of Elizabethan song.' In his *Handbook* (1946; 1970: Date, above) he links the *Song* with *L'Allegro* and *Il Penseroso* (and in *Poems*, 1953, remarks that 'The lilt of lines 5–9 associates it with "L'Allegro"'). 'Its purer lyric style, free from conceit and verbal curiosity, is a result of Milton's writing for the moment in the classic Jonsonian rather than in the Fletcherian tradition. He was evidently at this time and for several years to come an eclectic follower of many masters. The return to lighter themes may be a reaction from his failure to complete *The Passion*.'

Brooks and Hardy (1951, 123–4): 'The opening lines of this charming aubade, or dawn song, are not merely emptily pretty. They convey quite precisely a double salute,' to both May Day and the month of May. And 'May is not merely...the month, but a girl in a May-day dance,' led in by another dancer, the planet Venus—appropriately for a traditional fertility rite. 'This implied metaphor of the May dance' helps to define the poet's role as 'spokesman for all of nature,' 'a member of the general chorus of rejoicing nature.' The '*ceremonial* character of the poem...is reflected in the careful formal organization': the ten lines comprise an introduction (1–4) of five-stress verse; the song proper (5–8) of four-stress lines; and the two-line conclusion. 'This little poem is simple, but it has that kind of simplicity which results from the most painstaking care in construction.'

III. NOTES

1–2 The *morning Star* is here, plainly, the sun. [This seems hardly possible. In common usage the sun is masculine (as it is in *Nat* 79–84 and 231, *L'All* 60, *IlPen* 132), and this *Star* is feminine; cf. *with her* (2). Presumably the *Star* is Lucifer or Venus (Bell, Hughes).] Warton compared, among other passages: 'yonder shines Aurora's harbinger' (Shakespeare, *Dream* 3. 2. 380, of the morning star); 'The dawning day forth comming from the East' (Spenser, *Astrophel* 34), and 'the golden Orientall gate / Of greatest heaven' from which 'Phoebus... / Came dauncing forth' (*F.Q.* 1. 5. 2); [and 'Daies herbinger,' of the cock, and 'the daies bright king came dauncing out' (Richard Niccols, *The Cuckow*, 1607, pp. 13, 12).] Todd added (with further relevance to 3–4): 'The lovely Spring / Comes dauncing on; the Primrose strewes her way' (P. Fletcher, *Apoll.* 5. 27). [Sandys, possibly echoing the phrase cited from Shakespeare, refers to Aurora as 'the Harbinger of Day' (*Ovid*, 1626, 309; cf. Ovid, *M.* 15. 191).]

3–4 Newton compared: 'violets... / That strew the green lap of the new-come spring' (Shakespeare, *R. II* 5. 2. 46–7). Warton added 'The fresh green lap of...Richard's land' (ibid. 3. 3. 47), and, *inter alia*: 'nature them forth throwes / Out of her fruitfull lap' (Spenser, *F.Q.* 2. 6. 15); 'faire May... / And throwing flowres out of her lap around' (ibid. 7. 7. 34); 'Out of her [Flora's] fruitfull lap each day she threw, / The choicest flowers' (R. Niccols, *The Cuckow*, p. 2).

4 *the pale Primrose*. Warton cited 'pale primeroses / That die unmarried' (Shakespeare, *W. Tale* 4. 4. 122–3), which Milton certainly remembered in composing *Lyc* 142–50 (see n.), but here there is no suggestion of paleness due to unrequited love; the reference is only to colour (as in *Cym.* 4. 2. 221), *pale* in contrast to the deeper yellow of the cowslip. [Milton had used the primrose 'as pure emblem' in *FInf* 1–7. 'Here it is set beside "the yellow cowslip" and is clearly a flower of the English countryside. Neither cowslip nor primrose is found in classical pastoral poetry.' (Daiches, *More Literary Essays*, 105).]

5–10 In these lines Milton repeats the sentiments of *El* 5, and it is perhaps significant that Warton and Todd could detect no echoes from the poets such as abound in 1–4, save a remote one, if indeed it be an echo, from Chaucer: 'May, with alle thy floures and thy grene, / Welcome be thou, faire, fresshe May' (*Knight's Tale* 1510–11). [Apart from the graceful economy of Milton's phrasing, Warton and Todd might have cited abundant pastoral verse in praise of May and young love, e.g. *May* 1–36 in Spenser's *S.C.*]

On Shakespear. 1630

❦

I. DATE AND PUBLICATION

[While Milton's memory could err in regard to the dates of some early poems, we have no knowledge that warrants our questioning his '1630,' which Parker accepts (763, n. 54)], although 1630 may extend to March 1631, if he was using Old Style. The poem was printed, anonymously, in the Second Folio of Shakespeare (1632), under the title *An Epitaph on the admirable Dramaticke Poet, W. Shakespeare.* [The commendatory poems of both the First and the Second Folio are printed by Sir W. W. Greg, *A Bibliography of the English Printed Drama to the Restoration*, 4 v., London, 1939–59, 3, 1249–58. R. M. Smith's pioneer study, 'The Variant Issues of Shakespeare's Second Folio and Milton's First Published English Poem' (Lehigh University Publications, 2, No. 3, 1928), was corrected at points in W. B. Todd's minute analysis of the three states of the Second Folio printing (*SB* 5, 1952–3, 81–108).]

This was the first of Milton's poems to be printed [except the Commencement piece, perhaps *Naturam non pati senium*, mentioned in Milton's letter to Gill of 2 July 1628, *Works* 12, 11]. We do not know how the poem came to the hands of the publishers of the Folio. There seems to be no ground for the conjecture that Ben Jonson may have had a hand in the Folio and suggested the inclusion of these lines by the as yet unknown Cambridge student. [E. Saillens, giving no authority or evidence, turns nebulous conjecture into positive assertion: 'Milton's verse was inserted by Jonson, since it was Jonson who prepared the edition. Moreover, this verse he had not merely accepted but solicited....' (*John Milton*, New York, 1964, 35). M. Freedman ('Milton's "On Shakespeare" and Henry Lawes,' *Shakespeare Quarterly* 14, 1963, 279–81) thinks it unlikely that Milton was asked by the publishers or that—as Masson had suggested (*Life*, 1, 1881, 331)—Milton offered it to them. He proposes Lawes as the intermediary, an idea not in itself implausible, though the circumstantial support that he is able to give seems rather tenuous.]

When the poem was printed a second time, in *Poems: Written by Wil. Shakespeare* (1640), it was signed 'I. M.'; but it is doubtful whether the initials would have served to identify it if Milton had not included the poem in his volumes of 1645 and 1673. [The several texts are reproduced in Fletcher, *Facs.* 366–7.] H. W. Garrod ('Milton's Lines on Shakespeare,' *Essays and Studies* 12, 1926, 7–23) asserted (8, 9) that the 1640 text already had the principal variants which Milton introduced in 1645, but this is not quite correct: 1640 retains the extended title from 1632, and see below, 1 n., 10 n., 13 n., 15 n. [these items were recorded by Garrod, 10–12, in spite of his general statements]. Fletcher (*Facs.* 365) says: 'Milton himself apparently had nothing to do with the appearance of the poem in any of the folios [Second, Third (1663–4), and Fourth (1685)], though he may have been in some way connected with the printing of the *Poems* version of 1640, and may even have supplied new copy for it...'; but he finds no connection between even 1640 and the text of 1645 and 1673.

II. CRITICISM [D.B.]

Mark Pattison (*English Poets*, ed. T. H. Ward, 1880, 2, 294–5), who did not include the *Nativity* in his selections, pronounced *On Shakespear* 'the first piece of which it can be said that its merit does not lie chiefly in its promise.' In it the true Miltonic quality 'is already conspicuous.' 'This sublimity does not reside in the thesis which is logically enunciated, nor in the image presented. These are, as often in Milton, commonplace enough. The elevation is communicated to us not by the dogma or deliverance, but by sympathy. We catch the contagion of the poet's mental attitude. He makes us bow with him before the image of Shakespeare, though there is not a single discriminating epithet to point out in what the greatness which we are made to feel consists....Were we to suppress the feeling, and look only at the logical sentence, as Johnsonian criticism used to do, we should be obliged to say that the residuum is a frigid conceit in the style of Marini.'

Hanford ('Youth,' 1925, 124–5) sees 'Milton's work after 1629' as 'still eclectic in its inspiration and full of variety. The poem on Shakespeare, the two epitaphs on the University Carrier, and the elegy on the Marchioness of Winchester...exhibit a fresh range of contact with earlier English verse. Largely abandoning the manner of the Fletchers and definitely rejecting the "new-fangled toys and trimming slight" of the metaphysical school, Milton enrolls himself among the sons of Ben. *On Shakespeare* and the two Hobson poems (1630 and 1631) are in the vein of seventeenth century epigram.' 'The last lines of Browne's lyric [*On the Countess Dowager of Pembroke*]...supplied Milton with the conceit upon which he constructed the poem on Shakespeare' [see below, 13–14 n.].

Hanford (*Poems*, 1953, 74): 'Milton's attitude toward his greatest English predecessor is one of unfeigned but not uncritical enthusiasm. Shakespeare is for him, as he was for Jonson, nature's poet, but here, as in the later allusion in "L'Allegro," his want of art is regarded as no derogation from his genius.'

Tillyard (*Milton*, 1930, 50–1): 'Milton's lines *On Shakespeare* are his one successful venture in the more extravagant, and at that date (1630) more vital, type of seventeenth-century verse. Often referred to as illustrating Milton's early liberality of taste, they have not been sufficiently admired as a poem....Milton's praise is indeed extremely reverential, far more so than the politeness of a verse tribute absolutely demanded.' Milton may in his own mind have been 'modestly comparing' Shakespeare's 'easie numbers' with his own 'slow-endeavouring art.' But what strikes Tillyard is the extravagant and complicated analogy between men's wonder and a monument, a conceit which he elevates to sublimity, 'as he so painfully failed to do in *The Passion*.... Not merely does he say that our wonder, because it will not change, is a monument: he must explain with great exactness the nature of the process. Shakespeare's art prints itself on all our faculties, but it goes further, it robs our fancy of its active power, including that of effacing the impression. In this monument, frozen into marble yet covered with the impression of his verses, Shakespeare may meetly be interred. Displaying as it does an impassioned critical intelligence, this is the one poem of Milton that can be called metaphysical. Why this uniqueness?' Tillyard suggests some answers.

K. Muir (*John Milton*, 1955, 22–3): 'It is significant that Milton's first published poem was the tribute to Shakespeare.... The lines prove that he honoured Shakespeare's memory "on this side idolatry as much as any", and they indicate perhaps why it was impossible to imitate his work. A poet in the seventeenth century was compelled to explore new poetic territories.... Neither the conventional and misleading tribute in "L'Allegro" to Fancy's child, warbling "his native wood-notes wilde", nor Milton's discreditable sneer at Charles I for reading Shakespeare's plays in prison, nor even the tart dismissal of Shakespeare and his fellows in the preface to *Samson Agonistes*, where he speaks of the Athenian dramatists as "unequall'd yet by any", can affect the magnificence of his early tribute to "*my* Shakespeare". The poem ends with an ingenious conceit: "Then thou... wish to die." Shakespeare's readers, turned to marble by their admiration, provide him with a monument. The conceit was suggested by the opening lines of Jonson's elegy. ...He did not altogether disdain the conceit in his youth, but his conceits generally belong to the Italian tradition.'

Daiches (*Milton*, 1957, 50–1), citing Tillyard's epithet, 'metaphysical,' remarks: 'The first half of the poem, however, has a Jonsonian combination of formality with a note of deep personal affection, and the metaphysical element is only developed in the second half.'

'My' Shakespeare establishes a special relationship at once, but the most impressive thing about the poem—more impressive than the working out of the ingenious conceit—is the way in which it rises to the highly formal 'Under a Star-ypointing Pyramid' and then, after a pause, turns suddenly with a clearly audible shift in tone of voice and an almost visible gesture of affection and admiration to the strong line: 'Dear son of memory, great heir of fame.' The accent falls strongly on the first syllable (which is also the first and most important word) of the line, reversing the normal iambic rhythm and at once arresting our attention; while the balance of 'Dear son...great heir' helps to emphasize the grave emotion of the line.

'The shift in tone is dramatic and Shakespearean....But the poem returns almost immediately to an even more elaborate style of formal compliment than that in which it began, rising to a conventional complimentary climax.'

R. K. Das Gupta ('Milton on Shakespeare,' *Shakespeare Survey* 14, 1961, 98–101) enters a minority report. Opposing Pattison, Hanford, Tillyard, and Muir, he agrees with Hurd (in Warton, 317) that 'This is but an ordinary poem to come from Milton, on such a subject' and adds 'not only ordinary, but largely artificial'; intricate conceits do not evoke powerful feeling. Milton's good judgment stops short of adoration. The author inquires further into the lack of praise for Shakespeare elsewhere in Milton's writings, early and late, where we might expect to find it.

W. R. Parker (*Milton*, 1968, 90) is also severe: 'His poem *On Shakespeare* is one of his poorest, stiffly conventional and singularly uninformative. It is built around a conceit which other poets had used and exhausted, and it tells us almost nothing of Milton's attitude toward his subject. Shakespeare is praised, of course; that is what the verses were supposed to do. He is "my Shakespeare" (which implies nothing); his bones are "honoured" (which makes Milton's question about them purely rhetorical); his relics are "hallowed" (like those of a saint); he is a "son of Memory". We are told, moreover, that his lines are "Delphic" (in other words, poetic), and that they flow easily. Milton does not even suggest that he was a dramatist....A remarkable thing—this eulogy of a great playwright without a single reference to his plays.' [This last-named sin is shared at least by Matthew Arnold in his sonnet.]

III. NOTES

[Possible sources of some details are recorded below. What may be echoes of Tomkis, Jonson, Massinger, and the Stanley epitaphs were assembled by H. Mutschmann in an appendix (47–55) in his *Further Studies Concerning the Origin of Paradise Lost* (Tartu, 1934). Freedman (1 above) referred generally to parallels in image and word between Milton and the elegiac tributes of William Basse (*Oxford Book of Seventeenth Century Verse*, p. 238) and Jonson; but Basse was not printed before 1633. The epitaphs on the Stanleys, in the seventeenth century attributed to Shakespeare, were first cited—as one—by Todd (reporting F. Townsend). They are quoted here from Sir E. K. Chambers, *William Shakespeare* (Oxford, 1930), 1, 551:

> An Epitaph on Sr Edward Standly [Stanley]
>
> Not monumentall stones preserves our Fame;
> Nor sky-aspiring Piramides our name;
> The memory of him for whom this standes
> Shall out live marble and defacers hands
>   When all to times consumption shall bee given,
>   Standly for whom this stands shall stand in Heaven.

> On Sr Thomas Standly [Stanley]
>
> Ask who lies heere but doe not wheepe;
> Hee is not deade; Hee doth but sleepe;
> This stony Register is for his bones,
> His Fame is more perpetuall, then these stones,
>   And his owne goodnesse wth him selfe being gone,
>   Shall live when Earthly monument is nonne.

Quoting the first of these epitaphs, T. Spencer (*MLN* 53, 1938, 366–7) observed these resemblances between it and Milton's lines: '1) Both state the uselessness of a monument for preserving the memory of the dead; 2) in both, "fame" and "name" are rhymed; 3) "marble" is mentioned in both, and 4)—most striking of all—the one phrase in "Shakespeare's" poem that has life in it, "sky-aspiring Piramides," is echoed, both in idea and rhythm, by Milton's "star-ypointing pyramid." The first three resemblances are, of course commonplaces of epitaph poetry. But the last resemblance implies something more.' Probably Milton 'was consciously or unconsciously following a poem which, like his contemporaries, he believed Shakespeare himself to have written.']

1–4 Masson conjectured the possibility of some plan for a memorial to Shakespeare to which Milton here refers. But the idea of works of literature outlasting material monuments was a commonplace; cf. Horace, *C.* 3. 30. 1–2. And, among the verses printed in the First Folio, and reprinted in the Second, those of Leonard Digges speak of 'thy Workes, by which, out-live / Thy Tombe, thy name must: when that stone is rent, / And Time dissolves thy Stratford Moniment, / Here we alive shall view thee still' [(Greg, 1254; Chambers, 2, 231)].

1 *What needs*: *neede* in 1632 and 1640. Rolfe noted the common use of *what* for *why*, as in 'What need we any spur but our own cause...?' (Shakespeare, *Caesar* 2. 1. 123). [Cf. *Comus* 361, *PL* 2. 94, 329. H. C. H. Candy (*N&Q* 158, 1930, 310–12) cites Browne, *Brit. Past.* 1. 1. 9: 'What need I tune the swains of Thessaly?' cf. Lat. *quid.*]

3 *hallow'd reliques* ['implies that Shakespeare is a saint' (Brooks and Hardy, 127).]

4 *Star-ypointing Pyramid.* Some copies of the 1632 Folio have *starre-ypointed* (*Facs.* 366), the logically correct form, since *y* (Germanic *ge*) is the prefix of the perfect participle (*OED*: star, *sb.*^{1} 20, and Masson n.), but it fails to give Milton's exact meaning, 'pointing'—not 'pointed'—'to the stars' (*OED*, loc. cit.); [cf. the correct (though archaic) use of *y* with the perfect participle in *Nat* 155 and *L'All* 12]. Other copies have *ypointing*, as have 1640, 1645, and there can be no doubt that this is what Milton wrote and insisted on retaining. Todd quoted W. Browne's lines referring to the death of Spenser: 'A pyramis, whose head like winged Fame / Should pierce the clouds, yea, seem the stars to kiss' (*Brit. Past.* 2. 1. 1016–17). [Carey notes that Sandys (*Relation*, 1615, 129) quotes Propertius 3. 2. 19, *neque Pyramidum sumptus ad sidera ducti*, which he translated: 'Not sumptuous Pyramis to skies up-reard.' Cf. the epitaph on Sir E. Stanley quoted at the beginning of these notes. Baconian dealings with Milton's epithet are noticed by H. Darbishire.]

5 *Dear son of memory.* Newton (reported by Todd), recalling that in Hesiod (*Theog.* 53–62) the Muses are the daughters of Memory [cf. Milton, *Idea* 2–3], interpreted the phrase as making Shakespeare the brother of the Muses. This is adopted by Hughes [and Brooks and Hardy and Carey]; it seems doubtful, however, in the light of the co-ordinate *great heir of Fame*, which suggests rather being cherished in memory and heir to all that Fame can give [a meaning supported by the following line]. Todd noted that Browne calls the English poets 'sons of Memory' (*Brit. Past.* 2. 1. 1027), but there it is clear that, by satire, they are to perpetuate the memory of evil done.

6 *What need'st.* See above, 1 n. The 1632 Folio has *needst*; 1640, *needs* (presumably a misprint). For *weak*, 1632 has *dull*, but 1640 *weake*.

7-14 Garrod (15) quotes from *Albumazar* (1. 4. 3-4) by Thomas Tomkins (i.e. Tomkis), a comedy produced for James I's visit to Cambridge in March 1615 [not 1614, as Garrod says]: 'Wonder for me, admire, and be astonisht, / Marvaile thy selfe to Marble....' (*Albumazar*, ed. H. G. Dick, University of California Publications in English 13, 1944, 83). Garrod further (14) quotes [or rather misquotes] from Massinger and Field's *The Fatal Dowry*, also printed in 1632: 'He cannot rayse thee a poore Monument, / ...Thy worth, in every honest brest buylds one, / Making their friendly hearts thy funerall stone' (1632, sig. D2; 2. 1. 69-72; *Plays of Philip Massinger*, ed. F. Cunningham, London, 1868, 361).

8 *live-long*: 1632, *lasting*; 1640, *live-long*. *OED* explains the compound as normally an 'emotional intensive of *long*, used of periods of time' (cf. *L'All* 99 n.), but here as meaning 'that lives long or endures; lasting,' a nonce-use. [Garrod (11-12) thinks the change from *lasting* to *live-long* was prompted only by Milton's concern for sound.]

9-10 *whilst to th' shame...numbers flow.* Cf. *L'All* 132-4 and n. [Masson, Bell, Moody, and Carey quote the editors' preface to the First Folio: 'His mind and hand went together: And what he thought, he uttered with that easinesse, that wee have scarse received from him a blot in his papers.' Brooks and Hardy (127) remark that 'the sudden opening of the couplets in lines 9-12 is beautifully adapted to the idea of the "flow" of Shakespeare's "easie numbers." ']

10 *heart*: 1632, *part*; 1640, *heart*. [The word *part* may have been Milton's or a misprint. Garrod (11) defends *part* as equally good. Following Garrod, Tillyard (*Milton*, 50) says that *part* 'makes the encomium more explicit though it gives a less quickly obvious sense. Shakespeare would appeal not to the hearts of all his readers but to the reader's every part or faculty.' Brooks and Hardy (127) suggest that 'Perhaps Milton began by thinking of each reader as a *part* of the total monument.']

11 *unvalu'd Book.* Garrod (16) compares Chapman's lines in the postscript to his translation of the *Iliad*: '(repaid / With thine owne value) go, unvalu'd Booke, / Live and be lov'd' (*Chapman's Homer*, ed. A. Nicoll, 2 v., New York, 1956, 1, 498). The two meanings of *unvalued*—'of very great value, invaluable' (as in Shakespeare, *R. III* 1. 4. 27, 'Inestimable stones, unvalued jewels,' and as here) and 'not regarded as valuable'—were both in common use in Milton's day (examples in *OED*).

12 *Delphick lines.* Browne explains the epithet as 'oracular' (a common meaning by transference from the Delphic oracle), but Rolfe is probably right in taking it as 'inspired by Apollo' (from the same source) as better fitting the context. [Brooks and Hardy (126) assume both meanings.] *impression*: 'a strong effect produced on the intellect, conscience, or feelings' (*OED* 6b), but with a closer relation than is common in such figurative use to the stamping of a mark as with a seal on wax or here more probably the imprinting with type on paper (ibid. 3).

13 *it self*: 1632, *her selfe*; 1640, *our selfe*; 1645, *it self*. [Garrod (11) suggests that *our* may be a misprint for *her*, though '*our self* can be defended from other writers,' and that Milton's dislike of *her selfe* is clear from the 1645 reading. See the following note.]

13–14 It would seem that *our selfe* (1640) would give the clearer meaning: 'The strong impression made on our imagination causes us to lose consciousness of our self.' With *it self* one might paraphrase: 'The strong impression made on our imagination takes entire possession of it' [cf. *Comus* 259–60 (Todd)]. *conceaving.* The verb *conceive* could mean: (1) 'to take or admit into the mind; to become affected or possessed' with something (*OED* 6), or (2) 'to form a mental representation' of something, 'to imagine' (ibid. 8). The former would suit well with the context, the notion of a strong impression made; the latter, with *fancy* (or imagination), whose activity was to form mental images. Masson interprets: 'we, Shakespeare's readers, are the true marble of his tomb or monument.' [Brooks and Hardy (125–6) amplify Masson: 'we are turned to stone...with the labor of appreciation—"with too much conceaving," ' i.e. 'Not by losing all power of thought, but by being overwhelmed with thought; not by becoming dead, but by being awaked to more intense life....As Milton has developed his poem, both submeanings of *conceive* (to imagine and to become filled with life) are used.' Cf. Tillyard in 11 above.]

Editors compare *IlPen* 42, 'Forget thy self to Marble' (see above, 7–14 n. and cf. the epitaph on Sir E. Stanley quoted at the beginning of these notes). Hanford ('Youth,' 125; *Poems*), Garrod, and others quote the second half of W. Browne's *On the Countess Dowager of Pembroke* (*Poems*, 2, 294; the poem first appeared in Camden's *Remains, Concerning Britain*, ed. 1623): 'Marble piles let no man raise / To her name: for after days / Some kind woman born as she, / Reading this, like Niobe / Shall turn marble, and become / Both her mourner and her tomb.' [Garrod (15–16) also quoted (not quite correctly) the first lines of Browne's *On his Wife, an Epitaph* (*Poems*, 2, 293): 'Thou need'st no tomb, my wife, for thou hast one, / To which all marble is but pumex stone; / Thou art engrav'd so deeply in my heart, / It shall outlast the strongest hand of Art.' T.C.C. (*N&Q* 184, 1943, 314) saw Niobe behind Milton's 'marble imagery' here and elsewhere and cited parallels; R. Hussey (ibid. 381) rejected Niobe and cited Davenant's *The Witts* (acted 1634, pub. 1636): 'I have / Long since amaz'd my selfe e'ne to a Marble' (5. 1; sig. K).]

15 *dost*: so 1632, 1645; 1640, *doth*.

On the University Carrier

※

I. DATE AND CIRCUMSTANCES

Among his several titles to fame, Thomas Hobson (1544?–1631) must be unique among carriers in having a place in both the *Spectator* (509) and the *DNB*. According to Masson (*P.W.* 1, 126–8), he was a well-known figure in Cambridge for upward of sixty years. During that time he drove his own wagon weekly between the town and the Bull Inn, Bishopsgate Street, in London, carrying letters and parcels and an occasional traveller to and from the University. He also hired out horses, with full equipment for riding to London, and he always insisted on the customer's taking the horse nearest the door—whence the proverbial phrase, 'Hobson's choice.' He is further credited with the advice to impatient travellers: 'You will get to London time enough, if you don't ride too fast.' He was, in short, a character. The visitation of the plague in Cambridge in 1630, with the closing of the University, put a stop to his journeys; and though he escaped the plague, the breaking of his routine caused him—as was thought—to decline, and he died on 1 January 1631, shortly before the University reassembled.

Hobson's death occasioned a number of sets of verses (*Works* 18, 359, 590–2). [Parker (764–6, n. 57) gives a list.] G. B. Evans ('Milton and the Hobson Poems,' *MLQ* 4, 1943, 281–90) printed seven poems and two versions of a short epitaph; and in 'Some More Hobson Verses' and 'Correction' (ibid. 9, 1948, 10 and 184) printed four short epitaphs and mentioned another poem of 14 lines. Willa McC. Evans ('Hobson Appears in Comic Song,' *PQ* 26, 1947, 321–7) recorded a dialogue between Hobson and Charon, set to music. All these semi-comic pieces attest Hobson's fame and provide interesting background for Milton's superior efforts in the same vein. Two poems and possibly a third (see below) were written by Milton, one by William Hall of Christ's College, later to be associated with him in *Obsequies to the memorie of Mr Edward King*; the others, when not by unknown hands, were by persons who have no ascertained connection with Milton or Cambridge.

Milton's second Hobson poem (*Another on the same, Works* 1, 33–4) was printed in *A Banquet Of Jests* (6th ed., London, 1640, 129–31); and both the first and the second appeared in *Wit Restor'd In severall Select Poems Not formerly publish't* (1658, 84–6). [These printed texts are in Fletcher, *Facs.* 370–1.] The second poem was copied in a contemporary MS. collection of verse, now in the Bodleian Library (MS. Malone 21, fol. 69ᵛ: W. R. Parker, 'Milton's Hobson Poems: Some Neglected Early Texts,' *MLR* 31, 1936, 395–402; *Milton*, 766, n. 58). It was also copied in a pre-Restoration commonplace book now in the Huntington Library (MS. H. M. 116, pp. 100–1). The first poem 'occurs in Bodleian MS. CCC.E.309, fol. 48ʳ' (Parker, 766, n. 58) and in a commonplace book of about 1640–50 now in the Folger Shakespeare Library (MS. 1.21, fols. 79ᵛ–8oʳ: G. B. Evans, 'Two New Manuscript Versions of Milton's Hobson Poems,' *MLN* 57, 1942, 192–4). The variants are listed in the articles cited; those of critical interest are cited below.

The two poems are cited in this Commentary as *Carrier* 1 and 2.

Among the many poems on the subject, one, *Hobsons Epitaph*, occurs in *A Banquet Of Jests* (1640, 131–2), the collection that included Milton's second Hobson poem, and in *Wit Restor'd* (1658, 83–4), where Milton's first and second poems were reprinted, and this may possibly be by him (see below, *Hobsons Epitaph*).

[Textual variants in all three poems are given by Shawcross (*C.E.P.*, 550–2) and bibliographical data are summarized and augmented in his 'A Note on Milton's Hobson Poems' (*RES* 18, 1967, 433–7).]

Milton's two pieces, and the third tentatively ascribed to him, are, like their inferior fellows, *jeux d'esprit*. They are best described as applications of wit for comic (as in *On Shakespear* for solemn) effect, and as such they form a minor part of Milton's conscious experiment and practice in styles. It is plain, of course, that his feelings are largely disengaged, as they are in some of his other early verse. Considered in reference to their occasion, all the poems on Hobson might, by modern standards, appear somewhat heartless, and also at striking variance with the seventeenth century's own solemn and awestruck contemplation of death as one of 'the four last things.' But we may go along with Masson's opinion that 'through all their punning facetiousness, there is a vein of kindliness.' [Brooks and Hardy (129) remark: 'But more important than the meaning of any one of the conceits is the way in which all are especially designed for student appreciation. This is immediately apparent so far as the *matter* of Milton's wit is concerned....But it is also important to note that the poet has consistently maintained the proper *manner*—outrageous and somewhat irreverent, and yet completely guileless.']

II. NOTES (*Carrier 1*)

On the University Carrier, who sickn'd in the time of his vacancy, being forbid to go to London, by reason of the Plague.

The title states both the subject and the theme of the poem. There are no variants of critical interest in the text of the *Poems* of 1645; but the text in *Wit Restor'd*, apparently based on another and perhaps earlier MS., presents some substantive variants, recorded below (from Parker's complete list, *MLR* 31, 401) as 1658; and one in Folger MS. 1. 21 (from G. B. Evans' collation, *MLN* 57, 192), here recorded as Folger.

1   *old Hobson.* See headnote above.   *girt*: saddle girth (*OED* 1).

1–2   1658: 'Death hath his desire, / ...hath left him in the mire.'

5   *a shifter*: one who resorts to tricks or artifice (*OED* 3; the meaning derived from the verb *shift*, ibid. 6). Hobson was so old that he must have used every trick to evade death. In such a punning poem the noun could suggest other meanings of the verb *shift*: to elude, escape (ibid. 17), to manage matters (ibid. 4), arrange (ibid. 1), apportion, distribute (ibid. 2)—these in allusion to the habit that gave rise to the phrase 'Hobson's choice' (see headnote); and, in reference to his prospering in the world, to make a living by one's own devices, get on (ibid. 5), to shift for oneself (ibid. 7). [Lines 7 f. suggest that the word applies chiefly to the carrier's being so much in motion, on the road.]

8 *Dodg'd with him*: shifted position so as to baffle (*OED* 1b) him ⟨Death⟩, carrying on the primary idea in *shifter*. *Cambridge and the Bull*. See headnote. 1658: 'Dog'dd him 'twixt Cambridge and the London-Bull.'

9–13 See title and headnote.

13 *he had tane up his latest Inne*. [H. C. H. Candy (*N&Q* 158, 1930, 310–12) cited Browne, *Brit. Past*. 1. 3. 147: 'Now had the glorious sun ta'en [*taen* in original text] up his inn.']

14 *Chamberlin*: chamberlain, attendant in charge of the bed-chambers at an inn (*OED* 3). 1658: 'Death in the likenesse of a Chamberlin'; Folger: 'In craftie likenes of a Chamberlin.'

16 *took away the light*: an oblique reference to the ending of life. Cf. 'Put out the light, and then put out the light' (Shakespeare, *Oth*. 5. 2. 7).

Another on the same

✦

I. TEXTS

There are no variants of critical interest in *Poems* (1645). But, as we noticed above, the poem had already appeared in *A Banquet Of Jests* (1640), under the title *Upon old Hobson the Carrier of Cambridge*. This version, printed in *Works* 18, 349–50 (cited here as 1640), shows a number of variants. W. R. Parker (*MLR* 31, 1936, 395–402) gives a complete collation of 1640, 1658 (*Wit Restor'd*), and the version in Bodleian MS. Malone 21; and G. B. Evans (*MLN* 57, 1942, 192–4) adds collation for the version in the Huntington MS. Only substantive changes of some critical interest are recorded here. The title in Malone is *On Hobson ye Cambridge carrier who died 1630 in ye vacancy of his carriage by reason of ye sicknesse then hott at Cambridge*. Huntington gives the same information in slightly different words. Cf. the title of *Carrier* 1 above. Lines 15–20 and 25–6 are lacking in 1640, Malone, Huntington, [and St John's: see below] and lines 13–26 in 1658.

[Shawcross (*RES* 18, 1967, 433–7) describes a copy found in 'an anonymous poetical commonplace-book in the Library of St. John's College, Cambridge, MS. S. 32, on ff. 18ᵛ–19ʳ' (in which the poem is ascribed to 'Jo: Milton'). 'The variants are similar to those in the Huntington and Malone MSS.,' but this copy has some differences from any known text (see notes below, where this MS. is cited as 'St John's'). This miscellany was apparently compiled 'about the later 1630s.' The text of *Carrier* 2 'definitely was not taken from the 1645 *Poems*.' Shawcross's general conclusion is 'that the texts of the second Hobson poem resulted from two traditions: that which Milton printed (or else he altered the text before publication) and one which was changed by scribal or editorial error or emendation.']

II. NOTES (*Carrier 2*)

1 *lieth one*: 1640, *Hobson lyes* (also Malone, Huntington, St John's).

2 *could move*: 1640, *did move* (also Malone, Huntington).

4 *While*: [*So(e)* (Huntington, Malone, St John's).] *might still*: 1658, *could but.*

5 *sphear-metal*: the material of which the celestial spheres are composed. Keightley suggested a reference to the spheres' perpetual motion. Hughes compares *PL* 7. 353–6, where the sun is described as of celestial mould (substance), and sees a reference to Aristotle's doctrine (*Cael.* 1. 3, etc.) that the heavenly substance is indestructible [cf. Svendsen, *Science*, 55]. Both ideas are needed to give full force to Milton's conceit.

6 *revolution*: 1640, 1658, Huntington, St John's: *resolution.* *stay*: 1658, *made of stay.*

7 *Time numbers motion*: an allusion to the Aristotelian definition of time as the measure of motion. Editors cite Aristotle, *Cael.* 1. 9, *Physics* 4. 11–12, and Plato, *Timaeus* 37–8. What is here a conceit is later given a central place in Milton's theology (*DocCh* 1. 7, *Works* 15, 35).

7–8 (*without a crime* | *'Gainst old truth*): 1640, *without all crime*: without any violation of (this) old truth (now become a commonplace).

9 *an Engin*: a machine (*OED* 4), here of course a clock. For *an*, 1640, 1658, Malone, Huntington, and St John's read *some*. [For *with* St John's reads *by*.]

10 *principles*: source of motion, force which produces particular results (*OED* 1. 3). [*being*: *when* (St John's).] *ceast*: 1658, *once ceas'd.*

11 *Rest…life*: rest that gives refreshment for continued living, with a play on *rest*, cessation of movement. [For *men* 1640 reads *us*.]

12 *breathing*: time to breathe, rest (*OED*: vbl. sb. 2; *breathe*: v. 5).

13–26 1658 omits.

14 Taking the more general meaning of *vacation*, freedom from business or activity (*OED* 1), and the special meaning of *term*, extreme limit or end (*OED* 1 b), Milton makes an obvious but appropriate play on words. For *Too long* Malone reads *Too much*, which partly spoils the pun.

15 *drive…away*: banish, with an obvious pun.

15–20. Omitted in 1640, Malone, Huntington, St John's.

16 *quickn'd*: a play on *quicken*, restore life to (*OED* 1), and accelerate (ibid. 5).

18 *may not carry…ne're be fetched*: a special play on the common phrase 'fetch and carry,' since *fetch'd* here means restored to consciousness; cf. Bacon: 'For smells, we see their great and sudden effect in fetching men again when they swoon' (*Sylva Sylvarum* 694, *Works* 2, 556; *OED* 12 b and 2).

19 *the cross Doctors*: ['The Doctors of the University who are opposing (*OED* Cross, *a*. 5. a) Hobson's journeys to and fro' (Carey).]

20 *put down*: a play on the removal of a person from office (*OED*: *v.*¹ 41 c) and the destroying, killing, of a person (ibid. 41 g); [also perhaps on suppressing (ibid. 41 b, with reference, Wright thinks, to efforts to reduce the number of carriers on the roads) and on lowering a person's pride, 'taking down,' snubbing (*OED* 41 d)].   *bearers*: a play on *bearer* as porter (*OED* 1. 1) and as pall bearer (ibid. 1. 1 c).

21 Malone: *his disease & to judge aright*; Huntington: *his disease and (to judge aright.*

22 *heaviness*: [(1) weight, (2) sadness (*OED a, e*).]   *Cart went light*: 1640, *Carts were light*; Malone, Huntington: *cart was light*.

25–6 1640, Malone, Huntington, and St John's (as well as 1658: see 13–26 n.) omit.

26 *prest to death*. [There seems to be a grim reference to persons being pressed to death (a mode of execution: *OED*: press, *v.*¹ 1 b), who, to shorten their suffering, cry out for heavier weights.] The word also suggests ready (*OED*: prest *a*. 1; Keightley cited 'to battell…prest,' Spenser, *F.Q.* 5. 7. 27); and possibly the sense exemplified in 'men…pressed foorth to warre, against their will' (Fairfax, *Jerusalem* 20. 16). The word *waight* also involves a play on *wait*.

27 *But had*: 1640, 1658, Malone, Huntington, St John's, *For had*. [In St John's 27–8 appear between 12 and 13.]

28 *been an*: Huntington, *bene so sure an*.

29–34 Omitted in 1658.

29–31 The reference is to his *weekly course of carriage betwixt Cambridge and the Bull* (*Carrier* 1. 10 and 8), making up four journeys in each lunar month. Thus *Obedient to the Moon he spent his date* (the duration of his life: *OED* 4) and *In cours reciprocal*, like the tides.

30 *and had his fate*: Malone, *and in his fate*; Huntington, *& his fate*.

31 *Linkt to*: Malone, *Like to*. See above, 29–31 n.

32 Masson noted the 'pun on the two identical sounds, *wane*, wasting or diminution, and *wain*, waggon.' But there were other possibilities in the following recognized meanings available to Milton: *wain*: wagon or other wheeled vehicle (*OED*: *sb.*¹ 1 a–c); variant form of *gain* (ibid. wain *sb.*² and gain: *sb.*²); also the verb meaning to transport in a wagon (ibid. wain *v.* 1); *wane*: want, lack (ibid. *sb.*¹ 1); decrease, either in size (ibid. 4), especially of the waning of the moon (ibid. 5), or in power, especially as following upon a gradual increase (ibid. 6), all of these closely associated with the verb *wane*, one of whose particular meanings referred to the moon (ibid. wane *v.* 2), while another meaning, ebb, was applicable to the tides (ibid. 1 c). Likewise with the noun *increase* (also dependent upon the verb): from the basic meaning (ibid. *sb.* 1), growth in wealth (ibid. 4), or in extent, with special reference to the rising of the tide (ibid. 1 b), or in size, the waxing of the moon (ibid.).   *increase*: 1640, *disease*, which impairs the sense and limits the tissue of suggestions.

33 *deliver'd all and gon*: Huntington, *deliver'd, all are gone.*

33–4 The allusion is to Hobson's carrying letters between Cambridge and London (see headnote). A *superscription* is whatever is written above, as, in a letter, the address (*OED*: *sb.* 3; cf. *v.* 2), or, on gravestone or effigy, the epitaph (ibid. *sb.* 1). [For *this* (34) St John's reads *his*.]

[*Hobsons Epitaph*]

This poem appeared, after *Carrier 2*, in *A Banquet Of Jests* (6th ed., 1640, 131–2) and was included in *Wit Restor'd* (1658). It is printed in *Works* 18, 359, with full collation (ibid. 591) with the texts in *Wit Restor'd*, Bodleian MS. Tanner 465, British Museum MS. Add. 15–227, and British Museum MS. Sloane 542, supplied by W. R. Parker. Parker thought it possible that the poem, since it first appeared with *Carrier 2*, might also be by Milton, and that the poet might have thought that *Carrier* 1 and 2 were enough to print in his *Poems* of 1645 and discarded it. [In 1968 Parker (764, n. 57) says 'Probably also by Milton.'] If it is not by Milton it would appear to be 'the production of the same group of poets and wits at Cambridge to which he had belonged' (*Works* 18, 590). One should perhaps note an evident relation between this poem and one of 121 lines printed by G. B. Evans (*MLQ* 4, 1943, 286–8) from British Museum MS. Harleian 6057 (for examples see below, notes on 1–2, 5–6, 17–18) and a copy of the short attributed poem (Harvard MS. Eng. 686: Evans, 285) which provides a variant nearer to the long poem (see below, 1–2 n.). These facts may be thought to militate against Milton's authorship. Since the attribution is so speculative, it seems unnecessary to notice even substantive variants here, except in one or two instances; the interested reader may be referred to the complete collation. [The collation in Shawcross's *C.E.P.* (551–2) is enlarged in his article (*RES* 18, 1967, 433–7), based on his discovery of ten manuscript copies in addition to the eleven known before. He continues to regard Milton's authorship as 'an interesting possibility.'] The content of the poem turns wholly on Hobson's journeys between Cambridge and London. The word-play is much less constant and recondite than in *Carrier 2*.

1–2 *Here Hobson...of many letters.* Harleian reads *with some not his betters* (1) and *and yett a man of letters* (2), while Harvard reads *Hobson lies heare amongst his many betters.*

2–6 Evans (285, n. 10) notes that the writer seems to have had John Earle's character of 'A Carrier' in mind: 'Hee is the ordinary Embassadour betweene Friend and Friend, the Father and the Sonne, and brings rich Presents....He is no unletter'd man, though in shew simple, for questionlesse, hee ha's much in his Budget, which hee can utter too in fit time and place' (*Micro-cosmographie*, ed. G. Murphy, London, 1928, p. 25).

5–6 *His carriage...In Embassie twixt father and the Sonne.* Harvard reads: *oft hath he gon | On Embassi twixt father, and the sonne*; Harleian: *was approvd for hee hath beene | Ambassadors to all degrees of Kinn.*

17–18 *thou ever-toyling...Charls-waine.* Harleian reads: *thou everlasting Swaine | the Supreame Waggoner next Charles his wayne.* Other poems printed from MSS. by Evans make different play with this same image. One, from British Museum MS. Add. 15–227, reads: *Then I conjecture Charles ye Northerne Swayne, | Whisled up Hobson, for to drive his wayne. | Hee is not dead, h'has changed his mansion heere, | He has left the Bull, & flitted to ye Beare.*

L'Allegro and Il Penseroso

※

223

L'*Allegro* and *Il* *Penseroso*

🙰

I. DATE AND CIRCUMSTANCES

[Throughout discussions of these poems and some others, quoted references to Horton cannot be constantly altered or complicated, but the reader should bear in mind the discovery, based on legal documents, that from September 1632 to January 1635 (and perhaps for some time earlier or later) the Miltons were living in the London suburb of Hammersmith and did not move to Horton, near Windsor, until 1635 or thereabouts (H. F. Fletcher, *JEGP* 51, 1952, 154–9, and *Intell. Dev.*, 1, 1956, 405–14; French, *L.R.* 5, 1958, 380; and the summary of the data and related questions in Parker, 779–81). It is true that Milton himself, in the *Second Defence* (1654), spoke simply of leaving Cambridge and living at his father's house in the country (*Works* 8, 121), but, even if after twenty years he recalled the precise facts, he might well have avoided cluttering his brief account with insignificant details.]

On no better grounds than the rural setting, particularly of *L'Allegro*, the companion poems were once confidently assigned to the period of Milton's country retreat at Horton. Masson accepted that traditional association, but noticed the absence of the poems from the MS., whose commencement, with *Arcades*, he dated in 1633; accordingly, he placed the poems 'in the autumn or latter part of 1632' (*Life*, 1, 569; *P.W.* 1, 131). This date has been thought too late and too early. Grierson (*Poems*, 1925, 1, xviii–xxi) more ingeniously than convincingly explained their absence from the Cambridge MS., and, on the ground that their 'texture ...is that of the descriptive parts' of *Comus*, proposed to place them with the masque in 1633–4. This, however, is a minority opinion. Hanford ('Youth,' 131) declared for 'the very beginning' of Milton's residence at Horton (i.e. the summer of 1632), but thought it quite possible that the poems 'go back to some vacation interval in his university life.'

That the poems do thus go back was urged by Tillyard ('Milton: *L'Allegro* and *Il Penseroso*,' English Association Pamphlet No. 82, 1932; repr. in *M. Set.*, 1938). His argument turns chiefly on six considerations: (1) the absence of the poems from the Cambridge MS.; (2) their generalized landscape and the absence of any evidence in the poems themselves to support the traditional association with Horton; (3) the divergence of their holiday mood from what we know of Milton's life of study and preparation for his life-work undertaken there, and its consonance, on the other hand, with the spirit of a long vacation; (4) the fact that the poems, especially in their rhetorical openings, appear to suppose an academic audience; (5) the further association with Cambridge supplied by the dependence of both poems, especially *L'Allegro*, on *Prolusion* 1, 'Whether Day is more excellent than Night'; and (6) Milton's assertion in *Prolusion* 7 (*Works* 12, 249) that during the preceding long vacation he had enjoyed the highest favour of the Muses, which (if *Prolusion* 7 belongs to Milton's last year at Cambridge and these are the poems therein referred to) gives the summer of 1631 as their date.

All these points seem well taken. The third, indeed, might be considerably strengthened by a clearer apprehension of the pattern of Milton's poetic development from the *Nativity* to *Comus* and *Lycidas* and beyond, a recognition of the ethical and religious interests which dominate all the poems known to have been written after the retirement to Horton, or from *Sonnet* 7 onward. Only in the fifth point does Tillyard seriously overplay his hand in asserting that the memory of *Prolusion* 1 which clearly appears in the companion poems means that their real subjects are 'Day' and 'Night'; but this inference is a matter of interpretation and is dealt with below. To reject the interpretation does not much impair Tillyard's argument about the date. Indeed it permits us to recognize, and give due emphasis to, another fact which strongly supports his dating, namely, that if the imagery of the poems in some places reflects *Prolusion* 1, the theme of *Il Penseroso* has much in common with that of *Prolusion* 7 (Woodhouse, 'Notes,' 84–6, 88–9).

The precise relation of *Il Penseroso* to *Prolusion* 7 is again a question of interpretation and must be postponed [see Woodhouse under 1943–4 in III: Criticism]. Here it will suffice to say that *Prolusion 7*, *Il Penseroso*, and *Ad Patrem*—each with its own emphasis—all bear on the three subjects: leisure, learning, and poetry. The Prolusion starts by associating leisure and poetry and goes on to an eloquent defence of learning. *Il Penseroso*, assuming throughout, and exemplifying, the required leisure, dwells on the pleasures of learning but culminates in the hope that learning may issue in inspiration, while by virtue of its medium the whole piece is as it were encompassed by the idea of poetry—of poetry associated with leisure and learning. *Ad Patrem* deals specifically with the necessity of leisure for learning, and of learning for poetry. As an indication of contemporaneity such similarity of theme will carry weight only until it is confronted with much stronger evidence, internal or external, pointing to widely separated dates; and no such evidence has come to light. The preoccupations manifested by the three pieces would be entirely natural at the time when Milton was about to quit Cambridge and launch upon the private studies of the Horton period. [See also the Chronological Survey above, II and III.]

[Tillyard's argument for the summer of 1631, if not quite firm enough to establish certainty, seems to have been generally accepted, e.g. by Woodhouse (above), Hanford, Hughes, Shawcross, Parker, and Carey. F. W. Bateson's argument for 1629 (see III below, under 1950) was shown by J. B. Leishman ('*L'Allegro* and *Il Penseroso* in Their Relation to Seventeenth-Century Poetry,' *Essays and Studies 1951*, 2: this essay is repr. in Leishman's *Milton's Minor Poems*, London, 1969) to be untenable, but was endorsed by Fletcher (*Intell. Dev.*, 2, 1961, 479 f.); on the interpretation of *Elegy* 6. 89–90, which is crucial for Bateson and Fletcher, see J. Carey below, under *Sonnet* 1. E. S. Le Comte (*Yet Once More*, New York, 1953, 60–1) appealed to the full evidence of his book in seeing as specious Tillyard's relating of the poems to *Prolusion* 1: 'There is no span of years within his productive lifetime across which Milton will not and does not reach to borrow from himself. One could argue as well, probably better, that "L'Allegro" and "Il Penseroso" were written in the Horton period, because of the phrases connecting them with *Comus*.' E. Saillens (*Milton*, 37) accepts the summer of 1631 without question and also says, without question and without evidence, that Milton read the poems 'in the presence of the whole University.' Parker (1968: 98–103, 769–70) sees the poems as the final fruits of Milton's academic life and thoroughly representative of his mind and art in his last year at Cambridge. Like Woodhouse and Le Comte, he discounts Tillyard's use of *Prolusion* 1 but accepts his argument for an academic audience. He finds support for 1631 in the position of the twin poems in the printed texts, their closeness in rhythm to the *Epitaph*, and the affinity in mood of *L'Allegro* and the Hobson poems [this seems rather strained] and the May *Song*. Parker is tempted to see the genesis of the pair in the presentation, in *Elegy* 6, of 'two different yet complementary moods,' in the manner of an academic prolusion; the debate in each case is inconclusive, since Milton is not to be identified only with Il Penseroso.

The topography of the poems is not a matter of poetical interest, but there has been, chiefly in the past, some discussion of the supposed locality, most of it based on the assumption that they were written at Horton. It has also been noted that the scenery around Cambridge would fit the poems as well as that of Horton. The obvious conclusion, from the nature of the poems, is that the scenery is an eclectic mixture of common observation and idealization. The old question was revived by A. H. J. Baines ('The Topography of "L'Allegro,"' *N&Q* 188, 1945, 68–71), who fixed the scene in the Chilterns and saw L'Allegro beginning his walk from a hamlet on the edge of the Vale of Aylesbury, etc.]

II. BACKGROUND, SOURCES, AND ANALOGUES

L'Allegro and *Il Penseroso* are not so directly and obviously related to current or recent literary forms as are the sonnets, *Comus*, and *Lycidas*. [But, though they are essentially original, they have links with such various traditional genres as the academic debate, the encomium, the 'character,' the essay, and the pastoral. The academic debate is sufficiently illustrated by Milton's Prolusions and by the opposed themes he combined in *Elegy* 6. The encomium, usually ironical, was a genre cultivated by Renaissance humanists which had its most famous fruit in Erasmus' *Praise of Folly*; for such later English writers as Donne and Sir William Cornwallis the encomium was related to the paradox. The character, which had such a vogue in the first half of Milton's century, and the more spacious pastoral tradition, are noticed further along. Both of these genres could merge with the developing essay in such light 'characters' of the seasons, months, and hours as the *Fantasticks* (1604?) of Nicholas Breton (some of whose pastoral verse has been linked with *L'Allegro*). Milton's twin poems cannot of course be confined to any of these more or less special genres, and he may not have thought of them at all, but they were part of the general conditioning of any writer of his age. The two poems also belong to, indeed help to define, some other traditions or genres that will be mentioned shortly.]

1. Rural and Related Traditions

[The notion of the poems as complementary pictures of an ideal day was standardized by Masson; its inadequacy has been increasingly recognized, as the discussions in III below make clear.] Sara R. Watson ('Milton's Ideal Day: Its Development as a Pastoral Theme,' *PMLA* 57, 1942, 404–20) sought to connect *L'Allegro* and *Il Penseroso* with the tradition of the shepherd's ideal day, through illustrations of the theme extending from Theocritus (7 and 25) to Spenser and the Spenserians. But Milton's poems are not pastorals, although *L'Allegro* contains pastoral elements, and the ideal days sketched in them have little connection with the specimens adduced; nor do they at all imply a rejection of urban in favour of simple country life, a rejection which on Miss Watson's own showing is a constant feature of the tradition. However, such celebrations of rural or retired life may, in occasional particulars, illustrate what the notes in section IV amply prove, the way in which the companion pieces echo, and transmute in echoing, common themes and phrases. What must be rejected as source is often suggestive as analogue.

L'Allegro and Il Penseroso

[Maren-Sofie Røstvig links Milton's poems, especially *Il Penseroso*, with the tradition of rural, contemplative, and Stoic happiness whose Roman progenitors were Horace and Martial (*The Happy Man: Studies in the Metamorphosis of a Classical Ideal 1600–1700*, Oslo and Oxford, 1954). She sees William Habington as, at least in print, 'the first popularizer of the *Il Penseroso*-motif of contemplative solitude' (119), in a Horatian epistle, *To my noblest Friend, I. C. Esquire* (*Castara*, 1635, ed. Arber, London, 1870, 96–7; ed. K. Allott, Liverpool and London, 1948, 95–6). Miss Røstvig finds in Joseph Hall's 'character sketches of the Happy Man, the Humble Man, and the Wise Man, several distinct features of the type of happy man of which Milton's *Il Penseroso* is the best example' (51). Thus Hall's 'wise man' (*Heaven upon Earth and Characters of Vertues And Vices*, ed. R. Kirk, New Brunswick, 1948, 147–8)

seekes his quietnesse in secrecy, and is wont both to hide himselfe in retired-nesse, and his tongue in himselfe. He loves to be guessed at, not knowne; and to see the world unseene. . . . He stands like a center unmoved, while the circum-ference of his estate is drawne above, beneath, about him.

Miss Røstvig also (153–6) cites Virgil, *G*. 2. 475–512, for Il Penseroso's pursuit of learning and wisdom. About the relation of *Il Penseroso* to this tradition, perhaps some such qualification should be made as was made above about the pastoral tradition, although the conception of happy philosophic retirement seems a good deal closer to Milton.

H. M. Richmond (' "Rural Lyricism": A Renaissance Mutation Of the Pastoral,' *CL* 16, 1964, 193–210) propounds the 'thesis. . . that the later pastoral tradition produced an important offshoot in "rural lyricism," which came to fruition in the period between the birth of Ronsard and the death of Milton. . . .' 'The genre is one of lyrical praise of landscape, spoken at a particular time and place by a more substantial figure than the traditional shepherd—usually the poet in his own person.' The primary source of the tradition was Virgil's *Eclogues* and *Georgics*; and the primary modern adaptations of Virgil were Ronsard's odes. 'Milton's pastoral and rural poems possess a Virgilian smoothness and charm, but lack none of Ronsard's assured self-centeredness. *L'Allegro* and *Il Penseroso* merely purge the verse of Ronsard of its more labored classicisms, liberating the mood and personality of the author, for the moment, from even those conventional effects which he felt constrained to introduce into *Lycidas*.' But Milton's 'rural poetry marks a distinct evolution from the odes and elegies of Ronsard. The effects which Milton shares with Virgil and Ronsard...are controlled by new and significant formal intentions—the argumentative conflict between *L'Allegro* and *Il Penseroso* being a typical, if slight, illustration of this subordination of personal impressions to some kind of formal pattern.']

We may catalogue briefly some suggestions of more particular 'sources,' rural or miscellaneous, concerning both poems or either.

Two more or less audible echoes in Milton have long been recognized: from Marlowe's pastoral lyric and Marston's *Scourge of Villanie* (see, respectively, the notes on the last couplet of each poem and on *L'Allegro* 1–10 and *Il Penseroso* 11–16). The echo of Marlowe is perhaps chiefly significant in emphasizing that delight is the focus of both poems.

F. M. Padelford (*MLN* 22, 1907, 200) suggested as a source for *L'Allegro* the poem 'The Sunne when he hath spred his raies' (1–38), in *Tottel's Miscellany* (ed. Arber, Birmingham, 1870, 230; ed. H. E. Rollins, Cambridge, Mass., 1928–9, 1, 220). Lines 1–6 describe sunrise (*L'All* 60–2); 15–18 have 'mountaines hye,' 'towers strong,' 'The castels and the rivers long' (*L'All* 73–8); 31–2: 'The hunter then soundes out his horne, / And rangeth straite through wood and corne' (*L'All* 53–6); 35–8: 'Then lovers walke and tell their tale,...' (*L'All* 67–8). Cf. Keightley in *L'All* 67–8 n. (ii).

J. L. Lowes (*MLR* 6, 1911, 206–9) found in N. Breton's *Passionate Shepheard* (1604) passages parallel in grammar, metre, and image to passages in *L'Allegro*, and suggested that they inspired at least part of Milton's poem. With 41 f. he compared lines from the beginning of Breton's third section (1604 ed.; *Works*, ed. Grosart, 1879, 1): 'Who can live in heart so glad, / As the merrie countrie lad? / Who upon a faire greene balke / May at pleasures sit and walke? / And amidde the Azure skies, / See the morning Sunne arise? / While hee heares in every spring, / How the Birdes doe chirpe and sing: / Or, before the houndes in crie, / See the Hare goe stealing by: / Or along the shallow brooke, /

Angling with a baited hooke: / See the fishes leape and play, / In a blessed Sunny day....' With *L'Allegro* 25 f., Lowes compared lines from the second section: 'Come abroad you blessed Muses, / Yee that pallas chiefly choses....Haste yee therefore, come away: / ...Call the silvan Nimphes together, / Bid them bring their musickes hither.' Breton's third section ends with 'So I might but live to bee,' etc. [W. J. Courthope quoted Breton and briefly noted the resemblance (*History of English Poetry*, 2, London, 1897, 316–17).]

[In his introduction to a reprint of Edward Guilpin's *Skialetheia* (1598: Shakespeare Association Facsimiles, 2, 1931), G. B. Harrison found some resemblance between a passage on the contemplative life at the beginning of *Satire* 5 and the conclusion of *L'Allegro* (and Donne's *Satyre* 1). P. Reyher (*Revue Anglo-Américaine* 10, 1932–3, 137–9), citing Harrison and quoting the passage from Guilpin, linked it rather with *Il Penseroso* 77–120, remarking that 'Le parallélisme est frappant, malgré les différences qui sautent aux yeux.' Since the theme was so common, one may not see a significant likeness.

Nan C. Carpenter (*N&Q* 3, 1956, 289–92) put forward 'Spenser's "Epithalamion" as Inspiration for Milton's "L'Allegro" and "Il Penseroso."' While Milton of course would know the poem well, one may not think that the similarities, including the time scheme, are 'entirely too close to be accidental.']

2. The Traditions of Melancholy, Psychological and Literary

[The traditional kinds of melancholy and their reflections in literature belong obviously to the background of *Il Penseroso*, but, as various examples will show, the subject can embrace, or at least recognize, mirth.]

Burton's *Anatomy of Melancholy* (1621 and later enlarged editions: quoted from the edition of Holbrook Jackson, 3 vols., 1932) was of course the encyclopaedic and enthralling authority of Milton's age. Warton pointed to this work as a principal source, and later commentators have followed him, at least in regard to the prefatory poem, and in noting illustrative details. 'The Author's Abstract of Melancholy' (added to the third edition, 1628) presents, in octosyllabic couplets, a contrast between two kinds or degrees of melancholy, and their effects. From this contrast Milton may have taken the hint for his own contrast between Melancholy and Mirth. [Burton's poem was quoted in full by Francis Peck, *New Memoirs of...Milton* (London, 1740), 27–30.] Burton's painful melancholy is of the kind banished at the beginning of *L'Allegro*, not the 'divinest Melancholy' hailed in *Il Penseroso*, and some of Burton's pleasures of melancholy are distributed between Milton's pleasures of melancholy and pleasures of mirth. The following lines will sufficiently illustrate the nature of Burton's contrast and a comparison of the italicized phrases with the lines indicated in the companion pieces will suggest the degree of immediate relation:

> When to myself I act and smile,
> With pleasing thoughts the time beguile,
> *By a brook side* or wood so green,   (*L'All* 76, 129–30)
> Unheard, unsought for, or *unseen*,   (*IlPen* 65; cf. *L'All* 57)
> A thousand pleasures do me bless,
> And crown my soul with happiness.
>   All my joys besides are folly,
>   None so sweet as melancholy.
> When I lie, sit, or walk alone,
> I sigh, I grieve, making great moan,
> In *a dark grove, or irksome den,*
> With discontents and *Furies* then,   (*L'All* 1–10
> A thousand miseries at once
> Mine heavy heart and soul ensconce,
>   All my griefs to this are jolly,
>   None so sour as melancholy.
> Methinks I hear, methinks I see,
> *Sweet music, wondrous melody,*   (*L'All* 117 f., 135–44)
> *Towns, palaces, and cities fine;*
> Here now, then there; the world is mine,
> *Rare beauties, gallant ladies shine,*   (*L'All* 117–22)
> Whate'er is lovely or divine.
>   All other joys to this are folly,
>   None so sweet as melancholy.

L'Allegro and Il Penseroso

Methinks I hear, methinks I see,
Ghosts, goblins, fiends; my phantasy
Presents a thousand ugly shapes,
Headless bears, black men, and apes,
Doleful outcries, and fearful sights, (L'All 4)
My sad and dismal soul affrights.
  All my griefs to this are jolly,
  None so damn'd as melancholy.

As Warton noted, further suggestions occur in the body of Burton's work. Brief quotations dealing with the cure of melancholy—from *Anatomy* 2. 2. 4 (2, 71–93)—will illustrate the point. 'Of these labours, exercises, and recreations,...some properly belong to the body, some to the mind,...some with delight,... some within doors, some natural, some are artificial.' 'But the most pleasant of all outward pastimes is... *deambulatio per amoena loca* (strolling through pleasant scenery) ⟨L'All 53–99⟩, to make a petty progress..., see cities, castles, towns ⟨L'All 117, 77⟩,...to walk amongst orchards, gardens ⟨IlPen 49–50⟩,... arches, groves ⟨IlPen 133⟩, lawns, rivulets,...in a fair meadow, by a river-side, *ubi variae avium cantationes, florum colores, pratorum frutices* (to enjoy the songs of the birds ⟨L'All 41–4, IlPen 56–64⟩, the colours of the flowers, the verdure of the meadows ⟨L'All 75⟩).' 'What so pleasant as to see some pageant or sight go by, as at coronations, weddings, and suchlike solemnities...with masks, shows ⟨L'All 125–8⟩. ...' 'The country hath his recreations...May-games, feasts, wakes, and merry meetings, to solace themselves ⟨L'All 91–101⟩; the very being in the country, that life itself is a sufficient recreation to some men, to enjoy such pleasures as those old patriarchs did' ⟨i.e. their 'unreproved pleasures free': L'All 40–116⟩. 'The ordinary recreations which we have in winter...are...tales of errant knights,...lords, ladies ⟨L'All 119–24⟩ ...thieves, cheaters, witches, fairies, goblins, friars, etc...., which some delight to hear, some to tell, all are well pleased with' ⟨L'All 100–14⟩. 'Dancing,...masking,...stage-plays, howsoever they be heavily censured by some severe Catos, yet, if opportunely and soberly used, may justly be approved' ⟨L'All 131–4⟩. 'But amongst those exercises or recreations of the mind within doors, there is none...so fit and proper to expel idleness and melancholy, as that of study.' 'So sweet is the delight of study, the more learning they have...the more they covet to learn, and the last day is *prioris discipulus* (the disciple of the preceding)' ⟨*IlPen* 85–122, 170–4⟩. 'Whosoever he is, therefore, that is...carried away with pleasing melancholy and vain conceits ⟨cf. 'vain deluding joyes': *IlPen* 1⟩...I can prescribe him no better remedy than this of study, to compose himself to the learning of some art or science. Provided always that his melancholy proceed not from overmuch study; for in such case he adds fuel to the fire, and nothing can be more pernicious....' (All this is quoted by Warton, 95–6, with a few additions and deletions and inserted references.)

Later commentators have utilized Warton's notes and made some additions from Burton. G. W. Whiting (*Milton's Literary Milieu*, Chapel Hill, 1939, 129–76), who finds many parallels between Burton and Milton's writings in general, rejects Hughes's opinion that 'Burton counted many of L'Allegro's pleasures among...the prime satisfactions of melancholy' and that 'in *L'Allegro* no less than in *Il Penseroso*... Milton courted a melancholy of his own.' Whiting holds that his imagined pleasures all stem from Burton's suggested cures for melancholy (see extracts above from *Anat.* 2. 2. 4); and he quotes Milton's remark in *Tetrachordon*: 'No mortall nature can endure either in the actions of Religion, or study of wisdome, without somtime slackning the cords of intense thought and labour' (*Works* 4, 85; Whiting, 146).

W. J. Grace ('Notes on Robert Burton and John Milton,' *SP* 52, 1955, 578–83) finds in Burton, as in Milton, '*two* kinds of mirth and *two* kinds of melancholy': 'heart-easing mirth' and 'vain deluding joys,' 'loathéd Melancholy' and 'Divinest Melancholy.' 'The theme of "L'Allegro" is the replacement of "loathéd Melancholy" by "heart-easing Mirth," ' and that of 'Il Penseroso' the replacing of 'vain deluding joys' by 'divinest Melancholy' ⟨on the last phrase see below, *IlPen* 11–16 n.⟩. Grace finds the setting of 'loathéd Melancholy' representative of states of mind ascribed by Burton to the victims of religious melancholy ⟨see *L'All* 1–10 n.⟩ and concludes: ' "Heart-easing mirth" is the lawful distraction and pleasure which the pensive man can undertake to keep himself balanced and "lively and fit for any manner of employment" ⟨*Anat.* 2. 2. 6. 4: 2, 119⟩. The "vain deluding joys". . . are the pleasures undertaken to relieve melancholy but which become ends in themselves, as illustrated in the *Anatomy* ⟨2. 2. 6. 4⟩.' [Cf. Grace's *Ideas in Milton* (1968), 124–30.]

Each of the two widely different manifestations of Melancholy present in Burton and Milton has its history; the subject has been authoritatively expounded by L. Babb ('The Background of "Il Penseroso,"' *SP* 37, 1940, 257–73; *The Elizabethan Malady*, East Lansing, 1951; [and Babb's study of Burton, *Sanity in Bedlam*, East Lansing, 1959]). Melancholy is one of the four basic tempers recognized in the 'humours theory' of bodily and mental states as dependent on the predominance of one of the four humours, blood, phlegm, choler or bile, and (the cause of melancholy) black bile. This theory was traced back to Galen and to his view of melancholy belonged all those associations of lethargy, depression, fear, and madness that Burton and (by implication) Milton recognize. But in one of the *Problems* attributed to Aristotle (30. 1) a different view is taken: the question is asked why those who have succeeded in politics, philosophy, poetry, and the arts have been of a melancholy temper. In the Galenic system each of the humours is associated with certain qualities, the melancholy with dryness and coldness. But in the Aristotelian view melancholy may be associated with heat instead of cold, and that, apparently, makes all the difference. It is cold melancholy that issues in torpor and depression, while hot melancholy, if present in excess, leads to madness, but, if present in a moderate degree, may issue in poetic or prophetic inspiration, in the divine madness of the inspired poet or prophet of which Plato speaks. Where the melancholy is duly balanced by other humours and exists in a moderate temperature, there is a condition suited to intellectual attainment, whether active or contemplative; of 'mixed temperament' and 'moderate temperature' are men of genius. Such, evidently, is Il Penseroso, whose bent is for contemplation. It is melancholy of the Galenic tradition that is banished in *L'Allegro* and melancholy of the Aristotelian tradition that is welcomed in *Il Penseroso*.

[Dürer was cited by Bowle and Steevens (Warton, 69).] E. Panofsky's exposition of Dürer's *Melencolia I* (*Albrecht Dürer*, 2 v., Princeton, 1943, I, 156–71), though it has only one or two slight references to *Il Penseroso*, fills in much important background, and, with the plate (ibid. 2, plate 209), enables the reader to reach some interesting comparisons and contrasts. According to Panofsky, Dürer's Melancholy centres on the melancholy of the artist but draws on the whole complex of traditions that had grown up around the subject of the melancholy temper. In the Middle Ages these had been almost wholly pejorative. But in the Renaissance, especially in the Florentine school of Christian Platonists under the leadership of Ficino and Pico della Mirandola, the Aristotelian conception, read in close connection with the Platonic theory of inspiration, began to come into its own. It was accompanied by a revaluation of the role and influence of Saturn and the saturnine or melancholy temper. These became things of highest worth, though the attendant dangers were not altogether ignored as they are in *Il Penseroso*. While Aristotle had recognized that melancholy, duly tempered, might conduce not only to contemplation but to successful action, the whole emphasis of the Florentine school fell on contemplation, and so it is in Milton's poem. In Dürer, however, the outcome envisaged is the action of the artist, of the architect and builder, with geometry, not metaphysics and letters, as the basic subject of study. Here, despite Milton's own interest in mathematics, another contrast is evident: Il Penseroso is of the school of Pico, not of Dürer. But over Dürer's Melancholy hangs a heavy cloud of frustration: she is sunk in brooding inaction, not primarily because this is the inevitable outcome of her temper—as the Middle Ages (for which melancholy was a vice and closely related to *acedia*) would have assumed—but mainly because the task, the realizing of her aspirations (symbolized by her wings) was beyond her power, though such frustration might indeed be regarded as a danger incident to the temper. Thus the evidence of uncompleted work and disorder among her instruments is everywhere seen in the surroundings; and Dürer, further, is able and

excluded.' 'But Milton's sojourn in the realm of purely idyllic beauty could not, given his nature and education, be very long. For him the writing' of such poems, 'however exquisite the result, was in a sense a *tour de force*.'

In his *Milton* (1930, 65) Tillyard, like Hanford, deprecated a too serious reading of *L'Allegro* and *Il Penseroso*, which 'are poems of escape, of fancy,' and, 'if typical,...typical of only a part, and not a large part,' of Milton's mind. A paper of 1932 (reprinted in *The Miltonic Setting*, 1938) was largely concerned with the problem of dating and is summarized in I above. In this Tillyard argued that the poems grew out of Milton's first *Prolusion* (1628 or earlier) on the topic 'Whether Day is more excellent than Night,' a topic, Milton observed, more suitable for verse than prose. The poems, like the Prolusion, involved mythical genealogies (the 10-line preludes to the poems Tillyard takes as burlesque) and the familiar phenomena of dawn (these last in *L'Allegro*). The poems, while akin to each other, '*are* sharply contrasted'; 'In fact from first to last the poems are constructed on the contrasted eulogy of day and night.' Evidence of an academic setting is one of Tillyard's reasons for dating the poems in Milton's last long vacation, 1631, and he praises their 'social tone.'

D. C. Dorian ('The Question of Autobiographical Significance in *L'Allegro* and *Il Penseroso*,' *MP* 31, 1933–4, 175–82) cited two views of the poems, as objective summaries of Milton's aesthetic tastes (Hanford: see above) and as summaries of 'two possible attitudes toward life' (Moody, 24), and upheld the latter. 'Milton...was depicting the typical occupations, the habits, of a carefree man and of a pensive man; and... the two lives pictured are to some extent inconsistent with each other, contradictory and mutually exclusive' (177). 'L'Allegro is a self-portrait of a Milton who *might have been*; Il Penseroso, of essentially the Milton who *was to be*.' Probably one side of his nature would have to be sacrificed to the other; and the spirit of *L'Allegro* never appeared again in his writing. Milton's decision was reflected in *Comus* and sealed in lines 64–86 of *Lycidas*.

T. S. Eliot ('A Note on the Verse of John Milton,' *Essays and Studies*

21, 1936; repr. as 'Milton 1,' *On Poetry and Poets*, New York, 1957), arguing that Milton had an auditory rather than a visual imagination, quoted lines 63–8 of *L'Allegro* and remarked: 'The imagery in *L'Allegro* and *Il Penseroso* is all general....It is not a particular ploughman, milkmaid, and shepherd that Milton sees (as Wordsworth might see them); the sensuous effect of these verses is entirely on the ear, and is joined to the concepts of ploughman, milkmaid, and shepherd.'

Two comments on this view may be given here. Replying to Eliot ('Milton's Visual Imagination,' *UTQ* 16, 1946–7, 17–29), and dealing, like him, mainly with *Paradise Lost*, Phyllis MacKenzie pointed out Eliot's ignoring of Milton's purpose in *L'Allegro*. 'He began with a preconceived pattern, the pattern of a mood, and from nature recreated details to fit that pattern. In order, therefore, to subordinate the visual details to his total design, to limit the concrete visualization to the purposes of the poem, Milton has used, on the whole, generalized epithets. In a classical poem such as "L'Allegro" we should regard the natural details as a Platonist looks at the parts of the universe. They are the multiple bodyings-forth of an Idea in the mind of the poet. Part of the pleasure for the reader, therefore, is derived from the excitement of watching visual details spring to life, luxuriant and apparently real, which, none the less, bend and taper into the emergent design of the evolving whole. The Plowman, Milkmaid, Mower, and Shepherd..., along with the Cock, the Lark, and even the "labouring clouds"..., are like dancers in a dance. Each is characterized by stylized movements, executed against a stylized background; and both movement and background are keyed to the rhythm of the central mood....

'The world of "L'Allegro" is the world of the poem, and in that world all details are completely, but never disruptively visualized; for Milton, unlike Mr. Eliot in his own work antecedent to the *Quartets*, was not trying "to get beyond poetry."...Milton's description is profoundly evocative, but the emotion it evokes is ordered and controlled, regulated by the movement of the poem as a whole and inseparable from the total poetic experience.'

R. Tuve (*Images*, 1957, 20) remarks: 'For the subject of *L'Allegro* is every man's Mirth, our Mirth, the very Grace herself with all she can include. Therefore its images are not individualized.... Therefore Eliot will not find here his "particular milkmaid", for this one must instead be all milkmaids who ever sang; she must even be whatever fresh singing creature, not a milkmaid, does bring the same joy to the heart of him to whom milkmaids bring it not. The Plowman forever whistling, and the Mower who whets his scythe, do not exist thus simplified and quintessential in Nature, yet the fresh delight these catch for us lives in every such one we see—see with the eyes, that is, of one admitted of Mirth's crew. That is precisely the grace she confers.'

B. A. Wright (*Shorter Poems of John Milton*, 1938, repr. 1961, 126–7) remarks that 'L'Allegro and Il Penseroso are not two different characters; nor are they, as others have supposed, two different and incompatible attitudes towards life. Both are recognisably Milton himself.' 'The key to the poems is in the meaning of the term "melancholy." Milton uses it in the sense, now obsolete, of the serious, pensive mood; Il Penseroso is the solitary, meditative man.' The mood of *Il Penseroso* 'is the contemplative mood in which the poet abstracts himself into the world of thought and imagination,' hence the mood 'not only of study and meditation but of poetic composition'—as the word 'melancholy' is used by Thyrsis in *Comus* 545. The descriptions of nature in *Il Penseroso* 'suggest this mood of poetic reverie and at certain points reveal the poet's imagination, as it were, in the very act of creation.' *L'Allegro* depicts the corresponding mood of escape from study into social scenes. 'But L'Allegro too is the scholar and poet; he too finds much of his entertainment in the imaginative world of art, and the world he sees about him is full of literary romance and fiction. That is why the moods of the two poems, although subtly distinguished throughout, present no sharp contrast to each other.'

G. Wilson Knight ('The Frozen Labyrinth: An Essay on Milton,' *The Burning Oracle*, London, 1939, 59–113) sees *L'Allegro* and *Il Penseroso* as 'mosaics of impression. They resemble inlay-work or embroidery, choice pieces meticulously arranged according to a preconceived design' (59). 'Aspects of nature are often solidified into persons,

247

sometimes helped by reference to fabrics.... The ethereal and evanescent are rendered weighty (as in "labouring clouds") by images from human civilization, clothes, sculpture; something of nature's Shakespearian and dynamic otherness being lost nevertheless in the process. There is, moreover, little feeling for organic, pulsing life as such: all is levelled under a sculptural impressionism.... A smooth-surfaced and architectural delight in nature is apparent throughout, as in "smooth-shaven green" and "arched walks of twilight groves" ' (59–60). Such lines as *IlPen* 155–60 ('But let my due feet...dim religious light') exemplify 'Milton's love of architectural weight, dim light, and legendary colour suffused by religious solemnity...and the whole illustrates...Milton's innate sympathy with the weighty, monumental, and architectural' (60–1). The lines following those cited (161–6: 'There let the pealing organ blow...And bring all heaven before mine eyes') 'build a perfect condensation of the specifically Miltonic.... We are at the very heart of Milton here' (63). The two poems 'present a dualism of mood important to our understanding of Milton. But the texture of each is loose: no more is needed than a succession and addition of "objective equivalents" to the feeling in question. The poems are static. The images are themselves pictorially still, a sequential arrangement of tiny solids with no sense of any dynamic, evolving energy. The task of marrying movement and action to design, the realizing of an organic cohesion of motion and solidity, of the melodic and the architectural, remains unattempted: though the arts corresponding to each of these elements *in isolation* are insistently, almost excessively, emphasized' (64).

Chronological if not logical order may warrant the insertion here of some facts about the language of *L'Allegro*. R. M. Lumiansky ('Milton's English Again,' *MLN* 55, 1940, 591–4), using this poem, opposed the traditional view of Milton's diction as un-English (a view, to be sure, based mainly on *Paradise Lost*). *L'Allegro* contains 495 different words, of which 68 per cent are native (338 against 157). 'A more significant fact...is that all but 12 of the 495 words used appear in Middle English. If we consider as native any word in use before 1500, only approximately $2\frac{1}{2}$ percent of the total vocabulary of "L'Allegro" is borrowed.'

L'Allegro and Il Penseroso

Woodhouse ('Notes,' 1943-4, 85-8) opposed Tillyard's view that Milton took his double theme from his early *Prolusion* 1. 'They are not poems in praise respectively of day and night, but poems setting forth rival conceptions of a life of pleasure, the one active and social, the other contemplative and solitary, which adopt as their scheme of presentation the ideal day. L'Allegro's commences with sunrise and the song of the lark and extends to midnight, carrying (as Tillyard happily says) the glad spirit of day into the festivities of the evening and the reading of the midnight hour; Il Penseroso's commences with curfew and the song of the nightingale, extends through a night of study, and carries its spirit into the succeeding day. It is inconceivable that *Prolusion* 1 should have suggested the subject of these poems, or even their structural pattern, which is progressive while the prolusion remains perfectly static. The debt is real, but it commences when, having designed a pair of poems on rival conceptions of a life of pleasure, and hit on the device of the ideal day as furnishing the framework within which a whole series of contrasting parallels can be presented, Milton starts work on *L'Allegro*; nor does it extend much beyond the description of dawn in that poem, and the banishments and welcomes of Melancholy and Mirth. It is clear from the evidence which Tillyard amasses that at this point Milton turns back to his first *Prolusion* for several important suggestions in imagery....'

Passing by 'the companion aesthetic patterns, woven of landscape, myth and personification, reading, music and reverie,' Woodhouse speaks of 'some subtleties of differentiation between them, which have curiously escaped notice. In *Il Penseroso* the idea of a contemplative life, though pursued for its pleasure, reaches out towards the mystical and the religious; it is recognized as involving self-discipline and as culminating in inspiration. To his invoking of Melancholy, the natural temper and proper state of the studious, the Thoughtful Man adds: "And join with thee calm Peace and Quiet,...The Cherub Contemplation." These companions of Melancholy are much more than mere pieces of decorative imagery. Besides their derivation from Ezekiel 10. 1, 9-19, the last four lines quoted depend on the symbolic value traditionally attached to the angelic orders.' Woodhouse here gives an extract from Pico della Mirandola which is quoted below, in the note on 45–54.

'The process, as Pico goes on to make clear, while it implies a purging of the affections and a breaking of our bondage to earthly things, nevertheless uses a study of nature and man as a ladder of ascent to God; for through the work the Workman is known. It would be absurd to read the whole of this doctrine into Milton's image of the Cherub and the Throne, but not less absurd to ignore it altogether. The doctrine is clearly present in *Prolusion* 7, where that contemplation "by which our mind without the aid of the body, and as it were wrapped up in itself, copies the eternal life of the immortal gods with an extraordinary delight," is to be attained only after we are "saturated and perfected by knowledge and training" (*Works* 12, 254–5). In the light of this scheme one glimpses a deeper meaning in Il Penseroso's studies as they range through nature, the life of man (revealed in tragic poetry, or in allegorical "Where more is meant than meets the ear"), the spirit-world and the lore of the immortal soul; one sees the propriety of the Pythagorean asceticism, already alluded to in *Elegy* 6, and now rewarded by communion with the gods or vision of the Muses; and one understands the hope that study and discipline may issue at last in inspiration—"Till old experience do attain / To something like prophetic strain." These things do not constitute the subject of *Il Penseroso*, which is the pleasure, not the ultimate purposes, of the contemplative life; but they furnish some of its overtones and a hint of the direction which Milton's mind is preparing to take.'

'Then in the long vacation of 1631, in a setting briefly sketched in *Prolusion* 7, he produces the Companion Pieces. Into them goes more of himself. Here are moods that Milton has certainly experienced, with something of his favourite reading and of the scenes that have brought him delight, and in the overtones of *Il Penseroso*, something also of his deeper feelings and thoughts. But there is a complete absence of the problematical. One has no sense, as one is later so often to have in his poetry, of Milton's *dealing with* his experience as distinct from merely recording it in terms of an aesthetic pattern. The comparison of two ways of life does not involve, as in other circumstances it so easily might have done, the posing and making of a choice between them: indeed the comparison is simply a piece of patterning, with no extra-aesthetic reference. And this in turn is rendered possible because Milton is, for the time being, able to postpone his problems, to banish "sleepless cares and complaints" and "walk with heart secure." The phrases come not from the Companion Pieces, but from *Ad Patrem*, which, despite the momentous decision on which it depends, shows in remarkable degree the same tranquillity of spirit, the same power of abstraction from disturbing thoughts. This tranquillity and this power of abstraction are the essence of the purely aesthetic attitude which appears, not only in the Companion Pieces, but preeminently in *Arcades*, and establishes a kinship with them' (92–3). Some of these comments are briefly summarized in Woodhouse's *The Poet and his Faith* (1965), 93–4.

Cleanth Brooks ('*L'Allegro* and *Il Penseroso*,' repr. with slight revisions from Brooks's *The Well Wrought Urn*, 1947, in Brooks and Hardy, 1951, 131–44) finds that Dr Johnson perceived 'the essential character of the speaker in the two poems,' but that the body of later appreciative criticism, in taking their charm and beauty as obvious, has been 'quite useless.' Hence he welcomes Tillyard's remarks on 'social tone' and especially his connecting the poems with Milton's first *Prolusion*. Tillyard 'indicated how important are the day–night contrasts in determining the general architecture of the poem ['poem' means the two poems]. But the light–shade imagery...amounts to a symbolism, and this symbolism plays a part in determining the "meaning" of the poem, including its tone' (133).

In presenting 'the obvious contrast between mirth and melancholy, Milton obligated himself to bring them as close together as possible in their effect on the mind. For the tension between the two choices depends upon their presentation as choices which can appeal to the same mind.' Hence 'the "Mountain Nymph sweet Liberty" presides over "L'Allegro" and the "Cherub Contemplation" dominates "Il Penseroso,"' and these two figures 'have much in common and tend to merge into the same figure.' The 'more serious pleasures of Il Penseroso

...are hardly more *contemplative* than those which delight L'Allegro.' Throughout, parallel images and ideas tend to merge. 'Even more striking is the tendency for the items in opposition to cross out of their usual antitheses in a fashion which associates the same object with both mirth and melancholy' (137).

'But the most important device used to bring the patterns of opposites together—to build up an effect of unity in variety—is the use of a basic symbolism involving light.' Although 'Milton never declares this symbolism explicitly, he comes very close to it in the preamble of each poem: Melancholy is born "of blackest midnight"; the fancies of mirth are like "the gay motes that people the Sun Beams." ' 'In both poems, the spectator moves predominantly through cool half-lights. It is as if the half-light were being used in both poems as a sort of symbol of the aesthetic distance which the cheerful man, no less than the pensive man, constantly maintains' (138–9). Scenes presented must seem subdued to a mood, yet Milton skilfully gives 'at least the illusion of a real world.' More is said about light and darkness than can be summarized here. The essay contains much suggestive comment, but it has been criticized by later writers (e.g. below, Allen, R. Tuve, French) especially for emphasis on secondary things and neglect or misreading of ideas and symbols Milton inherited and utilized; some of these essential attitudes had already been set forth by Woodhouse in 1943 (see above). In his lecture *Milton the Poet* (Toronto, 1955, 5) Woodhouse remarked that Mr Brooks 'insists on the poem, the whole poem, and nothing but the poem, and then proceeds to isolate one strand in the pattern, the images of light and darkness (which of course spring quite inevitably from Milton's structural plan), and to find in them the meaning of the poems.'

W. Empson, in a review of *The Well Wrought Urn* (*Sewanee Review* 55, 1947, 691) described *L'Allegro* and *Il Penseroso* as 'ponderous trifles with a few good lines in them.'

K. Svendsen ('Milton's "L'Allegro" and "Il Penseroso," ' *Explic.* 8, 1949–50, Item 49) sees the unity of the two poems as deriving, not so much from Brooks's symbolism of light and shade as from Milton's 'progressive emphasis...on images of sound and music.' Through a detailed account of these images Svendsen shows that the thematic movement of the two poems is from comparative lightness to seriousness, which culminates in the last part of *Il Penseroso*, the first positive Christian allusion in the two poems: 'the many references to sound and in particular to music build toward this conclusion, so that structurally it is the end of a progressive development within both poems. The poet moves from communication through pagan mythology to the experience of Christian mysticism induced by Christian religious music....For the pensive man in his ecstasy experiences what Milton said in the nativity hymn could happen through the "holy Song" of the spheres and the angels. This force of musical harmony suggests further that feature of the Renaissance world-view in which man's perfect inner harmony would be correspondent to the harmony of nature and especially to that of the spheres. The two streams of imagery, light and sound, touch continually and reinforce each other.'

F. W. Bateson ('The Money-lender's Son: "L'Allegro" and "Il Penseroso," ' *English Poetry: A Critical Introduction*, London, 1950, 149–64) sees the two poems as the last and finest products of the young poet and wit of Cambridge, the gracious and unsoured heir of Spenser and the Renaissance who was for the moment at one with his audience. 'Milton's early poetic history is one of a surrender to Cambridge, and the Renaissance world that the University stood for, followed by a profound moral revulsion from it. In this psychological drama the key-poems are, I believe, "L'Allegro" and "Il Penseroso," though their significance has been misunderstood hitherto because they have been misdated' (154). Bateson assigns the poems to 'the late summer or autumn of 1629'—that is, some months before the *Nativity*. The evidence is found in the last lines of *Elegy* 6 (which Bateson takes to refer to these pieces, *cicutis* indicating pastorals), in the spelling of several words, and in the idea that 'This dating...gets over the difficulty of the "Anglo-Catholic" conclusion of "Il Penseroso" ' (which would have been impossible in 1631). This idea was disposed of by Leishman (*Essays and Studies 1951*, 2). Bateson does not attempt to define Milton's themes but to describe his aesthetic sensibility. 'The conflict between reason and passion that dominated the later Milton has not yet made its appearance. Instead we have a fusion of two elements that lay nearer the surface of his mind. They are (i) the world of classical mythology, and (ii) the English countryside' (157). The rest of the chapter develops these two lines. Milton was unlucky in reaching Cambridge at a time when 'the classic moment in English Renaissance poetry had already passed.'

[In II above, part of Leishman's study (1951) was summarized, and the more critical part, which carries on from that, is digested here, by Woodhouse.] Leishman collected valuable material, much of it naturally from earlier commentators, and brought it to bear on the relation of *L'Allegro* and *Il Penseroso* to seventeenth-century poetry. Though no other poet of the period, he says, could have written these poems, 'many of the most delightful characteristics of seventeenth-century poetry... are there more perfectly exhibited than elsewhere.' Milton is here 'further from Spenser...and nearer to some of the best seventeenth-century poets' than in any other of his 'major minor poems.' Not only does he adopt the octosyllabic couplet which they 'brought to perfection,' but he displays more 'wit' than anywhere else in his serious poetry, not in the narrower sense of ingenuity in devising 'analogies and comparisons..., but...as denoting a certain flexibility of mind and mood, a certain balance between seriousness and light-heartedness.' 'There is also some trace...of that dialectical, argumentative, and debating strain which is so strong in Donne and in some of his successors' (1). The debate is not between day and night, but mirth and melancholy, and in each poem (as Warton, 48, observed) 'there seem to be two parts: the one a day-piece, and the other a night-piece.' If the song from Fletcher's *Nice Valour* is a main source for the banishment motif, the idea of the contrast may have come from Strode's *Against Melancholy* when paired with it. After the initial invocations (where Strode's poem may have suggested the qualities personified in Mirth's train), the contrast in Milton is of course much less simple and emphatic. Like these poems, and unlike Donne's hyperbolic, paradoxical, and essentially less serious poems of persuasion, the companion pieces do not indulge in argument but merely show the advantages of the advocated state; and of the two source poems it is Fletcher's song that anticipates Milton's method of concrete example. The contrast between the pleasures of Mirth and Melancholy (and the idea of melancholy as a pleasurable state seems to have been a seventeenth-century development: see II above) is between those 'which, in some degree, take one, as the saying is, out of oneself' and those which are 'more introspective, more purely the pleasures of reverie and of solitary contemplation and imagination' (9). The eighteenth century admired the companion pieces as 'descriptive' poems. Actually they provide little detail and are evocative rather than descriptive in any full sense; but one must not (like T. S. Eliot in 'the most unfortunate of all his writings on Milton') overlook this power of evocation or the precision of outline which compensates for the absence of detail (17). By evocation Milton produces effects recognized by later poets as 'romantic'—effects which in their own hands would have been generally aimed at by elaboration. Examples are the allusions to 'the wandring Moon' and curfew sounding 'Over some wide-water'd shoar' (*IlPen* 67–76). If the poems eschew the detail of later descriptive poetry, they also avoid that pursuit of 'witty' analogies for their own sake which marks the descriptions of Donne and his school and is at its most charming in Marvell (for 'Marvell is as witty and ingenious as Donne, but, like Milton, he is also in love with what he is describing'). Nor is 'wit' in the form of apt analogies absent from *L'Allegro* and *Il Penseroso*. We find 'conceits' of various kinds: the sun's royal progress ⟨*L'All* 59–62 and n.⟩; 'Scatters the rear of darknes thin' ⟨ibid. 49–50 and n.⟩; the towers and battlements, with the inhabiting beauty, and a 'learned' image in the cynosure ⟨ibid. 77–80 n.⟩; the astrological image in the bright eyes raining influence ⟨ibid. 121–2 and n.⟩; and the Platonic in 'Untwisting all the chains that ty / The hidden soul of harmony' ⟨ibid. 143–4 and n.⟩; the play on blackness and beauty ⟨*IlPen* 12–21 and n.⟩; and 'Forget thy self to Marble' ⟨ibid. 41–2 and n.⟩. 'In every one of these passages the wit, the ingenuity, is strictly subordinated to the purpose of illuminating or sharpening the particular delight Milton is evoking....We never feel that any of these not very extreme examples of ingenuity is there merely *because* it is ingenious' (23). He observes a 'strict *decorum*...even in his wit.'

In the companion pieces Milton's greatest single debt is to Shakespeare (24–6). His if anyone's were the spectacles through which Milton viewed nature; and he adopts many of Shakespeare's phrases, sometimes combining them with echoes of other poets. See *L'All* 22 ('Roses washt in dew'); 33–4 ('trip it...fantastick toe'); 44 ('dappled dawn'); 72 ('nibling flocks'); 75 ('Daisies pide'); 96 ('Chequer'd shade'); 120 ('weeds of Peace'); *IlPen* 10 ('fickle Pensioners'); 14 ('hit the Sense'); 82 ('the Cricket'); 122 ('civil-suited Morn'); 141 ('Day's garish eie'). So numerous, and so integral to his effect, are Milton's echoes and adaptations of his predecessors that they suggest a deliberate collection of phrases that struck him in his reading and remind us in turn of his practice in his Latin poems. 'He sometimes complied with the contemporary academic taste for the ingenious comparison, but it would no more have occurred to him to cultivate in his English poetry that out-of-one's-own-head kind of originality which Carew praised in Donne than ...to try to write Latin poetry as though no one had ever written it before' (29). His power of transmuting more or less traditional phrases can be seen in *L'All* 24 ('bucksom...debonair'), 28 ('Nods...Smiles'), and *IlPen* 32 ('Sober...demure'), 67–8 ('Moon, / Riding'). Two examples of the transmuting of longer passages are *L'All* 148–50 ('Such streins...Eurydice') and *IlPen* 142–6 ('While the Bee...Sleep'). There is nothing pedantic or eccentric about Milton's originality, 'which consists simply in doing better...things which other poets had done, or had tried to do, before.' His art is in 'judicious selection and combination,' the 'observance of *decorum*, the subordination of the parts to the whole,...that sheer craftsmanship which is the foundation of all great poetry' (35).

Nan C. Carpenter ('The Place of Music in *L'Allegro* and *Il Penseroso*,' *UTQ* 22, 1952–3, 354–67) starts from Hanford's suggestion (*Handbook*, 150) that the two poems might be viewed as contrasting sections of a musical composition. The gamut of references is wide; in fact, 'all the important musical images and ideas...occur again in Milton's later writings' (363). 'The musical passages in these two poems point very clearly to their early composition and to their academic origin' (363). The author does not mention F. W. Bateson but apparently accepts (365) his notion (see above, under 1950) that the poems probably preceded the *Nativity*. She finds that music, 'far from being a mere pleasant accompaniment, is indispensably related to form, content, and meaning —is a means, indeed, of clarifying all three' (366). This claim had rather more penetrating support from Svendsen (under 1949–50 above).

D. C. Allen ('The Search for the Prophetic Strain: "L'Allegro" and "Il Penseroso," ' *Vision*, 1954, 3–23), more or less opposing Tillyard and Brooks, sees the poems, not as appendixes to a college Prolusion, but as 'deeply serious,' and he does not discern their 'social tone.' These 'poems of a solitary man...anticipate an even greater quest for creative solitude.' The 'temporal episodes have been variously admired as constituting the essence of the poem; yet they are mainly clichés of only ancillary importance. They have a total symbolic value, but in their separateness they are simply an alphabet of common experience easily recited by anyone' (5). 'The notion of the alert man seems to me to be stronger in these poems than that of the cheerful or the pensive man; it is the other side of the quiet solitary and it is the necessary component of the subsurface struggle.' *Il Penseroso* is 'more accomplished' and 'more mature' than *L'Allegro*. Because 'the poet lives to himself,' *Il Penseroso* 'gains in power; it is much more solitary and, hence, a more personal poem' (10), 'the poem of a poet who has found his way.'

Milton's allusion to 'thrice great Hermes' is one major clue to his thoughts and feelings, since it brings in the whole Neo-Platonic tradition of cosmic contemplation. 'The mind purified of its mundane excrescences becomes the music of God. The earthly expression of this experience—"There let the pealing Organ blow...And bring all Heav'n before mine eyes"—becomes in its ultimate experience a knowable reality. This knowable reality is not attained through an excess of religious emotions or through the exercises of the mystic, but through universal knowledge as a prelude to universal thought. Hermes displays the chart of necessary experiences.' (14)

'By a continued mounting of the slopes of the intellect from common experience, to intellectual experience, to religious inspiration, the poet trusts to arrive at the supreme poetic gratification: "Till old experience do attain / To something like Prophetic strain." For this reason, the dynamic symbol of the poem is the tower, solitariness and loneliness in itself, but truly much more than that' (17). 'The structure of the poems rests on the rising stairs of the tower. It is the symbol of the poet's program of artistic progress....' 'The first milestone in the course is measured by the common experiences recorded in "L'Allegro": the plowman, the milkmaid,...the theater, the orchestra.' 'The second milestone is the tower. Common experience is shut out and secular music is subdued because the experience here is of the mind and particular' (19). The meditative man is in quest of supramundane mysteries. At the end, the 'cloister is the synonym for the tower in Milton's lexicon of symbols' (22). ' "All Heav'n" takes the place of "Shallow Brooks, and Rivers wide." But there is still one more furlong in the journey. Common experience, intellectual experience, poetic experience are not enough. The "Prophetic strain" is the child of "old experience," which is all of this experienced over and over again. The direction of the poems is that of a continued venture....'

K. Muir (*J.M.*, 1955, 1960, 27–31): ' "L'Allegro" and "Il Penseroso" are written, except for the introductions, in the same exquisitely-managed octosyllabic couplets as the "Epitaph"; but Milton was able to put more of himself into these twin masterpieces.' Muir does not accept Tillyard's view that the prelude to *L'Allegro* is 'meant to be funny,' though it is 'intentionally grotesque,' or the same critic's 'argument that the real contrast is not between cheerful and melancholy, but between day and night. Day and night are merely used as appropriate backgrounds for the contrasting types.' There is little substance in Johnson's complaint, which others have echoed, 'that the cheerful man and the meditative man are too much alike.' 'For Milton is here contrasting, not the Cavalier with the Puritan way of life, but rather the two sides of his own character'; 'he praises in turn the two ways of life which could satisfy him as a poet and as a man,' and 'he himself enjoyed all the pleasures mentioned in both poems.' 'He implies that the complete man will be a synthesis of "L'Allegro" and "Il Penseroso", and we find in these poems the dialectical method he was afterwards to use so superbly in *Comus*.' Muir defends Milton against the charge that he 'saw nature through the spectacles of books and that he is inaccurate in some of his descriptions.' 'It is true that his descriptions of nature are mostly generalized, and that he combines direct observation with literary associations.' But so do Shakespeare and others, and 'most of the alleged mistakes in Milton's natural history rest on palpable misinterpretations.' Replying to T. S. Eliot's early strictures, he says: 'Milton does not describe what he sees. He depicts a generalized landscape by an accretion of detail from different sources. His spring morning is not a particular morning, any more than the public house in *The Waste Land* is a particular pub.' Like Eliot also, Milton makes pointed use of literary allusion.

J. W. Saunders' title, 'Milton, Diomede and Amaryllis' (*ELH* 22, 1955, 254–86), represents the conflict he sees in Milton between the attractions of courtly Renaissance poetry and its world and strenuous commitment to middle-class, religious, public causes (and his gradual shift from one ideal to the other). 'He used lyrical forms of the day to discuss with himself this inner conflict between Diomede and Amaryllis [the name Diomede comes from the epilogue to Milton's Latin elegies, in which he renounced the erotic for the Platonic]. *L'Allegro* and *Il Penseroso* are rather more than mere poetic versions of an academic prolusion on the relative merits of Day and Night, of Mirth and Melancholy. *L'Allegro* describes happiness which is open, unsuppressed, undisciplined; Zephir's love is open and frank; Corydon, Thyrsis and Phillis live in a flowery world where there are no restraining laws and where romance is real and immanent, from the cock-crow to the evensong of Hymen. Here courtly folk enjoy with carefree indulgence the delights of dance, drama, lyric poetry and, above all, courtly fellowship. *Il Penseroso* describes happiness which is controlled by melancholy and a sense of grave dedication to higher things; Saturn's love is demure and restrained; legends of inchantments drear follow tales of thwarted love;

and, at the end, the poet secretes himself from his fellows, alone with the nymphs of consolation, *waiting* for "old experience" to attain to the "Prophetick strain" of a victory worthy of Diomede. The courtly folk here are devoted, responsibly, to the graver pleasures of epic and tragedy and didactic poetry, and there is less fellowship, more solitariness. In these two poems Milton is asking the same question that he raises in *Lycidas*: which is the better life, one of service to Amaryllis, or one of service to Diomede? The first poem supposes Amaryllis victorious, uninhibited; in the second the shade of Diomede falls upon her. But both these poems are in the courtly tradition, patterned, metaphorical, lyrical, dramatic, and, this time, intensely personal.' (275–6)

D. Daiches (*Milton*, 1957, 53–4) follows Tillyard in taking the poems as 'in a sense exercises, a poetic development of the formal debate on the relative claims of day and night which was the subject' of Milton's *Prolusion* 1. He treats the poems briefly and casually, praising their 'grace and freshness and...happy stylization,' but slighting the deeper themes discerned by some of the critics above and below.

In *More Literary Essays* (1968), discussing Milton's early pastoral imagery, Daiches notes the 'exuberant, almost comic' use of classical myth in 1–10, the smooth use of it in 11–23, and the 'mutation to an English atmosphere' at 24 ('So bucksom'). There is the reference to Hebe (29), 'but in this context she is an English rustic wench. From this point on the landscape becomes more emphatically English,' all of it clearly 'from Milton's own experience of English country life.' Even the 'deliberately stately' allusion to the sun (60–2) has 'an English stateliness, with images drawn from English court and Great House ceremonial.' The next twenty lines of stylized rural figures and scenes bring us to Corydon, Thyrsis, Phillis, and Thestylis, but in the context these are mainly idealized English embodiments of pastoral content. Lines 100–14, on rural folklore, mark 'the high point of the poem's native imagery; Milton now begins to work back skilfully towards the classical world from a description of feats of arms in medieval romantic fashion, through wedding pageants, to drama, music, and poetry. As the arts take control the classical images grow, until at last we are with

L'*Allegro* and *Il* *Penseroso*

Orpheus and Eurydice.' In *Il Penseroso*, in keeping with its subject, 'the native tradition is represented only by the world of medieval romance and medieval English architecture' [but what of the nightingale, the moon, the curfew, the bellman, etc.?]; 'on the whole this poem is more consistently nourished from classical sources, both in imagery and in general use of language.'

In a discussion of *L'Allegro* (*New Republic*, 27 May 1957; *5 Pens in Hand*, New York, 1958, 33–53), Robert Graves—who, by the way, has the young poet writing in a cottage at Chalfont St Giles—invents first drafts of various bits, makes various naïve comments, and—for the benefit of scholars—suggests that lines 53–68 ('Oft list'ning...in the dale') got misplaced in Milton's manuscript (presumably remaining so for 13 or 14 years) and should follow line 114. The final title of this discourse was 'Legitimate Criticism of Poetry.' Graves's main suggestion was not endorsed by H. F. West (*Renaissance Papers 1958, 1959, 1960, 1961*).

Rosemond Tuve (*Images*, 1957, 15–36): 'The poems are not taken care of by saying that Milton portrays two moods, or two lives, or two men, or two days and nights, or Day and Night, or Light and Darkness; all these, assigned by critics as subjects, are instrumental.' The 'secret of the images' decorum (the much-discussed problem of their generalness) lies...in the relation of images to poetic subject....' For her own definition of the subjects, Miss Tuve claims only 'that it follows the text, that it would have occurred immediately to any intelligent seventeenth-century reader trained in a grammar school, and that it will take care of every image and word, in context, in each poem' (16–17). The subject of *L'Allegro* is Mirth, who 'is not a person; she is a personification, that is, she is a way of talking about the absolutely not the contingently real.' She is one of the three Graces, Euphrosyne (Gladness), sister of Aglaia ('splendor, brightness, or majesty') and Thalia ('flourishing or bourgeoning'). Behind her is a rich tradition of classical and Neo-Platonic symbolism. The 'sweet Liberty' who is joined with her is happy absence of responsibility, innocence. There is no problem of reconciling opposites, only 'the comprehending of things different,

261

and not in a pattern of antitheses but in a living and experiencing mind'
(19). The subject of *L'Allegro* 'is every man's Mirth, our Mirth, the
very Grace herself with all she can include. Therefore its images are
not individualized.' The generalness of the images 'is in no way at odds
with particularity, only with individual-ity' (22).

'The unindividualized character of the images is matched in the time-
structure of the poems.' There is not one simple round of twenty-four
hours; there are various days and seasons.

The prelude of each poem is not burlesque (Tillyard) nor ironical
contrast (Brooks); it is 'a banishing of the travesty of what is praised'
in the companion poem, 'a common rhetorical device' related to the
traditions of the *débat*, the pastoral 'choice,' and the like. 'In each case,
what is banished is quite real, not the subject of the other poem seen
in a different mood, or moral temper' (24).

Miss Tuve cites Panofsky, L. Babb, G. W. Whiting, and Leishman
(see above), and, for a representative of Renaissance discussion of
melancholy and contemplation, Cornelius Agrippa's *Occult Philosophy*.
'Light as the usual symbol for knowledge (the figure of the Cherub
Contemplation is light-filled) is never felt to be in opposition to these
and the other darkened images—the dim religious light, the fire-lit
gloom, the shadows brown, the lamp-lit lonely tower—because it is not
the *darkness* which is operating symbolically; it is the votary's retired,
solitary hiddenness, "Where no prophaner eye may look", where the
mind seeing by a different light from that of Day's garish eye learns the
things known to the Cosmic Mind, Melancholy's great father whom
Agrippa calls "a keeper of secret things, and a shewer of them." ' (28–9)

'That musical harmony and its power should come into the imagery
is to be expected because of the closeness of all these matters to the
imagery of the cosmic harmonies.' 'Milton's references to Musaeus and
Orpheus, to Hermes, and thence of course to Plato, to studies touching
the after-existence of "The immortal mind" and the planet-consenting
power of the elemental Daemons, make the frame of reference within
which he is speaking quite clear; his imagery evokes the major figures
in that group of *prisci theologi* who were thought to have foreshadowed

Christian revelation' (31). 'The poem ends firmly, with a climactic last representative of those who taste Melancholy's pleasures in the pursuit of wisdom; for certainly the hermit who spells out the secrets of the physical universe in his solitary cell is no concession to religiosity but the very type of the withdrawn seer who experiences the last pleasure: to know things in their causes and see into the hidden harmonies of the cosmos' (32).

'The major figure in each poem is, in each, the one true use of *symbol*.' 'For the two conceptions to which he has given a shape Milton found the names Mirth and Melancholy, inherited names for inherited figures. . . . The two personages are truly figurative in their action, the sole important *figures* of any scope, and each is the "dominant symbol" of her poem—not light nor darkness nor towers' (33–4). 'Each poem is "a praise", the form of "demonstrative oration" called *encomium*, taught to every grammar-school boy. . . The images flow directly out of this rhetorical structure, with its usual "places", of exordium, of praise by "what kind he came of"—what nation, ancestors, parents—praise by his "acts", his gifts of mind, of countenance or quality, friends, actions' (35). 'The reader who knew the structure (that is, every educated reader of its time) would not turn the great subject of *Il Penseroso* into "the pensive man's day", would take in the unity of each poem and something of its relation to the other with a single flash of recognition, and would understand and enjoy the very virtue of the images which has been so much rubbed and questioned—for long tracts of each poem consist of the rhetorical "circumstances" which can justly and delicately limn out the unseizable through the seizable. . . . The shapely perfection of *L'Allegro* and *Il Penseroso* depends most upon a central figurative conception at the heart of each, and these large formative images have been clarified to us as modern scholarship has cleared away obstructions present since the early 1700's.' (36)

J. M. French ('Light and Work in "L'Allegro" and "Il Penseroso," ' *South Atlantic Quarterly* 58, 1959, 123–7), opposing some of Brooks's data and opinions, argued that 'light is not uniformly shaded but ranges from blazing sunshine to blackest midnight'; that 'freedom from business appointments and dinner engagements' is 'natural but irrelevant'; that anyhow 'the poems are full of workers'; and that 'the dim religious light is natural, not manipulated.'

Carol Maddison (*Apollo and the Nine*, 1960, 318–20), while recognizing that Milton would not think of either poem as an ode, remarks on the presence of some features that belong to the tradition of the ancient and the humanistic ode or hymn. Thus in *L'Allegro* there is the exorcism of Mirth's opponent, who is identified by her parentage, birthplace, and attributes (1–10); the invocation of the deity hymned, Mirth, also identified and defined by alternative birth-myths (11–24); a further defining description of Mirth's *comitatus* (25–36); and finally a prayer to be admitted to the goddess's company and beneficence, the conventional proviso or talisman against *hybris* (37–40). (On these features, cf. R. Tuve above.)

Eleanor Tate ('Milton's "L'Allegro" and "Il Penseroso"—Balance, Progression, or Dichotomy?' *MLN* 76, 1961, 585–90) found the views of Tillyard and Brooks too simple or one-sided, R. Tuve's apparently inadequate, and Allen's most satisfactory, despite his overworking the image of the tower. Her own differentiating of the two poems may not seem altogether in focus: in *L'Allegro* 'a small-scale vision of the ideal, green comic world' is set against the dream-worlds of chivalry, myth, folklore, etc., while in *Il Penseroso* fancies are rejected for 'reality, the world of pain and tragedy.'

F. Berry ('The Voice of Milton,' *Poetry and the Physical Voice*, 1962, 83–113) discusses the change in Milton's 'voice' from, e.g. *L'Allegro* to *Paradise Lost*. His premise is 'that Milton conceived his poems as objects for performance, and for performance by his own physical voice. Milton, in composing, heard them *as if they were being sounded aloud by his own voice*. He therefore wrote within the bounds of his own voice and concentrated on what his own voice could most effectively utter' (101). Berry starts with the early biographers' testimony that 'Milton had a conscious musician's ear, a conscious musician's voice (it was "tuneable", i.e. it was obedient to Milton's will and knowledge of musical effects) and that, in his latter years, he played an organ'—which confirms what we infer from the poetry (86). Milton's concern with sound, which some critics, old and recent, 'have held as a limitation was in fact the condition of achievement' (87). In his time 'we are still within the living bounds of the great "oral tradition,"' when people's writing was determined more by words spoken and heard than by the printed page (92).

L'Allegro has 'a coolness and crispness inherent in the formality of his poetry,' a formality which 'pre-supposes a detachment between Milton and his material' (94). The 'aesthetic distance' (Brooks and Hardy) that he keeps, 'the formality consequent on that distance, demands a certain sharpness in the physical utterance of Milton's lines: the poem is to ring clearly and cleanly.' Berry sees a further reason in 'the nature and size of an actual or actually supposed audience' (95). He comments particularly on the punctuation and varying pitch of lines 25–8, etc. 'The timbre of Milton's voice, at this stage of his life not yet harsh, is exquisitely sharp. The lines must be said with the right tang' (96).

Marjorie Nicolson (*John Milton: A reader's guide to his poetry*, New York, 1963, 50–62) follows Tillyard in relating the poems to Milton's first *Prolusion* and—as further evidence of their academic background—in taking the opening lines as burlesque. The poems must be read closely together, in the way Milton wrote them, as a 'deft double-structure,' 'a little academic debate between two speakers.' In both we follow 'the "pleasures of a day," then the "pleasures of a night,"' all the details being artfully paralleled and contrasted. 'One poem is the other in reverse, in time sequence, the succession of light and shadow, of sounds.' In outline the two are identical 'except that, after the first ten lines, each section of *Il Penseroso* is just a little longer than the corresponding section of *L'Allegro*, since the serious man develops his ideas more thoughtfully and at more leisure.' The same reason explains the last two sections of *Il Penseroso* (155–74), for which there is no parallel in *L'Allegro*, that is, the theme of religious contemplation and old age. All these contrasts are expressed and enhanced by the contrasted metrical movement.

Kurt Schlüter (*Die englische Ode*, 1964, 66–77) develops in considerable detail a view briefly set forth by C. Maddison (above, under 1960). He insists strongly on the relation of the companion poems to the structure and substance of the Greek hymn. The two extravagant preludes may obscure that relationship, but the body of each poem follows the pattern of the hymn: an invocation of a deity, a recital of the deity's genealogy and attributes, and a catalogue of the gifts the petitioner seeks. This is the unifying scheme of both poems, although many critics have not seen the forest for the trees. Whatever the degree of direct influence from Greek or Latin originals, the traditional pattern is much more important than the various modern 'sources' cited by scholars. This pattern is the basis of the close parallelism between the two poems. The masses of detail are presented, not as information about accustomed activities, but as the enumeration of bounties to be bestowed upon the petitioner. While *L'Allegro* and *Il Penseroso* are not explicitly and devoutly religious like the *Solemn Musick*, they have a pervasive ideality; and the modes of life the poet craves reflect the pastoral tradition.

L. L. Martz (Summers, *Lyric Milton*, 1965, 16–20), following the emphasis of Svendsen and Allen (q.v.) on progression in the two poems, remarks that 'Their relation is...that of Younger Brother to Elder Brother'; they move 'from youthful hedonism toward the philosophic, contemplative mind.' [We might, perhaps, wish to qualify 'hedonism'; Milton's Mirth is the earthly counterpart of the heavenly Euphrosyne.] 'The first poem sums up a youthful Elizabethan world of poetry now past.' Leishman's article (quoted above under 1951) shows that 'most of the parallels with Elizabethan, Shakespearean, and seventeenth-century poetry are found in *L'Allegro*.' 'The spirit of Plato's "shady Academy" dominates *Il Penseroso*, from the opening salutation of the Goddess "sage and holy" to the grand musical close which extends this poem two dozen lines beyond the length of *L'Allegro*, to present a movement toward the "extasies" of Neoplatonic mysticism. All is, however, moderated and controlled by the quiet, detached tone of the poet.... Thus the two poems move from youth to age—the word "youthfull" is invoked twice in *L'Allegro*, and not at all in *Il Penseroso*—while in their

movement these two unequal but compatible companions suggest...
growth toward maturity....'

I. G. MacCaffrey's discussion carries on from her account of the
Nativity (above, under 1966). In the twin poems 'Milton opens a window
on the renewed innocence and redeemed nature made possible, at least
in imagination, by the descent of God to earth,' even though they are
not given such a setting. Forces of evil are banished 'in the two ritual
exorcisms with which the poems open.' The worlds of the two poems
'are really the same one seen from different points of view,' worlds of
youth and social diversion and of mature philosophic and religious contemplation and solitude. These complementary attitudes 'both partici-
pate in a realm of "unreproved pleasures."' Nothing, from liberty
to Lydian music, appears in a dangerous form. 'In a sense, then, these
poems represent Milton's first effort to render Paradise in his poetry.
Time is felt in both poems as a recurrent diurnal round, rather than
shunned as a path leading downward to darkness.' These are, to be sure,
'"literary" paradises, guarded not by watchful angels' but by the
idealizing poet. Yet even the 'domesticated worlds' of the two poems,
filled with natural and concrete images and sounds, 'are projected
against the backdrop of eternity.' The figures in the landscapes 'are
not frozen, like...the "fair attitudes" on Keats's Grecian urn. Their
measured, uninterrupted motion brings alive for us the rhythms of
untormented nature, evoked by but not modeled upon art.'

G. L. Geckle ('Miltonic Idealism: *L'Allegro* and *Il Penseroso*,' *TSLL*
9, 1967–8, 455–73) sums up his view in this paragraph: 'If we read
L'Allegro and *Il Penseroso* in terms of the sentiments expressed above
[in *Prol* 7], we again get a simple dichotomy: *L'Allegro* expressing the
life of the body (presided over by Mirth and Liberty), *Il Penseroso* that
of the mind (directed by Melancholy and the cherub Contemplation).
The companion poems do not, however, express simple contrasts. They
instead symbolize one principle, that of happiness, in two modes of
existence and on two levels of perfection. The complexities of the poems
result from the fact that each contains within itself the framework of the
other, but the other seen from a different perspective. The importance of

the *Seventh Prolusion* is threefold: it shows Milton's acquaintance with Platonic doctrine; it provides an example of simple contrast and therefore points up the subtlety of the companion poems; and it also illustrates the basic rhetorical structure of the poems.'

J. S. Lawry (*Shadow*, 1968, 41–51) relates the two poems to his general theme of Milton's 'matter and stance.' In dealing with universal and hence emblematic elements of man and life 'the speaker becomes a master of the ceremonies of celebration for Mirth and Melancholy.' He is 'doubly the center of the poem, not only presenting the song and thereby expressing the object of the ceremonies, but also leading the audience in its ceremonial responses.' 'The poems form a progress of man with nature (and its intimated Creator), very broadly conceived and orchestrated; joy and meaning in both man and creation are seen in their mutual delight.' The 'two poems stage a Platonic ascent from the joys of sense through joys of the mind to virtual unity with beauty and Being.' 'Although each is self-contained, they nevertheless are one in sequence, presenting two stages in an ascent.' Lawry takes the two opening exorcisms to be 'quite serious in associating discord with Satan's Hell.' His general approach is developed with special reference to the poet's guiding of the reader's reactions. The poetic process 'resembles the greater creative process in the Nativity Ode, where God's disposition of the dynamic universe also causes all materials, even those of discord, to take positions "serviceable" to the disposing mind. In the twin poems, elements from nature and human contemplation are stringently selected for their representative or emblematic properties, and are then set as carefully as the constellations of the ode....What is unusual here is that Milton's materials are so nearly free of direction from external myth or ritual. He probably is never again so free to choose and dispose.'

Ivy Dempsey ('To "Attain To Something Like Prophetic Strain,"' *Papers on Milton*, ed. P. M. Griffith and L. F. Zimmerman, University of Tulsa, Okla., 1969, 9–24), starting from D. C. Allen (above, 1954), emphasizes the progression from the light social pleasures of L'Allegro to Il Penseroso's deepest nocturnal meditations in and on a world of symbolic mystery, especially Hermetic and religious.

E. R. Gregory ('The Road Not Taken: Milton's Literary Career and "L'Allegro"-"Il Penseroso,"' *Discourse* 12, 1969, 529–38), noting that critics have related the two poems in terms of balance, progression, or dichotomy, sees Milton as uncertain about the direction his poetic talent should take and calmly contemplating two alternatives in a modest but praiseworthy genre. (Article not seen: summarized in *Milton Quarterly*— formerly *Newsletter*—4, 1970, 31–2.)

L'Allegro

※

IV. NOTES

1–10   The banishment of Melancholy [i.e. the morbid kind (see II above)], to be balanced by *IlPen* 1–10, the banishment of 'vain deluding joyes.' With these lines Warton compared Marston, *Scourge of Villanie* 3. 11 (ed. Davenport, 167) [a parallel rediscovered by S. F. Damon (*PMLA* 42, 1927, 873–4) and again by P. Reyher (*Revue Anglo-Américaine* 10, 1932–3, 137–9)]:

> Sleep grim Reproofe, my jocond Muse dooth sing
> In other keys, to nimbler fingering.
> Dull sprighted Melancholy, leave my braine
> To hell Cimerian night, in lively vaine
> I strive to paint, then hence all darke intent
> And sullen frownes, come sporting meriment,
> Cheeke dimpling laughter, crowne my very soule
> With jouisance...

[K. Muir (*J.M.*, 30) remarks: 'The point of this echo is that Marston's *Scourge of Villanie* is a representative of the fashionable melancholy of the late Elizabethans, enshrined in Burton's monumental *Anatomy*...—and Milton wished to indicate that he was dismissing an epoch as well as a state of mind.' This idea may seem over-subtle.]

   W. J. Grace (*SP* 52, 1955, 582–3: see II above) suggests that the accompaniments of *loathed Melancholy* symbolize the afflictions associated by Burton with religious melancholy and despair: '...a most intolerable pain and grief of heart seizeth on them;...they suffer the pains of hell, and...talk familiarly with devils, hear and see chimeras, prodigious, uncouth shapes,...fiends, hideous outcries, fearful noises, shrieks....' (*Anat.* 3. 4. 2. 6: 3, 424; see also below, 10 n.). In support of his idea that the banishments are parodies of academic verse (see above, III), Tillyard (*M. Set.*, 18–19) refers to Milton's *QNov* 139–50 [cited as a parallel by Verity] as the sort of verse here burlesqued. [While recognizing the obviously extravagant rhetoric, critics have reacted variously to the idea of burlesque. Parker (770, n. 63) accepts that idea, but not the notion of self-parody.]

L'Allegro and Il Penseroso

W. Elton (*N&Q* 192, 1947, 428–9) quoted lines 591–2, 601, 614, 646, 766–7, from a work of *c.* 1620, Thomas Robinson's *Life and Death of Mary Magdalene* (ed. H. O. Sommer, E.E.T.S., Extra Ser. 78, London, 1899), [but the commonness of the allusions in these scattered lines and the obscurity of the poem make a Miltonic connection unlikely].

2–3 *Of Cerberus... | Stygian Cave forlorn.* Classic myth has no such being as Melancholy. Milton invents her and her parentage, giving her for mother the classical primeval Night (if, as seems probable, Warton and Verity are right in identifying *blackest midnight* with her), and for father, not Erebus, the husband of Night (Hesiod, *Theog.* 123–5; Spenser, *F.Q.* 3. 4. 55; Milton, *QNov* 69, *Eli* 31–3), but Cerberus, the fifty-headed (or three-headed), brazen-voiced hound of Hades (Hesiod, *Theog.* 311–12) to whom Virgil assigns a cave over-looking the Styx (*A.* 6. 417–18) in the realm of Night (ibid. 390). Spenser made Cerberus the father of the Blatant Beast (*F.Q.* 6. 1. 8; Verity, 1–2 n.). There is of course no reason to suspect a mistake made by either Milton or the printer. Keightley observed that Milton 'evidently had in view the ordinary derivation of Cerberus, κῆρ βορός, *heart-devouring*. He was therefore a suitable sire for Melancholy'; the suggestion, then, is of the melancholy person eating out his heart in midnight meditations. This is consonant with Milton's other symbolic or allegorical genealogies in these poems, of Mirth (below, 13–24) and Melancholy (*IlPen* 22–30); there is precedent, as Keightley pointed out, in Spenser: 'Ignorance, / Borne in the bosome of the black Abysse, / ...begot amisse / By yawning Sloth on his owne mother Night' (*Teares* 259–63). [I have not come upon any authority for Keightley's derivation. N. Comes (*Mythologiae...Libri Decem*, ed. Padua, 1616, 3. 5), C. Stephanus (*Dictionarium Historicum*, etc., ed. Geneva, 1621), G. Sandys, and Alexander Ross, e.g., using a different etymology, make Cerberus a devourer of flesh. G. G. Loane (*N&Q* 175, 1938, 456–7) cited the parentage of the 'Fever' that struck Prince Henry in Chapman's *Epicede* 375: 'Begot of Erebus, and uglie Night' (*Poems*, 1941, 262). R. van Kluyve (*N&Q* 7, 1960, 220) suggested that Milton's substitution of Cerberus for Erebus might have been inspired by the three dogs' heads in Burton's arms in C. Le Blon's frontispiece in the third edition of the *Anatomy* (1628); this seems unlikely.] Browne, interpreting the name Styx as 'the hateful,' thinks that Milton used *Stygian* here without special reference to the river (or even, as often, to hell) but as a mere synonym for 'detested'; but Virgil's location of Cerberus' cave suggests that *Stygian* is to be taken literally. [For the *shreiks* (4) Carey cites Virgil, *A.* 6. 426–7, on the wailing of infants heard by Aeneas as he passes

Cerberus' cave, and he would therefore (like 'most modern editors': *Works* 1, 431) remove the full stop of 1673 after *forlorn* (there was no punctuation in 1645). This idea may be right, although Milton need not be thinking of the *shreiks* so precisely, but only as an appropriate element in his imagined scene; the immediate context in Virgil has no *horrid shapes* except Cerberus, or *sights unholy.*]

5 *uncouth*: desolate, wild (*OED* 5); *cell* here seems from the context to be a synonym for cave (which could not well be repeated). Todd noted the phrase in R.A., *The Valiant Welshman* (1615), 4. 6 (Tudor Facsimile Texts, 1913), a work perhaps echoed in *Comus* (612 n., 635–6 n.). [The phrase occurs also in *The Shepherd's Pipe* (1614), *Ecl.* 7. 17 (W. Browne, 2, 156).]

6 *brooding*: part of the metaphor of *darkness* as a huge bird spreading its wings over the scene (*OED*: brood v. 6; [cf. *PL* 1. 21]), but perhaps with a secondary suggestion of moody meditation (ibid. 7), although *OED*'s earliest example comes over a century later. *jealous*: i.e. of the intrusion of any light.

7 *night-Raven*: ['A nocturnal bird, variously identified as a night-owl, night-heron, or night-jar, or imagined as a distinct species' (*OED*). Cf. H. Ullrich, *Germanisch-Romanische Monatsschrift* 18 (1930), 74. Sir D'Arcy W. Thompson (*A Glossary of Greek Birds*, 2nd ed., London, 1936, 207–9) identified the *nycticorax* as 'A Horned or Long-eared Owl,' 'A bird of evil omen,' and remarked on 'an old confusion between this bird and the Night-Heron.' He cited Spenser, *F.Q.* 2. 12. 36: 'The hoars Night-raven, trump of dolefull drere' (cf. *Epithal.* 346, 'the night Raven that still deadly yels'; *S.C., June* 23, *F.Q.* 2. 7. 23); and Sir Thomas Browne, *Certain Miscellany Tracts*, 4 (*Works*, ed. Keynes, London, 1964, 3, 58–9): '*Nycticorax* we may leave unto the common and verbal translation of a Night Raven, but we know no proper kind of Raven unto which to confine the same, and therefore some take the liberty to ascribe it unto some sort of Owls, and others unto the Bittern....']

8 *Ebon shades*. The noun suggests partial (and often oncoming) darkness (*OED* 2a); the adjective intensifies the image (*OED*: ebon 2). Todd cites the burlesque phrase, 'Rouse up revenge from ebon den' (Shakespeare, *2 H. IV* 5. 5. 39); see *Comus* 134 and n. [Wright, who argues that for Milton *shades* commonly means trees, woods, or foliage (*N&Q* 5, 1958, 206; see below, *Comus* 62 n., 428 n.), says that Milton's italics show *Ebon* 'to be a proper noun or its adjectival form,' here 'the ebony tree,' and ' "ebon shades" corresponds to "cypress shades" in *Comus*, 520.']

8–9 *low-brow'd Rocks, | As ragged as thy Locks.* The governing image is that of a person with lowering, overhanging brows and long, unkempt hair, the figure of Melancholy herself as Milton here conceives her; and the congruity of the setting with the 'person' is thus heightened. The low, overhanging rocks shade her *cell* like brows. The image is helped by the ambiguity of the word *ragged*, and also *rugged*, in Milton's day: both could mean shaggy, covered with rough, tangled hair (*OED*: ragged 1, rugged 1), and *ragged* could also be applied to rocks, etc., with the meaning of rough or rugged. Todd cited 'the tops of the ragged rocks' (Isa. 2. 21) and 'ragged rockes' in the *Tragedy of Locrine* (Malone Society, 1908, 250). Browne added 'ragged fatal rock,' applied metaphorically to Richard, in Shakespeare, *3 H. VI* 5. 4. 27; and Rolfe, 'unto a ragged, fearful, hanging rock' (*T.G.V.* 1. 2. 121). Cf. *Lyc* 93 and n.

10 *dark Cimmerian desert.* In Homer, Odysseus' ship 'came to deep-flowing Oceanus, that bounds the Earth, where is the land and city of the Cimmerians, wrapped in mist and cloud. Never does the bright sun look down on them with his rays..., but baneful night is spread over wretched mortals' (*Od.* 11. 13–19, L.C.L.). In this land Ovid places the abode of Sleep, 'in a deep recess within a hollow mountain' (*M.* 11. 592–3), where the god reclines on an ebony couch (ibid. 610); but the whole tone of the description (which Spenser caught perfectly in *F.Q.* 1. 1. 39–41) is so utterly at variance with the effect Milton seeks that it is not easy to see why Warton and some later editors suppose Milton to be at all influenced by Ovid's picture or Statius' imitation (*Theb.* 10. 84–117), or by that of Sylvester (*D.W.W.* 2. 3. 1. 552 f., Grosart, 1, 169), which may indeed have coloured *IlPen* 5–10, as Warton also claims. References to Cimmerian darkness are so common in ancient and Renaissance poetry that it would be pointless to list examples. Two passages that harmonize in tone with Milton's image are Virgil, *Cul.* 231 f., and Spenser's paraphrase, *V. Gnat* 369 f.: *feror avia carpens, | avia Cimmerios inter distantia lucos; | quam circa tristes densentur in omnia poenae*; 'I carried am into waste wildernesse, | Waste wildernes, amongst Cymerian shades, | Where endles paines and hideous heavinesse | Is round about me heapt in darksome glades.' W. J. Grace notes the phrase 'Cimmerian darkness' in Burton's account of the power of superstition over the melancholy (*Anat.* 3. 4. 1. 2: 3, 340). [Milton uses the phrase for Roman friars in *QNov* 60.]

11–40 The welcome to Mirth, to be balanced by *IlPen* 11–60, the welcome to Melancholy. Milton has also to invent *heart-easing Mirth* and her parentage, though he suggests her identity with one of the Graces, Euphrosyne.

11–16 *But com…bore.* According to Hesiod the three Graces, Aglaia, Euphrosyne, and Thalia, were the daughters of Zeus and Eurynome, daughter of Ocean (*Theog.* 907–11; cf. Spenser, *F.Q.* 6. 10. 22), and were companions of the Muses (*Theog.* 63–4; cf. *Homeric Hymns* 27. 15). For Pindar the Graces give life its bloom (*Ol.* 7. 11): they are associated with the Muses (*Nem.* 9. 54); all three love song and dance (*Ol.* 14. 13–15) and assist at banquets (ibid. 8–9). This last item is in Horace (*C.* 3. 21. 22), who further links the Graces with spring (*C.* 4. 7. 5–6). There were, as the following notes indicate, other associations on which Milton could also draw. His only precedent for making the Graces the daughters of Venus and Bacchus is found, according to Keightley, in Servius' note on Virgil, *A.* 1. 720 (partly quoted in Osgood, *C.M.* 39). [But this parentage is recorded in some Renaissance dictionaries, e.g. that of C. Stephanus: D. T. Starnes and E. W. Talbert, *Classical Myth and Legend in Renaissance Dictionaries*, Chapel Hill, 1955 (hereafter cited as Starnes–Talbert), 251–2.] The Graces are associated in one way or another with Aphrodite or Venus: *Homeric Hymns* 3. 194–6, Pindar, *Pyth.* 6. 1–2, *Paean* 6. 3–4, Horace, *C.* 1. 4. 5–7, 1. 30. 6, Jonson, *Haddington Masque* 55 f.; with Dionysus (Bacchus, Liber), in Apollonius Rhodius 4. 424–5. Spenser (despite the orthodox genealogy of *F.Q.* 6. 10. 22) makes the Graces the sisters of Cupid (ibid. 2. 8. 6) and hence, as the context suggests, the daughters of Venus. With or without precedent, Milton clearly has a purpose in presenting this first genealogy of Mirth in the person of Euphrosyne: here Mirth is the offspring of Love and Wine—much in the spirit of Horace's linking of the Graces with Bacchus and Venus (*C.* 3. 21. 21–4): *te Liber et si laeta aderit Venus | segnesque nodum solvere Gratiae | vivaeque producent lucernae, | dum rediens fugat astra Phoebus.* [Cf. Milton, *El* 6. 13–54.]

11 *fair and free.* Warton cited 'A daughter cleaped Dowsabell, / a maiden fayre and free' (*Shepheards Garland* 8. 130–1, Drayton, 1, 88), and remarked on this as a stock phrase in the metrical romances. [He noted the phrase also in Jonson, *Epigram* 76 (*Ben Jonson* 8, 52).] *OED* defines *free* here as 'of gentle birth and breeding'; Keightley, as 'affable, courteous.'

12 *In Heav'n*: in the abode of the divinities of classical myth (*OED* 5 d). *ycleap'd*: called. The *y* (from the early prefix *ge*) was adopted by Spenser and others as a conscious archaism (*OED*: clepe 3, and Y-). Cf. *Nat* 155 and *Shak* 4.
13 *heart-easing*: a neat contrast with Melancholy if Keightley was right about the suggestion carried by Cerberus (above, 2–3 n.). For Mirth see above, 11.
14–16 See above, 11–16 n.

16 *Ivy-crowned Bacchus*. See *Comus* 54–5 and n.

17–24 'Euphrosyne...is invited to attend the poet because...she was the companion of the Horae. He rectifies her ancestry, making her, in the Baconian fashion, a kind of nature myth and as such more readily accessible to men' (Allen, *Vision*, 8). The second and preferred genealogy also has its symbolic or allegorical significance: the true sources of Mirth are found in simple pleasures and a rural setting, or (in Masson's words), 'it is the early freshness of the summer morning that best produces Cheerfulness.' While saying that 'Milton is the mythologist'—the *Sager* who sings—Warton cited Jonson's *Entertainment at Highgate*, in which Aurora and Zephyrus, with Flora, sing before Maia's bower: 'See, see, O see, who here is come a Maying! / ...Why left we off our playing? / To gaze, to gaze, / On them, that gods no lesse then men amaze' (*Ben Jonson* 7, 139). Jonson's coupling of Zephyr and Aurora seems to lack classical authority [A. H. Gilbert, *Symbolic Persons in the Masques of Ben Jonson*, Durham, N.C., 1948, 159], but the addition of Flora may remind us that, in Ovid's account of Zephyr's wooing of her (*F.* 5. 201–12), Flora has a role similar to that of Milton's Aurora. As in Ovid, myth in Milton is made to carry a charming allegory of springtime joy and freshness and flowers: the west wind blowing in the dawn over the dew-drenched beds of violets and roses gives life to the spirit of joy. [Cf. the opening of Campion's *Maske in honour of the Lord Hayes* (*Works*, ed. P. Vivian, Oxford, 1909, 64), and also Milton's youthful *CarEl* 9–12 (*Works* 1, 326) and notes in *V.C.* 1.]

18 *frolick*: joyous, sportive (*OED* 1). *breathes the Spring*: exhales (the odours of) spring, as in *PL* 2. 244–5: 'his Altar breathes / Ambrosial Odours and Ambrosial Flowers,' and *CarEl* 9: *rosa fragrantes spirat...odores*; see *OED* 10. Verity cites *Naturam* 55: *Trux Aquilo, spiratque hyemem, nimbosque volutat*. [Cf. Spenser, *F.Q*. 2. 5. 29. 9.]

19–20 *playing...a Maying*. Cf. Jonson as quoted in 17–24 n. Milton's phrase adds an erotic suggestion (*OED*: play 10c; cf. *PL* 9. 1027) absent in Jonson's.
   a Maying: celebrating the rites of May Day.

21–2 Cf. two earlier and partly similar pictures, in *Prol* 1 (*Works* 12, 136–8) and *CarEl* (ibid. 1, 326). Warton (reporting Bowle) cited Shakespeare, *Shrew* 2. 1. 173–4: 'as clear / As morning roses newly wash'd with dew.' Todd added other examples.

24 *So bucksom, blith, and debonair*. Warton (after Bowle) cited 'a female heir, / So buxom, blithe, and full of face' (Shakespeare, *Per.*, 1 prol. 22–3). Todd came closer with 'A Bowle of wine is wondrous boone cheere / To make one blith, buxome, and deboneere' (Thomas Randolph, *Aristippus*, 1630, p. 18; *Works*, ed. W. C. Hazlitt, 2 v., London, 1875, 1, 21: produced in 1625–6). *bucksom.* Verity interprets as 'lively, brisk,' and the original meaning (O.E. *bugan*, to bend) as pliable, submissive, then unresisting, as in *PL* 2. 842, 'Wing silently the buxom Air': cf. Horace, *cedentem aëra* (*S.* 2. 2. 13), Milton, *QNov* 208, *PL* 5. 270. Later it lost all evident connection with its original sense and became 'a vague term of compliment.' Cotgrave (*Dictionarie*, 1611) gave both *blithe* and *buxom* among the meanings of *joyeux*. Thus far Verity, supported by *OED*, which illustrates *buxom* 3 ('blithe, gladsome') with, e.g., an item from Florio's *Worlde of Wordes* (1598): 'Vago:...blithe...buckesome, full of glee.' *blith:* exhibiting gladness: jocund (*OED* 2). *debonair:* 'courteous, affable' (Lockwood), supported by Cotgrave (quoted by Verity): 'Debonnaire: courteous, affable;...of a sweet, or friendlie, conversation.' [Cf. Marlowe, of Hero (*H. and L.* 1. 288): 'So yoong, so gentle, and so debonaire.' G. W. Whiting (*N&Q* 193, 1948, 555–8) cited Henry Cockeram's *English Dictionarie* (1623: repr. New York, 1930; Menston, Scolar Press, 1968): 'Buxome, Pliant, obedient'; 'Debonaire, Milde, courteous, gentle.']

25 *Haste thee nymph, and bring with thee.* Cook (*MLN* 15, 1900, 320) noted a somewhat similar formula in Horace, *C.* 1. 30. 5–8. *nymph:* i.e. maiden (*OED* 2), really the feminine personification of Mirth, but with some suggestion of a minor divinity (ibid. 1) carried over from the account of her descent.

26–36 The companions of Mirth will be balanced by those of Melancholy (*IlPen* 45–55). Groups of personified attendants have been noted in other poets. Warton (after Peck and Newton) cited Statius' *Kalendae Decembres* (L.C.L., 1, 64), which calls on Saturn and *multo gravidus mero December / et ridens Iocus et Sales protervi* (5–6). Warton also (after Bowle) quoted some of Buchanan's *In Neaeram* (4) (*Opera*, 1725, 2, 346): *vos adeste rursus / Risus, blanditiae, procacitates, / Lusus, nequitiae, facetiaeque, / Ioci, deliciaeque, & illecebrae, / Et suspiria, & oscula, & susurri, / Et quicquid malesana corda amantum / Blandis ebria fascinat venenis: / Sic me vivere, sic mori suave est.* Todd added (after Dunster) Sylvester's attendants on 'Fair dainty Venus,' 'Whom wanton dalliance, dancing, and delight, / Smiles, witty wiles, youth, love, and beauty bright, / With soft blind Cupids evermore consort' (*D.W.W.* 1. 4. 406–10, Grosart, 1, 55). All these are far enough from Milton's 'unreproved pleasures free,' but they illustrate the device he is using. In the youthful Milton and the poetry of his day such personification was encouraged by the example of Spenser and emblem books and, later, masques. Verity noted in Shirley's *Triumph of Peace* (1634) the presence of 'Jollity in a flame-coloured suit, but tricked like a morice dancer,' and 'Laughter in a long side coat of several colours, laughing...' (*English Masques*, ed. H. A. Evans, London, 1906, 205; *A Book of Masques*, ed. T. J. B. Spencer et al., Cambridge, 1967, 283).

27 *Quips* usually carried the suggestion of a 'sharp or sarcastic remark directed against a person,' as in Lyly, *Campaspe* 3. 2. 30–1: 'what is a quip?...Wee great girders cal it a short saying of a sharpe witte, with a bitter sense in a sweete word' (*Works*, ed. R. W. Bond, 3 v., Oxford, 1902, 2, 334). But Milton's phrase seems to anticipate, and perhaps influenced, later usage by subduing or eliminating the earlier 'implication of sharpness' (*OED* 1) in the older examples cited by Warton (Shakespeare, *T.G.V.* 4. 2. 12; *1 H. IV* 1. 2. 51; Jonson, *Cynthia's Revels* 2. 4. 48) and by Verity (Spenser, *M. Hubberds Tale* 707; Shakespeare, *Much* 2. 3. 249; John Bullokar, *English Expositor*, 1616 [facs. repr., Menston, Scolar Press, 1967]: '*Quippe*, A quicke checke, a pretty taunt'), and also, as Warton partly noted, in Milton's prose (*Works* 3, 168, 286).

    Cranks: fanciful turns of speech, verbal tricks, conceits (*OED: sb.²* 3). Warton noted Milton's use of the word in the sense of turns or reversals of action issuing in contradictions (*Works* 3, 375). *wanton Wiles*. Milton relies on the context to relieve both words of the tone of reprobation that often accompanied them: *wanton* here has no suggestion of the undisciplined, the rebellious, or the un-chaste (*OED* 1 and 2); and *Wiles* no suggestion of deceit (*OED* 1 and 2) but merely of an innocent playful trick (ibid. 1 c).

28 *Nods, and Becks, and Wreathed Smiles*. Warton quoted from the verse translation in Burton, *Anat.* 3. 2. 2. 4 (3, 112): 'With becks and nods he first began / To try the wench's mind, / With becks and nods and smiles again / An answer he did find.' Milton's three expressions connote the sociability of Mirth: *Nods* in salutation (*OED* 1); *Becks*, gestures expressive of salutation, from a nod to a deep bow (*OED: sb.²* 3). *OED* cites 'And with a beck full low he bowed at her feete' (Surrey in *Tottel's Miscellany*, ed. Arber, 218, ed. Rollins, 1, 207), and Thomas Cooper's *Thesaurus* (ed. 1584): '*Nutus*...A signe that one maketh with his eyes or head: a becke: a nodde.' *Becks* (derived from the verb, a shortened form of *beckon*) might also mean gestures (*OED: sb.²* 2), but rather of command or admonition than, as here, of greeting. P. B. Tillyard (*TLS*, 25 July 1952, 485) objected to *OED*'s 'chiefly Scottish' 'bow,' as out of keeping with the context, and defined as 'an upward nod.' E. B. C. Jones (ibid. 8 Aug. 1952, 517), comparing 'beck and call,' defined *beck* as an 'upward movement of the head...⟨which⟩ surely corresponds to a beckoning by hand.' [Cf. Sylvester: 'And with a becke summons the Sunne away' (*Epithalamion* 28, Grosart, 2, 314).] *Wreathed Smiles*: cited in *OED*: wreathed 1c. Warton explained: '*Smiles* are *wreathed*, because in a smile the features are *wreathed*, or curled, twisted, &c.' Todd supported this by citing 'Whose Face with smyling Curles' (Drummond, 2, 36).

29 *Hebe's cheek*. Hebe, the cupbearer of Zeus and the other gods, was for the Romans Juventas, goddess of youth [the Greek name, as a common noun, means youth]. In Hesiod (*Theog.* 921–2) she is the daughter of Zeus and Hera; Ovid (*M.* 9. 416) calls her Jove's stepdaughter, *privigna*. For Milton she is a type of youthful bloom and beauty (cf. *Comus* 289).

30 *And love...dimple sleek*: dimple in a smooth plump cheek (*OED*: sleek 4). Warton compared 'a dimple chin / Made for love to lodge him in' (Richard Brathwait, *Shepheards Tales*, in *Natures Embassie*, 1621, 201). Todd added: 'That dympled chin wherein delight dyd dwell' (Gascoigne, *Works*, ed. Cunliffe, 1, 98). [Cf. the lines from Marston quoted above in 1–10 n.]

31–2 *Sport...sides*. Warton cited P. Fletcher (*P.I.* 4. 13): 'Here sportfull Laughter dwells, here ever sitting, / Defies all lumpish griefs, and wrinkled care....' Cf. also: 'And then the whole quire hold their hips and loffe' (Shakespeare, *Dream* 2. 1. 55).

33–4 *Com, and trip it...fantastick toe*. Newton (reported by Todd) cited: 'Before you can say "Come" and "Go," / ...Each one, tripping on his toe' (Shakespeare, *Temp.* 4. 1. 44–6). *trip*: move lightly and nimbly on the feet, dance (*OED* 1; cf. *Arc* 99). Verity explains *it* as a cognate accusative, common in the period, representing the action implied in the sense of the verb, as in 'dance it' (Shakespeare, *Dream* 5. 403), 'Foot it' (*Temp.* 1. 2. 379). The epithet *fantastick*, fanciful in conception (not necessarily grotesque as in *Comus* 144), is transferred from the dance to the foot that performs it—which does not seem to warrant the term 'arbitrarily' applied to Milton's use by *OED* 6b. Todd cited 'My pretty light fantastick mayde' (*Nimphidia* 29, Drayton, 3, 125). *you go*: [1645, *ye go*.]

35–6 *in thy right hand...sweet Liberty*. Newton's idea that Liberty is here called a Mountain Nymph 'because the people in mountainous countries have generally preserved their liberties longest' was rejected by Warton, but is repeated by some later commentators [e.g. J. W. Hales, *Longer English Poems*, London, 1872; Verity; and F. A. Patterson, *The Student's Milton*, rev. ed.,

New York, 1933]. Though Mirth is also represented as a nymph at 25 (where it is a mere adjunct of personification), Warton thought that *Mountain Nymph* was intended to suggest an oread such as those who danced on the mountains with Pan (*Homeric Hymns* 19. 19 f.); [cf. *Arc* 97 f.]. At any rate the *sweet Liberty* that L'Allegro desires is certainly not political but individual, the disengagement implied in the (apparently later) phrase 'at liberty,' and supported by *free* (40). [An anonymous commentator remarks (privately) on 'the common human reaction to mountains' and cites T. S. Eliot, *The Waste Land*, I. 17: 'In the mountains, there you feel free.'] Allen (*Vision*, 8) remarks that *libertas* connoted manumission, and suggests that what L'Allegro would be freed from is 'loathed Melancholy.' The *Mountain Nymph, sweet Liberty* will be balanced in *IlPen* (54) by 'The Cherub Contemplation'; *in thy right hand lead with thee* gives the same priority as 'first, and chiefest, with thee bring' (ibid. 51), and in each instance the idea embodied in the figure is central to the mood and movement of the poem.

38 *admit me of*: into the number of (*OED* 1 d). *crue*: crew, company; crew is 'elsewhere in Milton, as always in Shakespeare, a depreciatory word' (Verity). Cf. e.g. *Nat* 228, *Comus* 652, *PL* 1. 51, 4. 952, *PR* 1. 107, *SA* 891; but it is not so in Spenser, *F.Q.* 1. 4. 7, 3. 7. 11, 7. 6. 14. Thus in all cases the context, and in many a qualifying adjective, fixes the tone.

39 *her*: Liberty; *thee*: Mirth. See 35–6 n. on the centrality of the former, here raised to parity with the latter. Cf. below, 151–2 and n.

40 *unreproved*: blameless (Warton), unreprovable (Verity). Verity (on *Nat* 116) observes that in Shakespeare and Milton 'the force of participial and adjectival terminations is not rigidly fixed,' and cites examples; see notes on *Nat* 116, *Comus* 394, 792. Bell comments on the order—adjective, noun, adjective—as a favourite with Milton, citing 134 below and *Lyc* 42, and suggesting that the second adjective modifies the idea contained in the noun as modified by the first adjective. Here, however, it seems probable that *free* belongs rather to the verb *live* (*OED* c), i.e. live freely, live a free life (cf. 35–6 and n.).

41 *To hear the Lark*: hear, not see, because it is invisible as it soars in the half-light. Syntactically the infinitive depends on *admit* (38) and parallels *To live* (39), *To hear*, etc., being one of the activities of those who live with Mirth, or at least of L'Allegro if he is admitted to do so. Recognition of this structure is important in deciding the meaning of the lines introduced by the next infinitive, *to com* (45). At the same time *To hear* opens the list of pleasant activities that fill L'Allegro's day, and infinitives give place to present participles (53, 57) before we come to the normal indicative, 'Streit mine eye hath caught' (69). The theme progresses by a series of brief episodes or scenes with little dependence on syntax.

42 *startle*: alarm (Lockwood), and thus begin the routing of darkness, completed at 50. Warton remarked on the 'peculiar propriety' of the word: 'the Lark's is a sudden shrill burst of song.' [P. MacKenzie (*UTQ* 16, 1946–7, 19: see above, III, under Eliot, 1936) remarks: 'All the steps in the dance, however, are not as formalized as those of the Plowman–Milkmaid group....Frequently Milton thrusts through to the kernel of a more particular and immediate impression of the real, by means of a piercing word, twisted into a partial metaphor,' as in *startle* here, 'or by the more robust realism of the semi-comic picture of the "drudging Goblin"' in 111–12. *dull night*. Todd cited (after Steevens) 'Piercing the night's dull ear' (Shakespeare, *H. V* 4, Prologue 11). See 43 n.]

43 *watch-towre*. Cf. 'The Herald Lark / ...high towring to descry / The morns approach' (*PR* 2. 279–81) [and *caeli statione* (Ovid, *M*. 2. 115). E. Riggs (*Explic*. 23, 1964–5, Item 44) thinks 41 f. have been generally misread: if we disregard the comma after *night* as not in our mode of punctuation, the sense is that '*dull night* is startled from his watch-tower in the sky by the lark.' But, while such an idea is not in itself impossible, it requires that *night* be masculine ('*his* watch-towre'), and it is hard to recall any classical or later example of that. L. Lockwood (*Lexicon*, 317, col. 2) adopted the idea, taking *night* as masculine; but, among Milton's countless uses of the word, she found no other example (the one she offered, *Comus* 956, does not count, since 'monarch' is of either gender). A. Rudrum (*Milton: Comus & Shorter Poems*, London, 1967 [cited hereafter as *Comus*], 26)—who vouches for the accuracy of Milton's knowledge of the lark's habits (see 45–6 n. below)—remarks: 'If, as is usually thought, "his watch-towre in the skies" is the watch-tower of the skylark, this would constitute another piece of accurate observation (of the height to which the lark ascends, and the fact that it appears to hover almost stationary for quite long periods). But on balance it seems likely, in spite of the comma after "night", that Milton meant us to understand it as the watch-tower of night. This gives a military metaphor...carried on' in 49–50. (However, it may seem more natural to think of the lark singing from his watch-tower.)]

44 *dappled*: 'Marked with roundish spots, patches...of a different colour or shade' (*OED*). Verity cited: 'and look, the gentle day, / Before the wheels of Phoebus, round about / Dapples the drowsy east with spots of grey' (Shakespeare, *Much* 5. 3. 25–7).

45-6 *Then to com...bid good morrow.* Opinion has been divided between (i) those who hold that syntactically *to com* parallels *To live* (39) and *To hear* (41) and like them depends on *admit* (38), which makes *me* (i.e. L'Allegro) the subject of *to com*; and (ii) those who make *to com* depend on *To hear* or must in effect assume that the syntax may be ignored, having been already replaced by what amounts to a new construction, as it clearly is by the time we reach *Oft list'ning* (53). The first group, then, maintains that L'Allegro comes to his window and bids good-morrow—to whom is a question—through the overgrowing foliage (47-8). The second group, for the most part, will have the lark come, or seem to come, and bid good-morrow to L'Allegro, although (ii*b*) one or two, freed from the evidence of syntax, have made other suggestions. The problem seems not to have arisen with early editors. Without comment, and simply by the parallels he adduces, Warton places himself in group ii; so does Todd, who here cites no comment earlier than Warton's.

[Contributors to this recurrent debate are listed alphabetically in the Index under 'Lark (*L'All* 45-6).']

(i) Masson seemed to think that the lark held the field and referred vaguely to complaints made about Milton's apparent ignorance of the habits of larks (which do not sing as they descend to the ground); he later identified the chief offender as Mark Pattison (*Milton*, London, 1879, 24-5). This argument Masson dismissed as nonsense based on a false reading of the lines. The syntax makes it clear that L'Allegro, not the lark, comes to the window. This argument (see above) is the firmest ground of those who accept Masson's reading. But Masson goes on to claim that L'Allegro is presented as already abroad and 'coming to the cottage window, looking in, and bidding a cheerful good-morrow...to those of the family who are also early astir'; he even toys with the idea of some recent sorrow in the cottage, in spite of which L'Allegro gives his greeting. Browne simply stated the argument from syntax. Rolfe quoted Browne and Masson, even supporting Masson's second contention by arguing that not *come* but *go* would be the verb to signify moving from bed to window (an argument which would seem to cut both ways); but he ended by admitting that '*come* may refer to the lark after all.' J. LeG. Brereton (*MLN* 41, 1926, 533) reasserted the argument from syntax against Verity and Hustvedt (see ii below) and by implication answered the question about whom L'Allegro addresses by illustrating (as do two items quoted by Todd: ii below) the old custom of bidding good-morrow to the day itself: 'Good morning to the day' (Jonson, *Volpone* I. I. I); 'Good morrow to the Day so fair; / Good morrow, Sir to you' (Herrick, *The mad Maid's song: Poetical Works*, ed. L. C. Martin, Oxford, 1956, 156).

J. P. Curgenven (*TLS*, 18 Oct. 1934, 715) supported the argument from syntax (*to com* depends on *admit me*); to have the lark come would make *to com* depend on *To hear*, which in turn depends on *admit me* (a difficulty already admitted by Verity: ii below); as for parallels from Sylvester and Drayton (Todd, ii below), they simply have birds bid good-morrow generally, not come to one's window. Wright (ibid. 8 and 22 Nov. 1934, 775, 840), without offering new evidence, strongly asserted that the only tenable reading is that given by syntax, which involves no contradiction of fact concerning larks; and he found Grierson (ii below) guilty of ingenious private fancies. Tillyard (ibid. 15 Nov.) supported Wright, citing a passage in *Prol* 1 (to which he takes *L'Allegro* to be closely related); there (*Works* 12, 136) the cock summons men to come forth and greet the dawn (which seems at best equivocal support). In the note on 45–8 in his edition (1938) Wright said: 'The syntax and punctuation of the original editions indicate that it is the poet who comes to the window' (his own window, approached from within); this is the only reading that 'makes good poetic sense.' This view, that L'Allegro, inside his dwelling, approaches his own window, is held by other editors, e.g. [Oliver Elton (*Milton: L'Allegro*, Oxford, 1893), W. P. Trent (*John Milton's L'Allegro*, etc., New York, 1897),] Patterson, Hughes (1937), Hanford, [Bush, Prince, and Carey], and by Allen (*Vision*, 9) and K. Muir (*J.M.*, 29). [Moody remained neutral.]

(ii) We turn to those who support the lark. Warton simply gave from Sylvester two examples of birds bidding good-morrow: 'cease, sweet Chante-cleer, / To bid Good-morrow to the Morning' (*D.W.W.* 2. 3. 1. 548–9, Grosart, 1, 169); and 'But cheerfull Birds, chirping him sweet Good-morrows' (*D.W.W.* 1. 3. 1088, Grosart, 1, 49). Todd added: 'Our musick from the birdes we borrow; / They bidding us, we them, good morrow' (T. Heywood, *Pleasant Dialogues and Dramma's*, ed. W. Bang, *Materialien* 3, 1903, 200); 'The whistling Larke ymounted on her wings, / To the gray morrow, her good morrow sings' (*Shepheards Garland* 9. 89–90, Drayton, 1, 94). [J. W. Hales (*Longer English Poems*, 1872, 237) argued for the lark on the ground of its habits and thought it awkward that the poet should be out of doors, or, if indoors, should 'bid good morrow to the world at large!'] Verity admits that, for position (i), 'the grammar is satisfactory,' but he finds 'the sense...very forced' and decides against it. Against Masson's second contention, that L'Allegro approaches the cottage from without, he argues conclusively that *my window* must mean L'Allegro's own. He is afraid 'that the lark must be meant,' despite the contradiction of fact and the awkwardness of the construction that makes *to com* dependent on *To hear* (41), which is barely justified by his citations from Shakespeare: 'who heard me to deny it' (*Errors* 5. 1. 25); 'I had rather hear you to solicit that' (*Twel.* 3. 1. 120). [Bell thought that the difficulties 'disappear if we remember that Milton's references to nature are not always strictly accurate...; and that "to come" follows at some distance from "hear," thus rendering the introduction of "to" necessary as a sign of the infinitive.'] Grierson (*TLS*, 1, 15, 29 Nov. 1934, 755, 795, 856) insists that we are concerned with poetry, not science: L'Allegro, as he wakes to the singing of the bird and the smell of the sweet-briar, imagines that the bird, sharing his feelings, is bidding him good-morrow—an experience Dekker understood when he wrote: 'for joy whereof the Larke sung at his windowe every morning, the Nightingale every night' (*The Wonderfull yeare*, 1603, ed. G. B. Harrison, 1924, 16; *Thomas Dekker*, ed. F. D. Pendry, London and Cambridge, Mass., 1968, 32). On the question of syntax Grierson argues for a series of infinitives in apposition to one another: 'By my reading the new infinitive is in apposition to the infinitives applied to the lark: "to hear the Lark begin (inf.) his flight," to hear him "startle" (inf.) the dull night, to hear him then come (inf.) and "bid," &c.' ⟨Not only is the phrase *hear... Then to com* a difficulty in itself (cf. Verity, above), but *to com*, by paralleling in form *To hear* and not the other infinitives (without *to*), conceals and confuses the alleged structure.⟩ Grierson admits some difficulties in any interpretation, and confesses that, if we are not to have the lark (in the poet's imagination) as he still prefers, we had better take *to com* in its strict grammatical sense and adopt L'Allegro, although, in that case, we should expect *go*, not *come* (cf. Rolfe, in i above), and to be told to whom he is bidding good-morrow (cf. Brereton, in i above). [Other supporters of the lark are N. Frye (*Paradise Lost*, etc., New York, 1951) and R. Tuve (*Images*, 20–1), who seems to assume this idea as a matter of course.

The latest advocate of the lark is V. B. Halpert (*Anglia* 81, 1963, 198–200), who gives a brief summary of the debate and adduces these four arguments: (1) 'The infinitives *to live* and *to hear* introduce the lines in which they appear. If *to come* were to be in balanced parallelism with the two preceding infinitives, its line would not be introduced by the adverb, *then*. This adverb, *then*, more than any other element gives cogency to advancing the skylark as the subject of *to come*....' (2) If L'Allegro spoke of himself, he should say *go* rather than *come*. (3) It is more likely that a bird outside the window would offer a greeting than 'that the poet would reach out through all that foliage.' (4) 'Finally, there is implied some simultaneity of action between the coming of the lark, after beginning his flight, and the crowing of the cock. Again the word *then* is important. This time it is balanced by the word *while*....' But it is hard to see the logic of 1 and 4; 2 is not new; as for 3, why should anyone conceive of the poet as reaching through the foliage?]

(ii b) Finally, a few commentators who reject (i) are dissatisfied with the lark (ii) and seek a substitute. S. B. Hustvedt (*MLN* 38, 1923, 87–9) argued for dawn: 'dawn doth rise' (44) and is then 'immediately (or subsequently) to come… and at my window bid ⟨me, L'Allegro⟩ good morrow.' He anticipates (but does not dispose of) the objection of a false parallelism between *To live*, *To hear*, *to com*, and dismisses concern with punctuation. B. R. Rowbottom (*TLS*, 22 Nov. 1934, 840) also supported the dawn. T. Sturge Moore (ibid. 25 Oct., 8 Nov. 1934, 735, 775) noted that *to com* is the last in a series of three invocations: 'But com thou Goddess fair and free' (11) and 'Com, and trip it as you go' (33); these two are addressed to Mirth, and he suggests that the last is also. *Then* is the crucial word: *Then*, when the lark is singing, is the moment for Mirth to join L'Allegro. (But why the infinitive, instead of imperative, for the third invocation?) [H. Koziol (*Anglia* 84, 1966, 75), starting from Miss Halpert (ii above), revives the view that it is the dawn (personified in *Lyc* 187 and *Arc* 56–7) that comes to the window; he does not mention earlier proponents of this idea.

Woodhouse ended his summary without taking sides. The case for L'Allegro may be thought much stronger than the case for the lark.]

45   *in spight of*: in defiance, scorn, or contempt of (*OED*: spite 5), i.e. in defiance of sorrow's power, not in spite of an existing sorrow. The phrase may be used in the same general sense in *PL* 2. 393; *in despite of* also had this sense, and seems to have been more commonly used to express it (*OED*: despite 5), which suggests that *spight* here is really an abbreviation of *despite*. Dunster at first interpreted Milton's phrase in the light of Ps. 30. 5: 'weeping may endure for a night, but joy cometh in the morning'; but he preferred Sylvester's couplet (of which one line was quoted above in 45–6 ii): 'But cheerfull Birds, chirping him sweet Good-morrows, / With Natures Musick do beguile his sorrows' (*D.W.W.* 1. 3. 1088–9, Grosart, 1, 49). [B. R. Rowbottom (*TLS*, 22 Nov. 1934, 840) cited Matt. 5. 45: 'for he maketh his sun to rise on the evil and on the good….'] Allen (*Vision*, 9) evidently takes the phrase in its common modern meaning, for he asks 'Why is the poet…sad at the commencement of his progress?'

48   *twisted Eglantine*. 'Sweet-brier and Eglantine are the same plant. By the *twisted* Eglantine he therefore means the Honeysuckle' (Warton). Verity quoted John Gerard, *Herball* (1597), p. 1088: 'The Eglantine Rose…a kinde of Dogs

Rose...is a shrub growing like a tree, full of prickles...in English Eglantine, or sweete-Brier'; and William Turner (*Herball*, 1562, ii. 82) observed that 'Wodbynde or Honysuckle...windeth it self about busshes' (*OED*: woodbine 2). It may be noted that *twist* in this context could mean to prune or clip (*OED* 2a), so that *twisted* might possibly mean cut back (from the window). Shakespeare combines eglantine with woodbine and musk-roses (*Dream* 2. 1. 251–2; cf. *Lyc* 146 n.). [Carey cites G. G. Loane (*N&Q* 176, 1939, 225), who thinks Milton 'was misled by Spenser, *F.Q.* III vi 44 where ivy, caprifole (honeysuckle) and eglantine are combined,' and C. A. Knapp (ibid. 267), who 'insists that since "eglantine" derives from Latin *aculentus* ("prickly") M. must have known it was a plant with thorns.' D. Daiches sees a possible blend of the classical and English: thinking of some kind of creeping flower, Milton may have had in mind Theocritus' helichryse, 'a creeping plant with yellow flowers akin to the everlastings or immortelles of the seventeenth-century English gardener' (*More Literary Essays*, 106).]

49–65 *While the Cock...singeth blithe.* Warton (on 62) quoted Milton's *Prol* 1 (*Works* 12, 136): *At primus omnium adventantem Solem triumphat insomnis Gallus....* He further observed that, if later poets imitated the morning landscape of *L'Allegro*, Milton was anticipated in several details by William Browne (*Brit. Past.* 1. 4. 482–96) [—though he might have added that Browne's account of the cock, the ploughman, the baying of hounds, the milkmaid, and the sun gilding the landscape falls far short of Milton's total effect].

50 *Scatters the rear of darknes thin.* The image is that of an army in retreat, its meagre rear scattered by the approach, or shattered by the attack, of pursuing forces. Since this is effected by sound, we might expect the verb *shatter*, but, like *ragged* and *rugged* (above, 8–9 n.), *scatter* and *shatter* seem to have been in measure interchangeable (*OED*: scatter 2, shatter 1, and *Lyc* 5 n.). Warton missed the point of the image. Verity interprets it correctly except in making the light, not the sound, the agent of dispersal. Keightley quoted 'and scatter the darknesse that obscures him' from *Love Restored* 196–7 (*Ben Jonson* 7, 382).

52 *struts.* Todd (from Dunster) compared: 'a Peacock, prickt with loves desire, / To woo his Mistress, strowting stately by her' (Sylvester, *D.W.W.* 1. 4. 198–9, Grosart, 1, 54); cf. *OED* 7b. [One would like to think that Milton remembered Chaucer's Chauntecleer (*C.T.* 3180–1, 3191–2).]

53–6 The continuing image, having recorded the routing of night, now turns to the rousing of day; cf. *Arc* 56–8. *Oft list'ning*: see above, 41 n. *Chearly*:

blithely (*OED* B. 1). *Hoar Hill.* Verity explains as covered with hoar frost (*OED* 2b), appropriate enough in the hunting season. Keightley, and later Moody (24), objected to the implied shift of seasons from summer to autumn. H. B. Hoeltje (*PMLA* 45, 1930, 201–3) argued that the introduction of the hunt entailed no inconsistency at all, since in earlier literature hunting appears repeatedly as a summer sport; he cited, e.g., Surrey's *Prisoned in Windsor* (*Tottel's Miscellany*, ed. Arber, 14; ed. Rollins, 1, 12–13), Browne, *Brit. Past.* 1. 2. 827–34, and G. Turbervile, *Noble Art of Venerie.* And *Hoar* need not refer to frost: *OED* 4 explains as referring to woods 'Grey from absence of foliage: showing the bare grey stems,' which still leaves the scene autumnal or wintry. But the supposed inconsistency will trouble only those who insist that each of the companion poems presents a single ideal day. Hughes explains *Hoar* as describing the colour of the foliage (*OED* 2c) and cites, in *Hamlet* 4. 7. 169, the willow 'That shows his hoar leaves in the glassy stream'; but grey foliage is more or less peculiar to the willow, which does not grow on hills. Wright glosses 'grey with age,' and compares 'Cyllene hoar' (*Arc* 98), thus avoiding the dilemma of either having to ignore or to accentuate the shift in season. It is not necessary to involve *the high wood*: the notes reverberate from the bare *side of som Hoar Hill* and the echo is heard *Through the high wood.* [Milton may be thinking of a grassy hillside hoary with dew in the early morning; cf. Virgil, *G.* 3. 325 (quoted in *Lyc* 29 n.).]

57 *Som time walking.* See above, 41 n. At this point, apparently, L'Allegro quits his window and begins his progress through the idealized landscape. Hurd (reported by Warton and Todd) made the first of many comments on *not unseen*: 'In the *Penseroso*, he walks *unseen*, v. 65. Happy men love witnesses of their joy: the splenetic love solitude.'

59–60 *Right against...his state.* The image is that of a monarch or other high dignitary coming forth attended by liveried retainers. Here *state* virtually means procession of state (though no other example has been cited); *begins his state* is most closely related to 'hold one's state...appear in pomp and splendour' (*OED* 19c), as in Shakespeare, *H. VIII* 5. 2. 23–5, where however the phrase is ironical. Dawn's *Eastern gate* is a poetic commonplace: editors cite Shakespeare, *Dream* 3. 2. 391 ('the eastern gate, all fiery red'), Spenser, *F. Q.* 1. 5. 2, Drayton, *Poly.* 13. 48–9, Browne, *Brit. Past.* 1. 5. 69, 2. 5. 180, Fairfax, *Jerusalem* 14. 3, Milton, *QNov* 133 (and Ovid, *M.* 2. 112–14).

61–2 *Roab'd in flames...Liveries dight.* Todd compared *Hymne of the Passion*

1–3 (Drummond, 2, 14): 'farre in the East yee doe behold / . . . the Sunne to rise, / With rosie Robes and Crowne of flaming Gold.' *Amber*: of the colour and clearness of amber (*OED*: *sb.* III. B); cf. *Comus* 332, 862 and n., *PL* 3. 359, *PR* 3. 288. Warton cited Milton's description in *Prol* 1 of the clouds attending the sun: *nubesque juxta variis Chlamydatae coloribus, pompa solenni, longoque ordine videntur ancillari surgenti Deo* (*Works* 12, 138). *Liveries*: the distinctive dress of someone's servants or retainers (*OED* 2), here not only bright but varied (cf. *thousand*), as befits the followers of the Sun. *dight*: clothed, adorned (*OED* 10); cf. *IlPen* 159.

63–8 [See the comments by T. S. Eliot, P. MacKenzie, and R. Tuve, quoted above in III, under Eliot, 1936.]

67–8 *And every Shepherd tells his tale / Under the Hawthorn in the dale*. The phrase *tells his tale* has had alternative explanations. (i) Warton [who in his 1785 edition favoured 'telling stories' as the common meaning and as a traditional pastoral amusement, though he cited Dryden and Lyly (see below), in 1791] championed the idea that the phrase means 'counts the number of his sheep.' In support he quoted W. Browne, *Shepherd's Pipe* 5. 7–10: 'When the shepherds from the fold / All their bleating charges told, / And (full careful) search'd if one / Of all their flock were hurt or gone.' [Along with that morning scene he might have quoted a bit about evening (ibid. l. 795–6): 'Sever we our sheep and fold them, / 'Twill be night ere we have told them.'] Warton argued that Milton is presenting a series of realistic activities typical of early morning in the countryside, whereas the trite and general image of telling stories or singing belongs only to ideal shepherds and is not especially a morning diversion. Warton also cited Lyly, *Gallathea* 2. 1. 53: 'nor keepe sheepe till I could tell them'; and Dryden's version of Virgil, *E.* 3. 51 (34 in Virgil): 'takes the tale of all the Lambs.' [Here the flock is counted twice a day; in Virgil, *E.* 6. 85, *numerumque referre* is an evening practice.] Warton has been followed by Todd, E. Hawkins (*Poetical Works*, 4 v., Oxford, 1824), [Hales, T. I. Bennett (*N&Q*, Ser. 5, 2, 1874, 94)], Bell, Browne, Verity (in his earlier editions: see below), Trent, Moody, J. M. Hart (*Nation*, New York, 94, 1912, 32), [Patterson, M. H. Nicolson (*Milton: Poems and Selected Prose*, New York, 1962), I. G. MacCaffrey, Prince. Hughes, Frye, and Carey incline this way.] S. Beauchamp (*N&Q*, Ser. 5, 2, 1874, 153), agreeing with Bennett (above), said that *tell* as *count* and *tale* as *total number* were still used by shepherds in his locality. That meaning of the verb has been further illustrated from Gen. 15. 5, Ps. 22. 17, 48. 12; and *tale* (as *number*) from Exod. 5. 8, 18, etc. *OED* (tale 6) adds other examples, one from *Cursor Mundi* 7174 (ed. R. Morris, E.E.T.S., London, 1874 f.), in which verb and noun occur together.

(ii) Keightley rejected Warton's interpretation. He cited, *inter alia*: 'Then lovers walke and tell their tale, / Both of their blisse and of their bale' (*Tottel's Miscellany*, ed. Arber, 231; ed. Rollins, 1, 221), but saw no reason to assume that the tales told here are especially of love: the image in the poet's mind may have been the same as in *Nat* 85–7, 91–2. [A. Ainger (*N&Q*, Ser. 5, 1, 1874, 406) upheld love.] Masson, Rolfe, and Hanford may be said to be neutral, though inclining more or less to (ii); Elton accepted it. *OED* (tell 17), in a special note on Milton's line, pronounces against the idea of numbering and in favour of 'tells his story.' It finds no instance of ' "tell his (or a) tale" in a numerical sense' before the 19th century, 'while the expression in its ordinary sense has been common since the 13th century.' It quotes the *Complaynt of Scotlande* (1549), 6. 63: 'I thynk it best that euyrie ane of vs tel ane gude tayl or fabil, to pas the tyme quhil euyn....' *OED* further observes that, in Browne's *Shepherd's Pipe* (cited above), the shepherds, having already counted their sheep, 'Underneath a hawthorn by them, / On their pipes thus 'gan to play, / And with rhymes wear out the day' (5. 44–6). [Cf. Browne, *Brit. Past.* 1. 3. 355–6: 'Full many a shepherd with his lovely lass / Sit telling tales upon the clover grass.'] Verity, in his later editions, accepted the arguments of *OED* as decisive. Wright by implication accepts (ii) and is untroubled by the context: 'This is the ideal shepherd of pastoral poetry.' [Bush cites examples of both meanings from G. Wither: 'A Tale already told this Morne well neere' (*Shepheards Hunting* 3, Juvenilia, Part 2, Spenser Society, 1871, 520); and, in an evening scene, 'before these Ewes be told' (*Faire-Virtue*, ibid. Part 3, 746).]

The context seems to favour Warton's explanation, (i), as do the lines he quotes from Browne's *Shepherd's Pipe*; but the same poem illustrates the fact that even realistic pastoral in the general tradition of Spenser is entirely tolerant of echoes from classical pastoral (as indeed Milton himself illustrates when, at 83–8, he gives pastoral names to his rustics). The argument against (i) and in support of (ii) seems less conclusive than *OED* makes it. Though the exact combination of verb and noun in the numerical sense may not occur, they certainly do separately, and Milton has supplied *OED* with more than one 'first.' On the other hand, 'Pelagius' (*N&Q*, Ser. 5, 2, 1874, 378) seems to be correct in saying that elsewhere in Milton 'tell a tale' means speaking or narrating, not counting (e.g. *Works* 3, 47; 4, 17). All that is certain is that the shepherds were sitting *Under the Hawthorn*. (For the *Hawthorn* Warton cited Shakespeare, *3 H. VI* 2. 5. 42–5: 'Gives not the hawthorn bush a sweeter shade / To shepherds looking on their silly sheep / Than doth a rich embroider'd canopy / To kings...?' Cf. Browne, *Shepherd's Pipe* 5. 44–6, quoted above.) But whether 'their loves, or else their sheep, / Was all that did their silly thoughts so busie keep,' the reader must decide for himself.

69 See 41 n.

70 *Lantskip*: landscape, 'A view or prospect of natural inland scenery such as can be taken in at a glance from one point of view' (*OED* 2). The word was introduced as a technical term of painters. In his poetry Milton consistently spells it as here (cf. *PL* 2. 491, 4. 153, 5. 142), adopting the slightly earlier, if less correct, form in *-skip* instead of *-scape* (*OED*). On the *t* for *d OED* does not comment, but it gives examples from Dekker: 'Dutch peece of Lantskop' (*Seven Deadly Sinnes of London*, ed. H. F. B. Brett-Smith, 1922, 3), 'good peeces of lantskip' (*Satiromastix* 1. 2. 125); and from Jonson, 'A Landtschap' (*Masque of Blacknesse* 24, *Ben Jonson* 7, 169). *Measures*: traverses (*OED* 11), but figuratively, with the eye (of which *OED* gives no example).

71–82 We have noticed the deliberate use of contrast, which heightens the ideal character of the landscape and gives an effect of composition and pattern which anticipates, and no doubt influenced, much of the nature poetry of the 18th century. [Cf. H. V. S. Ogden, 'The Principles of Variety and Contrast in Seventeenth Century Aesthetics, and Milton's Poetry,' *JHI* 10 (1949), 159–82.]

71 *Russet*: 'Of a reddish-brown colour' (*OED* B. 1). Verity argues at length for grey or ash-coloured: russet was the name of a coarse cloth 'of a reddish-brown, grey or neutral colour' (*OED* A. 1). Verity collects examples of the adjective where he thinks grey is the more appropriate colour; the least dubious would be Jonson's description of Boreas 'In a robe of Russet and White' were it not that he goes on 'his wings gray' (*Masque of Beautie* 13–14, *Ben Jonson* 7, 181). The same objection applies with double force to taking *Russet* here as grey: throughout 71–82, where the whole scene is built up of contrasts, mountains and meadows, shallow brooks and rivers wide, castle towers and a cottage chimney, we must, inexorably, have reddish-brown *Lawns* and *Fallows Gray*.

Lawns: tracts of grass-covered land (*OED*: sb.^{2} 1 b; cf. *Nat* 85 n., *Comus* 568 n., *Lyc* 25 n.). *Fallows*: ploughed lands, in either a general sense (*OED*: sb. 1) or especially of lands ploughed but untilled and lying fallow (ibid. 2). Whichever the meaning here, the noun is derived from the adjective *fallow*, of a pale brownish or reddish yellow colour (ibid. a.^{1} 1): it thus becomes the more necessary for Milton, if he would distinguish the colour of this land from the *Russet Lawns*, to add *Gray*.

72 *Where the nibling flocks do stray*. Warton compared 'Thy turfy mountains, where live nibbling sheep' (Shakespeare, *Temp.* 4. 1. 62)—and *Mountains*, we observe, appear in the next line.

74 *labouring clouds*. Most editors are silent and *OED* ignores. Bell relates *labouring* to the birth of rain and storms from the clouds. Allen (*Vision*, 9) goes on from a similar idea to say: 'The calendar of Milton's writing would suggest that artistic sterility and the struggle for expressive birth were not far from his mind. The dismissals of the unfruitful melancholy and the infertile folly join in making firm this presumption.' An alternative reading would be a reference to the clouds' slow movement (*OED*: labour 14: 'To move or travel, *esp.* with implication of painful exertion or impeded progress'), the word *rest* suggesting a pause from labour, and the whole avoiding the implication of rain and storm, which, on the surface at least, conflicts with the tone of the poem. [While the Lat. *labor* was used of eclipses (cf. *PL* 2. 665, 'the labouring Moon'), Milton might be thinking here of the clouds blown by the wind as the trees are in Horace: *Aquilonibus | querqueta Gargani laborant* (*C.* 2. 9. 6–7). Carey remarks: 'The "barren" mountains are contrasted with the "labouring" clouds (bringing forth rain),' and cites *Passion* 56.]

75 *trim*: finely arranged (*OED* 2). Dunster cited: 'the Flowrs... | paint the Fields so trim' (Sylvester, *D.W.W.* 1. 3. 32–3, Grosart, 1, 40). *pide*: pied, of two or more colours, variegated (*OED* 1b). Editors quote 'daisies pied and violets blue' (Shakespeare, *L.L.L.* 5. 2. 904).

76-7 In view of the general character of the landscape there seems no reason to identify *Rivers wide* with the Thames (as Verity suggests), or *Towers, and Battlements* with Windsor Castle (Masson). Verity cites 'Royal Towred Thame' (*Vac* 100).

77 *it*: 'mine eye' (69); cf. 70.

78-80 Warton commented on the romantic effect of these residences of 'our Gothic ancestors': 'The embosomed battlements, and the spreading top of the tall grove...interest the fancy...: while just enough of the towering structure is shewn, to make an accompaniment to the tufted expanse of venerable verdure, and to compose a picturesque association'; they 'excite expectation by concealment.' Something like this was their effect on L'Allegro, who imagines the castle to contain *som beauty*, led thereto, as Todd implies, by the reading of romances. He quotes from *Palmerin of England* (tr. A.M., London, 1616), c. 98: Palmerin is brought 'to the place where Leonarda remained enchanted, where he beheld in a pleasant valley, a company of grave and stately Towers among the greene trees....'

78 *Boosom'd*: enclosed in the bosom, embosomed (*OED*: bosom v. 4). This definition, adequate enough for *Comus* 367 (the only other example cited from the 17th century), seems inadequate here. The qualifying *high* suggests rather, enclosed bosom-high (bosom thus discharging a dual function in the phrase).

    tufted: 'growing in a tuft or tufts; clustered' (*OED* 2). [Todd cited 'tufted Grove' (*Comus* 224) and 'tufted Planes' (Sylvester, *D.W.W.* 2. 4. 2. 170, Grosart, 1, 227).]

79 *lies*: dwells (*OED* 5), or is temporarily lodged, as in 'a litle Hermitage... / Wherein an aged holy man did lye' (Spenser, *F.Q.* 1. 10. 46), or as in Shakespeare, *Cor.* 1. 9. 81–2.

80 *Cynosure*: 'centre of attraction, interest, or admiration' (*OED* 2b). The derivation, as is well known, is Lat. *cynosura*, Gk. κυνὸς οὐρά (dog's tail), i.e. the constellation Ursa Minor containing the Pole Star, by which Phoenician mariners steered (cf. Ovid, *F.* 3. 107–8; [Sil. Ital. 3. 665; *Comus* 340–1 n. Starnes–Talbert (244) note the information in the dictionaries of C. Stephanus and A. Calepinus.]

81–2 The couplet, with its image of the smoke ascending between the two trees which frame the cottage, rounds out the effect of pattern in the whole scene (see 71–82 n.).

83–8 L'Allegro, whose pleasure in rural scenes is enhanced by literary associations, bestows on his rustics names culled from pastoral literature: Corydon and Thyrsis (Virgil, *E.* 7; cf. 2), Phillis (ibid. 3, 5, 7, 10), Thestylis (ibid. 2). The names often appear in later pastoral writing. [The use of them here is part of the general process of idealization.]

85 *Country Messes*. Originally *mess* meant in a general sense a prepared dish of food (*OED* 1), with no necessary suggestion of the humble or informal; it came to be used of liquid or pulpy food. The context suggests to *OED* 2 that *Messes* means dishes of soft food or boiled vegetables, though no other example is given. *Hearbs* (herbs) are presumably vegetables (*OED* 2), and *other Country Messes* may mean no more than other rural dishes. [Milton may be recalling Virgil, *E.* 2. 10–11: *Thestylis et rapido fessis messoribus aestu / alia serpullumque herbas contundit olentis*—a parallel supported by the fact that, while Phillis

replaces Thestylis, she hastens in 87–8 to join the latter in binding the sheaves.
Dunster (reported by Todd) cited the *messes–dresses* rhyme in Sylvester (*D.W.W.*
2. 1. 1. 108–9, Grosart, 1, 100).]

86 *neat-handed. Neat* here may mean either 'clean' or 'skilful' (*OED* 1, 8b);
'deft, dexterous' (Lockwood). The second meaning is supported by 'the neat
finger'd Artist' (a cook) in *Animad* (*Works* 3, 123). [Bell takes the word as 'a
kind of transferred epithet, referring not to the woman's hands but to the
appearance of the food prepared by her.' One might observe how fatal it would
be to have something like 'While greasy Joan doth keel the pot' (Shakespeare,
L.L.L. 5. 2. 930).]

87 *Bowre*: dwelling (*OED* 1: 'In early use *lit.* A cottage'). Milton would seem
to be reviving this early use and he certainly handed it on to the poets of the
18th century. The meaning 'inner room' or 'chamber (a woman's)' applies to
a mansion in which 'bower' is contrasted with 'hall' (cf. *Comus* 45 and n.);
it could be applied to the rustic Phillis's habitation only in playful irony. Verity,
with no hint of this reservation, adopts the second meaning; Bell, Trent,
Lockwood, Wright, and Hughes the first.

88–90 To bind the grain in sheaves, or, earlier in the season, to turn or load
the new-mown hay in the *Mead*, grassland given over to producing meadow
hay (*OED*: sb.² 1), where it lies in *Haycocks*, conical heaps (*OED*), browned by
exposure to the sun. [Line 89 is a reminder, if it is needed, that while the poem
goes through a day, it is not confined to one season.]

91 *secure*: Lat. *securus*, free from care (*OED* 1, 1c).

92 *up-land Hamlets*: 'little villages among the slopes, away from the river-
meadows and the haymaking' (Masson). This exemplifies once more the
principle of contrast in the landscape, which is enhanced here by the holiday
scene (91–9) set against the cheerful labour of the preceding lines. Milton idealizes
his simple up-land dwellers, unlike Puttenham (quoted by Verity), who speaks
of 'any uplandish village or corner of a Realme, where is no resort but of poore
rusticall...people' (*Arte of English Poesie* 3. 4: *Elizabethan Critical Essays*,
ed. G. G. Smith, 2 v., Oxford, 1904, 2, 150).

93–9 Here the festivity is apparently that of a whole parish on a traditional
feast day, with the church bells ringing merrily, and (though Milton omits this
detail) the clergyman presiding over the gathering. Warton quoted *The Sheepheards Consort* from *England's Helicon* (ed. Rollins, 1, 198):

L'eAllegro and Il Penseroso

> Harke jollie Sheepheards,
> harke yond lustie ringing:
> How cheerefully the bells daunce,
> the whilst the Lads are springing?
> Goe we then, why sit we here delaying:
> And all yond mery wanton lasses playing?

To the severe Puritan such scenes would be too suggestive of the hated *Book of Sports*. [C. W. Brodribb (*N&Q* 163, 1932, 201) suggested that Milton's two poems (which he took to be written *c*. 1634) were prompted by discussions of the royal *Declaration*, reissued in October 1633.] The ringing of the church bells would be in itself an offence; it was one of the sinful pleasures of the young Bunyan, as he tells us in *Grace Abounding*. But these two poems are notably free from Puritan prejudices (cf. *IlPen* 155–66). In *Areopagitica* Milton showed that he had not lost sympathy with these innocent pastimes, when, reducing censorship to absurdity, he said: 'The villages also must have their visitors to enquire what lectures the bagpipe and the rebbeck reads ev'n to the ballatry, and the gammuth of every municipal fidler, for these are the Countrymans *Arcadia's* and his Monte Mayors' (*Works* 4, 317).

94 *rebecks*: commonly defined as rudimentary fiddles, usually with three strings (*OED*); see the sentence quoted from *Areop* in 93–9 n. [Cf. *Rebec* in *Grove's Dictionary of Music and Musicians*, 5th ed., ed. E. Blom, 10 v., London and New York, 1954–61.] To show that they were strung with gut, Warton cited 'wiëry Cymbals, Rebecks sinews twin'd' (Sylvester, *D.W.W.* 2. 1. 4. 566, Grosart, 1, 127). The rebeck seems to have become associated with shepherds in poetry: Warton cited the *Shepheards Garland* 2. 104 (Drayton, 1, 53) and *The Sheepheard Arsilius, his Song to his Rebeck* (*England's Helicon*, ed. Rollins, 1, 144).

96 *Chequer'd shade*. Richardson (reported by Todd) quoted: 'The green leaves quiver with the cooling wind / And make a checker'd shadow on the ground' (Shakespeare, *Tit*. 2. 3. 14–15).

98 *Sunshine*: sunny (*OED* 5). Cf. 'All in a sunneshine day' (Spenser, *S.C.*, *January* 3), and *Comus* 958. The word is used figuratively for 'cheerful, prosperous' in 'many years of sunshine days' (Shakespeare, *R. II* 4. 1. 221: *OED* 5b).

99 *live-long*: 'an emotional intensive of *long*, used of periods of time,' as in 'Where dreary owles do shrike the live-long night' (*2 Return from Parnassus* 3. 5. 1422, *The Three Parnassus Plays*, ed. J. B. Leishman, London, 1949: *OED* 1). Originally two words, *lief* (dear) and *long*, the compound *livelong* was formed

when in the later 16th century *lief* (leve) was confused with *live* (*OED*). Cf.
Milton, *Shak* 8 n. [Quoting lines 95–9, E. E. Stoll remarks: 'The last line, with
its retarded movement, suspended couplet, and liquid lapse of melody, dies
away as with a sigh' (*Poets and Playwrights*, Minneapolis, 1930, 193).]

100   *Then*. The rural festivities have carried L'Allegro to early evening.   *Nut-
brown* (of the colour of a ripe hazel-nut) was an epithet sometimes applied to
ale (*OED* 1 c). Warton took Milton's phrase to refer to the combination of ale,
nutmeg, sugar, toast, and roasted crab-apples called lambs-wool, the 'gossip's
bowl' of Shakespeare, *Dream* 2. 1. 47.

101–14   We have now left classic myth (1–24), the persons of emblem or
masque (25–40), and rural landscape, with overtones from pastoral and romance
(41–100), and come to native folklore, echoes from the world of *A Midsummer
Night's Dream* but somewhat more robust than Shakespeare's diminutive fairy
court.

101   *feat*. Though often meaning simply a deed, an act (*OED* 1), *feat* sometimes meant an exceptional or noteworthy deed, as in 'feats of Arms' (*PL* 2. 537:
OED 2). Here the idea of a noteworthy incident, as involving the supernatural,
is uppermost; there seems to be no recorded parallel.

102–3   *Faery*: fairy. Milton's spelling varies, without discernible significance
(see *Comus* 297 n.).   *Mab*. Verity, following or followed by most modern editors, cited Mercutio's fantasy (*Romeo* 1. 4. 53 f.) as the '*locus classicus* on Queen
Mab,' though actually, apart from the name, it has nothing in common with
Milton's lines and it was significantly omitted by Warton and Todd. It was
Shakespeare who popularized, and perhaps invented, Mab as queen of the
fairies [M. W. Latham, *Elizabethan Fairies*, New York, 1930, 194], an idea
taken up by Jonson and others. The various efforts to trace the name to a Celtic
original glanced at by Verity may be safely ignored as irrelevant to Milton's
lines (and themselves infirmly based: W. P. Reeves, 'Shakespeare's Queen
Mab,' *MLN* 17, 1902, 20–7; [and Latham, loc. cit.]). Warton was clearly right
in saying that 'almost all that Milton here mentions...appears to be taken'
from Jonson's *Entertainment at Althrope* (*Ben Jonson* 7, 122):

> Not so nimbly as your feet,
> When about the creame-bowles sweet,
> You, and all your Elves doe meet.
> This is Mab the mistris-Faerie,
> That doth nightly rob the dayrie,...
> Shee, that pinches countrey wenches,
> If they rub not cleane their benches.

Ancient Pistol, masquerading as Hobgoblin, confirms this last activity and adds: 'Our radiant queen hates sluts and sluttery' (Shakespeare, *Wives* 5. 5. 50), which characterizes the narrator in 103. Jonson, Browne (*Brit. Past.* 1. 2. 396–404), and Drayton (*Nimphidia* 67–8) all noticed the gifts as well as punishments bestowed by Mab, which points to Bishop Corbet's famous *Farewell rewards and Fairies*, but this Milton omits. Bell, Verity, and Wright explain *junkets* as dainties (*OED* 3), but the tradition clearly associates Mab with the dairy, and *junkets* means cream-cheeses or other preparations of cream (*OED* 2). *She*: one of the typical recounters of feats.

104 *And by the Friars Lanthorn led*: in 1645: *And he by Friars Lanthorn led.* This is the only significant variant between the two texts. Masson took the later reading as a misprint, on the ground that, 'though the construction is difficult with the other reading ⟨1645⟩, it would be hopeless with this ⟨1673⟩.' But it seems clear that the change, little as readers may approve it, was deliberate: when *he* is omitted the metre is preserved by the addition of *the*. It is of course barely possible that both changes were made by the printer, but the Errata of 1673 offer no correction. Nor is it true that the original construction is 'difficult' or the revised one 'hopeless.' In 1645 *he* parallels *She* (103; [cf. Lat. *ille, illa*]), and we get the impression of a second member of the company breaking in with his story, though it is just possible to read the line as a part of what *she sed*, referring to the adventure of her lover or husband. In 1673 the adventure belongs to the narrator herself. We may remember an exploit, not indeed of the *Friars Lanthorn*, but attributed to Mab in Jonson's *Satyre* (*Ben Jonson* 7, 123): 'This is shee, that empties cradles,... / Traynes forth mid-wives in their slumber,... / And then leads them, from her borroughs, / Home through ponds, and water furrowes.' We may further recall that Nashe (cited by Todd) groups together the supernatural visitations experienced by the narrator of 1673: 'The Robbin-good-fellowes, Elfes, Fairies....Then ground they malt..., pincht maids in their sleep that swept not their houses cleane, and led poore Travellers out of their way notoriously' (*Terrors of the night*, *Works* 1, 347). The change of 1673 perhaps simplifies the syntax of 103–14 by reducing the whole to the account of a single narrator and making *she* (understood) the subject of *Tells* (105). But the absence of any punctuation after *led* in each text leaves the syntax at this one point somewhat obscure and suggests a degree of carelessness in both readings. See further the beginning of 105–14 n. below.

The *Friars Lanthorn* has presented problems. Warton identified it with 'the *Jack and lantern*, which led people in the night into marshes and waters,' a phenomenon whose cause is conjectured, and effect described, in *PL* 9. 634–42. Warton avoided all reference to Friar Rush, a will o' the wisp that led astray such later commentators as Keightley and Verity. Friar Rush, of German origin (Bruder Rausch), was a devil who sought service in a monastic order and distracted the monks from their religious duties; he passed into English legend in the prose romance *The Historie of Frier Rush*, etc. (see C. H. Herford, *Studies in the Literary Relations of England and Germany in the Sixteenth Century*, London, 1886, and Kittredge, below). Perhaps the first person who associated Friar Rush with the Will o' the Wisp was Sir Walter Scott (*Marmion* 4. 1. 30–1, and Scott's note), who applied the idea to Milton. This confusion was charged to Milton by Keightley, who cited his own *Fairy Mythology* (ed. 1850, 347). Browne quoted Keightley. Masson adopted Warton's explanation [and apparently Friar Rush as well] but rejected Keightley's comment. Verity defended Milton but, like Keightley, invoked Samuel Harsnet's *Declaration of egregious Popish Impostures* (London, 1603, 134–5), which he also misunderstood, though in a different way. Various confusions were exposed by G. L. Kittredge ('The Friar's Lantern and Friar Rush,' *PMLA* 15, 1900, 415–41). The 'Frier' Harsnet referred to had nothing to do with Friar Rush (as Keightley supposed); nor was Robin Goodfellow called 'the Frier' (as Verity said). Harsnet's 'Frier' was a real friar, who had an assignation with a dairymaid, and the provision of a bowl of cream for Robin Goodfellow served them for a repast and offered a convenient explanation for any noise that might disturb the household. There is no reason to suppose that Milton had read Harsnet, or, if he had, that he would have misunderstood him. Milton's identification of a *Friars Lanthorn* and the Will o' the Wisp is sufficiently accounted for by the alternative name, Jack o' the Lantern, coupled with the idea that apparitions frequently presented themselves in monkish garb and with the fact that in folklore attributes and activities were not at all firmly fixed, so that those of one figure were often attached to another—a fact illustrated in Puck's assumption of a wandering fire as one of his disguises (Shakespeare, *Dream* 3. 1. 110–14; cf. 2. 1. 39), in Mab's leading midwives astray, and in the general catalogue of acts ascribed by Nashe to 'Robbin-good-fellowes, Elfes, Fairies....' Such in essence was Kittredge's argument. Recent editors, e.g. Hughes and Wright, return to Warton's explanation and ignore Friar Rush [though Carey cites him again].

105–14 *Tells.* The subject is *she* (understood) in the 1673 reading of 104; but, almost certainly, *he* (understood) in the 1645 reading (see 104 n.). The *drudging Goblin* is Robin Goodfellow, most familiarly characterized in Shakespeare,

L'Allegro and Il Penseroso

Dream 2. 1. 33–57, etc., where he is given two more of his many names, 'Hob-goblin...and sweet Puck.' Warton, *inter alia*, cited Burton: 'A bigger kind there is of them ⟨fairies⟩ called with us hobgoblins and Robin Goodfellows, that would in those superstitious times grind corn for a mess of milk, cut wood, or do any manner of drudgery work' (*Anat.* 1. 2. 1. 2: 1, 193). [The fullest account of Robin Goodfellow, which illustrates all that Milton says about him (including his hairiness), is in the book already cited, M. W. Latham's *Elizabethan Fairies* (1930), 219–62. He was 'the most famous and the most esteemed of all the spirits...who haunted England,' 'the national practical joker,' 'a universally recognized member of English country life and an accepted figure in literature and on the stage, where his existence was referred to as frequently and as casually as that of the moon or the stars.' While Shake-speare first put Robin into fairyland, and was mainly responsible for making the fairies diminutive, he kept Robin's large size—as Jonson, Burton, Milton, and others did.]

105–6 The *Cream-bowle* was the traditional reward left for Robin. R. Scot (quoted by Verity) spoke of 'his messe of white bread and milke,...his standing fee' (*The discoverie of witchcraft*, 1584, 4. 10, pp. 85–6).

107–9 Warton quoted the play *Grim the Collier of Croydon* 4. 1 (pr. 1662: Tudor Facsimile Texts, 1912, 51): 'Enter Robin Good fellow in a suite of Leather close to his body, his Face and Hands coloured russet-colour, with a Flayle'; and he declares (55) that 'my Flayle shall never lin' [cease]. Verity (supported by *OED* 1a) thinks his *Flale* is *shadowy* because unsubstantial, but the *drudging Goblin* is so substantial a being that 'Screened from observation' (ibid. 2c) seems a more likely meaning.   *end. OED: v.*² (doubtfully recorded by Verity) suggests that this does not mean finish, bring to an end, but is another word, perhaps a variant or corruption of the verb *inn* (lodge) influenced by *end*, and means to put (grain, etc.) into (a barn, stack, etc.), as in Shakespeare's figurative use: 'holp to reap the fame / Which he did end all his' (*Cor.* 5. 6. 35–6). If this explanation is correct, the meaning is that the Goblin threshes more grain in one night than ten human labourers, working all day, could bring into the barn.

110 *Lubbar Fend.* [Since Robin, although so often beneficent as well as prank-ish, was a sort of devil (Latham, 224, etc.), the word 'fiend' is appropriate.] He is called 'thou lob [i.e. bumpkin] of spirits' (Shakespeare, *Dream* 2. 1. 16). '"Lob" and "lubber" are distinct words, but their meanings have long been associated' (Hughes, 1937).

111–12 Robin's dress, though always rustic, varied, and often he had none [Latham, 242], as these lines—and the close-fitting leather suit of *Grim the Collier*—suggest. R. Scot (*Discoverie*, 4. 10, p. 85) reported the belief that he would be angry if clothes were laid out for him beside his bread and milk. For his hairy body, cf. 'Puck-hairy' in *The Sad Shepherd* 3. 1 (*Ben Jonson* 7, 42). [Line 111 suggests his human, or superhuman, size (Latham, 240, etc.).]

Chimney has the old meaning of fireplace, and old fireplaces were large.

113 *Crop-full*: filled to repletion (*OED*). The word *crop* was on occasion used literally or figuratively for the stomach (ibid. crop 2). In the expressive *flings* (moves violently, rushes: *OED* 1) the context reinforces the idea both of haste (114) and clumsiness (cf. *Lubbar Fend*). [A. Oras discusses Milton's uses of the word ('Notes,' 37–40).]

114 *his Mattin rings.* The matin was originally 'One of the canonical hours of the breviary; properly a midnight office, but sometimes recited at day-break' (*OED* 1a). [The word 'matin' was used for public morning prayer in the Church of England after the Reformation (ibid. 1c).] It could be a synonym for morning (*OED* 3). Verity cites Shakespeare, *Ham.* 1. 5. 89: 'the glowworm shows the matin to be near,' but this is not the meaning here. *OED* 4 explains as a 'morning call or song (of birds),' citing only Milton's line and phrases influenced by it. Wright, no doubt correctly, emphasizes the close association with the ecclesiastical meaning (for which there is precedent in such phrases as Spenser's 'The merry Larke hir mattins sings aloft': *Epith.* 80). The time of service was announced by a bell; hence *rings*. Bowle (reported by Warton) compared Spenser, *F.Q.* 5. 6. 27: 'What time the native Belman of the night, / The bird, that warned Peter of his fall, / First rings his silver Bell t'each sleepy wight....' At the approach of dawn ghosts and fairies departed (cf. *Nat* 232–6), their signal being the first cock-crow (Shakespeare, *Ham.* 1. 1. 150–6).

116 *whispering Winds.* Todd noted the phrase in Sylvester, *The Maidens Blush* 171 (Grosart, 2, 106).

117–34 [The question has been raised whether L'Allegro is supposed (1) to see these sights or (2) to retire and read about them. Among supporters of (1) are Verity, Moody, and Hanford; of (2), Masson, Bell, and Trent—though Trent's instincts favour (1). The question seems idle, since throughout the poem L'Allegro is assumed to be in person an observer of the scenes he describes (that, as Verity says, is part of his social character), and there is no reason to make this passage exceptional.] The lines contrast pointedly with what immediately precedes them, in offering sophisticated urban pleasures, with at least a strong literary colouring, and a type of the romantic altogether different from that of the popular superstitions recounted over the ale-drinking. For there is contrast within *L'Allegro*, in order to heighten the sense of variety in the pleasures of the carefree, as well as the major contrast between the two poems, supplied in this instance by *IlPen* 85–120.

117 *Towred Cities.* Cf. *turrigerae urbes* (Virgil, *A.* 10. 253); [and Milton, *El* 1. 73–4]. The obvious meaning of *then* would seem to be 'when the Tales are done'; and this is understood by Masson, who holds that Milton is describing an ideal day and presents L'Allegro as visiting city, court, and theatre only in imagination as he reads masque and comedy. Verity denies that he is doing either and interprets *then*, both here and at 131, as 'on another occasion,' citing Shakespeare, *A.Y.L.* 3. 2. 436–8: 'would now like him, now loathe him; then entertain him, then forswear him; now weep for him, then spit at him.' But this is not really like Milton's construction, which has no 'now' to start the series, and whose once recurring *Then* (for it is impossible to draw in the *Then* of 100) is separated from its fellows by 13 lines. On the point of syntax the honours are with Masson [though not on his other points (see 117–34 n.); and one may see warrant for linking *then* with the *Then* of both 100 and 131, since each surely means 'next,' although Milton is not thinking of the activities of a single day. Here, L'Allegro is turning from country diversions, which end early in the evening, to the later and more sophisticated gatherings of the city.]

118 *busie humm.* Warton cited Sylvester's phrase about the crowded streets of London, 'busie-buzzing swarms' (*D.W.W.* 2. 1. 1. 364, Grosart, 1, 102). Todd added lines about bees (ibid. 2. 3. 4. 365 f., Grosart, 1, 201) which contain the same phrase and other words possibly echoed in the Miltonic lines: 'The ...busie-buzzing swarm, / With humming threats throngs from the little gates / Of their round Towr.'

119–24 *Triumph* in this kind of context usually meant 'a spectacle or pageant; especially a tournament' (*OED* 4, which cites Shakespeare, *R. II* 5. 2. 52: 'What news from Oxford? Do these justs and triumphs hold?'). Cf. Bacon, *Of Masques and Triumphs* (*Works* 6, 468): 'For justs, and tourneys, and barriers; the glories of them are chiefly in the chariots, wherein the challengers make their entry...; or in the devices of their entrance; or in the bravery of their liveries; or in the goodly furniture of their horses and armour. But enough of these toys' (cited by Browne, Masson). The connecting of *triumphs* with masques by

Bacon and Milton (125–30) was not arbitrary. *OED* 4 cites a connecting phrase from R. Johnson's translation of Botero: cf. John Fletcher, *The Noble Gentleman* 2. 1: 'You shall not see a maske, or Barriers, / Or tilting....' (*Comedies and Tragedies*, 1647, 32; *Works*, ed. Dyce, 10, 135). Relics of chivalry survived in Renaissance pageantry and entertainment, and that Milton's *triumphs* carried such a suggestion is supported by *the prise,* / *Of Wit, or Arms* (122–3). Perhaps he had in mind something like Prince Henry's Barriers (1610), when, after challenges were duly delivered, the Prince, with a group of peers and knights, defended with pike and sword the Barriers set up in the Banqueting House at Whitehall, against those who took up the challenge. For this occasion the weeds of Peace, 'Pearles silks and other necessaries,' cost nearly £2000 (*Ben Jonson* 10, 509), and Jonson wrote his *Speeches at Prince Henries Barriers*. Even more germane, in view of what follows, would be a memory of Jonson's *Hymenaei: or The solemnities of Masque, and Barriers, at a Marriage* (1606), the *Masque of Hymen* being performed on the wedding night, while on the next night, after speeches by Truth and Opinion, their champions (sixteen on a side) were led into the hall and marshalled on each side of the bar, where, with a good deal of ceremony, they fought with pikes and swords (ibid. 7, 229 f.).

120   *weeds of Peace.* Todd cited 'To see great Hector in his weeds of peace' (Shakespeare, *Troi.* 3. 3. 239). If *triumphs* means tournaments, *weeds of Peace* are not contrasted with armour as such, a tournament being, not a hostile encounter, but a display of martial skill. In a general sense *weeds* meant apparel, but could contextually take on specialized meanings, including armour (*OED* 4). Ample evidence indicates that costuming was rich and gay.

121   *store.* Annotators agree that the primary meaning is abundance (*OED* 4), *store of Ladies* being parallel to *throngs of Knights and Barons* (119). An obsolete meaning was 'a body of persons' (*OED* 3). Wright finds a secondary suggestion of 'precious' (ibid. 6). Warton compared 'store of faire Ladies' (Sidney, *Astrophel* 106: *Poems*, ed. W. A. Ringler, Oxford, 1962, 236). Todd added 'Of Lords and Ladies infinite great store' (Spenser, *F.Q.* 5. 3. 2).

121–2   *bright eies | Rain influence.* Milton combines two images: of eyes as stars (cf. Shakespeare, *Romeo* 2. 2. 13–22) and of the stars as affecting men's fortunes, the 'supposed flowing...from the stars...of an etherial fluid acting upon the character and destiny of men' (*OED*: influence 2), which explains the verb *Rain.*

122–4   There is no need of illustrating the chivalric custom of having the prize at a tournament awarded by a lady of the court. Milton extends the contest from *Arms* to *Wit*, *Wit* meaning inventive fancy and expressive skill. Although speeches accompanied *Prince Henry's Barriers* (above, 119–24 n.), Milton was perhaps thinking less of his own period than of medieval courts of love—as in the fourth book of Boccaccio's *Filocolo*, where Fiammetta is chosen as queen and Filocolo proposes the first of a series of questions to be discussed. The tradition was not unknown to the 17th century: witness Marston's *The Fawn* (1606), of which the denouement involves the staging of a Parliament of Love, and Massinger's *The Parliament of Love* (1624); see W. A. Neilson, *The Origins and Sources of the Court of Love* (Boston, 1899), cc. 8 and 9. The tradition had a more substantial continuation in the element of dramatized debate which was a feature of many masques and like entertainments, e.g. the debate of the Sphinx and Love in Jonson's *Love Freed from Ignorance and Folly*, or that of the two Cupids in his *Challenge at Tilt* (*Ben Jonson* 7, 359 f., 389 f.).

123–4 Syntactically, *both* seems to refer to *Wit* and *Arms*, so that the contest would be between brain and brawn. But, since there could hardly be such a contest, it seems more natural to take *both* as referring loosely to the two contestants in *Wit* or *Arms*. In either case the contest is for the *Grace* (favour) of the lady who is by general consent the admired judge of literary or martial prowess. Warton compared, for the rhyme words, Henry Peacham's *Nuptiall Hymnes* 4 (*The Period of Mourning*, 1613, sig. F 3ᵛ): 'where Art and Cost with each contend, / For which the Eye, the Frame should most commend.'

125–6 *There*: in this same quasi-chivalric setting. The word marks the transition from triumphs to masques and at the same time carries forward the note of love to the point of marriage, for it is a wedding masque that Milton proceeds to describe. Later 'wedded Love' will be contrasted with 'Court Amours / Mixt Dance, or wanton Mask' (*PL* 4. 750, 767–8), but here he is happy to see them (freed from all opprobrium) oft conjoined. *Hymen*, the god of marriage, wore a saffron robe (*croceo...amictu*, Ovid, *M.* 10. 1), which became a commonplace, e.g. Sylvester, *Epithalamion* 40 (Grosart, 2, 314); Browne, *Brit. Past.* 2. 5. 786; [Sidney, *Arcadia*, *Works* 1, 332]. Editors supply many references to the god's appearances, with or without his robe and torch: Spenser, *Epith.* 25–7; Beaumont and Fletcher, *Philaster* 5. 3. 55–7; Shakespeare and Fletcher, *Two N.K.* 1. 1, s.d.; Jonson's *Hymenaei*, *Haddington Masque*, *Challenge at Tilt* (*Ben Jonson* 7, 210–11, 255 f., 394). When Milton writes of Hymen's *Taper clear*, he perhaps remembers that the torch's smoking was a fatal omen at the marriage of Orpheus and Eurydice (Ovid, *M.* 10. 6–7; [cf. *EpWin* 18–20.

Sandys, in his comment on the Ovidian passage (1632), speaks of the 'mantle ...of saffron' and the torch's burning 'not clearely.']

127–8 *pomp*: ceremonial procession (Lat. *pompa*; *OED*; cf. *SA* 1312). The contestants at barriers or tilt entered in procession (cf. Jonson, *Hymenaei*); and the masque had its processional elements. *feast*: festal entertainment or banquet (*OED* 3, 5). *revelry*. Milton was probably thinking of the revels, theatrical entertainments at court (Verity), the business, Hughes and Wright add, of the Master of the Revels. Certainly the word here has a suggestion of ceremonious festivity which it altogether lacks in other contexts (e.g. *Comus* 103) but the implied reference to revels seems more likely to have been to the dances, in which the masquers took partners from the audience and danced galliards, corantos, and other lively measures, and which were known as 'the revels' (Evans, *English Masques*, xxxiv). This meaning of revels, missed by *OED*, can be abundantly illustrated from Jonson's masques (*Ben Jonson* 7, 470, 490, 524, 644). In Shakespeare, *Twel.* 1. 3. 120, when Sir Andrew says he delights 'in masques and revels,' Sir Toby proceeds to ask about his skill in the galliard, coranto, etc. *mask*: the alternative and apparently earlier spelling of masque. Verity contrasts the tone of Milton's words here with his later contemptuous reference to 'a Masking Scene' and 'the old Pageantry of some Twelf-nights entertainment at Whitehall' (*Eikon, Works* 5, 67, 68). *Pageantry* is used collectively of pageants, the epithet *antique* confirming their allegorical import and suggesting their derivation from classical myth or medieval romance. [Prince glosses *antique* as 'grotesque.' Cf. *IlPen* 158 n.]

129–30 *Such sights* sums up everything suggested from 125—perhaps from 119—onward, and thus the rest of the couplet refers to the imagination of the poet, youthful like Milton himself and so in sympathy with the spirit of L'Allegro. Verity and Wright explain *haunted stream* by a reference to *Nat* 184, i.e. a stream haunted by the water-nymphs; but it is rather the Muses of whom Milton is now thinking, and the relevant parallel is the utterance of age and blindness: 'Yet not the more / Cease I to wander where the Muses haunt / Cleer Spring....' (*PL* 3. 26–8).

131–4 However *Then* be taken (see 117 n.), it marks the transition from triumph and masque to comedy. Verity considers the absence in Milton, as yet, of Puritan prejudice against the theatre, and notices his later attitude and his apparent preference of Shakespeare's comedies to his tragedies (cf. *IlPen* 101–2 n.). It is in keeping with 'decorum' that comedies should appeal to L'Allegro's taste.

Masson seems to be justified in citing the opinion expressed in the *Theatrum Poetarum* (1675) of Milton's nephew, Edward Phillips, whose 'tastes in poetry' he had formed, and whom he 'had probably helped...with hints for this very book.' [S. Golding ('The Sources of the *Theatrum Poetarum*,' *PMLA* 76, 1961, 48–53) rejects this idea: 'A careful study of the sources and methods of composition of this book has convinced me that not only did Milton have *no* hand in the work but that even his influence, if any, was negligible. Actually, the *Theatrum* was a hasty, careless piece of hack work, derived for the most part from a few convenient reference works, with a minimum of effort on the part of the compiler.' Cf. Parker, *TLS*, 28 Feb. 1942, 108.] Phillips (in addition to a similar remark near the end of his preface) said (194): '...though some others may perhaps pretend to a more exact Decorum and œconomie, especially in Tragedy, never any express't a more lofty and Tragic heighth; never any represented nature more purely to the life, and where the polishments of Art are most wanting, as probably his Learning was not extraordinary, he pleaseth with a certain wild and native Elegance' (partly quoted by Warton).

Jonsons learned sock designates his comedy (the sock, the low-heeled slipper of the Greek comic actor, standing for comedy itself: *OED* 3). Cf. Jonson on Shakespeare in the First Folio: 'Or, when thy Sockes were on, / Leave thee alone, for the comparison / Of all, that insolent Greece, or haughtie Rome / sent forth, or since did from their ashes come.' Shakespeare's *native Woodnotes wilde* apply chiefly to his romantic comedies: Verity thinks to *Dream* and *Temp.* (which Milton often echoes), but surely also to *A.Y.L.* Jonson, emphasizing Shakespeare's 'small Latine, and lesse Greeke,' inevitably suggests a contrast with himself, on which Milton seizes. With learning criticism grouped art (conscious endeavour and writing to rule). Milton's assertion (*Shak* 9–10) that 'to th'shame of slow-endeavouring art' Shakespeare's 'easie numbers flow' is reinforced by the allusion here; but, though he is contrasting the two poets, he does not follow the lead of Jonson, who had written: 'Yet must I not give Nature all: Thy Art, / My gentle Shakespeare, must enjoy a part... / For a good Poet's made, as well as borne. / And such wert thou.' (55–65). The view to which Milton contributed became in the next century one of the worn counters of criticism: 'In all debates where Criticks bear a part, / Not one but nods, and talks of Johnson's Art, / Of Shakespear's Nature....' (Pope, *Imitations of Horace, Ep.* 2. 1. 81–3: *Poems* 4, London, 1939, 1953, 201). [This contrast had become a commonplace in the early seventeenth century: see, e.g., in *Ben Jonson* 11, the lines from 2 *Return from Parnassus* (364), F. Beaumont (374–8), Heywood (404), J. Mayne (454), O. Felltham (461), R. West (468), H. Ramsay

(472), L. Digges (496).] The epithet *sweetest* (133) again echoes Jonson's tribute: 'Sweet Swan of Avon.'

In interpreting the phrase *fancies childe* we must remember: (1) that, in Milton's day and long after, fancy and imagination were commonly used as synonyms (until the Romantic period there were only occasional and sporadic attempts to differentiate them); and (2) that, however named, fancy was recognized as an important element in the natural endowment of the poet (Shakespeare himself had described 'the poet' as 'of imagination all compact': *Dream* 5. 1. 7–8), though it had not yet achieved the full character of undisputed primacy bestowed upon it by Romantic criticism. It is emphasized here as part of the implied contrast between Shakespeare's natural gifts of imagination and Jonson's acquired learning. Cf. the same idea of inheritance in 'Dear son of memory, great heir of Fame' (*Shak* 5 and n.). The phrase 'child of fancy' occurs in Shakespeare, *L.L.L.* 1. 1. 171 (Warton). For *native Wood-notes wilde*, the metaphor of the spontaneous and untrammelled song of birds, cf. Phillips above; Todd cited *boscareccie inculte avene* (Tasso, *G.L.* 7. 6), and Verity 'wild music burthens every bough' (Shakespeare, *Sonn.* 102).

135   *And ever*. Besides the suggestion of a steady temporal progression of particular happenings, which most readers find reinforced by the repeated use of *then* (45, 100, 117, 131) and 'Streit...Whilst' (69–70), there is a counter-suggestion of the typical but (generally) intermittent, conveyed by 'Som time' (57), 'Some times' (91), 'oft' (125), 'And ever' (135). As in the other instances, the phrase is transitional—this time from drama to a kind of music which finds its contrast in *IlPen* 161–6. With *eating Cares* Keightley compared *dissipat Euhius / curas edaces* (Horace, *C.* 2. 11. 17–18) and *curis animum mordacibus angit* (Lucan 2. 681); Browne cited Horace, *C.* 1. 18. 4: *mordaces aliter* ⟨i.e. except for the gift of Bacchus⟩ *diffugiunt sollicitudines*. In both the phrases quoted (which Milton seems to combine in *Mordaces curas*, *EpDam* 46) Horace is referring to the power of wine to dispel cares and beget the 'mirth' Milton in effect repudiated at line 17.

136   *Lap*: enfold as in a garment (*OED*: *v.*² 1). With their acute sense of the effect of music (and the words that it accompanied) on the affections, the Greeks condemned the *Lydian* mode as sentimental and conducing to effeminacy, in contrast to the martial Phrygian and solemn Dorian (cf. *PL* 1. 550 and n.). *Lydian* came to denote modern music of like effect, with, or as here without, a suggestion of condemnation. Thus Edward Phillips says that 'the Lydian mood is now most in request' (*Theatrum Poetarum*, 1675, Preface **3: quoted by Warton), and praises Henry Lawes' skill in 'The Dorick Sage, and the mild Lydian, / . . .the Phrygian mournfull strain' (Lawes, *Ayres and Dialogues*, 1653, Aᵛ: cited by Todd). Hughes (1937) notes Milton's ironic remark: 'No musick must be heard, no song be set or sung, but what is grave and Dorick' (*Areop*, *Works* 4, 317). In *MLN* 40 (1925), 129–37, Hughes had discussed Milton's preference for *Lydian* in *L'All*, indicating that the word was a standard term of reproach in the Renaissance (G. Cinthio, *Secondo dialogo della vita civile*, in *Hecatommithi*, Venice, 1580, 2, 36; cf. Spenser, *F.Q.* 3. 1. 40), but that from this tradition (grounded ultimately on Plato's *Rep.*, which allowed only Dorian as alone conducive to temperance) Milton broke away. He would find precedent in Horace, *C.* 4. 15. 30–2. [Martz (Summers, *Lyric Milton*, 18) is perhaps alone in thinking that 'Milton subtly recalls the condemnation, while seeming to ignore it,' and that 'the words "wanton," "giddy," and "melting" recall the implications of the *Republic*.' H. W. Howard (*Explic.* 24, 1965–6, Item 3) argues that for Milton *Lydian* was not just one of the Greek modes but was one of the ecclesiastical modes which had superseded the Greek but kept the Greek names; Greek Lydian was a descending scale, the other an ascending one. Since the *Lydian Aires* support mirth and are not really sensuous, 'we must interpret this reference primarily in terms of musical brightness and ascension and not in terms of the downgrading sensuous meaning attached to the Greek modes.' This seems rather esoteric for the context; and Milton's *Aires* are *soft*.]

137 *Married to immortal verse*. Cf. 'Voice, and Vers, / Wed your divine sounds' (*SolMus* 2–3). Warton gave other examples of the image: 'Marrying his sweet notes with their silver sound' (Browne, *Brit. Past.* 1. 5. 312); 'To marry mine immortall Layes to theirs' (Sylvester, *D.W.W.* 1. 5. 684, Grosart, 1, 67); 'marrying their sweet tunes to th' Angels layes' (ibid. 2. 1. 1. 126, Grosart, 1, 100). Rolfe added 'the true concord of well-tuned sounds, / By unions married' (Shakespeare, *Sonn.* 8. 5–6). Browne came closer to Milton's sense: 'They are the Mariage-rites / Of two, the choicest Paire of Mans delights / Musique and Poesie: / French Aire and English Verse here Wedded lie' (*Ben Jonson* 8, 401). For Milton is celebrating music and poetry, thinking of them together in the Greek way. Verity quoted Campion's famous phrase (Campion, *Works*, 115): 'to couple my Words and Notes lovingly together'; and referred to Milton's concern with this matter in his sonnet to Lawes. [Cf. Sandys, *Ovid*, 1626, 14: 'Immortall Verse from our invention springs.']

138 *the meeting soul*: 'Coming forward in response or welcome' (*OED*: *ppl. a.* 2). Leishman (*Essays and Studies 1951*, 34) notes that *meeting* here has the same sense as Lat. *obvius*, as in *cui mater...sese tulit obvia* (Virgil, *A.* 1. 314). [Cf. Keats's phrase about 'Things semireal...which require a greeting of the Spirit to make them wholly exist' (*Letters*, ed. H. E. Rollins, Cambridge, Mass., 1958, 1, 243).] *pierce*: penetrate, permeate (Lockwood); cf. *SolMus* 2–4; [and *El* 6. 45–8].

139 *bout*: turn or involution (Lockwood). *OED* explains the word as apparently a specialized sense of *bought* (*sb.*¹: a bend, curve, etc.) possibly influenced by *about*, but ignores this and cites no other example of its application to music. In the absence of other evidence, then, we may assume that this is a figurative use peculiar to Milton. Todd's illustrations from Spenser (*F.Q.* 1. 1. 15, 1. 11. 11; *V. Gnat* 255), copied by later editors, are useless since the spelling is *bought* and they apply literally to the folds of a dragon or serpent. Possibly Milton intends to suggest figuratively a serpentine movement in the music, but, more probably, a pattern that turns back on itself and repeats its phrases.

140 *Of lincked...drawn out.* Verity quotes Milton's later remark on 'true musical delight' in poetry as depending on 'the sense variously drawn out from one Verse into another' (*PL*, 'The Verse,' *Works* 2, 6).

141 *wanton heed, and giddy cunning.* 'The adjectives describe the appearance, the nouns the reality' (Browne). *wanton*: uncontrolled by plan or purpose, hence spontaneous (*OED* 3). *heed*: care. *giddy*: incapable of steady attention (*OED* 3). *cunning*: (applied) skill (*OED* 3), as in Ps. 137. 5, 'let my right hand forget her cunning,' which 'Sandys rightly paraphrases, "Let my fingers their melodious skill forget" ' (Todd). With an eye to the rhyme, Todd cites: 'While the speedy wood came running, / And rivers stood to heare his cunning' (P. Fletcher, *Sic.* 4, Chorus: 1, 246). Fletcher's reference is to Orpheus, to whom Milton next turns.

142 *melting*: 'Liquid and soft, delicately modulated' (*OED: ppl. a.* 1 c). The idea sorts well enough with *Lydian Aires* (136), but so would that of touching the feelings to love or compassion (*OED*: melt 11), which would look on to the effect of such music on Pluto (148–9); perhaps this latter may be accepted as a secondary suggestion. Todd cited 'To melt the ravisht eare with musicks strains' (P. Fletcher, *Pisc. Ecl.* 3. 14: 2, 190). Browne observes that the accompanied voice is meant: 'otherwise there would be melody, but not harmony' (cf. 144). *mazes*: suggested by the labyrinthine paths of the maze, and reinforcing the image in *many a winding bout* (139 and n.). [Hanford remarks that 'Milton is referring to the complexities of Italian and English madrigals.' D. R. Roberts ('The Music of Milton,' *PQ* 26, 1947, 328–44) says:

'No better epitome [than 139–44] could be conceived of the character of the madrigal—its delicacy, subtlety, artifice, and gentle movement. In speaking of the madrigal as "drawn out"...Milton appears to refer to its rhythmical rather than its polyphonic character, or more accurately to the manner in which the interplay of voices is used to produce an effect of quiet, continuous, forward movement, with one voice taking up the rhythmic burden before it has been dropped by another.' N. C. Carpenter (*UTQ* 22, 1952–3, 355) thinks that *Lydian Aires* might 'refer to the English song or air, a type of composition for solo voice with instrumental—often lute—accompaniment,' but that Milton's lines 'call strongly to mind the florid Italian aria with its virtuoso passages' trills, roulades.']

143–4 Warton's paraphrase is 'that, as the voice of the singer runs through the manifold *mazes* or intricacies of sound, all the *chains* are *untwisted* which imprison and entangle the *hidden soul*, the essence or perfection, of harmony. *OED* 7 defines *soul* here as 'the essential...or animating...element.'

145–50 Despite the period at 144 (perhaps a misprint carried over from 1645), these lines clearly depend on and complete the preceding ones: the music is to be such as might arouse Orpheus in Elysium to listen to strains more effective than his own. The story of Orpheus, son of the Muse Calliope (see *Lyc* 58 n.), and Eurydice was evidently a favourite with Milton [for whom Orpheus is the archetypal poet]. In Ovid (*M.* 10. 1–77), after their inauspicious nuptials (see above, 125–6 n.), Eurydice, walking with attendant naiads, was fatally bitten by a serpent; the mourning Orpheus braved the terrors of the nether world in quest of her; he pleaded with Pluto and Proserpina, accompanying his words with music that enthralled the shades and drew tears even from the Eumenides, and finally won his suit, but with the condition attached that he should not look back as they left Hades; he looked back and lost his bride. In Ovid (11. 61–6) the slain Orpheus does not sleep on asphodel; he rejoins Eurydice and, as they wander together in the world of shades, he may look back upon her when he will. But Ovid's conclusion would not have suited Milton's purpose.

145 *Orpheus self. Orpheus* is a possessive; the modern equivalent would be 'Orpheus himself.' In earlier usage *heave* meant simply to lift without the added suggestion of effort (*OED* 1), but in the various contexts in which Milton speaks of heaving the head (*Comus* 884, *PL* 1. 211, *SA* 197) there is always some hint of impediment, here that of sleep.

146 *golden slumber.* Todd quoted the song in Dekker's *Patient Grissil* 4. 2. 99: 'Golden slumbers kiss your eyes.'

147   *Elysian flowres.* In Homer (*Od.* 11. 539, 24. 13) the Elysian fields are covered with asphodel. On the classical Elysium see *FInf* 38–40 n. and *Comus* 975 n.

151–2   *These delights...to live.* Todd (3, 381) quoted the ending of Marlowe's lyric: 'If these delights thy minde may move, / Then live with mee, and be my love'; repeated with slight variations in Ralegh's *The Nimphs reply to the Sheepheard*. Cf. *IlPen* 175–6 and n.

Il Penseroso

On the date, circumstances, and sources see above, *L'Allegro* and *Il Penseroso*, I and II; for general criticism, III.

V. NOTES

Title [M. Pattison (*Milton*, 23–24; followed by R. Garnett, *Life of John Milton*, London, 1890, 22) made a double complaint: that Milton's *Penseroso* was an incorrect form and should have been *Pensieroso*, and that he gave it an incorrect meaning, 'thoughtful, or contemplative,' whereas it meant 'anxious, full of cares, carking.' Pattison was wrong on both points, as Verity said. Verity cited W. H. David (*N & Q*, Ser. 7, 8, 1889, 326), who quoted a French–Italian dictionary (Geneva, 1644): '*Pensif*, penseroso, che pensa....' Verity also cited Skeat (ibid. 394), who quoted Florio's *A Worlde of Wordes*, 1598, 266) for three forms, *pensoso*, *pensoroso*, and *pensieroso*, meaning 'pensive, carefull, musing, full of care or thought.' The three Italian words were repeated, and their meaning somewhat altered ('pensive, sad, full of care and thought, thought-full'), in Florio's *Queen Anna's New World of Words 1611* (Facsimile Reprint, Menston, Scolar Press, 1968, 366).]

1–10 The banishment of *vain deluding joyes* parallels the banishment of 'loathed Melancholy' in *L'All* 1–10. See above, II: Sources, for the song 'Hence all you vaine Delights.' Bowle (reported by Warton) cited: 'Hence, hence false Pleasures, momentary Joyes; / Mock us no more with your illuding Toyes'] (Sylvester, *Henry the Great* 331–2, Grosart, 2, 242).

2 *brood of folly.* Verity cited: 'See, the Muses pure, and holy, / By their Priests have sent thee ayde / Against this brood of Folly' (*Love Freed* 272–4, *Ben Jonson* 7, 367). *without father bred.* No genealogy parallels that of Melancholy: *vain deluding joyes* are bred of folly alone.

3 *bested*: avail. *OED* records only one example of the intransitive use, from Clough [presumably an echo of Milton].

4 *fixed mind*: constant, steadfast (*OED* 2). Todd compared: 'Yet nothing could my fixed mind remove' (Spenser, *F.Q.* 4. 7. 16), though there the context specifies the object on which the mind is fixed, as it does only less definitely in *PL* 1. 97. *toyes*: idle fancies (cf. B. Googe, *Eglogs*, etc., ed. Arber, London, 1871, 7, p. 59: 'But yf a toye com in your Brayne, / your mynde is altered quyght'; and *OED* 4), rather than trifles (*OED* 5), as assumed by Verity ('A very common meaning in Shakespeare') and Wright.

5–10 Warton traced the images in these lines to the description of the Cave of Sleep in Sylvester (*D.W.W.* 2. 3. 1. 564 f., Grosart, 1. 169): 'Confusedly about the silent Bed / Fantastick swarms of Dreams there hovered, / .... They make no noyse, but right resemble may / Th' unnumbred Moats which in the Sun do play.' See the following notes.

6 *fancies*: here the faculty; *shapes*: the images it forms, as in *PL* 5. 100–13. Hughes (1937) compares Spenser, *F.Q.* 2. 9. 50–1. *fond*: foolish (*OED a.* 2). *gaudy*: (excessively) gay, showy (*OED a.*² 3), but perhaps with the added suggestion of deceptive from *gaud* (*sb.*² 1). Cf. *Nat* 33.

7–8 Besides Sylvester (above, 5–10 n.), Warton compared Chaucer, *Wife of Bath's Tale* 868: 'As thikke as motes in the sonne-beem'; but by Milton's day the simile was a commonplace.

9 *hovering*: 'hanging poised in air' (Lockwood; *OED*: *ppl. a.*a); perhaps also wavering, uncertain (*OED* b).

10 *fickle*: changeful, inconstant (*OED* 2), with perhaps a suggestion of false, deceitful (ibid. 1). *Pensioners*: a company of military courtiers formed by Henry VIII and at first called Spearmen, but after 1539 Pensioners (*OED* 2). Warton cited 'The cowslips tall her ⟨Titania's⟩ pensioners be' (Shakespeare, *Dream* 2. 1. 10) and 'yet there has been earls—nay (which is more) pensioners' (*Wives* 2. 2. 79). *Morpheus*: the god of dreams (not of sleep). According to Ovid (*M.* 11. 633–49), he was one of the thousand sons of Somnus (Sleep), whose special function was to represent the human form and voice, while other shapes were the office of other sons. *train*: company of attendants.

11–54 The welcome to Melancholy, with her genealogy and her companions, parallels and contrasts with the treatment of Mirth in *L'All* 11–36. For the meaning of Melancholy here welcomed, in contrast with that banished in *L'All* 1–10, and for the traditions behind Milton's figure, see 11 above.

11–16 Warton noticed Marston's invoking of Melancholy: 'Thou nursing Mother of faire wisedomes lore, / Ingenuous Melancholy, I implore / Thy grave assistance, take thy gloomie seate, / Inthrone thee in my blood... / Black

Cypresse crowne me' (*Scourge of Villanie*, Proemium). Melancholy is *sage* because conducive to contemplation and wisdom, *holy* because viewed here as a *Goddess*, though there is no such classical divinity. The Latin epithet would be *sacra*. Unlike *L'All*, *IlPen* has some religious overtones, *Saintly* (13), *Nun* (31), and (more important) her attendant *Contemplation* (54 and n.) is definitely religious; and the hoped-for culmination of Il Penseroso's studies is 'something like Prophetic strain' (174). All this justifies the epithet *divinest*. W. J. Grace (*SP* 52, 582) notes that Burton speaks of divine melancholy in connection with ecstasy: ' "Ecstasis is a taste of future happiness, by which we are united unto God"; "a divine melancholy, a spiritual wing"...to lift us up to heaven' (*Anat.* 3. 4. 1. 2: 3, 343).

14–16 *hit*: suit, fit (*OED* 15), adopted by Verity (with a dubious comparison with Shakespeare, *Macb.* 3. 6. 1–2) and Wright. But Browne may be right in explaining as 'meet, touch,' as in *SA* 1568 and Shakespeare, *Antony* 2. 2. 217: 'A strange invisible perfume hits the sense' (*OED* 11), the meaning assumed by Warton, who explains that to human sight the bright countenance of Melancholy appears dark—in a degree, indeed, 'Dark with excessive bright' (*PL* 3. 380)—and therefore represented as *Ore laid with black* (16), which means 'darkened, made black; not covered with a black veil' (Keightley). Among points in which Milton's Melancholy resembles Dürer's, Bowle (reported by Warton) mentioned 'the black visage.' Z. S. Fink (*PQ* 19, 1940, 309–13) argues for the dark visage (and against a dark veil) with citations from Burton's *Anatomy*, to illustrate a common opinion that the melancholy temper induced a leaden or black colouring. He further (311–13) explains *staid Wisdoms hue* in this context as referring to the traditional recognition of the melancholy temper as conducive to philosophy, citing Aristotle, *Problems* 30. 1, Cicero, *Tusc.* 1. 33, and again Burton [who cites Dürer: see II. 2 above] and concludes: 'By bringing the second traditional view to bear on the first, Milton intellectualized the idea that melancholy caused a blackness of the skin and transformed it from the mere pathological symptom which it originally was.' [Cf. Panofsky, *Dürer*, 1, 163. *weaker*: 'somewhat weak,' the absolute use of the comparative, derived from Latin and common in the period; cf. 'prophaner' (140).]

17–18 The general sense is clear: Melancholy is *Black, but* beautiful, as Memnon's sister was (cf. 'I am black but comely, O ye daughters of Jerusalem,' Song of Sol. 1. 5). The verb *beseem* may mean simply seem, appear (*OED* 1), with *Prince Memnons sister* as subject, or befit, become (ibid. 2), with *sister* as dative object. There are numerous classical references to Memnon, son of Eos

(Aurora) and Tithonus and king of Ethiopia, who fought on the Trojan side and was killed by Achilles (Hesiod, *Theog.* 984–5; Pindar, *Ol.* 2. 83, *Isth.* 5. 41, 8. 54; etc.), and to the statue of black marble erected to his memory (Philostratus, *Imagines* 1. 7, Callistratus, *Desc.* 9). While dark of hue (Virgil, *A.* 1. 489), he was the ideal of manly beauty (Homer, *Od.* 11. 522). Browne credited R. C. Trench with discovering that Memnon, in late tradition, had a sister, and cited Dictys Cretensis. E. Venables (*N&Q*, Ser. 8, 1, 1892, 149–50) summarized from Dictys the account of the sister, Himera or Hemera. [See R. M. Frazer, *The Trojan War: The Chronicles of Dictys the Cretan and Dares the Phrygian* (Bloomington and London, 1966), 126.] Trent cited Dictys; Verity quoted a phrase about her from Guido (see below). Mabel Day (*MLR* 12, 1917, 496–7) summarized and amplified the data, citing Dictys (6. 10), who does not mention Himera's beauty; Benoit de Sainte-Maure, who does (*Roman de Troie* 29361–6: ed. L. Constans, 5 v., Paris, 1904–12), but was not printed in Milton's day; *The "Gest Hystoriale" of the Destruction of Troy* 13788–9 (E.E.T.S., v. 39 and 56, London, 1869–74); Guido de Columnis, who speaks of *mire pulchritudinis... sororem suam* (*Historia Destructionis Troiae*, ed. N. E. Griffin, Cambridge, Mass., 1936, bk. 33, p. 269 [Miss Day says bk. 8]; and Lydgate's *Troy Book* 5. 2887–906 (pr. 1555; ed. H. Bergen, 3, 1910, pp. 855–6). [Here and in *RES* 23 (1947), 144–6, Miss Day suggested that a memory of Lydgate's lines might be reflected in Milton's picture of Melancholy in 11 f., but the likeness seems remote.] D. C. Allen suggests that Milton may have derived Memnon's sister from some scholium not yet identified.

19–21 As an alternative comparison Milton presents Cassiopeia, wife of Cepheus, king of Ethiopia, and mother of Andromeda. [J. W. Hales (*Longer English Poems*, 1872, 245), in saying that in the 'usual story' the queen boasted of her daughter's beauty, was perhaps initially responsible for the idea repeated or implied by some later editors (Moody, Verity, Hughes, Wright, Prince) that Milton departed from the orthodox version. The queen's boast of Andromeda's beauty appears, e.g. in Hyginus, *Fab.* 64 (*Fabularum Liber; Poeticon Astronomicon*, in *Mythographi Latini*, ed. T. Muncker, Amsterdam, 1681) and some modern dictionaries, but the orthodoxy of the other version—Milton's—is attested by a long line of writers, e.g. Ovid, *M.* 4. 687; Apollodorus, *Lib.* 2. 4. 3 (whom Osgood, *C.M.* 19, mistakenly links with the other version); Hyginus, *Poet. Astron.* 2. 10; G. G. Pontano, *Urania* 4. 310–13 (*Carmina*, ed. B. Soldati, 2 v., Florence, 1902); N. Comes, *Mythol.* 8.6; and the dictionaries of C. Stephanus and Calepinus; the last three are cited by Starnes–Talbert, 244–5.] Milton infers Cassiopeia's blackness from her being the wife of Cepheus and relies on the context, especially *Ethiope Queen*, to convey the idea [cf. Ovid, *H.* 15. 36, on Andromeda's blackness]. She is *starr'd* because she was later translated to the constellation that bears her name. Warton suggested that 'Milton seems to have been struck with an old Gothic print of the constellations, which I have seen in early editions of the Astronomers, where this queen is represented with a black body marked with white stars.' Verity observes that 'set with stars' would be a more natural meaning for *starr'd* than changed into a star; *OED* quotes the phrase as the earliest example of the latter meaning.

22 *Yet...descended.* In *L'All* 11–24 alternative descents are offered for Mirth, the second being preferred (17). Here (23 30) only one descent is given but a comparison is retained through that descent's being *higher far* than that of the figures previously mentioned.

23–30 As he had done for Mirth, Milton invents a descent for Melancholy. She is the daughter of Vesta, the chaste goddess of the hearth (identified with the Greek Hestia, daughter of Cronos and Rhea, the Roman Saturn and Ops) and of her father Saturn before he was overthrown by Jove; hence *long of yore* (23) and *While yet there was no fear of Jove* (30); cf. *PL* 10. 584. [Milton's comment on the marital customs of the gods (25–6) is paralleled in Ovid, *H.* 4. 131–4, *M.* 9. 498–9.] The imaginary genealogy would seem to be a complete departure from classic myth, since Hestia was, like his other children, swallowed by Cronos (Hesiod, *Theog.* 453–60; *Homeric Hymns* 5. 22); but Diod. Sic., who records this tradition (5. 70. 2), also records one more in harmony with Cronos as ruler in the golden age (5. 70. 1; cf. 5. 66. 4–6), which attributes to him and to his offspring, including Hestia, valuable gifts to men (5. 68. 1). There seems to have been no association of Cronos with the more famous Mount Ida near Troy, and Verity, followed by Wright, is perhaps correct in taking *woody Ida's inmost grove* to refer to the Cretan mountain of that name; Osgood (*C.M.* 75) notes that its woods are praised in Ovid (*Am.* 3. 10. 39) but that those of the Phrygian Ida are more famous. That it was not always possible to distinguish the two Idas is illustrated by Diod. Sic. (5. 64. 4–5) and (says Osgood) the Scholiast on Euripides, *Hipp.* 1252 [*Tragoediæ*, Geneva, 1602, 1, 593]. Diod. Sic. (5. 66) seems to make Crete the home of Cronos and his fellow Titans, but establishes no connection with the Cretan Ida except that Zeus, the youngest child of Cronos, was reared there in preparation for his father's overthrow (5. 70); this was perhaps enough for Milton, since he speaks of Saturn and Jove as 'first in Creet / And Ida known' (*PL* 1. 514–15). While, on the other hand, there is not even this tenuous connection of the Phrygian Ida with Cronos, Hestia (Vesta) is closely connected with Troy, whence her worship and her sacred fire were bequeathed by Hector to Aeneas to be taken to the city he would found (Virgil, *A.* 2. 293–7), and she is therefore called by Ovid *Troica Vesta* (*M.* 15. 730–1). This might well have led Milton to think of her as native to the region; and the epithet *woody* would well suit the Phrygian Ida.

In Roman religion Vesta was the patroness of hearth and home, as Hestia was with the Greeks (Pindar, *Nem.* 11. 1). She was vowed to virginity (*Homeric Hymns* 5. 21–32; Ovid, *F.* 6. 283–94), a fact emphasized in the worship of Vesta by the Vestal Virgins. Hughes notes that for N. Comes (*Mythol.* 8. 19) the important thing about Hestia was her enthronement in the heavens in an Orphic Hymn and in Plato, *Phaedrus* 247. Warton cited W. Warner (*Albion's England* 1. 1: Chalmers, *English Poets*, 1810, 4), who made Vesta the sister and wife of Uranos and mother of Saturn, and added that such a union was 'not then forbod'; but this was the elder Vesta (Terra), mother of Saturn (Ovid, *F.* 6. 267). [Cf. Starnes–Talbert, 278–80.]

Saturn (Cronos) is the ruler of the golden age (Hesiod, *W.D.* 111–29; Ovid, *M.* 1. 89–115), a period of innocence in which laws were needless and did not exist, an innocence otherwise described in Milton's later phrase, 'such pleasing licence, as in the fabl'd reign of old Saturn' (*DDD, Works* 3, 446). [Carey cites Propertius 3. 13. 25–46, Tibullus 2. 3. 69–74.] Another principal association with Saturn is the melancholy temper, recorded in the epithet *saturnine*, like jovial, mercurial, etc., traceable through the astrological influence of the various planets; cf. Burton, *Anat.* 1. 2. 1. 2: 1, 188 f., 198). The primary suggestion of *saturnine* is 'sluggish, cold, and gloomy in temperament' (*OED* 1 b), but it could involve different degrees of the temper and different implications, including the contemplative and speculative nature (see II above). [Bacon speaks of 'Saturn the planet of rest and contemplation' (*Adv., Works* 3, 294).] For a popular statement there is James Howell's contrast of two types, the one 'Active and Mercuriall,...Quick and Ayry...Discoursive and Sociable,' the other 'Speculative and Saturnine,...Slow and Heavy,...Reserved and Thoughtfull' (*Instructions for Forreine Travell*, 1642, ed. Arber, London, 1869, 30). The epithet *solitary* suits well with the other qualities of the saturnine temper and is indeed a more or less constant feature of the melancholy man (see II above) and one emphasized in *IlPen*.

As for the symbolic value of the invented parentage, Warton took Melancholy to be the daughter of 'Genius' (Vesta) and the god of saturnine dispositions; but there seems to be no reason to identify Vesta with Genius. Browne regards

Melancholy as 'the offspring of Retirement and Culture,' since to Saturn, father alike of Vesta and Melancholy, 'is attributed the origin of civilization.' Masson suggests but is not wholly satisfied with an emphasis on Vesta as goddess of the domestic hearth, so that 'Melancholy comes of solitary musings at the fireside'; he notes the association of Vesta with virginity and feels that 'here one is on the track of a peculiarly Miltonic idea.' [For Moody 'Milton implies that melancholy is the outgrowth of solitude and youthful purity or sanctity of life; or possibly of solitude and genius.'] There seems to be, as we saw, no ground for identifying Vesta and genius; but the other suggestions of retirement, of pure thoughts without offence, and of a life of learning and contemplation, the whole set in the light of the ideal life and liberty of the golden world, appear to have some validity and to be not ill-suited to Milton's situation if he wrote *IlPen* with retreat to Horton [*sc.* Hammersmith] in prospect, there to store his mind and discipline his character for his life-work in poetry.

27 *glimmering Bowres*: retreats overarched with trees (*OED*: *sb.*[1] 3), through which the light shines intermittently (ibid. glimmer *v.* 2).

31 *pensive*: full of thought, often with some tinge of melancholy. *Nun*. By their failure to annotate the word, editors appear to assume that *Nun* bears simply its common modern meaning, current from the Old English period; but from as early a date the word was also used of a pagan priestess or votaress (*OED*: *sb.*[1] 1b); cf. Marlowe, *H. and L.* 1. 45 (and 212, 319), 'Hero, Venus Nun.' Since Melancholy is presented as the daughter of Vesta, *Nun* here seems to be at least ambivalent. At first glance *robe of darkest grain* would appear to denote the garb of a religious, which Milton at this date could never have seen; but the description is general and stylized and serves mainly to re-emphasize the idea of blackness, with an added note of dedication and dignity. The association of monastic life, ideally conceived, with contemplation would be the contribution of *Nun* taken in the modern sense, as Keightley implies.

32 *demure*. [The word expresses, not the modern sense of affected modesty, but 'the reality of that virtue' (Keightley). To Warton's and Todd's illustrations he adds Shakespeare, *Lucr.* 1219, Spenser, *F.Q.* 2. 1. 6; a better one is cited below, 38 n.]

33 *grain*: dye or colour (*OED*: *sb.*[1] 11); [cf. *Comus* 749 n. and *PL* 5. 285, 11. 242].

34 *majestick train*. The train was a mark of rank, worn especially on ceremonial occasions, and conveying, as here, an impression of dignity or even majesty (*OED*: *sb.*[1] 5).

35 *sable*: black (*OED*: A. *sb.*² and B. 2a).   *stole*. Annotators have explained variously as robe, scarf, veil, hood (cf. *Nat* 220 n.). *Stole* as robe is grounded on the initial meaning (*OED*: *sb.*¹ 1), as in Lat. *stola*, the dress of Roman women of quality; and here a robe has already been mentioned (33). As scarf, the word seems to have been confined to the ecclesiastical vestment until a much later date, when it came to be used by analogy for an article of feminine wear (*OED*: *sb.*¹ 2 and 3). For *stole* as a veil covering head and shoulders (Warton), or as hood (Browne), there seems to be no reliable authority; for there is nothing to show that the head covering of Dürer's Melancholy (cited by Warton) was a stole, or that Una's stole (Spenser, *F.Q.* 1. 1. 4; cited by Browne) was a hood; in fact it clearly was a robe or mantle (ibid. 1. 1. 45). It is true that *stole* as veil seems to be supported by Spenser, *C.C.C.H.A.* 493–95: 'Whose goodly beames though they be over dight / With mourning stole of carefull wydowhead, / Yet through that darksome vale do glister bright' (cited by Keightley). The material, *Cipres Lawn* (see below), would suit well with veil and is compatible with mantle, but not with the ecclesiastical vestment, which was of silk or heavy linen and worn only by the clergy in administering the sacrament. The position, over the *shoulders drawn* (36), would seem to confirm *stole* as mantle, to which the other reliable evidence already points. The association of *stole* with religion and learning is apparent in Florio's definition (*Worlde of Wordes*, 1598): 'a roabe, garment or religious habit, a tippet, such as religious men and doctors weare upon their shoulders, a roabe of honor and dignity, a long vestment.'

Cipres Lawn. Cypress designated 'several textile fabrics originally imported from or through Cyprus' (*OED*³ 3) and most commonly (as here) lawn, fine linen resembling cambric (*OED*: lawn¹ 1). Apparently lawn (the name perhaps derived, as Skeat suggested, from Laon in France: *OED*: *sb.*¹) was commonly assumed to be white, and cypress to be black (Warton quoted 'Lawn as white as driven snow; / Cypress black as e'er was crow': Shakespeare, *W. Tale* 4. 4. 220–1); hence the qualifying *Cipres*, to reinforce *sable* and emphasize the black colour. See *EpWin* 15–22 n.

36 *decent*: Lat. *decens*, comely, well-formed, as in *pulcher ac decens...toto corpore* (Suetonius, *Domitian* 18; cf. Horace, *C.* 3. 27. 53, 4. 1. 13), or possibly 'seemly, becoming,' as in Quintilian 2. 15. 21, in which case the reference would be to the shoulders thus adorned and the force quasi-adverbial. Warton interpreted as decent because covered, not exposed (cf. *OED* 3).

37 *state*: condition (*OED* 1a), but with a strong secondary suggestion of dignity of demeanour or presence (ibid. 18) supported by the context. Warton cited 'State in wonted manner keepe' (Jonson, *Cynthia's Revels* 5. 6. 4). With the whole, cf. 'Haste thee nymph' (*L'All* 25).

38 *With eev'n step, and musing gate.* [With this and 32, cf. Spenser, *F.Q.* 1. 10. 12: 'With countenance demure, and modest grace, / They numbred even steps and equall pace.'] *musing gate*: the slow gait of one deep in thought.

39 *commercing*: conversing, holding communication with (*OED*: v. 2). [Cf. *commercia coeli*, Ovid, *A.A.* 3. 549.]

40 *rapt*: transported, enraptured (*OED: ppl. a.* 3). Todd cited 'Ah dearest Lord! does my rapt soul behold thee?' (P. Fletcher, *P.I.* 12. 73).

41 *passion*: a feeling powerfully affecting the mind (*OED* 6), the character of which is indicated by the context, or by a modifier, as here *holy* suggests a dedicated separation from the world (*OED* 1) and moral and spiritual purity (ibid. 4). Wright takes *still* to be an adjective, i.e. motionless (*OED a.* 1); it might however be adverbial and indicate continuance of the condition in time (ibid. *adv.* 4), [a meaning perhaps supported by *till* (42)].

42 *Forget thy self to Marble.* See *Shak* 13–14 and n.

43–4 *With a sad...earth as fast.* Todd cited 'But her sad eyes still fastened on the ground' (Spenser, *Epith.* 234). [Cf. Milton, *El* 4. 49: *paulum oculos in humum defixa modestos.*] *sad*: grave, serious (*OED* 4), or, possibly, settled, steadfast (ibid. 2); i.e. it either reinforces *Leaden* or further qualifies *cast*. *Leaden* is chosen for its astrological association with Saturn (above, 23–30 n.). Thyer (reported by Todd) cited 'In leaden contemplation' (Shakespeare, *L.L.L.* 4. 3. 321). *fast*: fixedly.

45–54 These companions of Melancholy are much more than pieces of decorative imagery; they symbolize the ideal accompaniments of the contemplative life, which, though pursued here for its pleasures, still reaches out toward the mystical and the religious. The desired leisure is marked by *Peace* and *Quiet* (45) and permits the enjoyment of gracious surroundings, here represented by *trim Gardens* (50). It seems absurd in connection with *trim* to expatiate, as Warton (1785) and Todd do, on the artificialities of the formal garden; there is no such suggestion in the lines. *Spare Fast* (46) introduces the Pythagorean ideal of plain and pure living and high thinking, a favourite theme of Milton's (cf. *El* 6. 55 f. and *Prol* 2, *Works* 12, 155). With that is combined (47–8) a memory of Hesiod's picture of the Muses (*Theog.* 2–4; quoted below in *Lyc* 15–16 n.); [cf. the same allusion in *Prol* 2, loc. cit.]. Then Milton moves up to the level of Christian Platonism, specifically to the symbolism of the angelic hierarchy, in the reference to the *Cherub Contemplation* (54). As Hurd first noticed (in Warton), *the fiery-wheeled throne* (53) which the *Cherub* (on whose *golden wing* see *FInf* 57 n.) is guiding, is based on the vision of Ezekiel (10. 1–2, 9–19: see extracts above in *Passion* 36–40 n.). The vision is of a sapphire throne, with coals of fire between its wheels, propelled and guided by cherubim, moving as they moved and lifted as they 'lifted up their wings to mount up from the earth.' But the significance of Contemplation as a Cherub, and indeed the purport of the whole image, are to be understood only in the light of such a passage as the following from Pico della Mirandola's *Oratio de Hominis Dignitate* [tr. E. L. Forbes, *The Renaissance Philosophy of Man*, ed. E. Cassirer et al., Chicago, 1948, 227–8; quoted, from trans. by C. G. Wallis, in Woodhouse, 'Notes,' 87]:

> The Seraph burns with the fire of love. The Cherub glows with the splendor of intelligence. The Throne [here the third in the highest triad of angels] stands by the steadfastness of judgment. Therefore if, in giving ourselves over to the active life, we have after due considera-tion undertaken the care of the lower beings, we shall be strengthened with the firm stability of Thrones. If, unoccupied by deeds, we pass our time in the leisure of contemplation, con-sidering the Creator in the creature and the creature in the Creator, we shall be all ablaze with Cherubic light. If we long with love for the Creator himself alone, we shall speedily flame up with His consuming fire into a Seraphic likeness....

> But by what means is one able either to judge or to love things unknown?...Therefore, the Cherub as intermediary by his own light makes us ready for the Seraphic fire and equally lights the way to the judgment of the Thrones. This is the bond of the first minds, the Palladian order, the chief of contemplative philosophy. This is the one for us first to emulate, to court, and to understand; the one from whence we may be rapt to the heights of love and descend, well taught and well prepared, to the functions of active life.

That Milton was familiar, not necessarily with this work, but with the sym-bolism of the angelic orders stemming from pseudo-Dionysius, *De Coelesti Hierarchia*, is apparent from his use of the titles here and in *Nat* (see notes on *Nat* 28, 112–13). Once this background of the *Cherub* image is recognized, there is seen to be a daring play on the word *throne*, whose primary meaning is literal but whose secondary reference is to the third angelic order: *Contemplation* directs judgment and action as the *Cherub* guides the throne. Further, the image is now seen to be integral to the structure of the poem: the *chiefest* com-panion of Melancholy and the last to be named, though the *first* in importance and in being foreseen from the beginning as the end is foreseen, is the power by which 'old experience' may at last 'attain / To something like Prophetic strain' (173–4 and n.). It is perhaps indicative of the degree to which this mode of thought had lapsed in the eighteenth century that to Newton (reported by Warton and Todd) Milton's *Cherub* appeared to be a figure like Cupid; and that Warton, while connecting Newton's evident confusion with the 'infantine

angel' of some 'dauber for a country-church' and of Shakespeare (at least in
H. VIII 1. 1. 22–3), still recognized no allusion to the angelic hierarchy and the
role of the Cherubim therein. Verity found the first such recognition in a note
by C. B. Mount, *N&Q*, Ser .7, 2, 1886, 323. He and later editors [e.g. Trent,
Hughes, Wright, Hanford, Carey] refer more or less briefly to medieval
angelology.

49 [The mistaken semicolon after *leasure* (1673) should be a comma, as in
1645. This is recorded in the notes in *Works* 1, 432, along with erroneous full
stops at the end of lines 81, 88, 143, and 156, but these four are corrected in
the text also.]

55 *And the mute Silence hist along.* There are two small problems here: one
of syntax, the other of the precise meaning of the verb *hist. OED* traces the
word to a 'natural exclamation...enjoining silence,' with variant forms
(cf. 'whist,' *Nat.* 64), and defines the verbal meaning here as 'To summon with
the exclamation "hist!"; to summon...without noise' (*OED: v.* 1). Masson,
followed by Wright, takes *hist* as an imperative addressed to Melancholy and
paralleling 'bring' (51). If this be correct, and the verb be taken as transitive,
the meaning would be 'bring the mute Silence with you' (Verity), admonishing
her to continue the while (Masson). Verity also suggests 'move stealthily
through (*along*) the silence'; this leaves the mood imperative but makes the
verb intransitive (for which *OED: v.* 2 offers only one late and dubious example).
It is not impossible, however, that *hist* does not parallel 'bring,' and that its
mood is the so-called optative subjunctive (expressing Il Penseroso's wish) with
Silence as its subject, the sense being 'And may Silence move along (with the
whole group) admonishing noiselessness the while.' This explanation has the
merit of providing for *along* without, incongruously, demanding action from
the detached and contemplative Melancholy, and without introducing another
and anticlimactic companion after the *Cherub Contemplation*, while at the same
time recognizing the twofold function of the line, namely, to reinforce *Peace*
and *Quiet* (45) by rounding off the whole passage with *Silence*, and to effect,
with the following lines (56–64), the transition to Il Penseroso's occupations.
[Cf. the Ovidian *muta silentia* in *QNov* 149.]

56 *'Less.* Even without the apostrophe (present also in 1645), the word was
used as a contraction of *unless* (Masson). [*OED* (less c) quotes this line.]

Philomel: the nightingale (Lat. *Philomela*). The Greek etymology, as
Milton would know, means 'lover of song' (Hughes). The myth of Tereus,
Philomela, and Procne (Ovid, *M.* 6. 412–674) hardly needs recounting. Verity

notes that Shakespeare used the form Philomel [he was not alone in that]. The nightingale here parallels the lark of *L'All* 41 and, like it, fixes the point at which the temporal sequence in the poem begins.

57 *plight*: either state of mind, mood (*OED*: *sb.*[2] 6) or possibly a plait (ibid. 2), something braided or intertwined, 'perhaps...to express the involution of the notes of the nightingale' (Keightley). Bell supports the latter explanation by comparing 'plighted clouds' (*Comus* 300), but is apparently wrong in regarding the two as different words. It may well be that Milton intends one as primary meaning, the other as secondary suggestion. Cf. 'Deare Quirister, who... sends / ...Such sad lamenting Straines, that Night attends / Become all Eare, Starres stay to heare thy Plight' (Drummond, 1, 26, *Sonn.* 25).

58 *Smoothing the rugged brow of night*. Todd cited: 'With like delightes sometimes may eke delay, / The rugged brow of carefull Policy' (Spenser, *F.Q.*, dedicatory sonnet to Hatton), where 'delay' means 'assuage' (*OED*: *v.*[2] 2) and 'rugged' means 'frowning,' as here and in *PR* 2. 164 (*OED*: *a.*[1] 3b). Verity cited Shakespeare, 'black-brow'd night' (*Romeo* 3. 2. 20, *Dream* 3. 2. 387) and 'black brow of night' (*John* 5. 6. 17), but black has here other associations for Milton (cf. 12–16 above).

59-60 *While Cynthia...accustom'd Oke*. In classical myth the dragon-drawn chariot belongs to Demeter or Ceres (Keightley), but Shakespeare has 'night's swift dragons cut the clouds full fast' (*Dream* 3. 2. 379)—which Verity took as Milton's probable source—and, in *Cym.* 2. 2. 48, 'Swift, swift, you dragons of the night' (Browne). Here, as in *Eli* 56–8 [cf. note in *V.C.* 1, 207], Milton transfers the dragons to the chariot of Cynthia, the moon (Masson). [The older partial explanations were superseded by D. P. Harding (*Milton and the Renaissance Ovid*, Urbana, 1946, 50), who cites Renaissance commentators on Ovid's tale of Medea. Ovid (*M.* 7. 218–19) tells 'how Medea's prayer to Hecate and other divinities was followed...by the descent of a dragon-drawn chariot.... Ovid does not explicitly state that the chariot belonged to Hecate. But apparently some of Ovid's Renaissance commentators thought that he strongly implied Hecate's ownership, for they do not hesitate to attribute the chariot to her': Harding cites Sandys, *Ovid* (1632), 255, and a note on 7. 398 [*sc.* 399?] in T. Farnaby's edition of the *Metamorphoses* (Amsterdam, 1650). Since Hecate was a moon goddess, with the triple identity of Luna, Diana, and Proserpina, 'Luna (Cynthia) is sometimes represented as driving a yoke of dragons' (Harding, 50). Some mythographers were cited by D. Bush, *PQ* 6 (1925), 296–7. One may add Marlowe's reference to the moon: 'That night-wandring pale and watrie starre / (When yawning dragons draw her thirling carre / From Latmus mount up to the glomie skie...)' (*H. and L.* 1. 107 f.); and, apropos of Milton's *Dragon yoke*, Sandys' 'my yoked dragons' (*Ovid*, 1626, 170: for *dracones*, *M.* 8. 795).]

The epithet *accustom'd* has reference to the observer, Il Penseroso, rather than to Cynthia and suggests to Masson and others that Milton may have had in mind a particular tree by which he had often paused to watch the slow progress of the moon, imagining her to linger as entranced by the nightingale's song. Verity and Wright compare *assueta seditque sub ulmo* (*EpDam* 15), where Milton is speaking of himself. But the landscape throughout the companion poems is generalized, and it is enough that the oak is a familiar landmark to Il Penseroso.

61-2 *Sweet Bird...most Melancholy*. As silence is associated with wisdom, so *noise* here with folly; but it is possible, as Keightley suggested by a cross-reference to *SolMus* 18 (cf. also *Nat* 97), that *noise* here means music, the gay music of folly as contrasted with the nightingale's song. On Milton's fondness for the nightingale, see the note on *Sonn* 1. 1-2. Editors suggest that he might recall classical descriptions of the bird's song, e.g. Sophocles, *O.C.* 670 f., Euripides, *Hel.* 1107 f., Virgil, *G.* 4. 513-15: *illa | flet noctem, ramoque sedens miserabile carmen | integrat*. *Even-song*. [With the ecclesiastical overtone, cf. 'Ere the first Cock his Mattin rings' (*L'All* 114).]

65 *unseen*: in contrast to 'not unseen' (*L'All* 57 and n.).

66 *smooth-shaven Green*. [Dunster (reported by Todd) cited 'new-shav'n Fields' in Sylvester (*D.W.W.* 2. 4. 1. 951, Grosart, 1, 221).]

67 *wandring Moon*. Keightley compared *vaga Luna* (Horace, *S.* 1. 8. 21) and *canit errantem lunam* (Virgil, *A.* 1. 742). Browne cited 'swifter than the wand'ring moon' (Shakespeare, *Dream* 4. 1. 101).

68 *highest noon*. *OED* 4b explains as 'The place of the moon at midnight,' the 'noon of night' being a fairly common synonym for midnight. But this does not suit the time sequence (see 74 and 85-6) or indeed the present image, where *highest* suggests position, and *noon* could be used of the highest point reached (*OED* 5), the explanation given by Hales, and as 'the moon's meridian' (Wright). [Milton says *neer*, not *at*, though *neer* may be at this point an overstatement.]

69-70 *Like one... | ...pathles way*. ['He was a passionate admirer of nature; and, in a single couplet of his, describing the moon,...there is more intense observation, and intense feeling of nature (as if he had gazed himself blind in looking at her) than in twenty volumes of descriptive poetry.' (Hazlitt, 'On Milton's Lycidas,' *Works*, ed. P. P. Howe, London: Dent, 1930–4, 4, 33).]

71–2 *And oft...fleecy cloud.* Dunster (reported by Todd), Keightley, and Masson comment on the accuracy with which Milton observed the optical illusion whereby the motion of the clouds seems to be transferred to the moon as seen through them, so that she seems 'sometimes to stoop among them' (Masson). [While *fleecy* needs no source, cf. Virgil, *G.* 1. 395–7, 3. 391–3.]

73 *Plat*: a variant form of plot, a small piece of ground, a patch (*OED*: *sb.*³ 1).

74 *Curfeu*: curfew, here the bell itself, rung at a fixed hour in the evening, originally as a signal to 'cover fire' for the night (*OED* 1a). As 76 indicates, *sound* is a verb.

75 *shoar*: the land bordering, not the sea only, but a larger lake or river, the idea of size being emphasized here by the epithet. The word *some* has discouraged annotators (not quite effectively) from the attempt to identify the locality.

76 *Swinging...sullen roar.* Masson, arguing that *shoar* implies the sea, toys with the idea that it is the sea and not the bell that is thus described; but this is to miss the accuracy and vividness of Milton's rendering of the effect of the slow-swinging bell. The word *sullen* had *solemn* as one of its meanings (*OED* 2), as in 'Sounds ever after as a sullen bell, / Rememb'red tolling a departing friend' (Shakespeare, *2 H. IV* 1. 1. 102–3; cf. 'the solemn curfew,' *Temp.* 5. 1. 40: both cited without comment by Browne). The word *roar* is applied in a transferred sense to any loud sound (*OED*: *sb.*¹ 2), but here it seems to reinforce the more common meaning of *sullen*. [Quoting lines 67–76, E. E. Stoll observes: 'There the sense of space and distance, with a sight or a sound to lure the imagination on, is quite in the vein of the Romantic poets, from Collins to Keats and Shelley' (*Poets and Playwrights*, 291).]

77 *Ayr*: weather (Wright). *OED* 4: 'A special...condition of the atmosphere, as affected by temperature, moisture...; approaching the senses of *weather* and *climate*.'

78 Warton took *still* as an adjective qualifying *place*. It may, however, be an adverb qualifying *removed*, which (as Warton recognized) means 'remote, secluded' (*OED*: *ppl.* 2a). The meaning may then be 'some (other) place, provided it is still secluded.'

80 *Teach light...gloom*: 'the light of the fire is so soft as to be a kind of darkness' (Verity); or perhaps the *glowing Embers* seem to intensify rather than illumine the gathering darkness *through the room*.

81–4 *Far from . . . harm.* It is significant that *mirth*, which is not utterly banished (above, 1 n.), is allowed this limited contribution to Il Penseroso's serious but not uncheerful mood. The chirping of the cricket is noticed by Shakespeare, but in a very different context (*Macb.* 3. 2. 42–3). Warton illustrated *the Belmans drowsie charm* from Herrick's *The Bell-man* (ed. L. C. Martin, 121): 'From noise of Scare-fires rest ye free, / From Murders Benedicitie. / From all mischances, that may fright / Your pleasing slumbers in the night: / Mercie secure ye all, and keep / The Goblin from ye, while ye sleep. / Past one aclock, and almost two, / My Masters all, *Good day to you.*' [C. W. Brodribb (*N&Q* 182, 1942, 273) cited Dekker's *Belman of London* (Temple Classics, 110): 'I began to talke to my Bell-man, and to aske him, why with such a Jangling . . . hee went about to waken either poore men . . . or sick men. . . . hee made answere unto me, that the Ringing of his Bell, was not . . . to fright the inhabitants, but rather it was musick to charme them faster with sleepe: the Beating at their doores assured those within that no theeves were entred . . .' C. L. Wrenn ('The Language of Milton,' *Studies in English Language and Literature Presented to . . . Karl Brunner, Wiener Beiträge* 65, 1957, 256–7) remarks that here (and in *PL* 4. 642) *charm* combines the sense of Lat. *carmen* ('magical song or incantation') with that of the 'purely English word of identical form derived from Old English or Anglo-Saxon Anglian *cerm*, meaning the noise of birds'—a word still surviving in dialects. Cf. Spaeth, *Music*, 88.]

85–6 *Or let . . . lonely Towr.* Warton noticed the imaginative picture created by this way of saying that Il Penseroso studies all night. Allen (*Vision*, 17) finds this tower 'the dynamic symbol of the poem' (see above, III: Criticism, under 1954).

87 *out-watch the Bear.* Since *the Bear* (Ursa major) never sets but becomes invisible with daylight, the phrase implies 'keep watch till daybreak' (Keightley). To watch is to keep awake (*OED* 1a), but with the added idea of purpose (ibid. b), and carries the further suggestion of a vigil, a devotional act (ibid. 2) —here devotion to high studies. Allen (*Vision*, 13) notes that for Hermes Trismegistus (see 88 n. below) 'this constellation is a symbol of perfection, of a never declining motion that makes an exact circle around Polaris. "The Bear who revolves upon herself, and carries round with her the whole Kosmos" (*Poimandres* 5. 4).'

88 *With thrice great Hermes*: i.e. reading the philosophic writings, probably of the second and third centuries A.D., which were ascribed to the Egyptian king and philosopher Thoth, identified by Alexandrian Greeks with Hermes and called Trismegistos, 'thrice great' [cf. *Ter magnus Hermes* in Milton's *Idea* 33. The standard edition (with a French translation) is *Corpus Hermeticum*, ed. A. D. Nock and A.-J. Festugière (4 v., Paris, 1945–54; 2nd ed., 1960 f.)]. Ficino finished his Latin translation of the *Corpus* in 1463. John Everard translated *The Divine Pymander* (London, 1650 [1649]). References to Hermes are frequent in the 17th century, e.g. Bacon (*Adv., Works* 3, 263); Jonson, *Neptunes Triumph* and *Fortunate Isles* (*Ben Jonson* 7, 684, 715). The *Hermetica* have been more or less related to the mystical or occult strain in Robert Fludd, Thomas and Henry Vaughan, Sir Thomas Browne, and Henry More. [Frances A. Yates gives a succinct account of the origins, growth, and doctrines of Hermeticism in the early chapters of her *Giordano Bruno and the Hermetic Tradition* (London and Chicago, 1964).]

88–96 These lines, which belong to the Neo-Platonic current touched in 88 n., have their starting point in Plato's *Phaedo* and *Timaeus*. In the former (114 B–C) Socrates discourses of the existence of the soul after death: 'those who are found to have excelled in holy living are freed from these regions within the earth and are released as from prisons; they mount upward into their pure abode and dwell upon the earth,' i.e. the True Earth, already described as above our earth [see Wright in *Comus* 1–4 n.]. In the *Timaeus* (41–2) it is said that, from the same elements that went to the making of the World Soul, but diluted, the Creator made 'souls equal in number to the stars, and each several soul He assigned to one star'; and that 'he that has lived his appointed time well shall return again to his abode in his native star, and shall gain a life that is blessed and congenial' (L.C.L.). These passages are perhaps enough to explain the 'unsphering' of the *spirit of Plato* and the desire to know more of the region inhabited by immortal souls (88–92). *OED* takes *unsphear* to be merely figurative, which is misleading if it conceals the basis in Platonic theory: implied are the residence of the soul in a star and the location of the star in its appropriate sphere.

There remains the question of those *Daemons* associated with the elements and the planets. Warton (1785) recognized here 'some reference to the Gothic system of Demons, which is a mixture of Platonism, school-divinity and christian superstition.' He referred particularly to Antonio de Torquemada's *The Spanish Mandevile of Myracles* (London, 1618, 126), which distinguished six grades of spirits: those in the highest region of air, called 'angels of fire, because they are neere unto that region, and perchance within it. The second kind...is from the middle region of the ayre, downeward towards the earth. The thirde on the earth it selfe. The fourth, in the waters. The fift, in the Caves and hollow vautes of the earth' (this last satisfactorily accounting, as Warton implied, for the phrase *or under ground*). Warton (1785) cited Drayton, *Poly.* 5. 178 f., which links the theory of spirits loosely with Platonism (and also with the fallen angels). Drayton protests that he does not 'selfe-conceited, play the humorous Platonist' and assert that spirits assume bodies and 'commix with frail mortalitie...beneath this lower Sphere / Of the unconstant Moone; to tempt us dailie here.' He continues: 'Some, earthly mixture take; as others, which aspire, / Them subt'ler shapes resume, of water, ayre, and fire, / Being those immortalls long before the heaven, that fell....' Todd added Burton's *Anatomy* (1. 2. 1. 2: 1, 180–202), where the association of evil demons with the four elements is noted, and also a subterranean class (1, 196). Warton concluded his valuable note, on which later editors have drawn, with the fact that the demons associated with the different elements were thought to control them and to be in turn controlled by magic: he cited Shakespeare, *Temp.* 5. 1. 33–57; Tasso, *G.L.* 13. 7; Fletcher, *F. Shep.* 4. 4. 36–8. E. C. Baldwin (*MLN* 33, 1918, 184–5) pointed out that only lines 89–92 (*The spirit of Plato...fleshly nook*) can be explained by reference to the *Phaedo* or any other work of Plato himself, and that 93–6 (on the Daemons) demand recourse to the *Hermetica*. He cited especially *Definitions of Asclepius to King Amon* (13–14), where the different strata of the cosmos are said to be peopled with innumerable daimons, ranked beneath the stars 'in equal number with each one of them'; through the daimons the stars exercise their influence on the lives of men, and the daimons 'watch over the affairs of men, and work out things appointed by the Gods.' Baldwin does not attempt to account satisfactorily for Milton's knowledge of this specific passage, though he thinks some knowledge of Hermetic ideas might have been gleaned from other old writers, e.g. Lactantius, who in *D.I.* 1. 6. 1 [*sc.* 2. 15–18, Migne, *Pat. Lat.* 6, 530–45?] seems to refer to the passage cited. But there were editions of the *Hermetica* in the sixteenth century; Ficino's translation was mentioned above.

[G. L. Finney (*Musical Backgrounds*, 105–6), quoting 93–6 (and also 151–4), remarks: 'By a "personalizing" of world spirit Ficino, in his commentary on Plato's *Symposium*, explained the musical sirens of the spheres and the demons that inhabit every element—an explanation frequently attributed to Plato, as it was by Milton. These spirits appear in heaven as angels, in the spheres as sirens, in the elements as demons, through the world as genii, man's tutelary spirits. And all are musical.' See *Marsilio Ficino's Commentary on Plato's Symposium*, tr. S. R. Jayne (Columbia, Mo., 1944), 6. 3–4. F. A. Yates (*Giordano Bruno*, 280: see 88 n. above) quotes *IlPen* 85–96 and comments: 'These lines (which to my mind have a Brunian ring through the mention of the Bear, where the reform of the heavens begins in the *Spaccio*) brilliantly suggest the atmosphere of the Hermetic trance, when the immortal mind forsakes the body, and religiously consorts with demons, that is to say, gains the experience which gives it miraculous or magical powers.' M. Y. Hughes ('Devils to Adore for Deities,' 244: reference in *Nat* 173 n.) cites Augustine's *City of God* as translated by John Healey (8. 26: Everyman's Lib., 1, 251) and remarks: 'The Hermetic citations by both St. Augustine and Lactantius may have stimulated Milton's youthful interest in Hermes Trismegistus, to whose authority Lactantius appealed for regarding all the idolatrous cults as the work of wicked angels....' Julia Humphreys-Edwards (*N&Q* 16, 1969, 93) finds 'a close parallel' between *IlPen* 93–4 and 'several lists of daemons...in late Greek sources,' e.g. *Orphei Hymni*, ed. G. Quandt (Berlin, 1962), 1. 32 f.]

97–102 *Som time...Buskind stage.* Philosophy now gives place to poetry, and first to ancient tragedies. Though Renaissance critics commonly ranked epic as the supreme genre, it is clear that Milton set a high value upon tragedy, as practised by the Greek tragic poets. In *Educ* (*Works* 4, 285) he was to group with heroic poems 'Attic Tragedies of stateliest and most regal argument'; and in the preface to *SA* (ibid. 1, 331) he was to declare: 'Tragedy, as it was antiently compos'd, hath been ever held the gravest, moralest, and most profitable of all other Poems'; and at the same time he belittled the modern tragic stage. In *El* 1. 37 he had personified Tragedy as bearing a blood-stained sceptre, and there too he had specified the same subjects as in *IlPen*, the house of Pelops, Troy, and Thebes. Thebes is the scene of tragedies about Oedipus and members of his family; descendants of Pelops include Agamemnon, Orestes, Electra, and Iphigenia; and Troy—called *divine* because built by the gods (Newton, Verity), or after Homer, *Od.* 11. 86, 17. 293 (Osgood)—supplied Euripides with the themes of the *Trojan Women* and other plays and Sophocles with *Ajax*. *Tragedy* is *Gorgeous* (i.e. magnificent) because of its royal or exalted characters; *Scepter'd* is a synonym for regal; her *Pall* (Lat. *palla*) is the mantle of the tragic actor, the invention of which Horace (*A.P.* 278–9) attributed to Aeschylus. The buskin, the high boot of the Greek tragic actor, designated tragedy, as the sock comedy (*L'All* 132).

101 *though rare.* [Hurd's 'Just glancing at Shakespeare' (in Warton) has been more or less confidently endorsed by Todd, Hales, Masson, Browne, Bell, Verity, Trent, Rolfe.

103–8 *But, O sad Virgin...Love did seek.* Next comes lyric verse, but with overtones of the Orphic mysteries. The *sad* (grave: *OED* 4) *Virgin* (above, 31 n.), Melancholy, is to bring back Musaeus and Orpheus. Orpheus' song won the conditional release of Eurydice from Hades (cf. *L'All* 145–50 and n.), drawing from Pluto *Iron tears*, because of the hardness of the heart from which they were wrung. Osgood (*C.M.* 66) cites Ovid, *M.* 10. 45–6, where the cheeks of the Eumenides are wet with tears, and Seneca, *Herc. Fur.* 578: *deflent et lacrimis difficiles dei* [there is a suggestion of iron—though *ferrugineus* means 'of the color of iron rust'—in Claudian's words about Pluto, *ferrugineo lacrimas deterget amictu* (35. 275: 2, 338)]. While the fact is not alluded to, it is not merely as singer and musician that Orpheus might be appropriately summoned, but in his religious character as reputed founder of the Orphic mysteries and author of the Orphic hymns [see D. P. Walker, 'Orpheus the Theologian and Renaissance Platonists,' *JWCI* 16 (1953), 100–20. While Orpheus as a 'type' of Christ does not come into Milton's allusion, one may cite some references for that tradition from D. C. Allen (*JEGP* 60, 1961, 618–21): Fulgentius, *Mythol.* 3. 10 (*Opera*, ed. R. Helm, Leipzig, 1898); Boccaccio, *Genealogie Deorum Gentilium Libri* (ed. V. Romano, 2 v., Bari, 1951), 5. 12; 'Thomas Walleys' (i.e. P. Berchorius), *Metamorphosis ovidiana Moraliter...explanata* (Paris, 1509), fol. lxxii^v; Gavin Douglas, *Poetical Works*, ed. J. Small (4 v., Edinburgh, 1874), 2, 18; G. A. dell'Anguillara and M. G. Horologgi, *Metamorfosi di Ovidio* (Venice, 1575, 190, 205; 1584, 357, 387); N. Comes, *Mythol.* 7. 14 (Padua, 1616: 401–2, and 548); G. Fletcher, *C.T.* 1. 7; Alex. Ross, *Mystagogus Poeticus* (1648), 334–7. Among these interpreters, Berchorius, Douglas, Fletcher, and Ross seem to be the only ones who draw an explicit parallel with Christ. Milton's various allusions are placed in their setting by K. R. R. Gros Louis, 'The Triumph and Death of Orpheus in the English Renaissance,' *SEL* 9 (1969), 63–80.]

Likewise *Musaeus*, the mythical lyrist, whose name betokens the servant of the Muses, was sometimes described as the son of Orpheus and priest of the mysteries of Demeter. In Elysium Aeneas encounters him with Orpheus, 'the long-robed Thracian priest,' in a fragrant laurel grove (the *bower*, as Osgood suggests, to which Milton alludes) where the company is chanting, with Musaeus pre-eminent and the centre of the vast throng who gaze up at him (Virgil, *A.* 6. 639, 645, 657–8, 667–8). Warton cited Milton's other allusions to Orpheus, and his nephew's words, 'that noblest thing call'd Education, this is that Harp of Orpheus' (Edward Phillips, *Theatrum*, *3). This, if Warton is right in attributing the idea to Milton or his influence, suggests a third association of Orpheus for the poet, not with the lyric and religious only, but also the educational, which is likewise consonant with the theme and rendering of *IlPen*. [But Phillips' phrase is probably only an echo of Milton's own praise of true education—'that the Harp of Orpheus was not more charming' (*Educ*, *Works* 4, 280) —and Warton's rightness is dubious (see *L'All* 131–4 n.): this 'third association' seems pretty remote from the context.]

106 *warbled to the string. OED* 3c gives no example of *string* in the singular as designating a stringed instrument.

109–15 If we wonder at Il Penseroso's reading Chaucer's *Squire's Tale*, which might seem to belong rather to L'Allegro, the answer is partly to be found in the *F.Q.* 4. 2. 30–3. 52, where Spenser, with due apology, completes the story. As Verity points out, Spenser imagines the end of Chaucer's tale to have been lost, while Milton speaks of it as *left half told*. But that he remembered Spenser's version is evident from the phrase *And who had Canace to wife*, which echoes 'For Triamond had Canacee to wife' (*F.Q.* 4. 3. 52); *the Tartar king* echoes Chaucer (266); and *the vertuous Ring* reflects the emphasis in both poets on the ring's 'vertue,' i.e. inherent virtue or power (*OED* 11; Warton cites 'That vertuous steele,' the sword Morddure, and the Palmer's 'vertuous staffe' in *F.Q.* 2. 8. 22, 2. 12. 86). But the significance of the memory of Spenser is that he had deliberately turned the tale to allegorical purpose—a type of reading consonant with Il Penseroso's interests—and further made Canace 'the learnedst Ladie in her dayes, / Well seene in everie science that mote bee, / And every secret worke of natures wayes, / . . . In power of herbes, and tunes of beasts and burds' (*F.Q.* 4. 2. 35), which comes close to Il Penseroso's own ideal (cf. 170–2 below). Allen (*Vision*, 12–13) finds a similar suggestion in Chaucer (149–54) in the knowledge conferred by the magic ring, which includes the language of birds and 'every gras that groweth upon roote.' Finally, Milton groups the half-told tale with Spenserian allegory; see 116–20 and n. (Woodhouse, 'Notes,' 88, n. 34).

[A word may be added about names. Our texts of Chaucer have Cambalo and Cambyuskan. For the former Spenser used chiefly Cambell, sometimes Cambello, so that Milton's *Camball* is no problem. Milton's use of Cambuscan is explained by the presence of that form in all the black-letter editions of Chaucer, including the one Milton owned, that of Speght, 1602 (F. P. Magoun, *MP* 25, 1927–8, 133–4). F. W. Emerson (*MLN* 47, 1932, 153–4), without reference to Magoun, suggested that Milton got his *Cambuscan* (with its second-syllable accent) and *Camball* from the continuation of the *Squire's Tale* written by John Lane, a friend of John Milton senior (a work also mentioned by Magoun). For an account of Lane see Parker, 715–16, n. 54.]

116–20 *And if ought els...meets the ear.* Warton recognized that the principal allusion is to Spenser and the *Faerie Queene*, but observed that among 'other great bards...of the romantic class...Tasso and Ariosto pretend to an allegorical and mysterious meaning.' He added Francesco Berni, who 'allows, that his incantations, giants, magic gardens, monsters, and other romantic imageries, may amuse the ignorant: but that the intelligent have more penetration': *Ma voi c'havete gl'intelletti sani | Mirate la dottrina che s'asconde | Sotto queste coperte alte & profonde* (*Orlando Innamorato* 25. 1, Venice, 1545, 88ᵛ). Warton also recalled Milton's report of the growth of his youthful idealism as his moral and religious concern led him from Ovid to Dante and Petrarch and then to

> those lofty Fables and Romances, which recount in solemne canto's the deeds of Knighthood founded by our victorious Kings; & from hence had in renowne over all Christendome. There I read it in the oath of every Knight, that he should defend to the expence of his best blood, or of his life, if it so befell him, the honour and chastity of Virgin or Matron. From whence even then I learnt what a noble vertue chastity sure must be, to the defence of which so many worthies by such a deare adventure of themselves had sworne.... So that even those books which to many others have bin the fuell of wantonnesse and loose living, I cannot thinke how unlesse by divine indulgence prov'd to me so many incitements as you have heard, to the love and stedfast observation of that vertue which abhorres the society of Bordello's. (*Apol, Works* 3, 304–5)

No one in Milton's day doubted the importance of Spenser's allegory, though Henry Reynolds said that 'some good judgments have wisht, and perhaps not without cause, that he had therein beene a little freer of his fiction, and not so close rivetted to his Morall' (*Mythomystes*, in J. E. Spingarn, *Critical Essays of the Seventeenth Century*, Oxford, 1908–9, 1, 147). Tasso's avowed allegory was also accepted. Milton might have found it harder to take at its face value Harington's claim that the *Orlando Furioso* (trans. 1591) is 'full of Christen exhortation, doctrine, & example' (G. G. Smith, *Eliz. Crit. Essays*, 2, 213)—[though there is Ariosto's notable episode of temptation and the temperate man]. With *sage and solemn tunes* compare 'our sage and serious Poet Spencer' (*Areop, Works* 4, 311); Warton discerned here a reference to the 'dignity of his stanza' as well as to his 'morality.'

118 *Turneys*: tournaments (*OED* 1). *Trophies*: the spoils or other memorials of victory, sometimes displayed in advance to be contended for, e.g. Duessa and Sansfoy's shield in *F.Q.* 1. 5. 5.

119   *Forests, and inchantments drear* are met as early as Virgil, *A.* 6. 136 f., and Lucan 3. 399–425, but Milton was no doubt thinking especially of Tasso's enchanted forest [*G.L.* 13 and 18; cf. below, 151–4 n., and *Comus* 38 n.] or the grove in Spenser where the monster Error lived (*F.Q.* 1. 1. 7 f.: Hughes).

120   *Where more is meant then meets the ear.* See notes on 116–20 and 119, and *Comus* 512–18 and 514 n. Bowle (reported by Warton) cited *in quibus plus intelligendum est quam audiendum* (Seneca, *Ep.* 114: L.C.L., 3, 300).

121   *Thus night...career* concludes the account of Il Penseroso's night hours.
  career: course, usually implying swift motion and applied to the movement of the sun or other body across the heavens (*OED* 3; *PL* 4. 353). Night's course is *pale* because it is identified with, or dimly lighted by, the moon.

122   *Till civil-suited Morn appeer* introduces the occupations of the day. The word *civil*, applied to dress, means 'Not gay,...sober' (*OED* 10). Editors quote: 'Come, civil night, / Thou sober-suited matron' (Shakespeare, *Romeo* 3. 2. 10–11).

123–4   *Not trickt...to hunt.* Here, as in *El* 5. 49–52, Milton takes only a passing glance at the story of Aurora's love for Cephalus, an Athenian prince and ardent hunter (Ovid, *M.* 7. 690–865); he ignores the tragic outcome as alien to his purpose. The suggestion of artifice which usually accompanies *trickt*, adorned (*OED*: *v.* 5)—though not always (cf. *Lyc* 170)—is heightened by *frounc't*, curled (of the hair). Warton cited: 'Some frounce their curled haire in courtly guise' (Spenser, *F.Q.* 1. 4. 14). [An example of *trickt* is in the excerpt from Shirley in *L'All* 26–36 n.]

125   *Cherchef't...Cloud*: covered by a cloud as with a kerchief.

126   *rocking Winds...loud.* Warton cited 'the winds, piping to us in vain' (Shakespeare, *Dream* 2. 1. 88). *Piping loud* indicates the whistling wind (*OED*: *ppl. a.* 2) of a blustery morning. Hence *rocking* means that the winds agitate tree-tops, etc., with a less gentle motion than that associated with rocking a cradle. [Cf. 'rocking windes' in Sandys, *Ovid*, 1626, 141 (*M.* 7. 585–6).]

127–30   *Or usher'd...Eaves.* The *Morn* is said to be *usher'd*, introduced, *with a shower*, in the same figurative sense of *usher* as in 'the blushing Dawne out of the chearfull East / Is ushering forth the Day' (Drayton, *Poly.* 3. 2–3). The word *still* is an adjective meaning gentle, quiet, subdued; cf. 'Still music' (Shakespeare, *A.Y.L.* 5. 4. 113, stage direction), and Milton, *Passion* 28. The meaning was not uncommon (*OED*: *a.* and *sb.* 3 and 4) and Milton was not unique in applying it to the sounds of nature; cf. 'The gentle blasts of Westerne winds, shall...breath / Still Musick' (Carew, *Rapture* 48–50, cited by *OED* 3 b). In contrast with the rocking and whistling wind, which has now blown itself out, there remains the rustling of the leaves, a sound replaced after the still shower by the dropping of water, minute by minute, from the eaves. *Eaves* could mean simply edge without reference to a roof (*OED* 2), even the over-hanging edge of a wood or grove (ibid. 1 b), and Malone (reported by Todd) suggested that Milton might be remembering 'like winter's drops / From eaves of reeds' (Shakespeare, *Temp*. 5. 1. 16–17); but it seems needless to go beyond the common meaning. [While the interpretation of *minute* as 'falling at inter-vals of a minute,' accepted from Warton onward, is doubtless right (though examples of this meaning in *OED* are mostly late), it is perhaps possible that the word has its common Latin and English meaning, 'small.' Cf. Pontano: *stillae paulo ante minutae* (*Meteora* 362); Erasmus: *Minutula pluvia imbrem parit...id est, Minutae guttulae imbrem parientes* (*Adagia, Opera*, ed. J. Clericus, Leyden, 1703–6, repr. London, 1962, 2, 112).]

131–2 *the Sun...beams.* Warton cited: 'When Phoebus with a face of mirth, / Had flong abroad his beames' (*Muses Elizium* 1. 1–2, Drayton, 3, 252). Todd added 'flaring beames' (Marlowe, *H. and L.* 2. 332).

132 *Goddess*: i.e. Melancholy.

133–4 *arched walks of twilight groves.* Warton compared 'Now wanders Pan the arched groves' (Browne, *Brit. Past.* 2. 4. 747), which possibly suggested Milton's phrase and also the following reference to *Sylvan* (134 n.).

134 *shadows brown.* The adjective was early applied to any dark shade (*OED* 1) and, fortified no doubt by Milton's influence (cf. *Lyc* 2, *PL* 9. 1088, *PR* 2. 293, 3. 326), became conventional poetic diction. [This particular phrase is in Fairfax, *Jerusalem* 14. 37.] *Sylvan*: Silvanus, the ancient Roman god of forest and field, who was worshipped in groves surrounded by dark pines (Virgil, *A.* 8. 597–602), and was by later writers identified with Pan [cf. *El* 5. 121–2 and n., *V.C.* 1, 109].

135 *monumental*: 'like a monument' (*OED* 3), but surely rather 'Comparable to a monument in massiveness and permanence' (ibid. 4, where, however, the examples, all later, are figurative), with perhaps the secondary suggestion of a memorial of other times (Browne). [Saillens (*Milton*, 38, n. 1) takes the phrase as 'A good example of Milton's complexity of expression. Three simultaneous meanings—"colossal", "witness to the past", and "apt for construction". Chaucer and Spenser contented themselves with "builder oak".' Cf. Pattison, *Milton*, 25.]

331

136-7 *the rude Ax...Was never heard.* [Cf. *silva vetus nullaque diu violata securi | stabat, Maenalio sacra relicta deo* (Ovid, *F.* 4. 649–50); and the *Homeric Hymn to Aphrodite* 256–68, where, among the mountain trees that spring up at their birth, the nymphs dance among the immortals and mate with the Sileni and Hermes: 'and men call them holy places of the immortals, and never mortal lops them with the axe' (*Hesiod*, etc., L.C.L. 425). The trees named here are pines and 'high-topped oaks'; cf. *IlPen* 135.]

137-8 The *Nymphs* here are Dryads. The wood is *hallow'd* because it is their haunt.

139 *close covert.* The phrase combines the suggestions of a dense growth or thicket forming a shelter, and a secret retreat.

140 *prophaner.* [Cf. 'weaker' at the end of 14–16 n.]

141 *Day's garish eie.* The image of the sun as the eye of the world ([*mundi oculus*, Ovid, *M.* 4. 228]; *PL* 5. 171), of heaven (Shakespeare, *R. II* 3. 2. 37; Spenser, *F.Q.* 1. 3. 4), of day (*Sonn* 1. 5, *Comus* 977; Browne, *Brit. Past.* 1. 1. 79; Sylvester, *D.W.W.* 1. 4. 562, Grosart, 1, 57), was a poetical commonplace but evidently one that attracted Milton. The epithet *garish*, excessively bright (*OED* 2b, citing this example), is applied to the sun by Shakespeare (*Romeo* 3. 2. 25), but Todd, who gathers the English parallels given above, adds that the phrase *garishe eye* (used of a woman) occurs in Barnabe Rich's *Adventures of Don Simonides* (1581), sig. Qii^v.

142-6 *While the Bee...dewy-feather'd Sleep.* Warton compared: *Hyblaeis apibus florem depasta salicti | saepe levi somnum suadebit inire susurro* (Virgil, *E.* 1. 54–5), and, for the combination of brook and bee: 'See the small brookes as through these Groves they travell, | ...Mocke the sweet Notes the neighb'ring Sylvans sing, | With the smooth cadence of their murmuring. | Each Bee with Honey on her laden thye' (*Owle* 117–21, Drayton, 2, 483). Milton could hardly have forgotten the blend of sleep-inviting sounds, flowing water, and 'murmuring winde, much like the sowne | Of swarming Bees' in Spenser, *F.Q.* 1. 1. 41. Finley ([below, Sonnets 11] 33, n. 3) cites: *fontesque lymphis obstrepunt manantibus, | somnos quod invitet leves* (Horace, *Epod.* 2. 27–8). With *flowry work*, cf. *laboris | Floriferi* (Lucan 9. 289–90), in a passage about bees which Thomas May in his translation of 1627 rendered as 'flowery taskes' (Leishman, *Essays and Studies 1951*, 33–4). For *consort* (145) see *Nat* 132 n. *Sleep* is a winged figure (cf. 148); his dewy touch betokens pure and healthful slumber.

147–50 *And let som strange...eye-lids laid.* For the whole passage Verity quotes from a speech by Night in Jonson's *Vision of Delight* 44–54 (*Ben Jonson* 7, 464–5):

> Breake, Phant'sie, from thy cave of cloud,
>   and spread thy purple wings;
> Now all thy figures are allow'd,
>   and various shapes of things;
> Create of ayrie formes, a streame;...
> And though it be a waking dreame;
>   Yet let it like an odour rise
>   to all the Sences here,
>   And fall like sleep upon their eies,
>   or musick in their eare.

Todd reports the interesting emendation of *in Airy stream* to *an*, supported by 'winged dreames' (P. Fletcher, *Apoll.* 1. 6), which, with the requisite changes in punctuation (which seems faulty in any case), would help to clear the syntax but at the cost of introducing a second winged figure. In lines which rely entirely on suggestion, syntax is secondary to image, and paraphrase is more than usually inadequate; but the sense seems to be that the *strange mysterious dream*, airy and unsubstantial, but vivid in its representations, is wafted on the *dewy-feather'd* wings of *Sleep* and gently laid on the closed eyes of the sleeper. Browne notes, of the spirit raised by Archimago, that 'on his litle winges the dreame he bore' (Spenser, *F.Q.* 1. 1. 44). Warton cited 'on sleeping cyclids laid' (Shakespeare, *Dream* 2. 1. 170), and 'Sweetest slumbers, / And soft silence, fall in numbers / On your eye-lids' (Fletcher, *F. Shep.* 2. 1. 31–3). [Coleridge (Brinkley, 565–6) thought the lines confused and awkward and construed them thus: 'at his wings (dewy-feather'd) softly laid on my eye-lids let some strange mysterious Dream flow wavingly in aery stream of lively portraiture.']

151–4 *And as I wake...Genius of the Wood.* Warton cited the music heard by Ferdinand: 'Where should this music be? I' th'air, or th'earth? / ...I hear it now above me' (Shakespeare, *Temp.* 1. 2. 387, 407); and that heard by Antony's soldiers: 'List, list! / ...Music i' th'air. / Under the earth' (*Antony* 4. 3. 12–13 —though here the supernatural music is of ill omen). But Warton would trace such poetic use of hidden music to the actual use of music in court entertainments, especially to 'the machineries of the Masks under the contrivance of Inigo Jones.' He cited other examples: Apuleius' Psyche, 'sleeping on a green and flowery bank near a romantic grove,' who 'is awakened by invisible singers and unseen harps'; and 'Rinaldo, in Tasso's Inchanted Forest, hears unseen harps and singers. C. xvi. 67.' [This last reference, reproduced in Todd as

xxvi. 67, should be 18. 18–24.] Verity takes *good* as an adjective qualifying *mortals* and by implication associates the sounds with the music of the spheres, inaudible to men of 'gross unpurged ear' (*Arc* 73). This might perhaps be supported by reference to 'Spare Fast,' etc. (46–8); but it seems rather remote, since *mortals* may, at least as naturally, be read as a possessive, the music of immortal spirits being sent for the good of mortals. [In that case would not Milton have been likely to say 'for mortals good' or 'for mortal good'? Bell explains as 'good to mortals' and Trent seems to mean that in saying '*Good* limits "Spirit." ' Prince glosses as 'well disposed to men.'] The *Genius of the Wood* of course suggests *Arc* and thus perhaps the music of the spheres which he heard and would fain imitate (*Arc* 62–78).

155–60 *But let my due feet…dimm religious light.* It is most natural to read these lines as referring particularly to Cambridge. There seems to be no reason to regard (with Verity) the *Cloysters pale* as alone so doing, while *embowed Roof* would refer to 'one of the great Gothic Cathedrals' and the description of the service to what Milton might have heard 'at King's College Chapel or Ely.' We may think rather of Il Penseroso as walking in the cloister and at service time entering the college chapel. It has been often observed that when the poem was written Milton could not yet have developed his later extreme antipathy to the liturgy and its accompaniments of consecrated and beautiful building, choir, and organ (indeed the word *love* shows a directly contrary sentiment), though he is already critical of the Church for its exclusion of worthy Puritan ministers (*El* 4), still a main point in the indictment in *Lyc* ten years later. In his prose of the 1640s he speaks with contempt (as Verity notes) of 'painted Windows,' 'the chanted Service-Book,' the 'Singing men' and 'Organs' (*Eikon, Works* 5, 268, 263), and the 'deare Antiphonies that so bewitcht of late our Prelats, and their Chaplaines' (*Areop, Works* 4, 304). [Milton had been more violent in his first tract of 1641 (*Ref, Works* 3, 1 f.]

156 *studious Cloysters pale*: the enclosed space ⟨*Cloysters* being a possessive⟩ formed by the covered walk of a college (hence *studious*). Browne cited 'studious universities' (Shakespeare, *T.G.V.* 1. 3. 10). [E. H. Visiak (*Milton: Complete Poetry and Selected Prose*, London and New York, 1938, 827) takes *pale* as an adjective, meaning 'shadowy.']

157 f. Here Il Penseroso has obviously left the cloisters and is describing the chapel. *embowed*: vaulted (*OED*: *ppl. a.* 2). [Cf. 'the faire embowed or vawted roofs' (*Lycurgus, Plutarch's Lives*, tr. North, Temple Classics, 10 v., London, 1898–9, 1, 168).]

158 *antick* might signify either *antique* or *antic*; the words have a common origin and the spelling is no sure guide. Here *antique* would mean old and venerable (*OED*: antique 2), *antic*, grotesque, fantastically ornamented (ibid. antic 1 and 3). Editors are divided. Warton printed *antic*, Todd *antick*, without comment; Browne and Masson, *antique*, without comment; Bell prints and supports *antique*; Lockwood prefers *antique* but admits the possibility of *antic*; Trent and Verity are doubtful, though Verity seems to prefer *antic*; Wright, Hanford, Hughes, [Shawcross, and Prince] accept *antic*. [Carey, in his modernized text, reads 'antique pillars' massy proof,' glossing *proof* as 'impenetrability.'] The word occurs as (i) *antique* (*L'All* 128); and (ii) in 'the measure (in a wild rude & wanton antick' in *Comus*, MS. direction at 144, also in Br. (*Facs*. 402, 309), though not in the printed texts. But this is not conclusive. In (ii) the meaning is certainly fantastic, grotesque, but in (i) *antique* is at least as tolerant of the meaning fantastic as of antique or traditional (see *L'All* 128 n.). Perhaps the strongest support for *antic* in *IlPen* is the fact that as a noun applied to architecture (irrespective of spelling) the word signified grotesque ornaments (*OED* B. 1). *OED* (B. 1c) quotes P. Holland, *Historie of the World* (tr. Pliny), 1634, 2, 552: 'to set up Gargils or Antiques at the top of a Gavill end'; and—in an extension of this use to other objects—Spenser, *F.Q.* 2. 7. 4: 'Woven with antickes and wild Imagery' (which should perhaps have appeared under A. 3). Admittedly Milton is describing a Gothic building, and so far the context seems to favour *antic*. But it is clear that in the aspect he is considering it commands his unqualified acceptance, and it is open to question how far the classical and soberly religious Milton would select for special praise the feature of Gothic most repugnant to classical taste and least obviously in harmony with the solemnity of the scene, whereas to consider the chapel, supported by its ancient and massive pillars, as a venerable emblem of traditional faith raises no such question. In short, either meaning is possible, and the reader must be left to make his own choice.

massy proof. Milton never uses *massive*, but uses the older *massy* ten times in that sense (*Lyc* 110; *PL* 1. 285, 2. 878, 5. 634, 6. 195, 11. 565; *SA* 147, 1633, 1648). The question here is twofold: the meaning of *proof* and the reference in *massy*. Wright paraphrases: 'secure in their [the pillars'] massiveness.' Most editors are in general accord with [Bell ('proof against the great weight of the stone roof, because they are massive') and] Miss Lockwood, who explains, with hesitation, as 'massive and able to bear up the incumbent weight.' *Proof*, originally applied to arms and armour (as in *SA* 133–4) carries the idea of tested strength (*OED* 9 and 10). Perhaps the most helpful parallel in Milton, though it is figurative, is: 'Nature faild in mee, and left some part / Not proof enough such Object to sustain' (*PL* 8. 534–5). [Milton might have recalled, with a difference, a bit from Spenser's Cave of Mammon: 'Many great golden pillours did upbeare / The massy roofe' (*F.Q.* 2. 7. 43).]

159 *storied Windows*: stained-glass or painted windows depicting scriptural stories. See above, 155–60 n. Warton quoted: '...all images, shrines...and monuments of idolatry are remooved, taken downe, and defaced; onelie the stories in glasse windowes excepted' (*Harrison's Description of England*, ed. F. J. Furnivall, London, 1879, 1, 31). The phrase *richly dight* was a commonplace: Todd cited examples in J. Hall's *Satires* 1. 2 (*Poems*, ed. A. Davenport, Liverpool, 1949), where it is used satirically as an archaism; Browne, *Brit. Past.* 2. 3. 544; Drayton, *Owle* 478 (Drayton, 2, 492); Sylvester, *Wood-man's Bear* 3 (Grosart, 2, 307). See above, *L'All* 62 n.

160 *dimm religious light.* The light, subdued by its passage through the *storied Windows*, is so described as suited to the solemnity of the religious service. Verity quoted More's statement (in Robinson's translation) that the churches in Utopia 'be al sumwhat darke' and this 'by the counsel of the priestes,' 'that over much light doth disperse mens cogitations, whereas in dimme and doubtful lighte they be gathered together, and more earnestly fixed upon religion and devotion' (ed. J. R. Lumby, Cambridge, 1908, 155). [Oras ('Notes,' 66) finds no earlier instance of *religious* in the sense of 'inspiring with a religious feeling,' and remarks that in *OED*'s quotation from T. May's *Lucan* (1627)—'A sad religious awe'—'the adjective is applied to the feeling itself, not to its cause.']

161 *pealing*: resounding (*OED*: *v.*³ 1). *blow*: emit its sound (used of wind instruments, commonly of trumpet or bugle, as in Shakespeare, *Troi.* 1. 3. 256: *OED*: *v.*¹ 15).

163 *Anthems cleer.* Todd cited 'The Cherubims in anthems cleer' (T. Jordan, *A Defence for Musick*, in *The Muses Melody* [1680?]. *Anthem* is a corruption of late Lat. *antifona* (*OED*).

164 *with sweetness.* Here the contrast with the music desired by L'Allegro (135–50) is not unqualified. Both are marked by *sweetness* (*L'All* 140), but of a different order and to a different effect. The one is Lydian and secular, the other religious.

165–6 *Dissolve me...mine eyes.* John Smith, the Cambridge Platonist, was to write: 'In such sober kind of Ecstasies did Plotinus find his own Soul separated from his Body' (*Cambridge Platonists*, ed. E. T. Campagnac, Oxford, 1901, 138); quoted in *OED*: ecstasy 3a. In this mystical sense Milton uses *Dissolve*: i.e. the soul is loosened and separated from the body (*OED*: dissolve 1). With the emphasis on the *sweetness* of the music as effecting this result, Milton suggests, perhaps beyond his intention, an aesthetic rather than a religious experience [but the Catholic tradition, with which this passage is in harmony, had accepted the agency of the senses in promoting religious emotion]. Be this as it may, the result is to reveal heaven to his imagination. Verity compares *Vac* 33–5, but there the context is classical and heroic, not Christian. [G. L. Finney (*Musical Backgrounds*, 166–7) remarks that 'Music of world spirit sounds' in *IlPen*, and that, in these climactic lines, 'Milton completely avoided any suggestion of Neoplatonic love and of the eroticism implicit in the idea of penetrating and ravishing sweetness so congenial to Castiglione and Chapman, ...[and] Crashaw, whose soul "melts down in sweet desire" in the ecstasy of religious love. Milton avoided, too, any notion of complete ecstasy, for heaven is carried to the soul, not the soul to heaven.']

167–74 *And may at last...Prophetic strain.* Unlike L'Allegro, Il Penseroso is not content with a mere prolongation of present pleasure but looks to the future and aspires. 'By a continued mounting of the slopes of the intellect from common experience, to intellectual experience, to religious inspiration, the poet trusts to arrive at the supreme poetic gratification...To something like Prophetic strain' (Allen, *Vision*, 17). The end is to be read in the light of the beginning and particularly in that supplied by the image of the *Cherub Contemplation* when fully understood (see above, 45–54 n.). Milton is here summing up the whole process of self-education described in the poem, which, commencing with the study of nature (typified by the *Herb*: see above, 109–15 n.) and proceeding through the different levels of human experience, at last leaves these behind in an act of pure contemplation and inspired insight. This was the traditional Platonic scheme proposed in *Prol* 7: one begins with the study of the sensible world, gradually becoming 'saturated and perfected by knowledge and training,' and attains at last the state in which the 'mind, without the aid of the body, remote and as it were wrapped up in itself, copies the eternal life of the immortal gods with an extraordinary delight' (*Works* 12, 255).

175–6 *These pleasures...live.* For the formula adopted in this couplet see *L'All* 151–2 n. It is significant that here, as in the last phrase quoted in 167–74 n. from *Prol* 7, the emphasis falls on delight—the delight of study, not the profit. It is not in the abandonment of delight that *Il Penseroso* contrasts with

L'Allegro, but in the different objects and the higher quality of the delight, a delight wholly consonant with the overtones of poetic dedication and even of religious response; but delight remains the predominant note. ['The poem ends firmly, with a climactic last representative of those who taste Melancholy's pleasures in the pursuit of wisdom; for certainly the hermit who spells out the secrets of the physical universe in his solitary cell is no concession to religiosity but the very type of the withdrawn seer who experiences the last pleasure: to know things in their causes and see into the hidden harmonies of the cosmos' (R. Tuve, *Images*, 32).]